When should I travel to get the best airfare?
Where do I go for answers to my travel questions?
What's the best and easiest way to plan and book my trip?

frommers.travelocity.com

Frommer's, the travel guide leader, has teamed up with **Travelocity.com**, the leader in online travel, to bring you an in-depth, easy-to-use resource designed to help you plan and book your trip online.

At **frommers.travelocity.com**, you'll find free online updates about your destination from the experts at Frommer's plus the outstanding travel planning and purchasing features of Travelocity.com. Travelocity.com provides reservations capabilities for 95 percent of all airline seats sold, more than 47,000 hotels, and over 50 car rental companies. In addition, Travelocity.com offers more than 2,000 exciting vacation and cruise packages. Travelocity.com puts you in complete control of your travel planning with these and other great features:

> **Expert travel guidance from Frommer's** - over 150 writers reporting from around the world!
>
> **Best Fare Finder** - an interactive calendar tells you when to travel to get the best airfare
>
> **Fare Watcher** - we'll track airfare changes to your favorite destinations
>
> **Dream Maps** - a mapping feature that suggests travel opportunities based on your budget
>
> **Shop Safe Guarantee** - 24 hours a day / 7 days a week live customer service, and more!

Whether traveling on a tight budget, looking for a quick weekend getaway, or planning the trip of a lifetime, Frommer's guides and Travelocity.com will make your travel dreams a reality. You've bought the book, now book the trip!

A New Star-Rating System
& Other Exciting News
from Frommer's!

In our continuing effort to publish the savviest, most up-to-date, and most appealing travel guides available, we've added some great new features.

Frommer's guides now include a new **star-rating system.** Every hotel, restaurant, and attraction is rated from 0 to 3 stars to help you set priorities and organize your time.

We've also added **seven brand-new features** that point you to the great deals, in-the-know advice, and unique experiences that separate travelers from tourists. Throughout the guide, look for:

Finds	Special finds—those places only insiders know about
Fun Fact	Fun facts—details that make travelers more informed and their trips more fun
Kids	Best bets for kids—advice for the whole family
Moments	Special moments—those experiences that memories are made of
Overrated	Places or experiences not worth your time or money
Tips	Insider tips—some great ways to save time and money
Value	Great values—where to get the best deals

We've also added a **"What's New"** section in every guide—a timely crash course in what's hot and what's not in every destination we cover.

Other Great Guides for Your Trip:

Frommer's China: The 50 Most Memorable Trips

Frommer's Hong Kong

Frommer's Shanghai

Frommer's®

Beijing
2nd Edition

J. D. Brown

D0068386

Here's what the critics say about Frommer's:

"Amazingly easy to use. Very portable, very complete."

—*Booklist*

"The only mainstream guide to list specific prices. The Walter Cronkite of guidebooks—with all that implies."

—*Travel & Leisure*

"Complete, concise, and filled with useful information."

—*New York Daily News*

"Hotel information is close to encyclopedic."

—*Des Moines Sunday Register*

"Detailed, accurate and easy-to-read information for all price ranges."

—*Glamour Magazine*

Hungry Minds™

Best-Selling Books • Digital Downloads • e-Books • Answer Networks
e-Newsletters • Branded Web Sites • e-Learning

New York, NY • Cleveland, OH • Indianapolis, IN

About the Author

J. D. Brown has lived and worked in China and has written about China as a literary traveler, a travel writer, and a guidebook author. His work has appeared in such diverse publications as the *New York Times,* the *Washington Post,* the *Michigan Quarterly Review, Islands,* and *Newsday.* He is also the author of *Frommer's China: The 50 Most Memorable Trips and Frommer's Shanghai.* When he is not traveling in the Far East, he lives in Eugene, Oregon.

Published by:

Hungry Minds, Inc.

909 Third Avenue
New York, NY 10022

ISBN 0-7645-6523-0
ISSN 1520-5568

Editor: Lorraine Festa
Production Editor: Suzanna R. Thompson
Photo Editor: Richard Fox
Cartographer: Roberta Stockwell
Production by Hungry Minds Indianapolis Production Services

Special Sales

For general information on Hungry Minds' products and services, please contact our Customer Care department; within the U.S. at 800-762-2974, outside the U.S. at 317-572-3993, or fax 317-572-4002. For sales inquiries and reseller information, including discounts, bulk sales, customized editions, and premium sales, please contact our Customer Care department at 800-434-3422.

Manufactured in the United States of America

5   4   3   2   1

Contents

List of Maps

An Invitation to the Reader

In researching this book, we discovered many wonderful places—hotels, restaurants, shops, and more. We're sure you'll find others. Please tell us about them, so we can share the information with your fellow travelers in upcoming editions. If you were disappointed with a recommendation, we'd love to know that, too. Please write to:

Frommer's Beijing, 2nd Edition
Hungry Minds, Inc. • 909 Third Avenue • New York, NY 10022

An Additional Note

Please be advised that travel information is subject to change at any time—and this is especially true of prices. We therefore suggest that you write or call ahead for confirmation when making your travel plans. The authors, editors, and publisher cannot be held responsible for the experiences of readers while traveling. Your safety is important to us, however, so we encourage you to stay alert and be aware of your surroundings. Keep a close eye on cameras, purses, and wallets, all favorite targets of thieves and pickpockets.

New! Frommer's Star Ratings & Icons

Every hotel, restaurant, and attraction listing in this guide has been ranked for quality, value, service, amenities, and special features using a star-rating scale. In country, state, and regional guides, we also rate towns and regions to help you narrow down your choices and budget your time accordingly. Hotels and restaurants in the Very Expensive and Expensive categories are rated on a scale of one (highly recommended) to three stars (exceptional). Those in the Moderate and Inexpensive categories rate from zero (recommended) to two stars (very highly recommended). Attractions, towns, and regions are rated according to the following scale: zero stars (recommended), one star (highly recommended), two stars (very highly recommended), and three stars (must-see).

In addition to the rating system, we also use seven icons to highlight insider information, useful tips, special bargains, hidden gems, memorable experiences, kid-friendly venues, places to avoid, and other useful information:

(Finds   (Fun Fact   (Kids   (Moments   (Overrated   (Tips   (Value

The following abbreviations are used for credit cards:

| AE | American Express | DISC | Discover | V | Visa |
| DC | Diners Club | MC | MasterCard | | |

FROMMERS.COM

Now that you have the guidebook to a great trip, visit our website at **www.frommers.com** for travel information on nearly 2,000 destinations. With features updated regularly, we give you instant access to the most current trip-planning information available. At Frommers.com, you'll also find the best prices on airfares, accommodations, and car rentals—and you can even book travel online through our travel booking partners. At Frommers.com, you'll also find the following:

- Daily Newsletter highlighting the best travel deals
- Hot Spot of the Month/Vacation Sweepstakes & Travel Photo Contest
- More than 200 Travel Message Boards
- Outspoken Newsletters and Feature Articles on travel bargains, vacation ideas, tips & resources, and more!

What's New in Beijing

Between massive new construction projects to mark the 50th anniversary of the People's Republic of China and the unprecedented sprucing up of the capital to bolster its bid to host the **2008 Olympics**—a bid that was won in July 2001—Beijing has acquired a brand new face for the 21st century. Repeat travelers will hardly recognize the place. Much of the gray fog is lifting as Beijing becomes a vibrant, more international world capital.

PLANNING A TRIP TO BEIJING A revival of **temple fairs** has, for the first time, given travelers plenty to do in the winter weeks around **Chinese New Year** (Feb 12, 2002; Feb 1, 2003), but it's worth knowing that many offices and attractions close down during the three major holidays of the Spring Festival (Chinese New Year), International Labor Day (May 1), and National Day (Oct 1), each of which has been expanded to an official 5-day vacation. During Spring Festival, in fact, most Beijingers seem to take a 2-week leave of absence.

GETTING TO KNOW BEIJING The new terminal at the **Beijing Capital International Airport** (open Oct 2000) is a vast improvement in every way: modern, clean, more efficient, less crowded with touts. Your trip into town will be faster, too, thanks to the new **Airport Expressway** (which cuts transfer time down to a mere 30 or 40 min., barring traffic jams). Meanwhile, **China International Tourist Service** (CITS) is now headquartered

inconveniently west of downtown at 103 Fuxingmennei Dajie (© **010/ 6601-1122**). The 24-hour travel hot line remains © **010/6513-0828,** and its English-speaking operators are helpful. The best news for getting around town is the completion of the **new crosstown subway,** Metro Line 1, with 23 stops running east and west under Chang'an Avenue. Tickets are 3RMB (36¢) for new Line 1 and the old Loop Line; easy transfers are free.

Last but not least, on the frontiers of hygiene, the nightmarish old public toilets are closing for good, at least in downtown areas, and are to be replaced by new or portable units with flush or chemical appliances.

ACCOMMODATIONS It's still impossible to find good, basic hotel rooms at inexpensive rates, but for possible budget options check out the new listing of traditional courtyard inns in chapter 4, "Accommodations." The two newest hotels in Beijing cater to luxury travel: the five-star **Radisson Plaza State Guest House,** 9 Fuchengmenwai Dajie (© **800/333-3333** or 010/6800-5588), with a lobby worthy of the Taj Mahal, and the soon-to-open **Oriental Harbour Plaza Hotel,** 1 Dong Chang'an Jie (© **010/ 6436-1805**), another five-star tower in the heart of Beijing's newest and biggest shopping/office plaza. Other accommodations changes are largely cosmetic. The Sheraton-managed Beijing International Club Hotel has changed its name to **St. Regis Beijing,** 21 Jianguomenwai Dajie

(℗ **800/ 325-3535** or 010/6800-5588), doubled the number of private butlers for each floor, and is about to open a new office wing and fitness center. Thanks to another round of renovations, the historic **Beijing Hotel**, 35 Dong Chang'an Jie (℗ **010/ 6513-7766**) grows less historic by the day. Another old hotel downtown, the Peace Hotel, has a new international management team and a new name: the **Novotel Peace Hotel**, 3 Jinyu Hutong, Wangfujing (℗ **800/ 221-4542** or 010/ 6512-8833). Movenpick's airport hotel has also been renamed; now it's the **Sino-Swiss Hotel**, Xiao Tianzhu Village, (℗ **010/ 6456-5588**), still the best place by far to billet by the airport.

DINING   The two newest, trendiest places to dine in Beijing are the Cajun-inclined **Big Easy**, at the south gate of Chaoyang Park (℗ **010/ 6508-6776**) and the retro **Red Capital Club**, 66 Dongsi Jiutiao (℗ **010/ 6402-7150**), where the latest Chinese dishes are juxtaposed with a decor recalling the era of Chairman Mao. Looking to the West, China's first **Starbucks** opened at the China World Trade Center and never looked back, quickly opening more than 20 outlets, from the Friendship Store to Wangfujing Street. But **bubble tea** (made with tapioca pearls) is giving coffee a run for its money; there are bubble teahouses on every shopping block. And salsa, both the food and the dance craze, has found Beijing as well, first at a Cuban-style hangout, the **Havana Cafe**, north gate of Workers' Stadium (℗ **010/6586-6166**), and then at the upscale **Salsa Cabana** in the Lufthansa Centre (℗ **010/ 6465-3388**, ext. 5700). The newest Thai eatery is **Serve the People**, a fine bistro in the ever-changing Sanlitun Bar Street cafe lineup (℗ **010/ 6415-3242**). For street-food aficionados, the mainstay has long been the **Donghuamen Night Market** off Wangfujing. Like much of the Wangfujing shopping area, the night market has been spiffed up, too. The vendors' carts here have been renovated, making the street food here the most hygienic in Beijing (but bring your own chopsticks).

EXPLORING BEIJING   Temple-troupers will be delighted with the restoration of the **Eastern Peak Temple (Dong Yue Miao)** on Chaoyangmenwai Dajie (℗ **010/ 6553-2184**), where the 88 courts of Daoist punishment and reward are again in session. The gorgeous **Five-Pagoda Temple (Wu Ta Si)**, 24 Wutaicun (℗ **010/6217-3836**), is closed until sometime in 2002 due to the construction of a museum to protect its fine stone sculptures. Another place of worship, the previously obscured **St. Joseph's Church**, 74 Wangfujing Dajie (℗ **010/ 6524-0634**), has a brand new courtyard that opens wide to Beijing's number-one shopping street. Nearby, the **Lao She House**, 19 Fengfu Hutong (℗ **010/6514-2612**), the courtyard home of one of China's best-known 20th-century writers, has just opened to visitors and is well worth a visit. The big new **China Millennium Monument** on Fuxing Lu is not worth visiting on its own, perhaps, but it is often the site of major exhibits of Chinese treasures. Two new attractions provide a more active way to experience Beijing: the **Beijing Aquarium**, 18 Gaoliangqiao Xie Jie (℗ **010/6217-6655**), the largest inland aquarium in Asia, has opened adjacent to the Beijing Zoo; and skaters can take to the ice year-round at the new indoor, state-of-the-art **Le Cool Skating Rink** in the China World Shopping Center, 1 Jianguomenwai Dajie (℗ **010/ 6505-5776**). If walks and strolls do a number on your feet, try one of the foot massage centers that are now catering to foreigners.

BEIJING STROLLS Beijing's number one place to window shop, and a great place for strolling, Wangfujing has changed considerably, largely to the benefit of visitors. For starters, there's the new **Wangfujing Pedestrian Mall.** Along Wangfujing you can now visit a century-old renovated church courtyard, a major writers private-alley residence, and Asia's largest commercial complex, **Oriental Plaza,** with the site of Beijing's oldest human settlement preserved in the basement subway entrance.

SHOPPING The Sanlitun wicker and clothing market has folded up its stalls and moved indoors (a few blocks west), but the **Hongqiao Market,** already indoors at 16 Hongqiao Lu (© 010/6711-7429), is going strong, with cheap freshwater pearls and very cheap designer-label outdoor wear. The **Yabaolu Market,** commonly called the Russian market, has also had to move indoors (all part of a city campaign to "clean up" the streets); in fact, it has split into two markets: an upscale arcade on Yabao Lu just west of Ritan Park and a massive flea market housed under metal roofs at 16 Chaoyangmenwai Dajie. The Xidan intersection, west of the Forbidden City, has new plazas on every corner and a mall called Times Square, but the upscale place to shop is the new colossus, **Oriental Plaza,** 1 Dong Chang'an Jie (© **010/6526-3366;** www.orientalplaza.com). With five themed shopping malls, a Volkswagen showroom, Starbucks, and a children's science museum, it is Asia's largest such complex.

BEIJING AFTER DARK Locals and some visitors are buying tickets to Beijing performances online at **www. webtix.com.cn** or **www.66cities.com;** ticket delivery to your hotel is included. The cafe bar and dance club scene continues to expand. The newest location is at Chaoyang Park (the south gate), where you'll find the capital's hottest disco, **Rock 'n' Roll** (© **010/6592-9856**), going strong from midnight to dawn, and its best live jazz and blues club, Big Easy (© **010/ 6508-6776**). Sanlitun Bar Street continues to add and subtract cafe bars, recently adding **Public Space,** 50 Sanlitun Bei Jiuba Lu (© **010/6416-0759**), an elegant lounge, to its late-night roster. Other well-received openings around town include **The Loft,** 4 Gongrentiyuchang Bei Lu (© **010/6501-7501**), an ultra-modern restaurant and dance club, and **Vogue,** 88 Gongrentiyuchang Dong Lu (© **010/ 6416-5316**), currently the dance lounge favored by celebrities.

1

The Best of Beijing

Beijing is China's preeminent city, hosting more travelers than any other city in China—and for good reason, because no other city offers so many marvels, ancient and modern. Where else in China (or in the world, for that matter) can you gorge yourself on crispy Beijing (Peking) duck, walk the Great Wall like a modern sentinel, crisscross the haunting expanses of Tiananmen Square, and freely explore the splendors of the Forbidden City, all in a day or two? Shanghai and Hong Kong may be more vibrant, more thoroughly modern cities, but only Beijing can really show off the past 6 centuries of Chinese history, art, and culture.

While serving as the capital for imperial dynasties from the Ming to the Qing, Beijing has had its pick of the empire's glorious creations, many of which it has guarded over the centuries. Beijing was the capital in the 13th century, when Kublai Khan built his palace there and when Marco Polo first paid a visit. It reigned supreme from the 15th century, when the Ming rulers built the Forbidden City, to the 18th century, when the Manchu rulers built the Summer Palace. Beijing continued as the capital until 1923, when the last of China's emperors was evicted from the Forbidden City, and it was reanointed as the city of China's rulers in 1949, when Mao Zedong established the People's Republic of China. No city is more important in recent Chinese history—and more of that history is on display here than anywhere else.

The Forbidden City still stands at the center of Beijing, its golden tiled roofs and vast white courtyards glittering in the sun like an ancient giant's crown. The Summer Palace has survived, too, at the northwest edge of the city, as has the Temple of Heaven to the south, along with dozens of delicate monuments, old temples, and the courtyard houses in little alleyways (*hutongs*) that were once the hallmark of ordinary city life.

Add to this Beijing's and China's number one attraction: the Great Wall, Asia's answer to the pyramids and China's paramount monument to its romantic and turbulent past. As the popular saying has it, "You haven't been to China if you haven't stood on the Great Wall."

Beijing's temples, parks, and historic sites all sing wonderfully and powerfully of the dream that was Old Cathay, but in the same hallowed space there's a new Beijing taking shape. Just outside the exquisite walls of Beijing's historic monuments, steel and concrete are steadily replacing silk and carved wood. This transition can be jarring. Beijing is transforming itself before our eyes—reborn as the capital of the most populous (and, potentially, the most powerful) nation on earth. Just since the turn of the new century, the Beijing cityscape has been enlarged almost daily with the appearance of yet another skyscraper. This building boom's cumulative effect to the eye: a fresher, larger, and—for the first time—very modern Beijing.

For some visitors, this reconstruction in the old capital is more a tragedy than a triumph, but in fact, the modern cityscape imparts much energy to the city. Construction projects tromp through this Beijing of the future like mechanical Godzillas, pounding antiquated neighborhoods into oblivion block by block. At dawn the city parks are still filled with Beijingers sleepwalking through their old tai chi exercises, but the surrounding streets are now packed with millionaires as well as street sweepers, with Mercedes as well as bicycles, with enterprising touts as well as destitute beggars. Beijing today is two cities in one, a crazy scroll of skyscrapers and shacks, of Pizza Huts and teahouses, unwinding in a chaotic sprawl.

Beijing is in the midst of remaking itself on a scale that can scarcely be believed, and this rapid modernization against a backdrop of ancient treasures gives Beijing a wild East–West flavor that is exhilarating. It is a city with two faces, both endlessly fascinating to the traveler. With all its celebrated historical attractions, Beijing may well be the capital of China's past, but it is also the capital of China's future, a city dedicated to becoming both modern and international, and it is here that one can see in broad and determined strokes both what China has been and what it means to become.

1 Frommer's Favorite Beijing Experiences

- **Walking Up and Down the Great Wall:** The three most popular sections of the Great Wall (at Badaling, Mutianyu, and Simatai) make for spectacular treks and photo opportunities. All three were built during the Ming Dynasty (1368–1644) and are located in beautiful mountain forests outside Beijing. Make time to walk beyond the crowds. The least-visited section, at Simatai, is the best of these three, as it's the only one that remains largely untouched by modern restoration. See Chapter 10, "The Great Wall & Other Side Trips from Beijing," for details on visiting the Wall.

- **Getting Lost in the Forbidden City:** The vast inner city of emperors and eunuchs for 500 years (1423–1923) is China's most impressive treasure house. It's best enjoyed on your own, rather than as part of a group tour, particularly at the small pavilions off the beaten path that house unusual royal treasures, from toys to clocks. See chapter 6, "Exploring Beijing," for details.

- **Crossing Tiananmen Square:** The very center of the People's Republic of China and the largest public square on earth, Tiananmen reverberates with the ghosts of recent history—from the Great Hall of the People to the Monument to the People's Heroes, where students encamped before the TV cameras of the world in 1989. It's at its best at sunset, when the flag is lowered. See chapter 6, "Exploring Beijing," for details.

- **Meeting Chairman Mao:** At Chairman Mao's Mausoleum, located dead center on Tiananmen Square, visitors are allowed 60 seconds of uncanny silence in which to contemplate the last real emperor as he lies in state on a bed of granite, preserved for the ages. See chapter 6, "Exploring Beijing," for details.

- **Going to Market:** Beijing's most famous street market, Silk Alley, is a tourist trap, but an interesting one, with a gauntlet of stalls offering the latest designer fashion labels, particularly in outdoor wear. The most fascinating market is held Sunday morning at dawn: the open-air Dirt Market (also called the Ghost Market) offers Beijing's wildest and most wide-ranging collection of collectibles, family heirlooms, Qing Dynasty furniture, and curios. Perhaps the best selection for clothing and jewelry, however, is the indoor Hongqiao Market (Pearl Market), five floors of potential bargains near the Temple of Heaven. See chapter 8, "Shopping," for the complete lowdown on Beijing's markets.

- **Exploring the *Hutongs*:** Don't miss a chance to explore the fast-disappearing *hutongs*—the twisting alleyways in the courtyard neighborhoods of Old Beijing—whether on an organized tour by tricycle taxi or on your own by rented bicycle. See chapter 6, "Exploring Beijing," for details on joining an escorted tour.

- **Whispering in the Temple of Heaven:** Venturing beyond the miraculous temple itself, explore the byways and whisper your name at Echo Wall. These and other nooks are favored by the locals for exercising, recreational sports, and family picnics. The park is an ideal place to see Beijingers at leisure. See chapter 6, "Exploring Beijing," for details.

- **Burning Incense in the Temples:** The Lama Temple is rated number one by tourists and foreign residents alike, and it has all the hallmarks of a typical large and active Buddhist temple, as well as some exotic (and erotic) aspects all its own. A livelier shrine, more frequented by locals, is the White Cloud Temple, where ancient beliefs and superstitions are alive and flourishing, the incense is always burning, and hundreds of Beijingers converge to kowtow and pray for a dozen different wishes (from good health to more wealth). See chapter 6, "Exploring Beijing," for details on Beijing's temples.

- **Going to Church with the Chinese:** Foreigners can now attend Christian services in the 19th- and early-20th-century churches and cathedrals of Beijing, where locals in increasing numbers pray and masses in Latin are still practiced. See chapter 6, "Exploring Beijing," for details.

- **Shadowboxing in the Parks:** Every morning before heading to work or school, thousands of Beijingers perform tai chi and other traditional, even more mysterious exercises, such as swinging from tree limbs, in the city parks. A growing number of early-risers are even practicing Western ballroom dancing. These are sights not to be missed. See chapter 6, "Exploring Beijing," for details on Beijing's parks.

- **Enjoying a Sunset at the Ancient Observatory:** This remnant of the city wall, an island in the busy downtown thoroughfare of Chang'an Avenue, houses 17th-century astronomical instruments on its roof. It's the perfect place to overlook the heart of the city and enjoy a sunset. See chapter 6, "Exploring Beijing," for details.

- **Rowing Your Boat at the Summer Palace:** The most beautiful spot in Beijing has a Long Corridor painted with thousands of scenes of China and its mythology. After seeing the sights on land, you can rent a rowboat for a dreamy afternoon on Kunming Lake. See chapter 6, "Exploring Beijing," for details.

- **Stilt-Walking at a Temple Fair:** You don't have to walk on stilts (although they're for hire) to enjoy Chinese New Year at one of the fairs in Beijing's parks and temples. This old tradition has come back in a big way in the capital, but you can only enjoy these gala, yet homespun, festivities for the 2 weeks of the Spring Festival each winter. See chapter 2, "Planning Your Trip to Beijing," for dates and locations.

- **Touring the Eastern Qing Tombs:** The Ming Tombs are still a major tourist stop on the way to the Great Wall, but at the Eastern Qing Tombs, a longer excursion, you'll find a more fascinating, less congested display that reveals how emperors and their concubines entered the afterlife in style. See chapter 10, "The Great Wall & Other Side Trips from Beijing," for details on getting there and visiting the tombs.

- **Window Shopping on Wangfujing:** Beijing's top shopping street in the heart of the capital now offers everything from art galleries and scroll shops to wedding stores and chic boutiques. Aging department stores compete with state-of-the-art shopping plazas. Plenty of McDonald's have sprung up, along with Starbucks (the new Chinese favorite), but the best native fast food and tea are served from stalls in the night market off Wangfujing (at Donghuamen Yeshi). See chapter 7, "Beijing Strolls," for a walk through Wangfujing, and chapter 8, "Shopping," for complete details on Beijing shopping.

- **Banqueting on Beijing Duck:** Plenty of restaurants serve it, a half-dozen specialize in it, and it's worth sampling this signature dish of Northern China several times over, preferably with a group. This is what Beijing banqueting is all about. See chapter 5, "Dining," for recommended places to try Beijing duck, and even tips on how to eat it.

- **Dining on the Moat:** There's no doubt about it, the best place for a fine dinner or a casual drink is at Beijing's most acclaimed restaurant, **The Courtyard** (95 Donghuamen Lu, Dongcheng District; (© **010/6526-8881**), with its stunning view of the moat that rings the Forbidden City. See chapter 5, "Dining," for details.

- **Barhopping in Sanlitun & Beyond:** The Sanlitun diplomatic district is home to more than 50 bars that cater equally to foreigners and locals. Many have live pop music from midnight to dawn. See chapter 9, "Beijing After Dark," for a complete guide to Beijing nightlife.

- **Bicycling through Old Beijing:** Although riding a bike in Beijing, with 8 million riders in motion, looks dangerous, it isn't difficult to get into the flow. This is a city meant for bike riding, which is the best means to explore the capital on your own. See chapter 3, "Getting to Know Beijing," for tips on renting a bike and navi-gating Beijing on two wheels.

- **Lingering in the Teahouses:** The teahouse tradition has staged a comeback in Beijing, with tea and snacks served in old teahouses to the accompaniment of singing, dancing, comedy, acrobatics, and magic. The best place to soak up Qing Dynasty atmosphere is the **Tian Qiao Happy Teahouse** at A1 Beiwei Lu (#113 Tianqiao Market), Xuanwu District (© **010/6304-0617**), where one's teacup is always full and the intimate stage is filled with opera singers and acrobats. See chapter 9, "Beijing After Dark," for details.

China

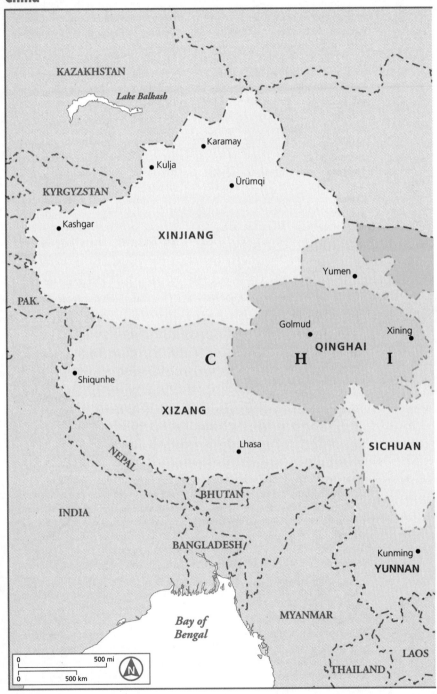

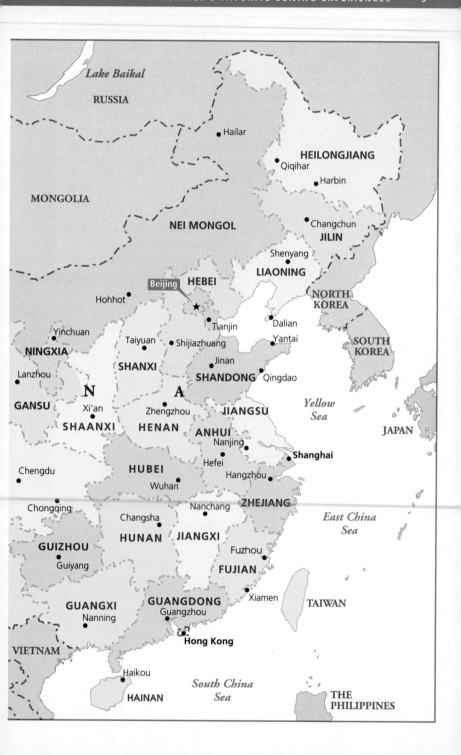

2 Best Hotel Bets

For complete hotel listings, see chapter 4, "Accommodations."

- **Best Hotel Hands Down:** The honor goes to **China World Hotel** (1 Jianguomenwai Dajie; ℰ **800/942-5050** or 010/6505-2266). No hotel in Beijing has perfect service, but China World comes closest, combining good help with excellent facilities—from its health and fitness facilities to its full-service, 24-hour business center.

- **Best Business Hotel (East Side):** Stay right next door to Big Sister (the China World Hotel) and enjoy that hotel's five-star guest facilities at no extra charge from the highly efficient four-star **Traders Hotel Beijing** (1 Jianguomenwai Dajie; ℰ **800/942-5050** or 010/6505-2277), a more intimate favorite of foreign business travelers trying to save a nickel, all the while keeping one of the most prestigious addresses in town.

- **Best Ring Road Business Hotel (Northeast):** The tried-and-true favorite is the highly experienced **Beijing Hilton Hotel** (1 Dongfeng Lu, Third Ring Road North; ℰ **800/445-8667** or 010/6466-2288) with its no-nonsense breakfast buffet, stylish restaurants, jazz theme decor, large business center, and room renovations, which began in 2001.

- **Best New Kid on the Block:** The **Kerry Centre Hotel Beijing** (1 Guanghau Lu; ℰ **800/942-5050** or 010/6561-8833) has made a uniformly impressive debut with its friendly staff, bright modern rooms, and first-class fitness facilities, including an outdoor in-line and jogging track. It's probably the most kid-friendly hotel in town.

- **Best Resort Hotel:** Beijing has no resorts, but the one that comes closest is the **Sino-Swiss Hotel Beijing** (Xiao Tianzhu Village, Capital Airport; ℰ **010/6456-5588**). It's far enough from the city to have noticeably better air, more blue sky, and a resident camel, and it offers plenty of outdoor activities on its spacious grounds (including beach volleyball). This is one place where Beijing's resident foreigners come in the summer for barbecues and horseback riding.

- **Best Hotel Lobby for Pretending You're a Foreign VIP:** With millions of dollars invested in marble alone, this new top-of-the-line Sheraton, the **St. Regis Hotel Beijing** (21 Jianguomenwai Dajie; ℰ **800/325-3535** or 010/6460-6688), has the most spectacular lobby in Beijing. Celebs and various VIPs drop in here for a casual drink or high tea, and the ballroom at the top of the winding marble staircase is a favorite for diplomatic receptions.

- **Best Hotel Lobby for People-Watching:** Any expat who's worth watching or talking to will, at some time, pass through Beijing's liveliest reception area, located at the venerable **Jianguo Hotel** (5 Jianguomenwai Dajie; ℰ **800/223-5652** or 010/6500-2233). The lobby is a favorite gathering place for afternoon tea; its Sunday buffets with classical music are a mainstay.

- **Best Hotel for Travelers with Disabilities:** More and more Beijing hotels have rooms equipped for travelers with disabilities, but the **Swissotel** (Hong Kong Macau Centre, Dong Si Shi Tiao Li Jiao Qiao; ℰ **800/637-9477** or 010/6501-2288) devotes the entire fourth floor to such travelers, with some of the best barrier-free architecture in Asia.

- **Best World Unto Itself:** This odd category fits to a tee the hotel complex known as the **Holiday Inn Lido** (Jichang Lu, Jiangtai Lu; ✆ **800/465-4329** or 010/6437-6688). As the largest Holiday Inn on Earth, the Lido contains everything a foreign traveler or resident could desire in one vast complex, from shoe repair and a bowling alley to an international school and kindergarten.
- **Most Efficient Hotel:** Nearly everything runs like clockwork, including Beijing's most frequent, wide-ranging hotel shuttle, at the **Kempinski Hotel,** (Lufthansa Centre, 50 Liangmaqiao Lu; ✆ **800/426-3135** or 010/6465-3388).
- **Best Room Decor:** Luxury hotel rooms begin to all look alike around the world, but the **Radisson SAS Hotel** (6A Beisanhuan Dong Lu; ✆ **800/333-3333** or 010/6466-3388) stands out with no less than three sterling choices,

all quite stylish: Chinese, Art Deco, and High-Tech.

- **Best Hotel Art:** Beijing is drab, but the nine-story atrium of the **Crowne Plaza Beijing,** 48 Wangfujing Dajie (✆ **800/465-4329** or 010/6513-3388), reveals that this is a hotel dedicated to contemporary Chinese artists—with its own fine art gallery on the first floor and an art salon on the mezzanine.
- **Best Hotel Shopping Arcade:** The elegant **Palace Hotel** (8 Jinyu Hutong, Wangfujing Dajie; ✆ **800/262-9467** or 010/6559-2888) maintains several floors of exclusive designer-name shops (Armani, Cartier, Hermès); it's a Beverly Hills outpost in the heart of the Chinese capital.
- **Best Hotel Garden:** Traditional gardens are seldom a feature of Beijing's modern hotels, but the **Shangri-La Hotel** (29 Zizhuyuan Lu; ✆ **800/942-5050** or 010/6841-2211) is a notable exception, with a romantic garden of arched bridges, pavilions, ponds, and resident rabbits and birds.

3 Best Dining Bets

For complete restaurant listings, see chapter 5, "Dining."

- **Best Restaurant (Hands Down):** **The Courtyard** (95 Donghuamen Lu, Dongcheng District; ✆ **010/6526-8881**) has it all: superb fusion cuisine, an excellent staff, a contemporary Chinese art gallery in the basement, and upstairs, a cigar divan with breathtaking views of the Forbidden City.
- **Best Beijing Duck:** The capital's most famous dish, roasted duck, is served up at a chain of duck restaurants. **Quanjude Kaoyadian,** nicknamed "Big duck," at 32 Qianmen Dajie, Chongmen

District (✆ **010/6511-2418**), south of Tiananmen Square, is the largest and most elegant of the group.

- **Best Beijing Cuisine:** For steamed buns, pastries, sliced duck, and noodles in the Northern Chinese style, **Sihexuan** (in the Jinglun Hotel, 3 Jianguomenwai Dajie, Chaoyang District; ✆ **010/6500-2266,** ext. 8116) offers unsurpassed quality in a rustic but relaxed setting.
- **Best Imperial Cuisine:** Served in a courtyard compound in a *hutong* neighborhood, the imperial dishes at the **Li Family Restaurant** (11 Yangfang, Deshengmennei Dajie,

Xicheng District; ✆ **010/6618-0107**) are so popular that reservations can be backed up for weeks.

- **Best Chinese Decor:** Fangshan (Beihai Gongyuan Nei, Xicheng District; ✆ **010/6401-1879**) was the first restaurant opened by former cooks from the Forbidden City, and its setting is pure Old Cathay: a courtyard mansion with views of Beihai Lake.
- **Best Chinese Dinner with a Side Order of History:** The fun is in the setting (1950s Mao redux), the stories that go with each dish, and the food (elegant modern Chinese fare) at the new **Red Capital Club,** 66 Dongsi Jiutiao (✆ **010/6402-7150** or 010/8401-8886).
- **Best Romantic Dinner:** The cuisine is French, the dress code is formal, and the mood is set by candlelight and a string quartet at elegant **Justine's** in the Jianguo Hotel, 5 Jianguomenwai Dajie, Chaoyang District (✆ **010/6500-2233**, ext. 8039).
- **Best Business Lunch:** For Cantonese dim sum in a power-lunch setting, make reservations at **Horizon** (1 Guanghua Lu, Kerry Centre; ✆ **010/6561-8833,** ext. 41). For Western fare, the continental fixed-price lunches at **Bleu Marine,** 5 Dongdaqiao Lu, Chaoyang District (✆ **010/6500-6704**), are also good (and a good deal).
- **Best Sunday Brunch:** The international hotels all have lavish Sunday spreads in their lobbies, but the most elegant and expensive is at the **Swissotel** (Hong Kong Macau Center, Dong Si Shi Tiao Li Jiao Qiao, Chaoyang District; (✆ **010/6501-2288,** ext. 2232) where guests feast on unrestricted portions of caviar and Moët & Chandon champagne.

- **Best Grill:** A hip jazz bar with a top Continental grillroom, **Aria** (China World Hotel, 1 Jianguomenwai Dajie, Chaoyang District; ✆ **010/6505-2266**) attracts the capital's VIPs, East and West. On its second floor, there's a secret nook that hovers above the busy hotel lobby, like a private box at the opera—perfect for people-watching.
- **Best Wine List:** Home of New American cuisine with a Cajun flare, **Louisiana** (Beijing Hilton Hotel, 1 Dong Fang Lu, Third Ring Road North; ✆ **010/6466-2288,** ext. 7420) has the city's largest wine list, cited for its excellence by *Wine Spectator* magazine.
- **Best Burgers:** A cheerful American-style bar and grill, **Henry J. Bean's** (China World Hotel, 1 Jianguomenwai Dajie, Chaoyang District; ✆ **010/6505-2266,** ext. 6334) consistently turns out a savory bacon cheeseburger with all the trimmings.
- **Best Coffee Spot:** Starbucks has launched its invasion of the Land of Tea with resounding success. The best and busiest latte dispatchers are located at the upscale China World Trade Center (✆ **010/6505-2288,** ext. 8122), in the spacious Full Link Plaza (✆ **010/6588-05030**), and at the casual Friendship Store (✆ **010/6586-4796**).
- **Best Ice Cream: Häagen-Dazs** has opened its own little cafe, with some of the richest ice creams and sauces in Beijing, in the diplomatic zone at the Beijing International Club (21 Jianguomenwai Dajie, Room 196, Chaoyang District; ✆ **010/ 6532-6661**).
- **Best Cajun:** Beijing's best version of Bourbon Street is found at the

ultra-trendy **Big Easy** located at Chaoyang Park south (✆ **010/6508-6776**).

- **Best Cantonese:** There are plenty of excellent Southern Chinese restaurants in Beijing, but the **Summer Palace** (in the China World Hotel, 1 Jianguomenwai Dajie, Chaoyang District; ✆ 010/**6505-2266,** ext. 34) blends service, selection, and quality with near perfection.

- **Best French:** Superb French restaurants in China are not an incongruity. Beijing has its own Maxim's, but for maintenance of the old traditions with just a twist of Asian invention, head downtown to **Plaza Grill** in the Crowne Plaza Beijing (48 Wangfujing, Dongcheng District; ✆ **010/6513-3388,** ext. 1132).

- **Best Indian:** Beijing's first Indian restaurant with an Indian chef, **Shamiana** (in the Holiday Inn Downtown, 98 Beilishi Lu, Xicheng District; ✆ **010/6833-8822,** ext. 7107) flies in fresh ingredients from India and knows how to produce top curries and somosas.

- **Best Italian:** There are plenty of top contenders, but few can equal the simple charms of the Naples-style dishes in the new **Danieli's** in the Beijing International Club Hotel (21 Jianguomenwai Dajie; (✆ **010/6460-6688,** ext. 2355). A less expensive, but quite superb, contender is **Peppino's** in the

Shangri-La Hotel (29 Zizhuyuan Lu; ✆ **010/6841-6727**).

- **Best Japanese:** Beijing's first *robatayaki* (grill) restaurant, **Nishimura** (in the Shangri-La Hotel, 29 Zizhuyuan Lu, Haidian District; ✆ **010/6841-2211,** ext. 2702), and **Nadaman** (in the China World Hotel, 1 Jianguomenwai Dajie; ✆ **010/6505-2266,** ext. 39), are both Japan-based restaurants that have made successful transits to China. For fine (but cheaper) sushi and tempura, resident Westerners prefer **San Si Lang** in Tuanjiehu Park (✆ **010/6506-9625**).

- **Best Sichuan:** The longtime expatriate favorite, for good reason, is **Berena's Bistro** (6 Gongrentiyuchang Dong Lu; ✆ **010/6592-2628**), where the waiters wear red and the entrees are heat-rated.

- **Best Thai:** Long regarded as Beijing's top Thai restaurant, **Borom Piman** (in the Holiday Inn Lido, Jichang Lu, Jiangtai Lu, Chaoyang District Northeast; ✆ **010/6437-6688,** ext. 2899) imports its spices and cooks from the Land of Smiles.

- **Best Vegetarian:** Nothing on the Chinese menu contains meat, despite appearances, and everything is fresh and tantalizing at Green Tianshi, located at 57 Dengshikou Lu (off Wangfujing), Dongcheng District (✆ **010/6524-2349**).

2

Planning Your Trip to Beijing

Here are the basics for designing a trip to Beijing and entering China with the right documents in hand, as well as tips on how to navigate smoothly through the airport and arrive in the capital with the fewest hassles.

1 Visitor Information

Foreign travel to the People's Republic of China (PRC) is handled by an official government agency, **China International Travel Service,** referred to by the initials **CITS.** In Chinese, CITS is called *guoji luxingshe.* CITS can set up international and domestic air flights, train and bus reservations within China, and hotel reservations for Beijing, as well as provide English-speaking guides and group or individual sightseeing tours through its Beijing branch offices (often located in hotels). **China Travel Service (CTS)** and a host of other governmental and private travel services also cater to foreign travelers.

CITS OVERSEAS CITS has opened China National Tourist Offices (CNTO) abroad to provide tourist information and services.

- In the **United States:** China National Tourist Office, 350 5th Ave., Suite 6413, New York, NY 10118 (© **212/760-9700;** fax 212/760-8809); 333 W. Broadway, Suite 201, Glendale, CA 91204 (© **818/545-7507;** fax 818/545-7506).

- In the **United Kingdom:** China National Tourist Office, 4 Glentworth St., London N.W. 1 (© **020/7935-9427;** fax 020/7487-5842).

- In **Australia:** China National Tourist Office, 44 Market St., Sydney NSW 2000 (© **02/9299-4057;** fax 02/9290-1958).

For the locations of CITS offices in Beijing, see "Orientation," in chapter 3, "Getting to Know Beijing."

BEIJING ONLINE One way to receive fairly up-to-date information on Beijing before departure is by logging onto the Internet. CITS maintains a helpful planning and reservations site at www.citsusa.com. Online editions of local English-language magazines with current dining and entertainment listings are available at www.cbw.com/btm (*Beijing This Month*), www.metroNET.com.cn (*Metrozine*), and www.citweekend.com.cn (*City Weekend*). Two other useful websites for visitors to Beijing are www.surfchina.com and www.chinanow.com.

2 Entry Requirements & Customs

ENTRY REQUIREMENTS

All visitors to Beijing and the People's Republic of China are required to have a valid passport that does not expire for at least 6 months after date of arrival. A special **tourist visa** or **business visa** is also required. Tour groups are usually issued a group visa,

> **Tips   Visas Online**
>
> Americans can download visa application forms and instructions from the Chinese embassy's website, **www.china-embassy.org**.

with the paperwork handled by the travel agency (check with your agent). Visas for individual travelers and business people can be obtained from certain travel agents overseas and in Hong Kong, and from the Chinese embassy or consulate in your country. Unless you are entering China through Hong Kong, where securing a visa from the Hong Kong CTS or local travel agent is easy, the safest way to secure a visa to China is by doing the paperwork required by the overseas consulate several months before your trip. Telephone, fax, or mail a request for a visa application to the Chinese embassy or consulate in your home country and follow the printed instructions. You will be required to mail a completed visa application form, one passport photograph, your valid passport (good for at least 6 months), and payment.

Payment depends on the visa you select. A 30-day single-entry tourist visa is the most economical; 60-day, 90-day, 6-month, and 12-month visas, permitting single or multiple entries, are also available. Currently U.S. passport holders can obtain a single-entry 30-day visa (expiring 3 months after the date of issue) for $30; a double-entry 30-day visa (expiring 3 months after the date of issue) for $45; a multiple-entry 6-month business visa (expiring 9 months after the date of issue) for $60; and a multiple-entry 12-month visa (expiring 15 months after the date of issue) for $90. Applications submitted by mail are assessed a $5 handling fee.

Express visa service is also offered at an additional cost. The visa prices and options can change without notice, and visas of special duration can be arranged by calling your nearest Chinese embassy or consulate.

GETTING A VISA IN HONG KONG   Many U.S., Canadian, Australian, New Zealand, Irish, and British citizens enter China through Hong Kong. Although Hong Kong is now part of China, residents of these nations are required to have only a valid passport to enter Hong Kong. Visas for the rest of China can be secured at countless travel agencies, including the highly efficient branch of China Travel Service (CTS) at 27-33 Nathan Road, Kowloon (© **852/2315-7149;** fax 852/2721-7757), second floor of the Alpha Building (entrance on Peking Rd.).

EXTENDED STAYS   The Foreign Affairs Section of the Public Security Bureau (the police), located at 85 Beichizi Dajie (© **010/6525-5486**) in downtown Beijing, has the power to extend visas. You must apply in person at the bureau for an extension. Those who overstay are fined about $50 per day.

CUSTOMS

Travelers are allowed to bring into China four bottles of alcoholic beverages and three cartons of cigarettes. Guns and illicit drugs are forbidden. There is no limit on the amount of foreign currency (although amounts above $10,000 must be declared on a customs form). No vaccinations or inoculations are currently required (although an AIDS test certificate is required for those planning on living in China for more than 6 months). Upon departure, note that antiques purchased in China must have a red wax seal for export. Customs declaration slips must be filled out prior to arrival and departure.

Returning **U.S. citizens** who have been away for 48 hours or more are allowed to bring back, once every 30 days, $400 worth of merchandise duty-free. You'll be charged a flat rate of 10% duty on the next $1,000 worth of purchases. Be sure to have your receipts handy. On gifts, the duty-free limit is $100. You cannot bring fresh foodstuffs into the United States; tinned foods, however, are allowed. For more information, contact the **U.S. Customs Service,** 1301 Constitution Ave. (P.O. Box 7407), Washington, DC 20044 (© **202/ 927-6724**), and request the free pamphlet *Know Before You Go.* It's also available at www.customs.ustreas.gov/ travel/kbygo.htm.

U.K. citizens returning from a non-EC country (PRC, in this case) have a customs allowance of 200 cigarettes; 50 cigars; 250 grams of smoking tobacco; 2 liters of still table wine; 1 liter of spirits or strong liqueurs (over 22% volume); 2 liters of fortified wine, sparkling wine, or other liqueurs; 60 cubic centimeters (ml) of perfume; 250 cubic centimeters (ml) of toilet water; and £145 worth of all other goods, including gifts and souvenirs. People under age 17 do not have a tobacco or alcohol allowance. For more information, contact HM Customs & Excise, Passenger Enquiry Point, 2nd Floor Wayfarer House, Great South West Rd., Feltham, Middlesex, TW14 8NP (© **020/ 8910-3744;** from outside the U.K. 44/181-910-3744; www.open.gov.uk).

For a clear summary of **Canadian** rules, write for the booklet *I Declare,* issued by **Revenue Canada,** 2265 St. Laurent Blvd., Ottawa K1G 4KE (© **613/993-0534**). Canada allows its citizens a $500 exemption, and you're allowed to bring back duty-free 200 cigarettes, 2.2 pounds of tobacco,

40 imperial ounces of liquor, and 50 cigars. In addition, you're allowed to mail gifts to Canada from abroad at the rate of Can$60 a day, provided they're unsolicited and don't contain alcohol or tobacco (write on the package "Unsolicited gift, under $60 value"). All valuables should be declared on the Y-38 form before departure from Canada, including serial numbers of valuables you already own, such as expensive foreign cameras. *Note:* The $500 exemption can only be used once a year and only after an absence of 7 days.

The duty-free allowance in **Australia** is A$400 or, for those under age 18, A$200. Upon returning to Australia, citizens can bring in 250 cigarettes or 250 grams of loose tobacco, and 1,125 milliliters of alcohol. If you're returning with valuable goods you already own, such as foreign-made cameras, you should file form B263. A helpful brochure, available from Australian consulates or Customs offices, is *Know Before You Go.* For more information, contact **Australian Customs Services,** GPO Box 8, Sydney NSW 2001 (© **02/9213-2000**).

The duty-free allowance for **New Zealand** is NZ$700. Citizens over age 17 can bring in 200 cigarettes, 50 cigars, or 250 grams of tobacco (or a mixture of all three if their combined weight doesn't exceed 250g); plus 4.5 liters of wine and beer, or 1.125 liters of liquor. New Zealand currency does not carry import or export restrictions. Fill out a certificate of export, listing the valuables you are taking out of the country; that way, you can bring them back without paying duty. Most questions are answered in a free pamphlet available at New Zealand consulates and Customs offices: *New Zealand Customs Guide for Travellers, Notice no. 4.* For more information, contact New Zealand Customs, 50 Anzac Ave., P.O. Box 29, Auckland (© **09/359-6655**).

3 Money

Chinese currency, the *yuan*, is called Renminbi (*RMB*). Six large bills are in wide circulation; they're clearly marked as 100, 50, 10, 5, 2, and 1 yuan. The current exchange rate is about 8.3 yuan to $1, making the yuan worth about 12¢. In addition, there are smaller bills worth less than 1 yuan in denominations of 5, 2, and 1 jiao (10 jiao = 1 yuan). Even smaller bills and coins have denominations in fen (100 fen = 10 jiao = 1 yuan). Commonly the yuan is called *kwai* and the jiao is called *mao*. Beijing is still a cash society, so most of your ordinary transactions in shops and cafes require Chinese currency. It is useful to carry a quantity of 10, 2, and 1 yuan notes to pay for taxis, bottled water, admissions, and other small daily purchases. Prices in China are usually marked with "RMB" or "Y" for yuan.

TRAVELER'S CHECKS   Traveler's checks are the easiest and safest way to bring money into China. Traveler's checks, as well as cash, can be converted to RMB at nearly all hotels, many banks, and some restaurants and stores (particularly the Friendship Store). Hotels and banks charge a small fee for conducting exchanges and credit card transactions, but hotel desks offer convenience and charge very little more than banks. Note that the exchange rate for traveler's checks is slightly better than for cash. It's usually not possible to get Chinese currency before you leave home.

You can get traveler's checks at almost any bank. **American Express** offers denominations of $10, $20, $50, $100, $500, and $1,000. You'll pay a service charge ranging from 1% to 4%. You can also get American Express traveler's checks over the phone by calling ℂ **800/221-7282;** by using this number, Amex gold and platinum cardholders are exempt from the 1% fee. AAA members can get checks without a fee at most AAA offices.

Visa offers traveler's checks at Citibank locations nationwide, as well as several other banks. The service charge ranges between 1.5% and 2%; checks come in denominations of $20, $50, $100, $500, and $1,000. **MasterCard** also offers traveler's checks. Call ℂ **800/223-9920** for a location near you.

CREDIT CARDS   In general, it is easiest to exchange traveler's checks for RMB at your hotel and to use a credit card to pay the hotel bill. Most fine restaurants and large stores in Beijing where tourists go now accept major credit cards, too, but the practice is not as common as in North America and Europe. You can also withdraw cash advances from your American Express, Visa, MasterCard, and Diner's Club card at most Bank of China branches and at a few select ATMs (although you'll start paying hefty interest on your advance the moment you receive the cash, and you won't get frequent-flyer miles on an airline credit card).

⸨Tips⸩ Packing for Security

Pickpockets are the bane of many a world's capital, including Beijing, so be sure to tuck traveler's checks, excess cash, airline tickets, and your ID, especially your passport, into a concealed pouch or money belt—not into a purse or backpack. Leave one copy of your passport and traveler's check receipts at your hotel (in a safety-box or room safe) and carry another copy with you.

The Chinese Yuan, the U.S. Dollar & the British Pound

For U.S. Readers   At this writing, $1 = approximately 8.3 RMB (or 1 RMB = 12¢). This was the rate of exchange used to calculate the U.S. dollar rates given in this book (rounded off). Exchange rates at hotels are usually 8.2 RMB per $1.

For British Readers   The rate of exchange used to calculate the pound values in the accompanying table was £1 = 13RMB (or 1RMB = 8p).

Check the current exchange rates before your arrival and use the following table as a guide only:

RMB	U.S.$	U.K.£	RMB	U.S.$	U.K.£
0.10	0.01	0.01	100	12.00	8.00
0.50	0.06	0.03	150	18.00	11.30
1.00	0.12	0.08	200	24.00	15.10
2.00	0.24	0.15	250	30.00	18.90
3.00	0.36	0.23	300	36.00	22.70
4.00	0.48	0.30	400	48.00	30.25
5.00	0.60	0.38	500	60.00	37.80
6.00	0.72	0.45	600	72.00	45.40
7.00	0.84	0.53	700	84.00	52.90
8.00	0.96	0.60	800	96.00	60.50
9.00	1.08	0.68	900	108.00	68.00
10.00	1.20	0.76	1,000	120.00	75.60
15.00	1.80	1.13	2,000	240.00	151.20
20.00	2.40	1.50	3,000	360.00	226.80
25.00	3.00	1.90	4,000	480.00	302.40
30.00	3.60	2.27	5,000	600.00	378.00
35.00	4.20	2.65	6,000	720.00	453.60
40.00	4.80	3.03	7,000	840.00	529.20
45.00	5.40	3.40	8,000	960.00	604.80
50.00	6.00	3.80	9,000	1,080.00	680.40
75.00	9.00	5.70	10,000	1,200.00	756.00

You will need your PIN at an ATM and your passport at the bank when using your credit card for cash withdrawals. If you've forgotten your PIN or didn't even know you had one, call the phone number on the back of your credit card and ask the bank to send it to you. It usually takes 5 to 7 business days. Some banks will supply the number over the phone if you tell them your mother's maiden name or pass some other security clearance.

Many ATMs honor only Chinese-issued credit cards, but American Express has a 24-hour ATM at the China World Trade Center (1 Jianguomenwai Dajie). Visa cardholders can withdraw RMB from any ATM labeled Visa/Plus, as well as from many banks. ATM locations for Visa/Plus machines include the airport, the CITIC Building, the Palace Hotel, and Bank of China branches.

What Things Cost in Beijing	U.S. $	U.K. £
Taxi from airport to city center	12.00	8.00
Subway ride	36¢	23p
Local telephone call	6¢	3p
Double room at the China World Shangri-La (very expensive)	240.00	151.00
Double room at the Traders Hotel (expensive)	190.00	119.70
Double room at the Novotel Peace Hotel (moderate)	108.00	68.00
Double room at the Bamboo Garden Hotel (budget)	60.00	37.80
Lunch for one at Berena's (moderate)	8.00	5.00
Lunch for one at Gold Cat Jiaozi City (inexpensive)	5.00	3.15
Dinner for one, without drinks, at Li Family Restaurant (very expensive)	40.00	25.20
Dinner for one, without drinks, at Summer Palace (expensive)	30.00	18.90
Dinner for one, without drinks, at a Beijing duck restaurant (moderate)	20.00	12.60
Dinner for one, without drinks, at Sihexuan (inexpensive)	12.00	7.60
Glass of beer	3.50	2.20
Coca-Cola	1.25	.80
Roll of 100 ASA Fujicolor film (36 exposures)	6.00	3.80
Admission to the Forbidden City	7.20	4.50
Admission to the Lama Temple	2.40	1.50
Movie ticket	4.00	2.50
Theater ticket (good seat) to Peking Opera	20.00	12.60
Ticket to Three Tenors Concert at Forbidden City	200–2,000	140–1,400

ATMs   Many of Beijing's ATMs are linked to a network that most likely includes your bank at home. **Cirrus** (© **800/424-7787**; www.mastercard. com/atm/) and **Plus** (© **800/ 843-7587**; www.visa.com/atms) are the two most popular networks; check the back of your ATM card to see which network your bank belongs to. Before your trip, use the toll-free numbers to locate ATMs in your destination or ask your bank for a list of ATMs in China. Be sure to check the daily withdrawal limit before you depart, and ask whether you need a new PIN.

Personal checks are almost impossible to cash in Beijing. (Although personal checking accounts were authorized at several banks in 1995, at press time only a few dozen people in all of the capital had signed up.) **Western Union** (Beijing hot line: © **010/ 6318-4313**) has branches at the International Post Office and the Asian Games Post Office.

THEFT   Almost every credit card company has an emergency toll-free number that you can call if your wallet or purse is stolen. Your credit card company may be able to wire you a cash advance off your credit card immediately, and in many places it can deliver an emergency credit card in a day or two. In Beijing, MasterCard holders should call ✆ **10-800-110-7309;** Visa cardholders should call ✆ **10-800-110-2911.** American Express cardholders should visit one of the Amex offices in Beijing; see "American Express" under "Fast Facts: Beijing" in chapter 3 for a list of locations.

If you opt to carry traveler's checks, be sure to keep a record of their serial numbers, separately from the checks, of course, so that you're ensured a refund in just such an emergency.

4 When To Go

Beijing's busiest tourist periods coincide with its mildest weather in the spring and autumn. To avoid the big crowds and still enjoy decent weather, therefore, try to visit in late March or early November. Except for the long winter months, Beijing is usually filled with tourists and business travelers from May through October, but the crowds (largely of Chinese tourists coming to see sights of their nation's capital) can be interesting, too. In the low season, November through March, room rates fall, airfares plunge, and the crowds diminish, but the sights, shops, and cafes can be diminished as well, drained of color and energy, unattended, sometimes downright dreary. In the fall, from mid-October to mid-November, the leaves in the parks and along the avenues change color, the crowds linger, and everything is shaken to life. Whenever you visit, however, it is best to sightsee on weekdays (the weekends are crowded) and, at popular sites, early in the morning or late in the afternoon.

CLIMATE   Beijing, located on the 40th parallel north, possesses four distinct seasons. Spring, from mid-March to mid-May, is mild, although sometimes subject to dust storms. Summers, from mid-May to mid-September, are humid and hot, with heavy rains likely in July and August. Beijing's "Golden Autumn," from mid-September to mid-November, is dry, with mild days and chilly nights. The long winter, mid-November to mid-March, with Siberian winds, ice, and increased air pollution can be bitterly cold, but there is little snowfall and there are some days when the skies clear and turn refreshingly blue.

HOLIDAYS   National holidays observed in Beijing are January 1 (New Year's Day), Spring Festival/Chinese New Year (first day of the lunar calendar: Feb 12, 2002; Feb 1, 2003), March 4 (Arbor Day), March 8 (International Working Women's Day), May 1 (International Labor Day), May 4 (Chinese Youth Day), June 1 (International Children's Day), August 1 (Army Day), September 10 (Teacher's Day), and October 1 (National Day).

Spring Festival, the Chinese New Year, is the most important holiday.

Beijing's Average Temperatures & Rainfall

	Jan	Feb	Mar	Apr	May	June	July	Aug	Sept	Oct	Nov	Dec
Temp. (°F)	23.5	27.8	39.9	55.8	68.4	75.6	78.8	76.3	67.1	54.5	39.2	27.0
Temp. (°C)	-4.7	-2.3	4.4	13.2	20.2	24.2	26.0	24.6	19.5	12.5	4.0	-2.8
Days of Rain	2.1	3.1	4.5	5.1	6.4	9.7	14.5	14.1	6.9	5.0	3.6	1.6

Officially, it is a 5-day national holiday, meaning on the first 5 days banks, offices, and many workplaces are closed in Beijing, where temples hold large fairs. **National Day,** a 5-day observance of the founding of the People's Republic of China on October 1, 1949, is the second most important national holiday. It is particularly big in the capital, with celebrations held at Tiananmen Square, where fireworks and other special performances are staged. **International Labor Day** on May 1 has recently become the third official 5-day holiday, part of Beijing's attempt to give people the opportunity to travel, shop, and spend their savings to bolster the economy.

BEIJING CALENDAR OF EVENTS

Festivals and celebrations are not numerous in Beijing, and many are family affairs, but there are some opportunities to mix with the locals at city parks and other locations at annual public events.

Winter

Spring Festival. This is the time when the Chinese decorate their homes with red paper (signifying health, wealth, and prosperity), visit friends, settle the year's debts, visit temples, and enjoy family get-togethers. Beijing's temples have revived the traditional temple fairs, which are outdoor celebrations with folksy entertainment and markets. Begins the first day of the lunar calendar: February 12, 2002; February 1, 2003.

Lantern Festival. On the 15th day after Chinese New Year, on the first full moon, parks and temples display elaborate and fanciful lanterns, often accompanied by fireworks and folk dances. Beihai Park is worth visiting on this day. Locals mark the festival by consuming a sweet steamed dumpling called

xuanxiao. February 26, 2002; February 15, 2003.

Spring

Qing Ming Festival. Also known as Grave Sweeping Day, held in the 3rd lunar month, this event honors the dead, although in Beijing it usually means a mass run on the parks, where kite-flying goes into high gear. The holiday is locally known as the "Stepping on Greenery Festival," a rite of spring. April 5, 2002; April 5, 2003.

International Labor Day. Nearly everything is closed except hotels, cafes, and some shops on May 1. The holiday now stretches officially for 5 days, so some offices and businesses won't open for nearly a week. This holiday offers almost nothing for a traveler to see. May 1.

Chinese Youth Day. This is a colorful day to be in Beijing. The streets and parks are filled with flower displays to commemorate the May 4th Movement when students protested at Tiananmen Square, May 4, 1919.

Summer

International Children's Day. Nothing special for most tourists, as local school classes enjoy themselves on field trips on the first day of June.

Watermelon Festival. On this festival day unique to Beijing, which falls in late June, the city government organizes eating tours in the melon fields of Daxing County. Call ✆ **010/6924-3711** to book a place. Late June.

Autumn

Mid-Autumn Festival. Held on the 15th day of the 8th lunar month, the "Moon Festival" celebrates the harvest moon and revolt against the Yuan Dynasty. Beijingers visit their ancestral homes and enjoy eating moon cakes

Finds   Temple Fairs

Starting with Spring Festival in 2001, Beijing brought a thaw to winter with the continued revival of traditional temple fairs across the city. A staple of the annual Spring Festival (Chinese New Year) celebrations before 1949, temple fairs began their comeback in Beijing in 1999. The winter fairs have spread from temples to parks and amusement parks. These lively and crowded festivities turn temple courtyards into traditional markets with dozens of food stalls, tables featuring handicraft dealers, games of chance, stilt-walking, and stages for cultural performances (folk dances, plays, operas, acrobatics, martial arts demonstrations, dragon dances, and even pet shows). The largest turnouts are at Ditan and Chaoyang parks and at the temples of Baiyunguan, Longtan, and Changdian (Dongyue); more than 1 million visitors converge at each of these weeklong fairs. For information on individual temples, parks, and fairs, see chapter 6, "Exploring Beijing."

(round biscuits stuffed either with sweet, dense red bean paste and egg or with preserved fruits). Moon cakes are distributed to friends during the festival, a custom dating back to the Yuan Dynasty (1279–1368). September 21, 2002; September 11, 2003.

National Day. Be at Tiananmen or be square—this is Beijing and China's biggest mass patriotic demonstration, held every October 1.

"Red Leaf Festival." Whenever the autumn leaves turn, thousands of Beijingers throng the Fragrant Hills Park northwest of the city for this informal festival, the best time for tourists to enjoy the scenery, markets, and temples there. Late October through mid-November.

China International Jazz Festival. Although it may seem out of character, Beijing can swing; it has been the site of the annual China International Jazz Festival since 1993. At recent festivals, Chinese jazz bands and international groups played everything from big band swing to fusion, with performers ranging from the Danish Radio Jazz Orchestra and Australia's Ten Part Invention to American drummer Paul Motian and his Electric Bebop Band. Best spots to get into the swing next time around: nightly jam sessions at local bars and teahouses that regularly feature jazz performers such as CD Jazz, Keep in Touch, and the Sanwei Bookstore. Mid-November.

5 Health & Insurance

STAYING HEALTHY No **vaccinations** are required for entry to Beijing, but be sure that your **inoculations** are up-to-date, particularly for tetanus. Check updated information for travelers to China as provided by your doctor or local or national health agencies.

Probably the two most common ailments upon arrival, or shortly thereafter, are jet lag and colds. **Colds** can be picked up on the flight over or from exposure to Beijing's polluted air and whatever cold germs its citizenry may be carrying. Because common Western medications are not always easy to find, pack an ample supply of cold remedies (tablets and sprays), as well as generous supplies of your preferred pain relievers.

Because the flight to Beijing is long and crosses many time zones, **jet lag** is a problem (less so if you are flying westward). Take the usual precautions on the flight—avoid alcohol, drink plenty of non-carbonated fluids, and walk and exercise as much as space allows. Set your watch to Beijing time upon departure. Whether or not you can sleep on the way to Beijing, try to coordinate your schedule with the new time zone upon arrival, putting in a full day and sleeping (as much as possible) through the night. It can require several days to reset your biological clock.

Upset stomach and diarrhea are the bane of travelers to third-world countries—which China still is, to some extent. Avoid tap water and street food, and carry the remedies you depend on at home. Such diseases as malaria and hepatitis exist, but they are no longer considered serious health risks in China's major cities.

Due to the large number of foreign nationals serving as diplomats and working in the capital, there are several Beijing hospitals and clinics with special facilities for treating international travelers. The level of service and care is of international caliber. The doctors are expertly trained in Western medicine (although many foreigners try Chinese herbal medicines and other traditional remedies, sometimes with great success). See "Doctors & Dentists" and "Hospitals" in the "Fast Facts: Beijing" section of chapter 3 for a list of facilities catering to foreign visitors.

TRAVEL INSURANCE Hospitals, clinics, and physicians charge rates nearly on par with those in the West, so check with your health-insurance carrier to see if treatment in China is included in your coverage. Be sure to carry your medical insurance identification card with you. If you are not covered, consider purchasing a short-term policy to cover medical and dental emergencies. Most health-insurance companies offer special overseas coverage plans for travelers, as do a number of private insurers (see below).

Emergency medical evacuation is quite expensive ($20,000 or more from Beijing to the U.S.), so investing in a plan to cover this emergency is also wise. **International SOS Assistance**, P.O. Box 11568, Philadelphia, PA 11916 (© **800/523-8930** or 215/244-1500), has ties to the

---

Tips A Dose of Your Own Medicine

Three special items I always carry to China, regardless of my mandate to travel light, are prescriptions, extra contact lenses/glasses, and syringes.

Many prescriptions can be filled at hospitals that cater to foreigners, but because this is costly and time-consuming, it is best to bring all prescriptions with you. Pack prescription medicines in your carry-on luggage. Carry written prescriptions in generic, not name-brand form, and dispense all prescription medications from their original labeled vials.

If you wear contact lenses, pack an extra set in case you lose a lens.

Because the hygiene in many medical facilities (especially if you travel out of the city) is not up to Western standards, carry a sterile syringe or two. Having taught at a medical university in China—and having seen a number of wards and clinics—I always carry two syringes, packed in an envelope with my doctor's prescription, in my luggage to China.

International Medical Center (IMC) in Beijing.

Trip-cancellation insurance is a good idea if you have paid a large portion of your vacation expenses upfront. Trip-cancellation policies cost approximately 6% to 8% of the total value of your trip.

If you require additional insurance, try one of the companies listed here. But don't pay for more than you need. For example, if you need only trip-cancellation insurance, don't purchase coverage for lost or stolen property. *Rule number one:* Check your existing policies before you buy any additional coverage. Among the reputable issuers of travel insurance are **Access America,** 6600 W. Broad St., Richmond, VA 23230 (© 800/284-8300); **Travel Guard International,** 1145 Clark St., Stevens Point, WI 54481 (© 800/826-1300); **Travel Insured International, Inc.,** P.O. Box 280568, East Hartford, CT 06128 (© 800/243-3174); and **Columbus Travel Insurance,** 279 High St., Croydon CR0 1QH (© 020/ 7375-0011 in London; www2. columbusdirect.com/columbusdirect).

6 Tips for Travelers with Special Needs

FOR TRAVELERS WITH DISABILITIES Despite the fact that China has more citizens with disabilities than any nation on Earth, amenities for travelers with disabilities in Beijing can best be described as sporadic. Nevertheless, the Chinese have made notable efforts in addressing the needs of the people with disabilities (spearheaded for several decades by the son of former Supreme Leader Deng Xiaoping, who is in a wheelchair as a result of persecution endured during the Cultural Revolution). Many Beijingers get around via special motorized carts, sections of some major sidewalks are now equipped with "raised dots" to assist the blind, and modern buildings and some major tourist sites have elevators. But the bottom line is that Beijing is a city of long stairways (even in the subway) and crowded, crumbling sidewalks. Even so, travelers with disabilities frequently make their way through the Beijing obstacle course and enjoy its many sights.

Contact **Mobility International USA,** 45 W. Broadway, Eugene, OR 97405 (© 541/343-1284, voice and TDD; www.miusa.org) for more information about visiting Beijing, especially since this group has led several special tours to Beijing and China. Annual membership for Mobility International is $35, which includes their quarterly newsletter, *Over the Rainbow.* You can also join the **Society for Accessible Travel & Hospitality** (SATH), formerly the Society for the Advancement of Travel for the Handicapped, at 347 Fifth Ave., Suite 610, New York, NY 10016 (© 212/447-7284, fax 212-725-8253; www.sath.org) for $45 annually, $30 for seniors and students, to gain access to a vast network of connections in the travel industry. This group provides information sheets on travel destinations and referrals to tour operators that specialize in tours for travelers with disabilities. Its quarterly magazine, *Open World for Disability and Mature Travel,* is full of good information and resources. A year's subscription is $13 ($21 outside the U.S.).

FOR SENIORS The Chinese respect age far more than their Western counterparts, but don't expect to find a plethora of "senior discounts" at tourist attractions or in stores. If you book a hotel from an international hotel chain overseas, inquire about senior discounts. In Beijing, brace yourself for tiresome stairways at museums and temples, long walks at all tourist sites, and impatient crowds at your elbows everywhere.

Golden Companions, P.O. Box 5249, Reno, NV 89513 (© **702/ 324-2227**), helps travelers 45-plus find compatible companions through a personal voicemail service. Contact them for more information.

The Mature Traveler, a monthly 12-page newsletter on senior citizen travel, is a valuable resource. It is available by subscription ($30 a year) from GEM Publishing Group, Box 50400, Reno, NV 89513-0400. Another helpful publication is *101 Tips for the Mature Traveler,* available from Grand Circle Travel, 347 Congress St., Suite 3A, Boston, MA 02210 (© **800/221-2610** or 617/350-7500; fax 617/346-6700).

FOR SINGLE TRAVELERS The most common difficulties that solo travelers, male or female, encounter in Beijing are their own feelings of loneliness and isolation and having to fend off a variety of touts met in the streets, at tourist sites, or even in hotel lobbies. These freelancing entrepreneurs have a variety of come-ons, usually involving the purchase of whatever they are selling (art works, souvenirs, and so on). Sometimes, of course, the Chinese are simply trying to be friendly or practice their English. Sexual harassment cases involving foreign visitors are quite rare. Single travelers are, however, an inviting target for "street merchants," and Beijing is less annoying and far more fun when travelers are in a small group. Restaurants are more interesting, too, when you dine with companions. Nevertheless, I frequently travel alone throughout China and in Beijing, where befriending other solo or independent travelers is not difficult.

FOR FAMILIES While many children are not delighted with museums, temples, and the architecture of the Forbidden City, there are plenty of sites to dazzle them in Beijing. Beijingers are family-oriented and friendly toward all children. For Western kids, there are hundreds of familiar fast-food and foreign-style eateries, several amusement and theme parks, the ancient observatory, the zoo, indoor playgrounds and toy stores in shopping centers, a wax museum, a do-it-yourself craft center, a Beijing version of "Universal Studios," a natural history museum with dinosaur exhibits, and plenty of parks for rowing, kite-flying, and in-line skating. Many hotels in Beijing allow children to stay free with their parents, and some hotels provide babysitting services (usually at an hourly fee). Travelers with infants and small children may well find themselves the center of attention at times, as Beijingers are often quite open about talking to and even touching very young visitors from faraway places.

Although there are often no discounts for kids at many of Beijing's attractions, amusement parks, recreational facilities, the zoo, and some museums do have discount tickets for children.

Several books offer tips to help you travel with kids. Most concentrate on the U.S., but two, *Family Travel* (Lanier Publishing International) and *How to Take Great Trips with Your Kids* (The Harvard Common Press), are filled with good general advice that can apply to travel anywhere. Another reliable resource, with a worldwide focus, is *Adventuring with Children* (Foghorn Press).

FOR GAYS & LESBIANS Beijing is tolerant of gay and lesbian travelers, but dating or sexual involvement with locals of the same sex can be dangerous. In sexual matters, gay or straight, Chinese society is quite puritanical, although walking hand and hand with a same-sex partner won't raise any eyebrows since it is deemed a sign of

Beijing for Business Travelers

Thousands of foreign businesspeople arrive in Beijing every year; some stay for extended periods in the capital. Business travelers on a short stay should try to book an international hotel with a large 24-hour business center located near their work site or relevant local offices. Take plenty of business cards, with one side printed in English, the other in Chinese. Some Beijing hotel business centers offer this service.

A special business visa (the "F" visa) is required for entry into China. Your business visa application must be accompanied by a formal invitation or authorization letter from Chinese authorities or institutions, along with a cover letter from your company. For more on visas, see "Entry Requirements & Customs," earlier in this chapter.

Keys to business success in Beijing include patience, flexibility, and the cultivation of strong, friendly connections (*guanxi*) with Chinese associates, so read up on China and Chinese business before you arrive. Three books that business travelers to Beijing should read are *Beijing Jeep: A Case Study of Western Business in China* by Jim Mann (Westview Press), *The Business Guide to China* by Laurence Brahm (Butterworth-Heinemann), and *Managing in China: An Executive Survival Guide* by Stephanie Jones (Butterworth-Heinemann).

The **U.S.–China Business Council**, 1818 N Street NW, Suite 200, Washington, DC 20036 (© **202/429-0340**; fax 202/775-2476), provides business information and consulting. Its office in Beijing is in the CITIC Building, Room 26D, 19 Jianguomenwai Dajie (© **010/6500-2255**; fax 010/6512-5854; www.uschina.org).

friendship. Beijing has a homosexual community, but it is not organized or officially sanctioned in any way. Because foreigners are perceived as "different" from Chinese in the first place, gay and lesbian travelers should experience little discrimination in Beijing. Recently, several nightspots have even come to be identified by their gay, lesbian, and transgender clientele.

The **International Gay & Lesbian Travel Association** (IGLTA) (© **800/ 448-8550** or 954/776-2626; fax 954/776-3303; www.iglta.org) links travelers up with the appropriate gay-friendly service organization or tour specialist. With around 1,200 members, it offers quarterly newsletters, marketing mailings, and a membership directory that's updated quarterly. Membership often includes gay or lesbian businesses but is open to individuals for $150 a year, plus a $100 administration fee for new members. Members are kept informed of gay and gay-friendly hoteliers, tour operators, and airline and cruise-line representatives. Contact the IGLTA for a list of its member agencies.

General gay and lesbian travel agencies include **Family Abroad** (© 800/999-5500 or 212/459-1800; gay and lesbian), **Above and Beyond Tours** (© 800/397-2681; mainly gay men), and **Yellowbrick Road** (© 800/642-2488; gay and lesbian).

FOR STUDENTS Student travelers, like visiting seniors, should not expect special rates or other discounts in Beijing, although some museums and attractions do sell student tickets (requiring your student identification).

For students who want to party or exercise, Beijing has an increasingly interesting nightlife (discos, bars, live music, cinema) and a variety of outdoor and athletic activities, which are supported by an equally active resident population of foreign students studying at Beijing's universities.

The best resource for student travelers is the **Council on International Educational Exchange,** or CIEE (www.ciee.org). They can set you up with an International Student Identity Card (ISIC), and their travel branch, **Council Travel Service** (© 800/ 226-8624; www.counciltravel.com), is the biggest student travel agency in the world. It can get you discounts on air tickets and the like. The Council Travel Service office in Beijing is located at 2-101 Shaoyuan, Beijing University (© 010/6275-1287; fax 010/6275-7001; gkulacki@public.sta. net.cn).

7 Getting There by Air

More than 30 international airlines, from Aeroflot to Yugoslav Airlines, serve Beijing. It can be a long trip (10 hr. from London, 11 hr. from San Francisco, 13 hr. from Sydney, 15 hr. from New York—longer with stopovers and connections). Leading airlines serving Beijing from North America, England, Australia, and New Zealand include:

- **Air China** (© 310/335-0088; www.airchina.com.cn), China's largest airline, offers flights from 28 countries, including 4 nonstops from San Francisco and Los Angeles weekly. Beijing office: 15 Xi Chang'an Jie, © 010/ 6601-6667 or 010/6601-3336.
- **All Nippon Airways** (© 800/ 235-9262; www.ana.co.jp) flies nonstop daily from Tokyo (3 hr.). Beijing office: Fazhan Dasha, Room N200, 5 Dongsanhuan Bei Lu 1 Jianguomenwai Dajie, © 010/6590-9174.
- **British Airways** (© 800/247-9297 in the U.S., 03/4522-2211 in England, www. british-airways. com) flies nonstop from London three times a week (10 hr.). Beijing office: Scitech Tower, Room 210, 22 Jianguomenwai Dajie, © 010/6512-4070.
- **Canadian Airlines International** (© 800/426-7000; www.cdnair. ca) flies nonstop from Vancouver 6 days a week (10½ hr.). Beijing

office: Lufthansa Center, Room C201, 50 Liangmaqiao, © 010/ 6462-3349 or 010/6468-2001.
- **China Southern Airlines** (© 800/888-338-8988; www. cs-air.com), China-owned and managed, has branched out to offer international flights from the U.S. Beijing office: Minghang Yingye Bldg., 15 Xi Chang'an Jie, © 010/6501-7596.
- **Dragonair** (© 800/223-2742; www.dragonair.com), partly owned by Cathay Pacific Airlines, offers the best flight from Hong Kong (3 hr.). Beijing office: Henderson Center, Office Tower 1, Room 1710, 18 Jianguomenwai Dajie, © 010/6518-2533.
- **Japan Airlines** (© 800/525-3663; www.jal.co.jp) flies nonstop from Tokyo (3 hr., 40 min.) 5 days a week and from Nagoya and Osaka less frequently. Beijing office: Changfugong Office Building, 26A Jianguomenwai Dajie, © 010/6513-0888.
- **Korean Air** (© 800/438-5000; www.koreanair.com) flies nonstop from Seoul 6 days a week (2 hr.). Beijing Office: China World Trade Center, Room C-401, 1 Jianguomenwai Dajie, © 010/ 6505-0088).
- **Northwest Airlines** (© 800/ 447-4747; www.nwa.com) flies nonstop daily from the U.S. four

times weekly from Detroit (13 hr.), with additional direct flights via Tokyo three times weekly. Northwest also code-shares flights with Air China inside China, enabling American passengers to purchase "seamless" tickets for travel from U.S. cities to many cities in China. Beijing office: China World Trade Center, West Wing, Room W501, 1 Jianguomenwai Dajie, ℂ 010/6505-3505.

- **Qantas Airlines** (ℂ **800/227-4500** in North America or 13-13-13 in Australia; www.qantas.com) flies nonstop from Sydney 4 days a week (13 hr.). Beijing office: Lufthansa Center, Room S120B, 50 Liangmaqiao Lu, ℂ 010/6467-3337 or 010/6467-4794.
- **SAS** (ℂ **800/221-2350;** www.sas.se) flies nonstop from Copenhagen five times a week. Beijing office: Henderson Centre, Office Tower 1, Room 1403, 18 Jianguomenwai Dajie, ℂ 010/6518-3838.
- **Singapore Airlines** (ℂ 800/742-**3333;** www.singaporeair.com) flies nonstop daily from Singapore (6 hr.). Beijing office: China World Trade Center, Room L109, 1 Jianguomenwai Dajie, ℂ 010/6505-2233.
- **Swiss Air** (ℂ **800/221-4750;** www.swissair.com) flies nonstop to Zurich 3 days a week. Beijing office: Scitech Tower, Room 201, 22 Jianguomenwai Dajie, ℂ 010/6512-3555.
- **United Airlines** (ℂ **800/538-2929;** www.united.com) has daily nonstop service from San Francisco and Los Angeles, and direct service from Chicago and New York City gateways. Beijing office: Lufthansa Centre, 50 Liangmaqiao Lu, ℂ 010/6463-8551 or 010/6463-1111.

AIRFARES Full-fare, unrestricted air tickets to Beijing are expensive. Some of the finest, most luxurious cabin service in the world is conducted on this route, particularly in the first-class and business-class sections; if travel comfort is a concern, it may be worth spending the extra money (or airline club miles) for an upgrade. Economy class is crowded on many flights (except during winter) and the seats are narrow (although the food and drink can be of reasonably good quality). The rub is that a first-class round-trip seat can cost over $5,000 and a business-class seat over $2,500. Full fare for economy class usually runs from $1,500 to $2,000—but you shouldn't have to spend that much to get to Beijing.

There are several ways to save hundreds, even thousands of dollars on a Beijing flight. First, plan ahead, so you can book a much less expensive **APEX** (Advance Purchase Excursion Fares) ticket. APEX tickets have various restrictions, depending on the airline; usually, they must be purchased several weeks or more in advance and are often nonrefundable. Keep in mind, too, that weekend flights cost more than weekday flights. An advance purchase round-trip ticket in economy class on a major airline, such as United, should be $1,200 or less, depending on how competitive flights to Asia happen to be at the time. My last two trips to China from the western coast of the U.S. (including connector flights to and from San Francisco), taken in high and low season and booked in advance through a local travel agent, have both cost well below $800 round-trip.

To save even more, shop around. Check the travel sections of major newspapers, particularly those on the western coast of the U.S. Dozens of travel agents, consolidators, and so-called "bucket shops" advertise deeply discounted tickets, sometimes as low

---

Tips **Flight Jargon**

Remember that a **nonstop** flight is quickest. **Direct** flights require at least one stopover along the way; this can mean a change of planes, adding hours to a trip to Beijing. Itineraries that involve **code-sharing** (where airlines cooperate in ticketing) can mean that a passenger must change airlines en route as well. Nevertheless, roundabout routes can be less expensive than nonstop service.

---

as $500. These tickets, which are usually purchased in blocks by consolidators from the airlines, carry about every restriction imaginable and are normally valid only on a few specific dates, but they are great bargains. The small, boxed ads usually run in the Sunday travel section at the bottom of the page. Before you pay, however, ask for a confirmation number from the consolidator and then call the airline directly to confirm your seat. Be prepared to book your ticket with a different consolidator—there are many to choose from—if the airline can't confirm your reservation. Also be aware that bucket-shop tickets are usually nonrefundable or rigged with stiff cancellation penalties, often as high as 50% to 75% of the ticket price.

Council Travel (☎ 800/226-8624; www.counciltravel.com) and **STA Travel** (☎ 800/781-4040; www.sta.travel.com) cater especially to young travelers, but their bargain-basement prices are available to people of all ages. **Travel Bargains** (☎ 800/AIRFARE; www.1800airfare.com) was formerly owned by TWA but now offers the deepest discounts on many other airlines, with a 4-day advance purchase. Other reliable consolidators include **1-800-FLY-CHEAP** (www.1800flycheap.com) and **TFI Tours International** (☎ 800-745-8000 or 212/736-1140), which serves as a clearinghouse for unused seats. "Rebators" such as **Travel Avenue** (☎ 800/333-3335 or 312/876-1116) and the **Smart Traveller** (☎ 800/448-3338 in the U.S. or 305/448-3338) rebate part of their commissions to you.

Certain airlines, especially those based in Asia, offer low fares from North America and Europe, but be aware that they cannot fly nonstop to Beijing; a stopover in the airline's home country is required on the way. Korean Air, for example, flies to Beijing from North America, but it must first stop in Seoul, lengthening the already-long trip by hours; in addition, foreign-based airlines depart only from a major gateway city, which can necessitate adding on an expensive, time-consuming connecting flight.

You can also search for cheap fares via the Internet. Many travel sites and the airlines themselves routinely advertise special Internet fares on their websites, so don't hesitate to browse for electronic bargains. (See "Planning Your Trip Online," later in this chapter.)

8 Booking a Tour Versus Traveling on Your Own

Whether you decide to visit Beijing independently or on a group tour depends on your experience and goals. Travelers who are experienced, especially with other third-world destinations, or travelers who want to experience Beijing in some depth, can comfortably explore Beijing on their own. While many people still believe that the People's Republic of China is run like a police state and that independent tourists are followed around by secret police, spied upon by authorities, or prevented from going to "prohibited" places on their own, this is simply not the case. It is quite possible for a foreign traveler to book an entire stay in Beijing by him- or herself and never deal with the authorities (except at customs and immigration); in short, independent travel in China is as viable an option as it is these days in Europe or South America.

On the other hand, touring Beijing without a net requires time, energy, resourcefulness, and a sense of adventure. If time is short, and one's intent is to sample Beijing's leading treasures in comfort, with a minimum of hassles, a group tour is the answer. Seeing the Forbidden City and the Great Wall, tasting Beijing Duck at an organized banquet, and perhaps venturing out on the streets to shop at Silk Alley are memorable experiences that group tours can deliver effectively. The crucial difference lies in the depth of the experience. The busy dawn-to-twilight group tour simply cannot allow more than an hour or two at even the major sites, barely giving you enough time to snap a picture and get a general sense of the place.

Dozens of tour operators in North America, Europe, Australia, New Zealand, and Hong Kong offer excellent group tours of Beijing and China. Some of the largest operators are **Globus** (© 800/221-0090), **Maupintour** (© 800/225-4266), **Pacific Delight Tours** (© 800/221-7179), **Travcoa** (© 800/992-2003), and **United Vacations** (© 800/328-6877). You can speak to these operators directly or use a travel agent.

Between the complete group tour and the completely independent traveler is a wide middle ground. Travel agents, including CITS and CTS in Hong Kong, Beijing, and

overseas, can book the essentials for independent-minded travelers who want to customize their trips. Hotel reservations, car and driver hires, airport transfers, personalized day tours with English-speaking guides, and other matters can be set up long before departure or upon arrival, although the price can exceed that of a group tour if too many pieces are ordered this way. Personal guides can be hired for the entire duration of a stay, which is a luxurious way to see the capital—and often a great way to gain an insider's view. Independent packages can be engineered by tour operators who specialize in China, such as **Asian Pacific Adventures** (© 213/935-3156) and **Orient Flexi-Pax** (© 800/545-5540).

Independent travel arrangements, as well as group tours of Beijing, in more depth are offered by **Helen Wong's Tours** (Level 18 Town Hall House, 456 Kent St., Sydney NSW Australia, © 02/9267-7833; fax 02/9267-7717; www.helenwongstours.com). Helen Wong offers 5-day group tours of Beijing, has pioneered special group packages for more extended stays in Beijing, and offers "plan-your-own-itinerary" services (accommodations, transfers, transportation, guides) for independent and business travelers.

Another option is to come to Beijing on a group tour that focuses on a special theme. If you are especially interested in Chinese cooking, acupuncture, shopping, architecture, education, tai chi, traditional medicine, art, or another topic, search magazines, newspapers, and the Internet for a small overseas group tour that meets your interest. Such tours are usually one-time offerings, led by experts in the field, so finding them requires research and some luck. Not only do thematic tours provide an opportunity to explore an interest area in some depth, but they also open doors that remain closed to independent travelers. Some of these tours also include a day or two of general sightseeing, such as taking in the Great Wall and the Forbidden City.

Fully independent travel in Beijing, on the other hand, depends on your energy, resourcefulness, and ability to act as your own tour guide and travel agent. It is easy to book the basics (flight and hotel) on your own. Beyond that, you can rely on information in this guidebook—which I've field-tested—to reach a wide variety of major sites and hidden delights. The Chinese language will present occasional difficulties, of course, but a good hotel staff (the concierges and bellhops, foremost) can help foreign travelers get around. And should you tire of being on your own or should you find that reaching a remote site stretches your tactical skills to the breaking point, Beijing hotels maintain tour desks. One tactic I've often employed when arriving in a strange Chinese city for the first time is to book a group tour at my hotel, using that tour to gain an overview. Then, if something I've seen is intriguing, I return to it on my own, properly oriented and prepared to deepen the experience.

9 Planning Your Trip Online

With a mouse, a modem, and a certain do-it-yourself determination, Internet users can tap into the same travel-planning databases that were once accessible only to travel agents. Sites such as **Travelocity, Expedia,** and **Orbitz** allow consumers to comparison shop for airfares, book flights, learn of last-minute bargains, and reserve hotel rooms and rental cars.

But don't fire your travel agent just yet. Although online booking sites offer tips and hard data to help you bargain shop, they cannot endow you with the hard-earned experience that makes a seasoned, reliable travel agent an invaluable resource, even in the Internet age. And for consumers with a complex itinerary, a trusty travel agent is still the best way to arrange the most direct flights to and from the best airports.

Still, there's no denying the Internet's emergence as a powerful tool in researching and plotting travel time. The benefits of researching your trip online can be well worth the effort:

- **Last-minute specials,** known as "E-savers," such as weekend deals or Internet-only fares, are offered by airlines to fill empty seats.

Most of these are announced on Tuesday or Wednesday and must be purchased online. They are only valid for travel that weekend, but some can be booked weeks or months in advance. Sign up for weekly e-mail alerts at airline websites or check megasites that compile comprehensive lists of E-savers, such as Smarter Living (smarterliving.com) or WebFlyer (www.webflyer.com).

- Some sites will send you **e-mail notification** when a cheap fare becomes available to your favorite destination. Some will also tell you when fares to a particular destination are lowest.

- The best travel planning sites are now **highly personalized;** they track your frequent-flier miles and store your seating and meal preferences, tentative itineraries, and credit card information, letting you plan trips or check agendas quickly.

- All major airlines offer **incentives**—bonus frequent-flier miles, Internet-only discounts, and sometimes even free cell phone rentals—when you purchase online or buy an e-ticket.

- Advances in mobile technology provide business travelers and other frequent travelers with the **ability to check flight status, change plans, or get specific directions** from handheld computing devices, mobile phones, and pagers. Some sites will e-mail or page a passenger if a flight is delayed.

TRAVEL PLANNING & BOOKING SITES

The best travel-planning and -booking sites cast a wide net, offering domestic and international flights and hotel and rental-car bookings, plus news, destination information, and deals on cruises and vacation packages. Keep in mind that free (one-time) registration is often required for booking. Because several airlines are no longer willing to pay commissions on tickets sold by online travel agencies, be aware that these online agencies will charge a $10 surcharge if you book a ticket on that carrier—or neglect to offer those air carriers' offerings.

The sites in this section are not intended to be a comprehensive list, but rather a discriminating selection to get you started. Recognition is given to sites based on their content value and ease of use and is not paid for—unlike some website rankings, which are based on payment. *Remember:* This is a press-time snapshot of leading websites—some undoubtedly will have evolved or moved by the time you read this.

- **Travelocity** (www.travelocity.com or www.frommers.travelocity.com) and **Expedia** (www.expedia.com) are the most longstanding and reputable sites, each offering excellent selections and searches for complete vacation packages. Travelers search by destination and dates coupled with how much they are willing to spend.

- The latest buzz in the online travel world is about **Orbitz** (www.orbitz.com), a site launched by United, Delta, Northwest, American, and Continental airlines. It shows all possible fares for your desired trip, offering fares lower than those available through travel agents. (*Stay tuned:* At press time, travel-agency associations were waging an antitrust battle against this site.)

- **Qixo** (www.qixo.com) is another powerful search engine that allows you to search for flights and hotel rooms on 20 other travel-planning sites (such as Travelocity) at once. Qixo sorts results by price, after which you can book your travel directly through the site.

SMART E-SHOPPING

The savvy traveler is one armed with good information. Here are a few tips to help you navigate the Internet successfully and safely.

- **Know when sales start.** Last-minute deals may vanish in minutes. If you have a favorite booking site or airline, find out when last-minute deals are released to the public. (For example, Southwest's specials are posted every Tues at 12:01am, central standard time.)

- **Shop around.** Compare results from different sites and airlines—and against a travel agent's best fare, if you can. If possible, try a range of times and alternate airports before you make a purchase.

- **Follow the rules of the trade.** Book in advance, and choose an off-peak time and date, if possible. Some sites tell you when fares to a particular destination tend to be cheapest.

- **Stay secure.** Book only through secure sites. (Some airline sites are not secure.) Look for a key

Tips **Frommers.com: The Complete Travel Resource**

For an excellent travel planning resource, we highly recommend **Arthur Frommer's Budget Travel Online** (www.frommers.com). We're a little biased, of course, but we guarantee that you'll find the travel tips, reviews, monthly vacation giveaways, and online-booking capabilities thoroughly indispensable. Among the special features are **"Ask the Expert"** bulletin boards, where Frommer's authors answer your questions via online postings; **Arthur Frommer's Daily Newsletter,** for the latest travel bargains and inside travel secrets; and Frommer's **Destinations archive,** where you'll get expert travel tips, hotel and dining recommendations, and advice on the sights to see for more than 200 destinations around the globe. Once your research is done, the **Online Reservation System** (www.frommers.com/booktravelnow) takes you to Frommer's favorite sites for booking your vacation at affordable prices.

(Netscape) or a padlock (Internet Explorer) icon at the bottom of your Web browser before you enter credit card information or other personal data.

- **Avoid online auctions.** Sites that auction airline tickets and frequent-flier miles are the number one perpetrators of Internet fraud, according to the National Consumers League.
- **Maintain a paper trail.** If you book an e-ticket, print out a confirmation (or write down your confirmation number) and keep it safe and accessible—or else your trip could be a virtual one!

ONLINE TRAVELER'S TOOLBOX

Veteran travelers usually carry some essential items to make their trips easier. Following is a selection of online tools to bookmark and use.

- **Visa ATM Locator** (www. visa.com/pd/atm) or **MasterCard ATM Locator** (www.mastercard. com/cardholderservices/atm). Find ATMs in hundreds of cities in the U.S. and around the world.
- **Foreign Languages for Travelers** (www.travlang.com). Learn basic terms in more than 70 languages and click on any underlined phrase to hear what it sounds like. *Note:* Free audio software and speakers are required.

- **Intellicast** (www.intellicast.com). Weather forecasts for all 50 states and cities around the world. *Note:* Temperatures are in Celsius for many international destinations.
- **Mapquest** (www.mapquest.com). This best of the mapping sites lets you choose a specific address or destination, and in seconds, it will return a map and detailed directions.
- **Cybercafes.com** (www.cybercafes. com) or **Net Café Guide** (www. netcafeguide.com/mapindex. htm). Locate Internet cafes at hundreds of locations around the globe. Catch up on your e-mail and log on to the Web for a few dollars per hour.
- **Universal Currency Converter** (www.xe.net/currency). See what your dollar or pound is worth in more than 100 other countries.
- **U.S. State Department Travel Warnings** (www.travel.state.gov/ travel_warnings.html). Reports on places where health concerns or unrest may threaten U.S. travelers. It also lists the locations of U.S. embassies around the world.

3

Getting to Know Beijing

The alien language and initial strangeness of China's vast capital can intimidate, as well as exhilarate, any foreign visitor. This chapter deals with the practical stuff you'll need to know about the city. The following facts, tips, and overviews are designed to help you demystify Beijing's layout, unlock its facilities, and decipher some of the mysterious signs in its streets.

1 Orientation

ARRIVING

BY PLANE

The Beijing Capital International Airport, China's largest and busiest airport (© 010/6456-3604), recently received a long-needed face-lift with the opening of a state-of-the-art terminal on October 1, 2000. For international arrivals and departures, passengers passing through Beijing's new terminal are hard-pressed to see much difference between it and the latest terminals in Europe and North America—besides the foot massage (reflexology) outlet and the Bank of China money-exchange counter (at gate 12), that is. As you would expect, there are duty-free shops, restaurants, business centers, moving sidewalks, and nonsmoking waiting halls. Before arriving at the Beijing airport, you should receive **health and customs declaration forms** to fill out on the plane. Have your **passport** in hand. It usually takes less than 10 minutes now to pass through the checkpoints and to retrieve luggage at the carousels. The **Arrival Hall** is not as congested and chaotic as in the past. Unless you are part of a group tour or are being met by a local, you still could become the target of roving taxi drivers and their advance men who will try every verbal stratagem to suck you into an overpriced taxi. As always, ignore these touts. Instead, try to exchange a small amount of money at the **Bank of China** counter (© 010/6456-3987), open daily from 6am to midnight, in Arrival Hall; the exchange rates here are good. Airport bellhops do not exist at present, so you'll have to haul your own luggage as you seek a transfer into the city.

GETTING INTO TOWN   The Beijing International Capital Airport is just 16 miles (25km) northeast of the heart of downtown Beijing; thanks to a new **Airport Expressway** built to complement the new airport terminal, the trip into town is fairly speedy (30–40 min., sometimes less; about twice as fast as in the past). There are three options for reaching the city, ranked here by convenience.

Hotel Shuttles   Hotel buses and limousines have service desks in the main terminal. Line up at your hotel desk for help. Someone will make sure that you get on the right hotel bus when it arrives. (When you make advance hotel reservations, be sure to include a request for shuttle service from the airport, if it is offered; your name will then appear on the list at the airport counter.) Some hotels charge a fee (less than taxi fare) for the transfer.

Tips Departing Beijing

Whether you return to the Beijing International Capital Airport by hotel shuttle, taxi, or bus, be sure you have enough RMB in hand to pay the **international departure tax.** The tax is currently **90RMB** for international departures, including Hong Kong (50RMB for domestic flights), payable only in Chinese currency. Credit cards and foreign currencies are not accepted. Go to the clearly marked departure tax counter just inside the International Departure Hall (to your left) to pay the tax. Be sure to arrive at least 2 hours early because departures require more time than arrivals. You must clear several levels of security, and the lines at airline check-in counters can sometimes be long. Before clearing immigration, you'll need to fill out a **departure form** as well. Although starting this process early is a good idea, I must admit that things went rather smoothly (and quickly) the last time I left Beijing. From the moment I left my hotel room downtown, it took me less than an hour to check out of the hotel, take a taxi to the airport, pay the departure tax, check in at my airline counter, clear security, and make the long walk to my gate. Of course, this was in the heart of winter, Beijing's lowest tourist season . . .

Airport Taxis   The legitimate taxis are lined up in a long queue just outside the Arrival Hall, to the right at the curb. Join the line. Taxis should charge 90RMB to 20RMB (about $11–$15); this includes a 10RMB ($1.25) expressway toll. Make sure that the meter is on. If it isn't, shout *"Da biao;"* if that doesn't work, get out and select another taxi. If you aren't able to change money at the bank counter at the airport, don't panic: Many taxi drivers accept foreign currency, and if they don't, they'll wait while you change money at your hotel. A tip should consist of a small bit of change (no more than a few RMB).

Airport Buses   Special airport buses serve the terminal every 30 minutes (8am–10pm) and cost 16RMB ($2). Tell someone at the airport bus service counter inside the terminal your destination, buy the ticket, and head outside in search of the bus. Someone on the curb outside may have to read your ticket and point you in the right direction. There are several routes to and from the airport, with terminals at the China Aviation Building, the China Art Gallery (downtown Beijing), and Zhongguancun (northwest high-tech district). Once in the city, it may be necessary to hail a taxi to reach your final destination. The airport bus may save you $5, but it's a tiring and trying way to get downtown.

By Train   If you arrive by train from another Chinese city, from Hong Kong via the 29-hour deluxe super-train (Train No. 97), or from Moscow on the Trans-Siberian Railway, you will have completed your immigration and customs procedures before arrival in Beijing. Whether your terminal is the old **Beijing Railway Station** (✆ **010/6563-4422**) or the new **Beijing West Station** (✆ **010/6321-4215**), you'll have to hail a taxi at the queues outside to reach your hotel.

Beijing train stations are crowded and messy, not the kind of places in which you want to linger. Foreigners holding soft-seat and sleeping-car (soft-berth) tickets can use the special lounges set aside for these passengers. Equipped with stuffed chairs, these rooms are quiet (but utterly boring) places in which to wait. Train stations typically lack ATMs, currency exchange outlets, and shops, but they do have counters for buying snacks, sodas, and sundries. Hundreds of taxis wait for passengers outside.

Beijing

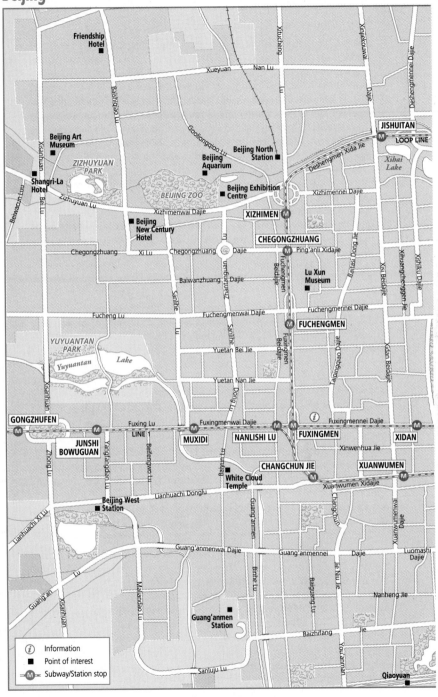

Friendship Hotel

Xueyuan
Nan Lu

Xiucheng

Xinjiekouwai

Deshengmennei Dajie

JISHUITAN
Ⓜ
LOOP LINE

Baishiqiao Lu

Gaoliangqiao Lu

Beijing Art Museum

ZIZHUYUAN PARK

Beijing Aquarium

Beijing North Station

Deshengmen Xida Jie

Xihai Lake

Xisanhuan Lu

Beiwachi Lu

Shangri-La Hotel

Zizhuyuan Lu

Bei Lu

BEIJING ZOO

Beijing Exhibition Centre

Xizhimennei Dajie

Xizhimenwai Dajie

XIZHIMEN Ⓜ

Beijing New Century Hotel

CHEGONGZHUANG

Chegongzhuang Xi Lu

Chegongzhuang Dajie

Zhanlanguan Lu

Ping'anli Xidajie

Ⓜ

Baitasi Dong Jie

Xsi Beidajie

Xihuangchenggen Jie

Xishiku Dajie

Lu Xun Museum

Baiwanzhuang Dajie

Fucheng Lu

Sanlihe

Fuchengmenwai Dajie

Fuchengmennei Dajie

FUCHENGMEN Ⓜ

Xidan Beidajie

YUYUANTAN PARK

Yuetan Bei Jie

Sanlihe

Fuxingmen Beidajie

Taipingqiao Dajie

Yuyuantan Lake

Yuetan Nan Jie

Dong Lu

Xisanhuan Lu

GONGZHUFEN Ⓜ

Fuxing Lu

LINE 1

Fuxingmenwai Dajie

Fuxingmen Beidajie

Ⓘ

Fuxingmennei Dajie

Ⓜ Ⓜ

Ⓜ **XIDAN**

Yangfangdian Lu

Beifengwo Lu

Baiyun tt

MUXIDI

NANLISHI LU

FUXINGMEN

Xinwenhua Jie

Zhong Lu

JUNSHI BOWUGUAN

CHANGCHUN JIE

XUANWUMEN Ⓜ

White Cloud Temple

Xuanwumen Xidajie

Changchun

Xuanwumenwai Dajie

Lianhuachi Donglu

Beijing West Station

Guang'anmen

Xuanwumenwai Dajie

Lianhuachi Xi Lu

Guang'anmenwai Dajie

Guang'anmennei Dajie

Luomashi Dajie

Malandao Lu

Binhe Lu

Baiguang Lu

Jie Niu Jie

Nanheng Jie

Guang'an Lu

Xisanhuan Lu

Guang'anmen Station

Baizhifang

Jie

You'anmen

Sanluju Lu

Qiaoyuan

Ⓘ Information
■ Point of interest
Ⓜ Subway/Station stop

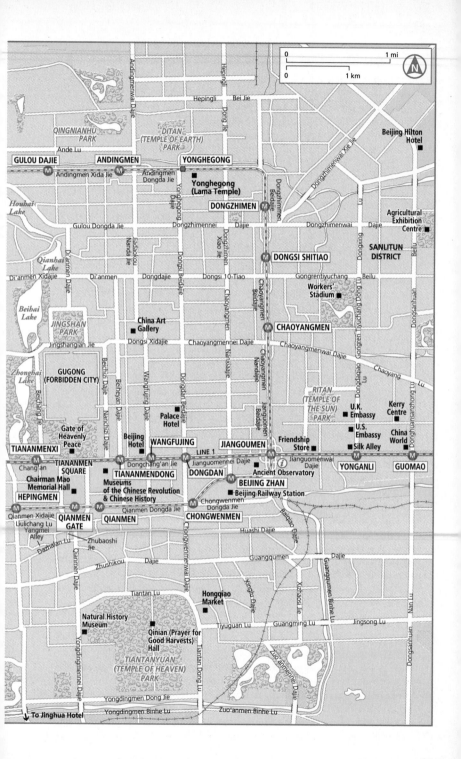

> **Fun Fact** **Bigger Isn't Always Better**
>
> The Beijing West Station, with its grand green-tile gate, is the largest train station in Asia, bigger than anything in Japan. Designed to wow international passengers (and costing $600 million), West Station opened to great fanfare in 1996. A subsequent investigation into corruption and shoddy building practices, however, has tarnished the terminal's state-of-the-art image. Platforms sunk (they were built on mud instead of concrete), elevators would grind to a halt, fire alarms failed, light fixtures and ceiling panels cracked, and the dazzling decorative tiles warped. The mess is patched up for now, though; for better or worse, West Station is the showpiece of China's railway palaces.

VISITOR INFORMATION

Beijing's official tourist bureau for foreign visitors, the **China International Travel Service (CITS),** does not have information services at the airport or train stations. The main office, however, can be quite helpful; it is located at 103 Fuxingmennei Dajie (✆ **010/6601-1122**), near the Fuxingmen subway stop. Office hours are Monday to Friday from 8:30am to 5:30pm. **China Travel Service (CTS),** another large government tourist agency, also provides information, ticketing, and tours through its office at 2 Beisanhuan Dong Lu (✆ **010/ 6462-2288**). The **Beijing Tourism Group (BTG),** located at 28 Jianguomenwai Dajie (✆ **010/6515-8652;** fax 010/6515-8603), is located 3 miles east of the Forbidden City, near the Jianguomen subway stop, and has a friendly staff. The **Beijing Tourism Administration** maintains a **24-hour Tourist Hot Line** (in English, Japanese, and Chinese) at ✆ **010/6513-0828.**

For most visitors, their hotel and its tour desk are their initial source of information. The best sources of current information on events, restaurants, and nightlife are the free English-language newspapers and magazines that are distributed to hotels, shops, and cafes. *Beijing This Month* (www.cbw.com/btm) is a glossy magazine published by the Beijing Tourism Administration; it includes feature stories, a city map, a monthly events calendar, and lots of useful ads. Also, keep an eye out for the twice-monthly *Metrozine* (www.metronet.com.cn), a stylish magazine of feature articles, gossip, advertisements, and extensive local dining and entertainment listings. Two other free papers, which cover much the same ground with a slant toward the expatriate community and the youth market, are *Beijing Journal* (a Hong Kong–based publication formerly called *Welcome to Beijing*) and *City Weekend* (twice-monthly; entertainment listings available at www.cityweekend.com.cn).

CITY LAYOUT

Beijing is a flat, sprawling metropolis in northeast China, lying inland on roughly the same latitude as New York City (about 40° N). The Beijing Municipality (it has a status separate from any province) consists of four urban districts, six suburban districts, and eight counties. More than 7 million inhabitants live in the city and its immediate suburbs; greater Beijing's population is usually cited as 11 million. Steep mountain ranges, girded by the Great Wall, lie to the north. What concerns the visitor most immediately is the center of this municipality—what was once the old city of Peking.

For 600 years, since the early days of the Ming Dynasty, the center of Beijing has been the Forbidden City, the grand Imperial palace that faces Tiananmen Square to the south. This is still the central landmark for the traveler today. Imagine one axis running north–south through the Forbidden City, an intersecting axis running east–west between palace and square, and two ring roads surrounding this graph: That's urban Beijing in a nutshell. Just add some orderly main streets and scores of oblique alleyways to complete the grid.

The east–west axis is Beijing's main thoroughfare, the wide and straight **Chang'an Avenue.** Chang'an, like most Beijing avenues, changes its name as it goes (becoming Jianguomenwai Dajie to the east and Fuxingmenwai Dajie to the west). Running north from Chang'an Avenue, almost on the axis through the Forbidden City, is **Wangfujing Avenue,** the city's main shopping street. And directly south of the Forbidden City and Tiananmen Square, again on the ancient axis, runs **Qianmen Avenue,** which leads to the Temple of Heaven.

This geometrically correct grid forms the outstretched arms and spine of Beijing past and present. Encircling central Beijing today are a **First Ring Road** and a **Second Ring Road,** surrounded in turn by a **Third Ring Road** and a newly completed **Fourth Ring Road** (with a Fifth Ring Road in the planning stages). The First Ring Road actually consists of no more than the streets encircling the Forbidden City/downtown core. The Second Ring Road, which changes its name frequently as it completes its circle, traces the route of the old city walls and the modern subway loop. The Third Ring Road is largely an expressway, elevated at points and the location of many of Beijing's top international hotels. While the diameter of the Forbidden City is less than a mile, that of the Second Ring Road is more on the order of 4 miles; that of the Third Ring Road is 7 miles. The circle line of Beijing's subway lies under the Second Ring Road; because its stops bear the names of the ancient city gates (some of which are still standing), you can see where the old walled city of Beijing was contained. A second subway line now runs beneath Chang'an Avenue, right under that imaginary east–west axis that divides Tiananmen Square from the Forbidden City.

Inside the Second Ring Road, and inside what was once the walled city, Beijing's four inner districts form four orderly quadrants. The Forbidden City is the center point. From there, **Dongcheng District** lies to the northeast, **Xicheng District** to the northwest, **Chongwen District** to the southeast, and **Xuanwu District** to the southwest. Beijing also has four outer districts (these lie outside

China's First Olympics

After losing out to Sydney for the 2000 Summer Olympics (largely due to China's human rights record), China regrouped and put on a vigorous bid for the 2008 Olympics. Its efforts were rewarded when the games were awarded to Beijing in July 2001 in a showdown vote.

Beijing has been gearing up for the Olympic bid for several years, concentrating on new construction in the capital, the creation of green ways, and reductions in industrial pollution and vehicle emissions. This revitalization is likely to continue unabated until 2008. And although the improvements will no doubt make the city a more pleasant place to visit, big questions remain about Beijing's (and China's) democratization and progress in human rights. As the 2008 Olympics near, the media will undoubtedly devote increasing attention to both issues.

Fun Fact **That Sinking Feeling**

No matter how heavy the air pollution, the sky is not falling in Beijing—but the ground is. Scientists recently determined that the entire city is sinking at an accelerating rate—now 20 millimeters (nearly 1 in.) per year—due to increasing exploitation of underground water resources by industry.

---

the Second Ring Road): **Chaoyang District** to the east, **Shijingshan District** to the west, **Haidian District** to the northwest, and **Fengtai District** to the southwest.

Within Beijing's eight urban districts are many neighborhoods and subdistricts. Although district and area names are difficult to pronounce and to remember, knowing them can be useful. Most addresses bear not only the street name, but also the district or neighborhood name; knowing where a particular area lies can help in locating an attraction, shop, or cafe.

MAIN STREETS

Chang'an Avenue (Chang'an Jie) is the main east–west street, running between Tiananmen Square and the Forbidden City. As it runs eastward, **Chang'an Jie** (*jie* means street) is quickly renamed **Dong Chang'an Jie** (*dong* means east), then **Jianguomennei Dajie** (*mennei* means within the gate, and *dajie* means avenue; the old gate was named *Jianguo*), and finally **Jianguomenwai Dajie** (*menwai*, means outside the gate). This eastern stretch of Chang'an Avenue contains many shops, hotels, and attractions (such as Silk Alley and the Friendship Store).

Parallel to and a few blocks south of Chang'an Jie is another major street, **Qianmen Avenue,** which runs by the historic Qianmen Gate (*men* means gate) at the southern end of Tiananmen Square. This street rapidly changes its name, too, becoming **Qianmen Dong Dajie** to the east and **Qianmen Xi Dajie** to the west (*dong* means east; *xi* means west).

North of Chang'an Jie there are several major east–west streets on the grid, all of which change names along the way, too. The first, **Jingshanqian Jie,** separates the north wall of the Forbidden City from the artificial hill that overlooks it (called Jingshan Park or Coal Hill). As it runs east toward the **Second Ring Road,** Jingshanqian Jie changes its name twice, becoming **Dongsi Xi Dajie,** then **Chaoyangmennei Dajie.**

Further north of the Forbidden City is another major east–west avenue, called **Di'anmen Xi Dajie** to the west and **Di'anmen Dong Dajie** to the east. When this street nears the Second Ring Road in the east, it changes its name, yet again, to **Gongrentiyuchang Bei Lu.** Here, you can find many cafes and the Sanlitun neighborhood of diplomatic compounds, the location of Beijing's liveliest bar scene.

The most important north–south street, for shoppers at least, is **Wangfujing Dajie,** the capital's number one street to browse. It begins 3 blocks east of the Forbidden City along Chang'an Jie. Other big downtown streets to the east are **Nanchizi Dajie** (along the Forbidden City's moat) and **Dongdan Bei Dajie** (a big shopping street 1 block east of Wangfujing). Heading west from the Forbidden City, the most important intersecting streets are **Xidan Bei Dajie** (a shopping street favored by locals, with immense new malls) and **Fuxingmen Bei Dajie** (the name of the Second Ring Road as it heads north).

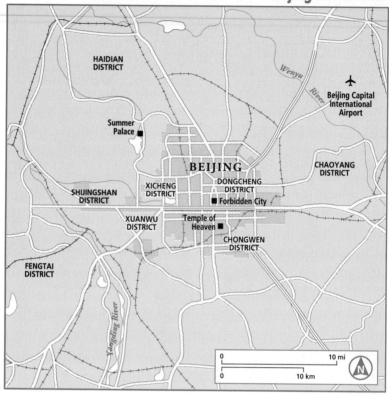

The ring roads are important streets in their own right; many restaurants, hotels, shops, and attractions are located on or near them. This is especially true of the northeastern stretches of the Second and Third Ring roads. At these busy points, the Second Ring Road is called **Chaoyangmen Bei Dajie;** the Third Ring Road is called **Dongsanhuan Bei Lu.**

FINDING AN ADDRESS

Even though the main streets are laid out in a checkerboard on north–south and east–west axes, it is possible to get lost. The blocks, which appear short and simple on any map, are in reality extremely long. What looks like a 10-minute stroll can stretch to an hour on foot. Moreover, the main streets are constantly intersected by other, sometimes very substantial streets, which can be mistakenly identified or may not appear on a map at all. The trick is to locate a street sign.

Fun Fact Here Comes the Sand

The legendary Gobi Desert is on its way to Beijing. In fact, the desert begins just 150 miles to the northwest of the capital. Due to accelerated erosion, the Gobi is advancing today at a menacing pace, coming 10 miles closer each year. Not even the Great Wall could keep out this advancing army.

Streetwise in Beijing

Unfortunately, the streets of Beijing are mouthfuls to pronounce and difficult to remember at first. After a few trips through the city, however, they begin to sort themselves out. One reason that the street names (which are written in *pinyin,* rather than English; see appendix B) seem so long is that the Chinese characters for directions (north, south, east, or west) and for various kinds of thoroughfares (street, avenue, alley) all run together into a single long street name that makes you think you're in Wales. In fact, a street named South Chizi Avenue is written on the street signs and maps in *pinyin* as Nan Chizi Dajie (where *nan* means south and *dajie* means avenue, or literally "big street"). Common elements in street names (and their English translations) are as follows:

bei	north	*lu*	road
nan	south	*hutong*	alley
dong	east	*wai*	outer
xi	west	*nei*	inner
zhong	central	*qiao*	bridge
jie	street	*men*	gate
dajie	avenue		

Nearly all of Beijing's big streets have signs on poles near intersections that give the names in Chinese characters and in *pinyin,* which is the alphabetical rendering of those characters (used on maps and throughout this book). The street signs can be obscured by the general chaos of the cityscape, by buses and traffic, and by their location, which may be as much as half a block from the actual intersection. Your neck and eyes can take a beating as you strain to find a crucial street sign. Because one big block of buildings is often indistinguishable from the next, architectural landmarks can be few and far between. You must be flexible and patient when navigating Beijing.

Actual street addresses can be even more difficult to discover, even on major buildings—and they often don't exist at all. Part of this obscurity arises from Beijing culture, which for centuries has not relied on maps or numeric addresses, but on intimate familiarity with a neighborhood. Fortunately, most cafes and shops that cater to foreigners now post their addresses; parks, temples, and other large sites can usually be identified by their traditional gates and the congregation of street vendors and taxis near their entrances.

MAPS   City maps (*ditu*) are indispensable. You can find them at hotel desks, in hotel gift shops and kiosks, and at bookstores. Street vendors sell maps, too, although they may be Chinese-language only. The best maps are trilingual, with streets and sights rendered in English, *pinyin,* and Chinese characters. The map I use most often is the ***Beijing China Regional Map,*** published by Periplus Editions and sold worldwide. (Be sure to get the newest edition possible.) No map is perfect—and none can keep up with the daily onslaught of new construction in this booming city—but with this guidebook and a trilingual map in hand, you'll be set to explore the city.

NEIGHBORHOODS IN BRIEF

In Beijing, the main districts are also the main means of determining and describing locations. The districts of most interest to the traveler are identified here.

Dongcheng The sector lying north of Chang'an Avenue and east of the Forbidden City contains many of Beijing's top attractions, including Tiananmen Square and Wangfujing Dajie, the chief shopping street. In its northern reaches, it encompasses Jingshan Park, the Lama Temple (Beijing's most popular), and the historic Bell and Drum Towers. Its northern and eastern borders are today enclosed by the Second Ring Road, which is where the city walls and gates once stood.

Chaoyang Farther east from Dongcheng District is what was once the great suburb of Chaoyang. Chaoyang is now one of the city's wealthiest urban districts. It encompasses the area along Chang'an Avenue (here called Jianguomenwai Dajie, after an ancient gate in the old city wall) that is home to Beijing's most famous open-air market (Silk Alley), the city's Friendship Store, the China World shopping center, and a row of grand international hotels. The northern reaches of Chaoyang are the location of Ritan Park, of a tree-lined embassy district, of Workers' Stadium, and of Sanlitun diplomatic district, which is lined with scores of bars and small cafes. On the northeast arc of the Third Ring Road, the

Chaoyang district also contains a number of international hotels, shopping plazas, and restaurants, including Beijing's Hard Rock Cafe.

Chongwen Located below Chang'an Avenue in the southeastern quadrant of the great Beijing grid, Chongwen is home to the Natural History Museum, the old Qianmen neighborhood, and a stellar attraction, the Temple of Heaven (Tiantan Park).

Xuanwu Occupying the southwestern quadrant of old Beijing, Xuanwu contains the city's largest Moslem neighborhood (near the Ox Street Mosque) and, in the Dazhalan subdistrict, the historic street of Liulichang, Beijing's best strolling and antique shopping row.

Xicheng Immediately west and mostly north of the Forbidden City, Xicheng is the site of some of the most extensive old *hutong* (alleyway) neighborhoods in Beijing. It is also the location of the city's most beautiful lakes: Beihai Lake (which Marco Polo praised) and the three "back lakes" of Xihai, Houhai, and Qianhai. The lakes are near some excellent temples and the lavish, once-private grounds of Prince Gong's Mansion.

Tips Which Way Do I Go?

When finding an address proves impossible, ask a local. Even if they do not speak English, they might be able to locate your destination on a map and point you in the right direction. In moments of complete disorientation, hail a cab; this is the quickest way to beam yourself back to your hotel, where you can start over. Becoming completely lost happens to the most experienced Beijing travelers, especially now that the city changes shape so rapidly. Cartographers, who used to do annual updates, are now forced to print new editions of city maps as often as every 3 weeks.

Haidian   Located far to the north-west on the way to the Summer Palace and the Western Hills, Haidian is best known as the capital's university district (site of China's Harvard, Beijing University) and its high-tech development zones. The zoo ranks as its most famous attraction, but Haidian is also the location of a new aquarium and an old temple that now houses the Beijing Art Museum.

2 Getting Around

Given the vastness of Beijing and the overcrowded condition of its public buses, taxis and the subway become indispensable for any sightseer. Fortunately, both are relatively inexpensive. An adventurous alternative is to travel as most Beijingers do, by bicycle.

BY SUBWAY

The Beijing subway (*ditie*), usually called the **Metro,** is the fastest way to cover longer distances, and it's incredibly inexpensive: 3RMB (36¢) per ride. Operating daily from 5am to 10:30pm, the subway has two lines: The **Loop Line,** which makes 18 stops, girdles Beijing under the Second Ring Road, and the crosstown **Line 1,** which makes 23 stops, runs east–west along Chang'an Avenue. The two lines intersect at **Fuxingmen Station** in the west and at **Jianguomen Station** in the east. Transfers are free at these two stations, but passengers must walk upstairs or downstairs to change lines.

When **Line 1** (the red line) opened in 1969, it constituted China's first subway. This line was recently extended 8 miles to the east, a godsend to visitors who can now use the Metro to visit such downtown attractions as the Xidan shopping malls (Xidan Station), the Forbidden City and Tiananmen Square (Tiananmen Xi Station or Tiananmen Dong Station), Wangfujing shopping (Wangfujing Station), Dongdan shopping (Dongdan Station), the Friendship Store (Jianguomen Station), the Silk Market (Yonganli Station), and the China World complex (Guomao Station). It also puts the hotels along the line as far east as China World within minutes of Beijing's central attractions.

The **Loop Line** also leads to major attractions. Many of its stations bear the names of the nine gates in the old city wall (the wall itself having been pulled down in the 1950s and replaced by the Second Ring Road and the Metro line). Moving clockwise from the Fuxingmen stop (western transfer point to the crosstown Line 1), the Loop Line provides stops for the zoo, the aquarium, the West Train Station (at Xizhimen), the back lakes and Soong Chingling's mansion (at Jishuitan), the Bell and Drum Tower area (at Guluo Dajie), the Lama Temple (at Yonghegong), Silk Alley and other sites along Jianguomenwai Dajie (at Jianguomen), the Beijing Train Station (at Beijing Zhan), southern Tiananmen Square (at Qianmen), and Dashalan and Liulichang Antique Street (at Hepingmen).

NAVIGATING THE SUBWAY   Using Beijing's Metro is simple. Every platform looks nearly the same, with trains running each direction on opposite sides. The station name in Chinese and *pinyin* is usually posted on pillars facing the tracks. Maps on tunnel walls indicate the next station on the route. Maps of the complete system are posted in each station and over each door inside the subway cars (always in Chinese and *pinyin*). In addition, a recording (usually quite audible), first in Chinese, then in English, announces each upcoming stop. Navigating with all these aids is simple; should you find yourself going the

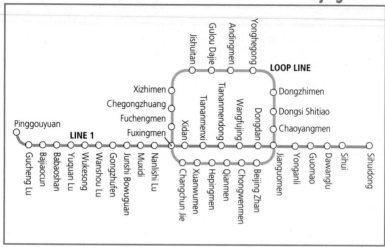

wrong way, simply exit at the next station, cross the platform, and board the train running in the opposite direction.

To make a line transfer at Fuxingmen Station or Jianguomen Station, exit your car and find a stairway marked (in English) as the transfer route to the other line. If you are transferring from the Loop Line to Line 1, go downstairs; if you are transferring from Line 1 to the Loop Line, go upstairs.

The cars, which are conventional in design, are a bit worn but cleaner than the streets and most taxis. They lack air-conditioning, but they are seldom jam-packed except on Sundays and during rush hours (and even then you can get on). It takes about 2 minutes to travel between stations.

To enter a subway station, walk down the stairs. (There are always stairs at the entrance and no elevators; escalators, often under repair, are provided only for exiting from stations.) Walk through the tunnel until you come to the ticket window (look for a sign and arrow in English). Push your cash through the ticket window and take your change and the paper ticket (there are no magnetic cards, passes, or tokens). Hand the paper ticket to the checker at the top of the final flight of stairs to the platform below and hold onto the torn chit, which is sometimes checked again when you exit. Bilingual signs on platform posts help direct you when choosing an exit. Your only problem upon exiting is determining what street you're standing on—not always easy until you locate a street sign or landmark.

Tips Finding the Subway

Finding a subway entrance can be tricky. First, study your map to see which intersection is nearest the station. There are usually at least four entrances, one on each side of the intersection (although not always on the corner). Look for a large sign with the letter D inside a circle. If you can't find the sign, look for a bicycle park on the sidewalk. The entrances always have chain-link gates that are closed at night. Anywhere you see people entering and walking down a wide set of stairs is probably a subway entrance (except for a few street underpasses).

BY TAXI

With 70,000 taxis in the street (the most of any city in the world), this is the most common means for visitors to get around Beijing. Expect to pay about 15RMB to 25RMB ($2–$3) for most excursions around town and up to 60RMB ($7.50) for a long crosstown trip. Tip your driver 1RMB to 2RMB (12¢–24¢). Credit cards are not accepted. To hail a taxi in the streets, stand on the edge of the sidewalk and stretch out an arm, raising an open palm. It's safest to ride in the backseat (especially for women traveling solo).

There are three levels of taxis. The old yellow minivans (*miandi*) have been phased out by the government, making the cheapest choice the tiny, Chinese-manufactured hatchbacks (known as *Xiali*). These are seldom clean or comfortable, but they charge just 10RMB ($1.20) for the first 3km (1.2RMB, or 13¢, per additional km). The next step up are the older but slightly larger and cleaner sedans, which charge 10RMB ($1.20) for the first 4km (1.6RMB, or 19¢, per additional km). The best taxis, which congregate at leading hotels, are new cars (usually Japanese imports or Chinese-produced VW Santanas). These charge 12RMB ($1.44) for the first 4km (2RMB, or 24¢, per additional km). Note that taxis charge 20% more after 11pm and that the meters, which click every 0.5 km, also click when in a traffic jam (charging for another 0.5km of travel every 2½ min. when motionless).

Always insist on using the taxi's meter; any negotiated price is a rip-off. Be sure that the meter is set at zero when you start. If the meter is not on, say *"Qing da biao!"* To stop, shout *"Ting che!"* Taxi complaints can be directed to the **Beijing Taxi Administration** (✆ **010/6835-1150**). Carry smaller bills to pay the driver (nothing over a 50RMB note). Receipts, which record the cab number, are printed from the meters upon request (say *"Fa piao"*). The **Beijing Taxi Dispatch Centre** has a 24-hour dispatching service, ✆ **010/6837-3399.**

BY BUS   Public buses (*gong gong qi che*) charge from 1RMB (12¢) for short hops and up to 11RMB ($1.21) for the longest hauls, but they are more difficult and uncomfortable than taxis and subways. Still, they can provide an inexpensive adventure. Tickets are sold on the bus; the conductor will want to know your destination to figure the fare. The red-and-white city buses service every bus stop. Electric trolleys cost the same as the buses. To figure out which bus number will get you to your destination, ask for help in your hotel. Buses 103 and 104, for example, run up and down the length of Chang'an Avenue. Be prepared to stand and be crammed during your expedition, and take care with backpacks and purses, as these can be inviting targets for thieves.

⎛*Tips* Talking to Taxi Drivers

Most taxi drivers speak little or no English. If you speak little or no Chinese, get your hotel desk clerk or bellhop to write your destination (and your hotel name and address) on a slip of paper when you set out. Most hotels now provide printed cards for taxi travel; the card has the hotel's name on it and a blank in which to fill in your destination. Many hotel doormen write out the taxi's ID number for you when the cab arrives, in case you have a complaint later.

Fun Fact **Renting a Car in Beijing**

There are plenty of car rental outlets in Beijing, but don't plan on picking yours up at the airport or anywhere else. Tourists are forbidden to rent cars (or motorcycles or scooters) in China because a Chinese driver's license (available only to foreigners with an official residency permit) is required. Of course, major hotels are only too happy to rent chauffeured sedans to their foreign guests by the hour, day, or week, at rates that would make Mr. Avis or Mr. Hertz blush.

BY PEDICAB

These human-pedaled "tricycle taxis" or "rickshaws" appeal to tourists, but they can be expensive. You must haggle with the driver over prices, which start in the 30RMB ($3.60) range and often end up far higher. When bargaining, determine from the outset if the price is per person, one-way or round-trip, and in RMB or U.S.$. Ask the driver how much (*"Dou shou?"*) and then bargain from there; try to get the driver down to about half his original fee. Unless you are exploring the narrow and winding back alleys (*hutongs*) of old Beijing on your own, pedicabs aren't worth using.

BY BICYCLE

A bicycle is the best way to see Beijing, especially its back streets, at your own pace. It may look intimidating and downright dangerous, but joining in with Beijing's millions of bike riders is not so difficult. The three keys to success: riding at a leisurely pace, staying with the flow, and using the designated bike lanes on the big streets. Some hotels rent good bicycles (usually newer mountain bikes) by the hour for 10RMB to 20RMB ($1.20–$2.40), with better rates by the half or full day. Be sure that the brakes are in good working order—you'll need them—and that tires are fully inflated. Should you have a flat or need a repair, sidewalk bicycle mechanics charge ridiculously low rates (1 mao–2 mao, or 1¢–2¢) on nearly every block. You'll also need a bicycle lock. Sometimes, the lock is built into the back tire. When you reach your destination or need to stop and explore on foot, look for a forest of bikes parked at a major intersection or near a park, attraction, or major store. These are bike parks. Wheel your bike over, lock it next to others, and pay an attendant, who will give you a paper receipt. Parking costs are no more than a few mao (cents).

ON FOOT

The best way to see Beijing and experience life at street level is to walk. Although certain shopping streets can be impossibly crowded at times, they are always fascinating. Just bear in mind that Beijing drivers, who drive on the right side of the street, do not give pedestrians the right of way. Even at red lights, vehicles don't stop when making a right turn, whether or not pedestrians are in the crosswalk. Bicycle riders don't give way to pedestrians, either. Cars also present an obstacle on the sidewalks—whether parked or returning to the street. Stay alert and you'll be fine—and watch out for imperfect sidewalks that seem to be designed to trip you up. Don't expect to sue anyone successfully if you take a tumble on a broken sidewalk.

FAST FACTS: Beijing

If you don't find what you're looking for in these listings, try the 24-hour Tourist Hot Line (© **010/6513-0828**) or inquire at your hotel desk.

Airport See "Arriving," under "Orientation" at the beginning of this chapter.

American Express Holders of an American Express card can make inquiries about currency exchange, emergency card replacement, personal check cashing, and 24-hour access to an ATM at the China World Trade Center, Tower 1, Room 2101, 1 Jianguomenwai Dajie (© **010/6505-2888**), but money exchange and other banking matters aren't handled here. Office hours are Monday to Friday from 9am to 5:30pm, Saturday from 9am to noon. American Express travel services are now handled at the new CITS office, Room 417, 4/F CITS Building, 103 Fuxingmennei Dajie (Fuxingmen subway stop), open Monday to Friday from 8:30am to 5:30pm (© **010/6607-1575** or 010/6608-7124).

Babysitters Most four- and five-star hotels can provide babysitting services, provided you give advance notice. Prices vary but average about $5 per hour.

Banks Convenient **Bank of China** locations for currency exchange and credit card cash withdrawals are the **Bank of China Headquarters,** 410 Fuchengmennei Dajie (© 010/6601-6688), open Monday to Friday from 9am to 4pm; the **Bank of China Beijing Branch,** 8 Yabao Lu (© 010/6519-9114), open Monday to Friday from 9am to noon and from 1 to 5pm, Saturday and Sunday from 9:30am to 3:30pm; the **Bank of China Capital Airport Office** (© 010/6456-3985), open daily from 6:30am to midnight; and the **Bank of China Lufthansa Center Office** (© 010/6465-3388), open Monday to Thursday from 9am to 4pm, Friday from 9am to 3:30pm. The **CITIC Industrial Bank** provides the same services at the CITIC Building, 19 Jianguomenwai Dajie (© 010/6501-3331), open Monday to Friday from 9am to noon and from 1 to 4pm.

Bookstores The **Foreign Language Bookstore,** 235 Wangfujing Dajie (© 010/6512-6911), has a large collection of English-language books (on the third floor); so does the attached **Foreign Imports Bookstore** next door. The **Friendship Store Bookstore,** 17 Jianguomenwai Dajie (© 010/6500-3311), carries a fine selection of imported magazines and travel guides, as well as Chinese books in English. Gift shops and kiosks in major hotels sometimes maintain a good collection of books about Beijing and China (as well as foreign newspapers). The Kempinski, Kunlun, and Traders hotel gift shops are worth browsing, as is the **World of Books** on the sixth floor of the Lufthansa Centre, 50 Liangmaqiao Lu (© 010/6465-3388).

Business Hours Since China adopted the 5-day work week in 1995, most banks and government offices are open Monday to Friday only, usually from 9am to 5pm, although some still close at lunchtime (noon–2pm). Bank branches and CITS tour desks in hotels often keep longer hours and are usually open Saturday mornings. Shops and department stores are open daily, typically from 9am to 7pm (later in the summer). Most hotels keep their money exchange desks open 24 hours a day. Most temples and parks are open daily from sunrise to sunset. Other tourist sites are typically open daily from 9am to 5pm, although some, such as museums, may close for a day or two during the week. Restaurants located outside of hotels are generally open daily at least from 6 to 9am, from 11:30am to 2pm, and from 5 to 9:30pm. Restaurants catering to foreigners may stay open later, and bars (which often include a cafe) don't close until the wee hours.

Business Services Kinko's, America's ubiquitous photocopy center, opened its first branch in Beijing in 1998. Running 24 hours a day, it provides the same services in China as elsewhere, including copying, self-service copying (6 mao, or pennies, per page), and scanning and binding, along with PC rentals (65RMB, $7.90 per hr.), conference room rentals (20RMB, $2.40 per hr.), and free pickup and delivery (Mon–Fri, 8am–6:30pm). Fax rates are 4RMB (50¢) a page to receive, 6.20RMB (75¢) a page to send locally, 10RMB ($1.25) a page to send within China, and 20RMB ($2.50) a page (plus phone charges) to fax overseas. You can receive faxes sent from any other Kinko's in the world free—definitely the way to office in Beijing. Kinko's Beijing is located 2 blocks north of the Jiangguang Centre on the Third Ring Road at A11 Xiangjun Bei Lu (© **010/6595-8020** or 6595-6388; fax 6595-8218; kinkos@bj.col.com.cn).

Camera Repair/Film Kodak, Fuji, and other imported camera films can be purchased at hotel kiosks, in megamall outlets, at department store counters, and in camera stores at prices on par with those in Western nations. There are 1-hour and next-day film processing outlets in hotel sand shopping centers, too. For reliable camera repair and film developing, try **Beijing Photography,** 263 Wangfujing Dajie (© **010/6525-7301**), open daily from 8:30am to 8pm.

Climate See "When To Go" in chapter 2.

Computers & Laptops Beijing lags behind Western capitals in installing dataports/modular plugs in hotel rooms, but it is quickly catching up. Most hotel business centers have computer (PC) rentals with up-to-date software, Internet access, and e-mail capabilities; you may also be able to plug in a laptop there. The top hotels are now wired so that you can plug in your laptop and even go online in the comfort of your own room.

Couriers International parcel and courier services with offices in Beijing are **FedEx,** Golden Land Building, 32 Liangmaqiao Lu (© **010/6468-5566**), with 4 flights weekly to the U.S.; **DHL-Sinotrans,** with branches at China World Trade Center, Room 111, 1 Jianguomenwai Dajie (© **010/6505-2173**), and Lufthansa Center, 50 Liangmaqiao Lu (© **010/6465-1208**); and **UPS,** Kelun Building, Tower 2, 12A Guanghua Lu (© **010/6593-2932**).

Credit Cards See "Money" in chapter 2 for details. **American Express, Visa, MasterCard,** and **JCB** are accepted at most hotels, hotel restaurants, and a growing number of stores and restaurants outside of hotels. **Diners Club** is accepted at many hotels and some restaurants. The **Eurocard** and the **Discover Card** are rarely accepted anywhere in Beijing. Representative offices for credit card companies include **American Express,** 2101 China World Trade Center Shopping Arcade, 1 Jianguomenwai Dajie (© **010/6505-2888**), and **Diners Club,** Room 101, Tower 1, Bright China Chang An

Bldg., 7 Jianguomennei Dajie (℃ **010/6510-1833** or 24-hr. hot line 010/6606-2227). MasterCard and Visa can be reached via the Beijing/China phone numbers as indicated on their cards.

Currency See "Money" in chapter 2 for an explanation of Renminbi (RMB) and conversion rates.

Currency Exchange Certain branches of the **Bank of China** and other banks can convert your traveler's checks and national currencies to RMB. The rate is fixed by a government agency. Hotel desks also do currency exchanges, usually on a 24-hour basis, at rates nearly as good as the banks offer. A passport is required. No private offices or kiosks offer currency exchange services.

Customs See "Entry Requirements & Customs" in chapter 2.

Doctors & Dentists Hotels can refer foreign guests to dentists and doctors versed in Western medicine. Some hotels have in-house doctors and small clinics. The following medical clinics and hospitals specialize in treating foreigners and provide international-standard services: **Beijing United Family Hospital,** 2 Jiangti Lu (near the Hilton Hotel), open 24 hours daily, has a pharmacy, dental clinic, and in- and out-patient care (℃ **010/ 6433-3960); Beijing International SOS Clinic and Alarm Center,** Building C, BITIC Leasing Center, 1 Xingfusancun Bei Jie, open 24 hours daily, has a pharmacy, ambulance service, 13 expatriate doctors, and 3 dentists (℃ **010/6462-9100);** and **International Medical Center (IMC),** Beijing Lufthansa Center, Regus Office Bldg., Room 106, 50 Liangmaqiao Lu, open 24 hours daily, has a pharmacy, ambulance service, dentists, and 25 doctors that speak various languages (℃ **010/6465-1561).** The **Hong Kong International Medical Clinic** at the Swissotel, Beijing Hong Kong Macau Center, 9th floor, also provides doctors and dentists at its 24-hour clinic, closed Sundays (℃ **010/6501-2288,** ext 2346). The **Peking Union Medical Hospital,** 53 Dongdan Bei Dajie (near the downtown Oriental Plaza), is staffed by Western-trained Chinese doctors who speak English and maintains a 24-hour "Foreigners Emergency Clinic" (℃ **010/6529-5269** or 010/6529-5284 for emergencies). The **Haisheng Dental Clinic,** Building 10, Anhua Xi Lu, 1st floor (℃ **010/6425-4777),** is a complete dental clinic headed by the personal dentist of former Premier Zhou En-lai; open daily from 8:30am to 5pm, it offers everything from crowns to "cleaning of teeth and removal of [bad] breath." A new international **VISTA** medical clinic opened in the Kerry Centre, 1 Guanghua Lu, in 2001. Medical charges at all these facilities are on par with those in Western nations.

Documents Required See "Entry Requirements," in chapter 2. Carry your passport and a copy of your passport at all times.

Drugstores See "Pharmacies," below.

Earthquakes Beijing is located in an earthquake-prone zone and anticipates a San Francisco–style disaster, perhaps in the near (but unpredictable) future. In 1976, the nearby city of Tangshan was struck by a major quake that killed over 250,000 residents, the most fatal earthquake in history. China's earthquake experts are charged with making predictions and deciding on when to order advance evacuations.

Electricity The electricity in Beijing is 220 volts, alternating current (AC), 50 cycles. Outlets come in a variety of configurations. You may have to supply your own transformers and modem adapters in some hotels, but better hotels now supply a range of standard adapters for electrical appliances and electronic devices. The most common adapters are the narrow round 2-pin, the slanted 2-prong, and the 3-prong types.

Embassies & Consulates The embassies of most countries are located in Beijing in the Jianguomenwai and Sanlitun Embassy Compounds (Chaoyang District), several miles east and northeast of city center. Visa and passport sections are open only at certain times of the day, so call in advance. Most embassies are open Monday to Friday only. The **U.S. Embassy** is at 3 Xiushui Bei Jie, Jianguomenwai Dajie (✆ **010/6532-3831/3431;** fax 010/6532-3297). The **Canadian Embassy** is at 19 Dongzhimenwai Dajie (✆ **010/6532-3536;** fax 010/6532-4072). The **Ireland Embassy** is at 3 Ritan Dong Lu (✆ **010/6532-2914;** fax 010/6532-2168). The **New Zealand Embassy** is at 1 Dong'erjie, Ritan Lu (✆ **010/6532-2731;** fax 010/6532-4317). The **Australian Embassy** is at 21 Dongzhimenwai Dajie (✆ **010/6532-2331;** fax 010/6532-4349). The **United Kingdom of Great Britain and Northern Ireland Embassy** is at 11 Guanghua Lu (✆ **010/ 6532-1961;** fax 010/6532-1937). (*Note:* Within the next few years, many of these embassies will move northeast to a new area near the Hilton Hotel, on the other side of the Third Ring Road, where ground is being broken.)

Emergencies The emergency phone numbers in Beijing are ✆ **110** for the police, ✆ **119** for the fire department, and ✆ **120** for an ambulance.

Holidays See "When To Go," in chapter 2.

Hospitals Consult the hospitals listed above in "Doctors & Dentists." These hospitals and clinics cater to the expatriate community and foreign visitors.

Hot Lines The **Beijing Tourism Administration** maintains a 24-hour hot line for tourist inquiries and complaints, with operators fluent in Chinese, Japanese, and English, ✆ **010/6513-0828.**

Information See "Visitor Information," above and in chapter 2.

Internet Access Business centers at major hotels provide online services, e-mail access, PC rentals, and familiar software programs; charges can be billed to your hotel room. In the city's luxury hotels, you may also get in-room Internet access using your laptop. There are cheaper alternatives at independent vendors throughout the city. The most convenient outlets for travelers are provided by **Unicom–Sparkice** Internet Cafes, at locations across the capital (✆ **800/810-8100** in China), including branches at the China World Trade Center (1 Jianguomenwai Dajie, 2nd floor (✆ **010/ 6505-2288,** ext. 8209), the Kempinski Hotel, 50 Liangmaqiao Lu (✆ **010/6465-3872**), and at Wantong Century Market, 2 Fuwai Dajie (✆ **010/6857-8794**). One of the largest Web-surfing emporiums is the student-friendly **Feiyu Internet Cafe** at the south gate of Beijing University, Haidian Lu (✆ **010/6263-1244**), with over a 100 PCs for rent 24 hours a day. Other choices include the **On/Off Restaurant and Bar,** 5 Xingfu Yicun Xili, in the Sanlitun area, where Internet connection is free (✆ **010/6415-8083**), and **11 Fans Cyber Cafe**, Basement, Full Link Plaza, 18 Chaoyangmenwai Dajie, open 24 hours a day, which charges 15RMB ($1.80) per hour (© **010/ 6588-0399**).

Laundry & Dry Cleaning Laundromats have not made a mark in Beijing. Your hotel provides full laundry and dry cleaning services, often same-day, with prices depending on the rating of the hotel.

Liquor Laws The drinking age in Beijing is 18. Bars keep irregular closing hours, some not closing until 4am or later. Supermarkets and some hotel shops sell beer, wine, and spirits. Beijingers don't drink much except on holidays, on special occasions, and at banquets. Follow your Chinese host's lead in drinking and toasting.

Lost Property First, contact the site where you think you lost an item. Then report the loss to your hotel staff and ask for their suggestions and assistance in calling around town. Items lost in taxis are sometimes returned to your hotel.

Luggage Storage The train stations have left-luggage counters but the subway and airport do not. Hotels provide storage (often for a small daily fee) at their bell desks.

Mail Most hotels sell postage stamps and will mail your letters and parcels. A few hotels even have small post offices. Overseas letters and postcards require 5 to 14 days for delivery. Overseas airmail rates are 4.20RMB (50¢) for a postcard, 5.20RMB (60¢) for an aerogramme, and 6.40RMB (75¢) for a letter (up to 20g, or 0.5 oz.). These rates are always subject to change. The main **International Post Office** is located near the Second Ring Road on Yabao Lu by the Jiangwai Diplomatic Compound, Jianguomen Bei Dajie, open Monday to Saturday from 8am to 6:30pm (© **010/6512-8120** or 010/6512-8114). There is also a post office branch located next to the Friendship store on Jianguomenwai Dajie. For private couriers offering overseas express mail and parcel service, see "Couriers," above.

Money See "Money," in chapter 2.

Newspapers & Magazines The official *China Daily* English-language newspaper appears Monday to Friday, with a special edition on Saturdays, and is available free at hotel desks. It is a national newspaper, giving official views, China and world news, and features, as well as a calendar of events and TV listings for Beijing. Monthly editions of English-language magazines and newspapers produced for travelers and expatriates in Beijing are also available at hotels and restaurants around town. Look for such titles as *Beijing This Month, Metrozine, Beijing Journal,* and *City Weekend.* Foreign magazines and newspapers, including *USA Today, International Herald Tribune, South China Morning Post,* and Asian editions of *The Wall Street Journal, Newsweek,* and *Time* are available at the kiosks in all large international hotels.

Pharmacies There are no 24-hour drugstores in Beijing. Hotel kiosks, modern department stores, and supermarkets sometimes carry Western amenities and remedies (cough drops, toothpaste, shampoo, beauty aids), but bring your own pain and cold remedies. The best outlet for Westerners is

Watson's at the Holiday Inn Lido, Jichang Lu, Jiangtai Lu (© 010/ 6436-7653), open daily from 9am to 9pm, and at Full Link Plaza, 18 Chaoyangmenwai Dajie (© 010/6588-2145), open daily from 10am to 9pm. The **Wangfujing Drug Store,** 267 Wangfujing Dajie (© 010/ 6524-9932), also has a selection of Western remedies and Chinese medicines. Prescriptions can be filled at the hospital pharmacies listed above under "Doctors & Dentists."

Police The Beijing police force is known as the **Public Security Bureau (PSB),** with the main office at 85 Beichizi, near the Forbidden City. The emergency telephone number is © **110.**

Post Office See "Mail," above.

Restrooms For hygienic restrooms, rely on the big hotels. Thousands of public restrooms are located in the streets, parks, restaurants, department stores, and the major tourist sites of Beijing, but these are not very clean and seldom provide tissues or soap. The restrooms in the newest shopping plazas, fast-food outlets, and deluxe restaurants catering to foreigners are much cleaner and often meet international standards. The common public restrooms charge a small fee (usually less than 1RMB), but seldom provide Western-style facilities or private booths, relying instead on squat toilets (porcelain "holes-in-the-floor"), open troughs, and rusty spigots. Look for "WC" signs at intersections pointing the way to these facilities. On the east side of the Forbidden City is a large public restroom, which charges a small fee, but its facilities (some Western toilets and booths) are not always particularly clean. Tourists often come armed with their own tissues and even a can of spray disinfectant. Be prepared to rough it if you are off the beaten track (meaning anywhere outside a major hotel).

Note: As part of a 2-year campaign to upgrade Beijing's public toilets, the cramped and filthy facilities found on nearly every city block are now subject to a rigorous rating system: Each public toilet will soon be assigned one to four stars. The four-star public restrooms "should have granite floors, sufficient lighting, lively music, facilities to wash hands, tissues, automatic flush, hand dryers, and bathrooms specially designed for disabled and old people," according to the official *China Daily* account. Requirements for lower-rated restrooms have not been made public. Also, there is a program to rid Beijing of all streetside public toilets except for the portable kind.

Safety Beijing is one of the safest capitals in the world for foreign travelers, but as the city modernizes and Westernizes, the usual precautions should be followed. Pickpockets and thieves do exist. At crowded public tourist sites, keep an eye on purses, wallets, and cameras. Always store valuables in a concealed safety pouch. Backpacks and fanny packs are targets in buses, on the subway, and in markets. Use hotel safety-deposit boxes or room safes, and do not open your door to strangers. Violent crimes and cases of sexual harassment against foreign visitors are quite rare, but they do occur, so use common sense. Travel with others when possible, rebuff strangers in the streets, and avoid unlighted streets after dark. Beggars are common on Beijing streets, as are touts hawking merchandise. The touts often speak a little English, may pose as "friends," and are not usually thieves, but they should be rebuffed quickly. Don't give strangers your hotel name or phone number, unless you want to be bothered later. If someone befriends you in the street and suggests going to a cafe, resist (for example, say you have an appointment to keep at your hotel); this is quite often a con game in which your "friend" and the cafe team up to present you with an outrageously inflated bill that you will feel obligated to pay. (This ruse has been used on me in my city wanderings on more than one occasion.)

Shoe Repair Streetside vendors repair shoes and other leather goods for a small fee. Most hotels provide the same service, and an increasing number of shoe-repair outlets are opening in modern shopping malls throughout Beijing.

Smoking China has more smokers (an estimated 350 million) than any other nation, accounting for one of every three cigarettes consumed worldwide. About 70% of men smoke. Recent antismoking campaigns have led to laws banning smoking on all forms of public transport (including taxis) and in waiting rooms and terminals. The ban is spreading to many public buildings. Fines can be levied, but enforcement is sporadic. Hotels provide nonsmoking rooms and floors, and more and more restaurants are setting aside nonsmoking tables and sections. At present, expect to encounter more smoking in public places in China than in the West.

Taxes Hotels levy a 15% service tax and a 70¢ per day per person City Development Tax on rooms. Many upscale restaurants and bars place a 15% service charge on bills. There is no sales tax. The other common tax tourists face is the international departure tax at the airport, currently 90 RMB ($10.80), payable only in Chinese currency in the departure hall before checking in.

Taxis See "Getting Around," earlier in this chapter.

Telephone & Fax The **country code** for China is **86**. The **city code** for Beijing is **010**. If you are calling a Beijing number from outside the capital but within China, dial the city code (010) and then the number. If you are calling Beijing from abroad, drop the first zero.

Local calls in Beijing require no code; just dial the 8-digit Beijing number (or the 3-digit emergency numbers for fire, police, and ambulance). Calls from Beijing to other locations in China require that you dial the full domestic city code (which always starts with **0**).

To call Beijing from the United States, dial 011 (the international access code) + 86 (the country code for China) + **10** (the city code for Beijing minus the initial 0) + the eight-digit Beijing phone number.

To make an international direct dial (IDD) call from Beijing (which you can now do from most Beijing hotel rooms), dial the international access code **(00)** + country code for the country you are calling + the area code and the local phone number. The country code for the U.S. and Canada is **1,** for the United Kingdom **44,** for Australia **61,** and for New Zealand **64.** To call the U.S. from Beijing, for example, dial 00 + 1 + the U.S. area code + the U.S. phone number. If you have questions, speak with the hotel operator or an international operator (© **115**).

You can also use your **calling card** (AT&T, MCI, or Sprint, for example) to make international (but not domestic) calls from Beijing. The local access number for **AT&T** is ✆ **10-811;** for **MCI,** ✆ **10-812;** and for **Sprint,** ✆ **10-813.** Check with your calling-card company or with your hotel for other local access numbers. The directions for placing an international call with a calling card or stored-value card vary from company to company, so check on the exact procedures before you leave home.

Most Beijing hotels have fax services for their guests (usually through a business center). Faxes are an efficient way to communicate overseas (and within Beijing and China). The charges for faxing overseas from Beijing, however, are higher than those for faxing to Beijing from overseas, owing not only to hotel charges but to the higher rates imposed on international communications by China. Starting in 2001, these high rates have begun to be lowered.

Television **Chinese Central Television** operates six stations (CCTV 1, 2, 3, 4, 6, and 8), and Beijing Television (BTV) has three stations. Nearly all programs (including commercials, sports, and news) are in Chinese. Hotels provide a spectrum of Western-language satellite stations and international broadcasting. International hotels typically offer 20 to 30 stations, including the Chinese channels, Hong Kong–based Star TV (in both English- and Chinese-language versions), video stations (such as MTV), news stations (such as CNN, CNBC, and BBC), sports stations (such as ESPN and Star Sports), and some international networks (such as Japan's NHK). Some hotels still provide in-room closed-circuit movie channels, but the most common options on the hotel TV dial are Asian versions of HBO and Cinemax.

Time Zone Beijing (and all of China) is 8 hours ahead of Greenwich Mean Time (GMT + 8), meaning it is 13 hours ahead of New York, 14 hours ahead of Chicago, and 16 hours ahead of Los Angeles. Beijing does not use daylight savings time, so subtract 1 hour from the above times in the summer. Because China is on the other side of the International Date Line, you lose 1 day when traveling west from the U.S., but you gain it back upon return (across the Pacific). For the current time in Beijing, dial ✆ **117.**

Tipping This practice is still officially forbidden in the People's Republic of China, so no tipping is necessary. In reality, however, Beijing hotel bellhops routinely receive 10RMB ($1) per bag; restroom attendants, 1RMB to 2RMB (10¢–20¢) per visit; taxi drivers, the change from a bill (1–5RMB, 10¢–50¢); guides on day tours from hotels, 10RMB to 20RMB ($1–$2); and waiters (where no service charge is added), hairdressers, and other service personnel, 10% of the bill.

Water Water from the tap is not safe for drinking (or for brushing teeth), even in the best hotels. The water that's available in hotel rooms in a flask or thermos has been boiled and is safe to drink. Most hotels provide a bottle or two of safe water. Clean bottled water (including the best imported brands) can be purchased almost everywhere, inside and outside your hotel, for 10RMB to 40RMB ($1.20–$4.80) per liter, even from street vendors.

Weather The *China Daily,* Chinese TV news programs, and some hotel bulletin boards furnish the next day's forecast. You can also dial Beijing's weather number, ✆ **121.**

4

Accommodations

Beijing offers more fine accommodations and international chain hotels than any other city in China (except Hong Kong), with higher prices to match. Even the budget hotels (there are no hostels, motels, or B&Bs) charge more in Beijing than elsewhere in China. Rates are highest from May to October.

The first foreign joint venture (JV) hotel in China opened in Beijing in 1982. The Jianguo Hotel on Jianguomenwai Dajie introduced Western management and services to the capital, became a favorite of expatriates and business travelers, and paved the way for such foreign groups as Holiday Inn, Shangri-La, and Sheraton. Foreign staffs manage all these high-end hotels.

The Chinese government now ranks hotels on a star system. **Five-star hotels** have the complete facilities and services of any international luxury hotel. The **four-star hotels** come close, often lacking only a few technical requirements (such as a large swimming pool or other amenities). Both levels are popular choices for Western travelers, providing English-speaking staff and clean, luxurious accommodations. The **three-star hotels** are almost always Chinese-managed and provide less consistent services, fewer amenities, and more basic rooms, with a reduced dedication to upkeep and maintenance. Some, however, are still adequate for the budget traveler who expects merely a decent place to spend the night. Few of the three-star hotels have experienced English-speaking staffs, though, and most have limited facilities that can best be described as drab or run-down.

Acceptable **budget hotels** are almost nonexistent in Beijing. Most Western travelers (and tour groups) must select from more expensive four-star and five-star accommodations. Hotels rated as two-star or below cater to the more rugged backpacking traveler who is not fussy; some offer dormitories and shared bathrooms; and most are not allowed by the government to accept foreign travelers.

HOW TO CHOOSE THE LOCATION THAT'S RIGHT FOR YOU

The bulk of Beijing's international-level four- and five-star hotels are located in three clusters: (1) in the **Dongcheng (City Center)** district near the Forbidden City, (2) in the **Chaoyang (East)** district between the Second and Third Ring roads along Jianguomenwai Dajie, and (3) in the **Chaoyang (Northeast)** district on the Third Ring Road North. The western and southern districts contain far fewer hotels.

On the face of it, one would think that the most desirable location would be in **Dongcheng,** nearest the Forbidden City, Tiananmen Square, and Wangfujing shopping street. The only real drawback to staying in the city center is the lack of adequate transportation. Although you can easily walk to some major sites and shops, taxis have a hard time getting in and out of the heart of the capital—and it can be a long walk to a subway entrance.

Some of Beijing's best hotels are found east of the city center in the **Chaoyang (East)** district (those with Jianguomenwai Dajie addresses). With the completion of the crosstown Metro **Line 1,** these hotels are within a few minutes' commute of the city center and the Forbidden City. They are already closer than the city center hotels to such attractions as Silk Alley and the Friendship Store.

Staying at one of the international hotels in the **Chaoyang (Northeast)** district on the Third Ring Road, a 10- to 20-minute taxi ride from the city center, has advantages, too. For instance, you can easily walk to the Sanlitun diplomatic district, Beijing's number one neighborhood for international cafes, bars, and nightlife. Plenty of restaurants, markets, and shops surround these hotels as it is, and guests out on the Third Ring Road Northeast have a head start in reaching out-of-town destinations, such as the airport (15–20 min. by taxi) and the Great Wall.

None of these three main international hotel districts really has an upper hand in convenience for the traveler. Even hotels in other districts do not suffer significantly by their locations because the main tourist sites are scattered around the sprawling city and, therefore, often must be reached by taxi. The main drawback to staying in a hotel outside the three main hotel precincts is that other neighborhoods are less developed and more isolated. There are fewer shops, tourist attractions, and restaurants nearby.

HOW TO GET THE BEST ROOM FOR THE BEST RATE

The hotel rates listed in this guide are **rack rates.** A rack rate is the maximum rate a hotel charges for a room. You may get that rate if you walked in off the street and asked for a room, but hardly anyone pays that price. Always ask politely whether a room less expensive than the first one mentioned is available—and don't be afraid to bargain. Specials occur year-round, and rack rates change with the seasons (they're lowest from mid-Nov to mid-Mar).

Many four- and five-star hotels in Beijing give travel agents discounts in exchange for steering business their way, so if you're shy about bargaining, an agent may be better equipped to negotiate discounts for you. Book your hotel overseas in advance when possible, either through a travel agent, the hotel chain, or a reservation service.

Reservation services work as consolidators, buying or reserving rooms in bulk, then dealing them out to customers at a profit. Most of them offer online reservation services as well. A few of the more reputable providers are: **Accommodations Express** (© 800/950-4685; www.accommodationsxpress.com), **Hotel Reservations Network** (© 800/96HOTEL; www.180096HOTEL. com), **Quikbook** (© 800/789-9887, includes fax-on-demand service; www.quikbook.com), and **Room Exchange** (© 800/846-7000 in the U.S., 800/486-7000 in Canada). Online, try booking your hotel through **Arthur Frommer's Budget Travel** (www.frommers.com) and save up to 50% on the cost of your room. **Microsoft Expedia** (www.expedia.com) features a "Travel Agent" that can also direct you to affordable lodgings.

Once in Beijing, keep your eye on the local city guides and monthly papers that are distributed free to hotels and restaurants. They frequently advertise tremendous hotel deals, with room rates far below published rack rates.

The hotel listings in this chapter are arranged first by location, then by price within each location. Prices do not include a **service charge** of 15% per night and a city development tax of 70¢ per night per person. All rooms include private baths, satellite television with foreign channels, and nonpotable tap water (unless otherwise noted). All hotels have private baths and **nonsmoking** rooms or floors. Hotel names are rendered first in English, then in *pinyin.*

(*Tips*   **Luxury Hotel Rooms on the Cheap**

In the slower tourist seasons (Nov–Apr), independent travelers who haven't booked a hotel before arrival can sometimes get superb deals by visiting the hotel desks in the Beijing airport. Last-minute rates offered there can sometimes translate into stays at a four-star luxury hotel for the price of a no-star dump.

The **Very Expensive** category lists hotels with rack rates over $230 per night; the **Expensive** category lists hotels with rack rates of $180 to $230 per night; the **Moderate** category lists hotels with rack rates at $90 to $180 per night; and the **Inexpensive** category lists rooms with rack rates of under $90 a night.

1 Dongcheng (City Center)

VERY EXPENSIVE

Beijing Hotel (Beijing Fandian) ⊛   This historic hotel consists of three parts: a seven-story middle section built in 1917 (known for decades as the Peking Hotel), a seven-story west wing added in 1954, and an 18-story east wing opened in 1974. In 1999, the two oldest sections were combined and extensively renovated, eliminating the old French-style guest rooms with their brocade wallpapers; in 2001, the west wing was also completely renovated. Thus, very few reminders of the Peking Hotel's glory days remain, except for the ornate ballrooms. Gone are almost all the older-style rooms (service desks on every floor) with high ceilings and black Qing-style furniture (except for a few "cheaper" rooms in Bldg. C). The hotel carries a five-star government rating, which it now merits based strictly on its lavish facilities. In reality, the amenities and services rate just above three stars, except when State guests and high-ranking delegations take over the floors. Recent renovations have brought an end to the extensive shopping arcade that once lined the hallways, and the Bosendoufer grand piano that has been in Beijing since 1900 and used to reside in the east lobby here has been retired as well. So much for a sense of history. What remains is a massive modern hotel with services and amenities that can be topped by other downtown hotels. The Beijing Hotel still has, however, the location nearest Tiananmen and the Forbidden City, as well as a few links to old Peking.

35 Dong Chang'an Jie (on corner of Wangfujing Dajie), Beijing 100004. © **010/6513-7766.** Fax 010/6513-7307. www.chinabeijinghotel.com.cn. 850 units. $180–$220 double (Bldg. C); $290–$390 double (Bldg. B). AE, DC, MC, V. Metro: Tiananmen Dong (East). **Amenities:** 4 restaurants (Cantonese, Beijing, Japanese, Western), lounge; indoor heated pool (not always open); exercise room; Jacuzzi; sauna; concierge; tour desk; business center; salon; 24-hr. room service; same-day laundry/dry cleaning; executive-level rooms. *In room:* A/C, TV, dataport, minibar, hair dryer, safe.

Grand Hotel (Guibinluo Fandian) ⊛   This 10-story 1990 addition to the Beijing Hotel is the closest hotel to the Forbidden City and provides luxury accommodations, although its staff and management are not quite as efficient as those of the other downtown five-star hotels managed by international groups. The centerpiece is its seven-story atrium (beginning on the 3rd floor) with its marble floor, three glass elevators, cascading greenery, and fountains with figures of the zodiac. The atrium's east wall retains the facade and white marble archway of the original Peking Hotel (1917). The best rooms are on the west side, with fine views of the Forbidden City. Rooms are of good size, elegant, with rosewood Chinese furniture and objets d'art. Bathrooms feature separate tubs and showers, phones, and makeup mirrors. There is no hotel shuttle bus, but taxis are always at the front door.

35 Dong Chang'an Jie (west wing of Beijing Hotel), Beijing 100006. ✆ **800/223-6800** or 010/6513-7788. Fax 010/6513-0048. 218 units (including 57 suites). $300 double; $500 suite. AE, DC, MC, V. Metro: Tiananmen Dong (East). **Amenities:** 2 restaurants (Cantonese; International), lounge, rooftop barbecue (in summer); heated indoor pool; health club; Jacuzzi; sauna; bike rental; concierge; tour desk; small business center; salon; 24-hr. room service; babysitting; same-day laundry/dry cleaning; executive-level rooms. *In room:* A/C, TV, dataport, minibar, coffeemaker, hair dryer, safe.

The Palace Hotel (Wangfu Fandian) 🤎🤎🤎 This is a modern palace fit for China's modern capital. The most luxurious of Beijing's city center hotels, the Palace shows off with its fleet of Rolls Royces and its stunning red marble lobby with two waterfalls. The services (presided over by the Hong Kong–based Peninsula Group) and considerable facilities are tops, too. This hotel pampers its guests in every way. The two basement floors contain about 40 of China's most exclusive shops and boutiques (mainland China's first Armani, for example), as well as a Bank of China branch. The gold-trimmed rooms are spacious, and robes, slippers, and bedside control panels are standard. The large marble bathrooms are equipped with safe drinking water dispensers (a rarity) and mist-free bathroom mirrors. There's a 24-hour medical clinic on the third floor. Westerners outnumber Asians among guests. Airport transfer is appropriately provided by a chauffeured Mercedes Benz ($55) or Rolls Royce ($100).

8 Jingyu Hutong (1 block east of Wangfujing Dajie), Beijing 100006. ✆ **010/6559-2888.** Fax 010/6512-9050. www.peninsula.com. 530 units (including 52 suites). $300 double; $380 executive level. AE, DC, MC, V. Metro: Tiananmen Dong (East). **Amenities:** 4 restaurants (Italian, German, Cantonese, International), 3 lounges (1 with high tea); large heated indoor pool (18m); large state-of-the-art health club; Jacuzzi; sauna; concierge; 24-hr. business center; shopping arcade; salon; 24-hr. room service; babysitting; same-day laundry/dry cleaning; executive-level rooms. *In room:* A/C, TV, dataport, minibar, coffeemaker, hair dryer, safe.

EXPENSIVE

Capital Hotel (Shoudu Binguan) 🤎 Since its $10 million renovation in 1996, this four-star, 20-story hotel near the south entrance to Tiananmen Square has been leaning toward achieving five-star status in its facilities and services. It certainly has the facilities to qualify. The imposing red marble lobby is a bit dark, but the garden goldfish ponds and walkways outside are pleasant and bright. The rooms have adequate space and counters. Writing desks, TVs with CNN and HBO, and separate showers and bathtubs are standard. There are two executive floors (14 and 15), a nonsmoking floor (12), and rooms for travelers with disabilities. The staff speaks fair English and is helpful. A hotel shuttle serves a few city locations (but not the airport). This is the best city center hotel on the south side of Chang'an Avenue, within a 30-minute walk of downtown sites.

3 Qianmen Dong Dajie (4 blocks east of Tiananmen Square), Beijing 100006. ✆ **010/6512-9988.** Fax 010/6512-0309. www.meritus-hotels.com. 326 units (including 37 suites). $180 double. AE, DC, MC, V. Metro: Chongwenmen. **Amenities:** 8 restaurants (includes Italian, Chinese, Japanese, International), garden barbecues (in summer); indoor heated pool; exercise room; sauna; bike rental; video arcade; 4-lane bowling alley; tour desk; air ticket office; business center; shopping arcade; salon; 24-hr. room service; in-room massage; same-day laundry/dry cleaning; executive-level rooms. *In room:* A/C, TV, dataport, minibar, coffeemaker, hair dryer, safe.

(*Fun Fact* **Best Barracks in Town**

Until ordered to sell off its business investments in 1998 and 1999, the People's Liberation Army (PLA) was the behind-the-scenes owner of the ultra-chic **Palace Hotel,** with a fleet of Rolls-Royces rather than tanks.

Beijing Accommodations

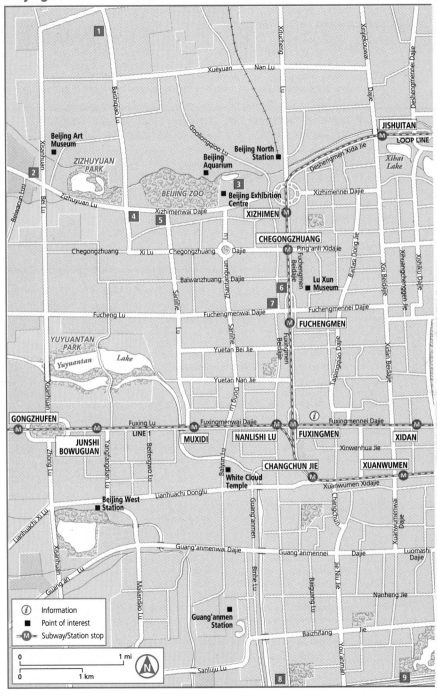

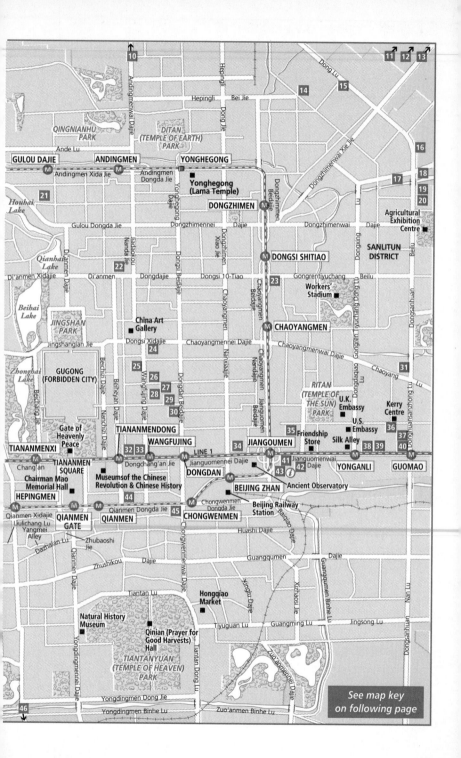

Key for Beijing Accommodations

Bamboo Garden Hotel **21**
竹园宾馆

Beijing Continental Grand Hotel **10**
五洲大酒店

Beijing Hilton Hotel **16**
希尔顿酒店

Beijing Hotel **33**
北京饭店

Beijing International Hotel **34**
国际饭店

Beijing New Century Hotel **4**
新世纪饭店

Beijing Song He Hotel **27**
松鹤大酒店

Capital Hotel **44**
首都宾馆

China Travel Service Tower **15**
中旅大厦

China World Hotel **39**
中国大饭店

Crowne Plaza Beijing **26**
皇冠饭店

Exhibition Centre Hotel **3**
北展饭店

Friendship Hotel **1**
友谊宾馆

Gloria Plaza Hotel **43**
凯莱酒店

Grand Hotel **32**
贵宾楼饭店

Grand View Garden Hotel **8**
北京大观园酒店

Great Wall Sheraton **20**
长城饭店

Harbour Plaza **13**
北京海逸酒店

Holiday Inn Downtown **6**
金都假日饭店

Holiday Inn Lido **12**
丽都饭店

Hotel New Otani Chang Fu Gong **41**
长富宫饭店

Jianguo Hotel **38**
建国饭店

Jing Guang New World Hotel **31**
京广新世界饭店

Jinghua Hotel **46**
京华饭店

Jinglun Hotel **39**
京伦饭店

Kempinski Hotel **18**
凯宾斯基酒店

Kerry Centre Hotel **36**
嘉里中心饭店

Kunlun Hotel **17**
昆仑饭店

Landmark Hotel **19**
亮马河饭店

Lusongyuan Hotel **22**
侣松园宾馆

New World Courtyard Beijing **45**
新世界万怡

Novotel Peace Hotel **29**
和平宾馆

The Palace Hotel **30**
王府饭店

Prime Hotel **24**
华侨大厦

Qiaoyuan Hotel **9**
侨园饭店

Radisson Plaza State Guest House **7**
国宾酒店

Radisson SAS Hotel **14**
北京皇家大酒店

Scitech Hotel **42**
塞特饭店

Shangri-La Beijing Hotel **2**
香格里拉饭店

Sino-Swiss Hotel Beijing Airport **11**
国都茂盛宾饭店

St. Regis Beijing **35**
北京国际俱乐部饭店

Swissotel **23**
港澳中心

Tianlun Dynasty Hotel **24**
天伦王朝饭店

Traders Hotel Beijing **37**
国贸饭店

Wangfujing Grand Hotel **25**
王府井大饭店

Xiyuan Hotel **5**
西苑饭店

Crowne Plaza Beijing (Guoji Yiyuan Huangguan Fandian) ★★   China's first Crowne Plaza (opened in 1991) consists of a skylit atrium open to all nine floors and an art theme underlined by a sales gallery of contemporary Chinese work off the lobby and an art salon on the second floor mezzanine. The service level is lifted by the presence of the most helpful bellhop staff in Beijing. (Ask them for sightseeing, shopping, and restaurant tips.) Every evening, live performances of classical music fill the atrium, a sweet enhancement for dining in the lobby or mezzanine restaurants. Half the rooms face into the high atrium, and the other half face the city shopping streets. Standard rooms on floors 3 to 6 are exceedingly small for a five-star hotel, but stuffed with lavish amenities such as plush robes and slippers. Counter space is minimal. Bathrooms (with phones) are clean and modern. The top floor is nonsmoking and contains guest rooms, a swimming pool, and health facilities with a panoramic view of downtown. By Beijing standards, this is a tiny five-star hotel with tiny rooms, but the service and city-center location are excellent.

48 Wangfujing Dajie (corner of Dengshikou Dajie), Beijing 100006. ℂ **800/465-4329** in U.S. and Canada, 1800/221-066 in Australia, 0800/442-222 in New Zealand, 1800/553-155 in Ireland, 0800/897-121 in U.K., or 010/6513-3388. Fax 010/6513-2513. www.crowneplaza.com. 385 units. $220 double. Children under 19 stay free in parents' room. AE, DC, MC, V. Metro: Tiananmen Dong (East). **Amenities:** 2 restaurants (French, Cantonese), coffee shop, lounge; heated indoor pool (with city view); small health club; Jacuzzi; sauna; bike rental; concierge; tour desk; small 24-hr. business center; salon; 24-hr. room service; babysitting; same-day laundry/dry cleaning; executive-level rooms. *In room:* A/C, TV, dataport, minibar, coffeemaker, hair dryer, safe.

Prime Hotel (Huaqiao Dasha) ★   Known as the Guangdong Regency when it opened in 1991, the nine-story Prime Hotel has been upgraded to five-stars, meaning its facilities are nominally on par with those of its nearest competitors. However, it ranks no higher than fifth (behind The Palace, Crowne Plaza Beijing, Grand Hotel, and Wangfujing Grand, in that order) in downtown hotels. The Prime receives many international tour groups these days and even has a group check-in area off its spacious white marble lobby. Its facilities are splendid. The rooms are fairly large, with bathrobes and spacious writing desks. There are a few rooms for travelers with disabilities. It's a long walk along Wangfujing to the subway, but there's plenty of window-shopping along the way.

2 Wangfujing Dajie (corner of Dongsi Xi Dajie), Beijing 100006. ℂ **800/223-5652** (Steigenberger Reservation Service) or 010/6513-6666. Fax 010/6513-4248. www.primehotel.com. 400 units (including 26 suites). $220 double. AE, DC, MC, V. Metro: Tiananmen Dong (East). **Amenities:** 4 restaurants (Cantonese, Mexican, Italian, International), lounge, deli; narrow indoor pool (15m); exercise room; sauna; bike rental; concierge; tour desk; small business center; salon; 24-hr. room service; in-room massage; babysitting; same-day laundry/dry cleaning; executive-level rooms. *In room:* A/C, TV, dataport, minibar, coffeemaker, hair dryer, safe.

Tianlun Dynasty Hotel (Tianlun Wangchao Fandian) ★   The Tianlun is a showy five-star hotel that claims to have the largest hotel atrium in Asia: It's a miniature Tiananmen Square with copies of the Arc de Triomphe and Roman and Greek palatial sculptures. There's a modern bowling alley in the basement, 13 Japanese 3-D video games, and a classy emporium of Asian snacks (Timeless Medley). But beyond the splash of big and trendy public spaces, the rooms, though recently updated, are just wide enough for a desk and small sitting area. Tour groups (mainly Asian) make up most of the guests. This hotel has had maintenance problems since its opening in 1991, but it has pulled itself back into shape under the direction of one of the very few female general managers in China. Its entrance is incredibly difficult to find, opening up midway in a dark alley a block east of Wangfujing. If you have a bit more money to spend, I suggest going across the street to the Crowne Plaza Beijing.

50 Wangfujing Dajie (on southeast corner of Dengshikou Dajie), Beijing 100006. ℂ 010/6513-8888. Fax 010/6513-7866. www.tianlunhotel.com. 408 units. $160–$180 double (Nov 16–Mar); $180–$200 double (Mar–Sept); $200–$220 double (Sept–Nov 15); executive-level room $20–$30 more. Children under 12 stay free in parents' room. AE, DC, MC, V. Metro: Wangfujing. **Amenities:** 6 restaurants (includes Cantonese, Sichuan, Dim Sum, Japanese, Western), lounge; indoor heated pool; outdoor tennis court; exercise room; Jacuzzi; sauna; game room; concierge; tour desk; large business center; shopping arcade; salon; 24-hr. room service; same-day laundry/dry cleaning; executive-level rooms. *In room:* A/C, TV, dataport, minibar, coffeemaker, hair dryer, safe.

Wangfujing Grand Hotel (Wangfujing Da Fandian) 🏨 At 14 floors, this five-star Chinese-managed hotel, opened in 1995, towers over the shops on the north end of Wangfujing, affording good views of the Forbidden City from half its rooms. The lobby of inlaid marbles is spacious and grand, with its fountain and hemispherical chandelier. The rooms are cheery but small (about the size of those in the nearby Crowne Plaza), with just enough room for a coffee table and two chairs. The gold furnishings and bird's-eye maple trim brighten things up. While the staff is not as efficient or as familiar with foreign travelers as those of the nearby Crowne Plaza or Palace hotels, some of this hotel's facilities are larger, including its shops and its pool—at 25 meters, it's the longest of any in the city center. Many large tour groups from Asia and Europe stay here. It's a luxurious place worth considering if you can negotiate a good deal on the room rate.

57 Wangfujing Dajie, Beijing 100006. ℂ **010/6522-1188.** Fax 010/6522-3816. 380 units. $200 double. AE, DC, MC, V. Metro: Tiananmen Dong (East). **Amenities:** 4 restaurants (Sichuan, Chaozhou, Korean, International), wine bar; large heated indoor pool; health club; Jacuzzi; sauna; game room; concierge; tour desk; 24-hr. business center; shopping arcade; salon; 24-hr. room service; in-room massage; same-day laundry/dry cleaning; executive-level rooms. *In room:* A/C, TV, dataport, minibar, hair dryer, safe.

MODERATE

Beijing International Hotel (Beijing Guoji Fandian) 🏨 This 29-story modern monolith, owned by the China National Tourism Administration, is one of Beijing's largest hotel complexes and receives many Western and Asian tour groups. Situated on the north side of Beijing's main street, the hotel is near some modern shopping complexes, but it's still almost half a mile from a subway stop and more than a mile east of the Forbidden City. Its facilities are four-star, but its room rates are relatively low, with 67 of the smallest standard rooms listing for less than $80. The deluxe double rooms are larger and modern, and the bathrooms are clean. The staff is familiar with international travelers, and the shops offer some variety, including a small supermarket stocked with some Western brands. It's a bit cold in feeling, but for the price, it's a relatively good deal.

9 Jianguomennai Dajie (northeast corner of Chaoyangmen Nanxiao Jie), Beijing 100005. ℂ 010/6512-6688. Fax 010/6512-9961. 1,008 units. $110 double. AE, DC, MC, V. Metro: Jianguomen. **Amenities:** 16 restaurants (including Cantonese, Shanghai, vegetarian Chinese, Japanese, Korean, Swiss, International), lounge; heated indoor pool; outdoor lighted tennis court; health club; Jacuzzi; sauna; 10-lane bowling alley; business center; shopping arcade; salon; 24-hr. room service; in-room massage; same-day laundry/ dry cleaning; executive-level rooms. *In room:* A/C, TV, minibar, coffeemaker, hair dryer, safe.

Beijing Song He Hotel (Songhe Da Jiudian) 🏨 This three-star hotel, under local management, tries hard to please. From 1993 to 1995, under Novotel's international management, it was rated by the city as the best hotel in its class. Its rooms are as large or larger than those across the street at the five-star Crowne Plaza, but its amenities are simple and relatively few (no hair dryer, no coffeemaker, no CNN). Bathrooms are clean and modern and even include telephones. The deluxe rooms are more spacious and worth the extra $10 per night. The top floor is reserved for nonsmoking guests; the executive floor has extra amenities and services. Guests are mostly Asian from overseas, but there is always a Western presence. There are cheaper three-star hotels in Beijing, but given the fine location and adequate maintenance level of the Song He, it has to rank as one of the city's top three-star hotels.

88 Dengshikuo Jie (near Wangfujing Dajie, south of the Crowne Plaza Beijing), Beijing 100006. ✆ 010/6513-8822. Fax 010/6513-9088. 310 units. $90 double. AE, MC, V. Metro: Tiananmen Dong (East). **Amenities:** 3 restaurants (Thai, Cantonese, International), 2 disco/karaoke bars; exercise room; sauna; tour desk; small business center; salon; 24-hr. room service; in-room massage; same-day laundry/dry cleaning. *In room:* A/C, TV, minibar, safe.

Novotel Peace Hotel (Heping Binguan) 𝄞𝄞   A new name, new international management team, and a recently remodeled east wing, make this the best bargain in downtown Beijing. The hotel (formerly the Peace Hotel), although thoroughly modern, has a history. Built on the site of a Qing Dynasty garden in 1952, it was rebuilt as a four-star, 22-story joint government venture in 1984. Today, the hotel is bustling, with enough Western guests to give it an international feel. The staff speaks some English. The better rooms (those in the east wing) are of average size, with space for a writing desk, a coffee table, and two chairs. Bathrooms are modern and clean; most have a tub/shower combination. Rooms have thermoses. A wide range of facilities (post office, air ticket counter, disco) and its downtown location make this a good choice for the price (two to three times cheaper than the deluxe Palace Hotel across the street).

3 Jinyu Hutong (1 long block east of Wangfujing, opposite Palace Hotel), Beijing 100004. ✆ 800/221-4542 in U.S. and Canada; 300/65-65-65 in Australia; 0800/44-44-22 in New Zealand; 44/181-283-4500 in U.K.; or 010/6512-8833. Fax 010/6512-6863. www.accorhotels-china.com. 344 units. $80–$100 double (west wing); $100–$150 double (east wing). Children under 16 stay free in parents' room. AE, DC, MC, V. Metro: Dongdan. **Amenities:** 4 restaurants (Sichuan, Chaozhou, Korean, International), lounge; disco; indoor heated pool; exercise room; Jacuzzi; sauna; concierge; tour desk; small business center; salon; in-room massage; 24-hr. room service; same-day laundry/dry cleaning; executive-level rooms. *In room:* A/C, TV, dataport, minibar, safe.

2 Chaoyang (East)

VERY EXPENSIVE

China World Hotel (Zhongguo Da Fandian) 𝄞𝄞𝄞   Frequently ranked by international business magazines as one of the top 100 hotels in the world—and as the best in Beijing—China World adds attentive service to its deluxe facilities. Although there are over a dozen five-star hotels in the capital, this one is the most assured in handling international guests. The hotel is part of the China World Trade Center complex, which means it is directly attached (via escalators and elevators) to a large shopping center with restaurants, offices, and even an ice rink. The hotel's grand lobby has a comfortable lounge; the mezzanine serves as a contemporary art sales gallery; and the expanded business center is the best in Beijing. Rooms are quite spacious, with plenty of counter space, a writing desk, table and chairs, bright lighting, and robes and slippers. The marble bathrooms with tub/shower combos are also roomy and well appointed. Nearly half the rooms are nonsmoking. The health and fitness facilities are also the city's best. Its distance from the city center is overcome by the new subway line, which connects seamlessly to the hotel via the basement shopping plaza. This is an efficient, luxurious international hotel where CEOs and world leaders often stay.

1 Jianguomenwai Dajie (northwest corner of Third Ring Road), Beijing 100004. ℂ **800/942-5050** in U.S. and Canada, 1800/222-448 in Australia, 0800/442-179 in New Zealand, 4420/8747-8485 in London, or 010/6505-2266. Fax 010/6505-3167. www.shangri-la.com. 738 units (including 56 suites). $235 double; suites $330 and up. Children under 18 stay free in parents' room. AE, DC, MC, V. Metro: Guomao. **Amenities:** 5 restaurants (Cantonese, Japanese, Continental, International, American), deli, lobby lounge with Sun brunch; large heated indoor pool; 2 driving ranges; putting green; 2 golf-simulator machines; 3 indoor tennis courts; squash courts; extensive health club; Jacuzzi; sauna; game room; video arcade; bowling alley; concierge; tour desk; large 24-hr. business center; underground shopping mall; salon; 24-hr. room service; in-room massage; babysitting; same-day laundry/dry cleaning; executive-level rooms, florist. *In room:* A/C, TV, dataport, minibar, coffeemaker, hair dryer, safe.

Hotel New Otani Chang Fu Gong (Chang Fu Gong Fandian) ⍟   This
neatly maintained 24-story, five-star hotel caters to Japanese visitors (70% of guests), but also hosts a considerable number of Europeans and Americans. A particularly attractive aspect is the large, traditional Chinese garden in the rear, with its ponds, bridges, waterfall, and classical pavilion. The modern rooms are all equipped with humidifiers. (The air can be very dry in Beijing.) Although the hotel is built with Japanese guests in mind (the four tour desks all offer tours in Japanese), it is quite Westernized, and the staff is confident in English.

26 Jianguomenwai Dajie (1 block east of Second Ring Road overpass), Beijing 100022. ℂ **800/421-8795** or 010/6512-5555. Fax 010/6512-5346. 500 units. $220 double. AE, DC, MC, V. Metro: Jianguomen. **Amenities:** 4 restaurants (Japanese, Cantonese, Continental, Western), bar with karaoke; large heated indoor pool; outdoor lighted tennis court; health club; Jacuzzi; sauna; concierge; tour desks; business center; shopping arcade; salon; 24-hr. room service; in-room massage; same-day laundry/dry cleaning; executive-level rooms. *In room:* A/C, TV, dataport, minibar, coffeemaker, hair dryer, safe.

Jing Guang New World Hotel (Jingguang Xinshijie Fandian) ⍟   At 52
stories, this fan-shaped, blue glass tower was the tallest building in Beijing when it opened in 1990. It still stands out. Restaurants and other public facilities are on the first seven floors, five-star hotel rooms are on floors 8 to 23, offices occupy floors 25 to 38, and apartments are located on floors 40 to 52. Hotel guests benefit from a wide range of services and facilities within a single tower, including a Bank of China office and a basement pharmacy. Rooms are bright, clean, and modern, trimmed in a rich mahogany with considerable counter space. Coffeemakers and hair dryers are standard, but such amenities as in-room safes and robes are available only on the executive floors (22 and 23), priced $40 higher. Guests are Western and Asian; many expatriates living in the apartments use the hotel services. The efficient staff is conversant in English. For the price, the Kerry Centre, Traders, and China World hotels are nearer the subway and shopping, but this is a fine international hotel with plenty of facilities.

Jingguang Centre, Hu Jia Lou (10-min. walk north of Jianguomenwai Dajie on Third Ring Road at Chaoyang-menwai Dajie), Beijing 100020. ℂ **800/228-9898** in U.S. and Canada, 0800/181-737 in U.K., 1800/222-431 in Australia, 0800/441-111 in New Zealand, or 010/6597-8888. Fax 010/6597-3333. www.newworld-intl.com. 446 units. $200 double. Children under 12 stay free in parents' room. AE, DC, MC, V. No subway station. **Amenities:** 3 restaurants (International, Cantonese, Korean), basement food court, deli, lobby bar; heated indoor pool; large health club; Jacuzzi; sauna; game room; video arcade; concierge; tour desk; large business center; small shopping arcade; salon; 24-hr. room service; in-room massage; babysitting; same-day laundry/dry cleaning; executive-level rooms. *In room:* A/C, TV, dataport, minibar, coffeemaker, hair dryer.

Kerry Centre Hotel Beijing (Beijing Jiali Zhongxin Fandian) ⍟⍟⍟ *Kids*
One of Beijing's newest hotels (built in 1999) and the third sister in the Shangri-La hotel cluster on Jianguomenwai Dajie, the Kerry is a five-star hotel with a thoroughly modern, quite friendly feel. The hotel is in the 23-story western tower of the Beijing Kerry Centre, an office and apartment complex rising from

a massive four-story platform. It's that four-story base that serves the hotel as a roof garden, encircled by a track for jogging and in-line skating. The roof garden also contains a children's play area and splash pool. Nearly half the guests are Western, and many of them are on business. The rooms are large and bright, with a high-tech edge to the spacious desks and ergonomic desk chairs; Internet access is provided. About half the rooms are nonsmoking. Bathrooms have separate tubs and showers. The hotel is directly linked to a two-story shopping center and the Kerry Sports Centre (free use for guests), one of the city's best. Local calls, airport transfer, laundry, and breakfast are free. The Kerry Centre Hotel has a warmer atmosphere than the nearby China World and offers plenty for children as well as adults.

1 Guanghua Lu (2 blocks north of China World), Beijing 100004. © **800/942-5050** in U.S. and Canada, 1800/222-448 in Australia, 0800/442-179 in New Zealand, 4402/8747-8485 in London, or 010/6561-8833. Fax 010/6561-2626. www.shangri-la.com. 487 units (including 51 suites). $250 double; $270 deluxe. Children under 18 stay free in parents' room. AE, DC, MC, V. Metro: Guomao. **Amenities:** 2 restaurants (Cantonese, International), lobby lounge; heated indoor lap pool; children's pool; 2 indoor tennis courts; squash court; basketball court; extensive health club; Jacuzzi; sauna; children's playground; concierge; tour desk; business center; shopping center (attached); 24-hr. room service; in-room massage; same-day laundry/dry cleaning; executive-level rooms. *In room:* A/C, TV, dataport, minibar, coffeemaker, hair dryer, safe.

St. Regis Beijing (Guoji Julebu Fandian) ★★★ With the nicest and most expensive rooms in Beijing—and the most opulent formal lobby—Sheraton's 19-story "boutique hotel" deserves its St. Regis upgrade. This is the hotel favored by the richest travelers, most of them from America. Every room entitles its guest to the services of a butler, a sort of personal concierge who will do anything from unpacking to pressing. The St. Regis has doubled its number of butlers to 35; some are quite skilled, and all are eager to help. But the hotel's glorious rooms and public spaces are its best features. The Great Hall banquet room at the top of the white marble lobby staircase, which caters to VIP functions and diplomatic receptions, underlines the high-class image the hotel projects. The large, bright double rooms (called "executive deluxe" rooms) have a writing desk, two excellent desk chairs, a walk-in closet, robe and slippers, and a separate deep bathtub and shower in the marbled bathrooms. The hotel doesn't have a pool or health club yet, but both are due by 2002 with the completion of an attached service apartment tower. A spa is also in the works. The location is good, within walking distance of the Silk Market, cafes, and the subway.

21 Jianguomenwai Dajie (entrance 1 block north on Xiushui Jie), Beijing 100020. © **800/325-3589** in U.S. and Canada, 00800/3254-5454 in U.K. and Ireland, 1800/814-812 in Australia, 0800/44-5309 in New Zealand. Fax 010/6460-3299. www.stregis.com. 273 units. $300 double; $400 suite. AE, DC, MC, V. Metro: Jianguomen. **Amenities:** 4 restaurants (Italian, Cantonese, Japanese, International), afternoon high tea, bar; small exercise room; concierge; 24-hr. business center; 24-hr. room service; same-day laundry/dry cleaning; 24-hr. personal butler service. *In room:* A/C, TV, fax (on request), dataport, minibar, coffeemaker, hair dryer.

Swissotel (Beijing Gang Ao Zhongxin) ★★ Expertly managed by the Swissair Swissotel Management Group, this immaculate 16-story five-star hotel has some of the best facilities in Beijing. The fourth floor, for example, has the best barrier-free architecture in the capital for travelers with disabilities. The respected International Medical Clinic is on premises, as are an airline ticketing office and courier service. The deluxe rooms are brightly decorated with bleached oak trim and are equipped with ample counter space and large desks. For a European atmosphere in the capital of China, this is the place to stay; the levels of service and upkeep are quite high. The subway station is quite close.

Dongsishi Tiao Li Jiao Qiao, Hong Kong Macau Centre (east side of the Second Ring Road overpass at Gongrentiyuchang Bei Lu), Beijing 100027. ⓒ 800/637-9477 in U.S. and Canada, 1800/062-155 in Australia, 0800/614-145 in U.K., or 010/6501-2288. Fax 010/6501-2501. www.swissotel.com. 421 units. $260 double. AE, DC, MC, V. Metro: Dongsishitiao. **Amenities:** 3 restaurants (Swiss, Shanghai, Cantonese), lobby brunch (Sun), Mongolian barbecues (in summer), bar; large indoor heated pool; outdoor lighted tennis court; health club; Jacuzzi; sauna; concierge; tour desk; 24-hr. business center; salon; 24-hr. room service; in-room massage; same-day laundry/dry cleaning; executive-level rooms. *In room:* A/C, TV, dataport, minibar, coffeemaker, hair dryer, safe.

EXPENSIVE

Jianguo Hotel (Jianguo Fandian) ★★   For 2 decades the Jianguo—the first joint venture hotel in China (opened in 1982)—was the expatriate community's favorite meeting place in Beijing, and the hotel still maintains a lively lobby under its golden chandelier. The four-story East Wing is linked to the nine-story West Wing at ground level by a floor of restaurants and services. Some rooms have views of a water garden and courtyard area, while the rooms facing south onto Jianguomenwai have outdoor balconies (unusual in Beijing—and nice in the summer). There is one executive floor in the East Wing. Rooms are of average size (though some appear a bit worn), with writing desks and clean bathrooms. The hotel has fine restaurants and bars, as well as an airport shuttle bus ($5 one-way); the facilities are a step above rooms and service.

5 Jianguomenwai Dajie (1 block east of Silk Alley), Beijing 100020. ⓒ 800/223-5652 in U.S. and Canada, 0800/898-852 in U.K., 1800/553-549 in Australia, or 010/6500-2233. Fax 010/6500-2871. www.hoteljianguo. com. 460 units, some with kitchenette. $190 double (including breakfast). AE, MC, V. Metro: Yonganli. **Amenities:** 2 restaurants (French, Cantonese), American bar, lobby brunch (Sun), karaoke; heated indoor pool; exercise room; Jacuzzi; sauna; bike rental; tour desk; 24-hr. business center; salon; 24-hr. room service; same-day laundry/dry cleaning; executive-level rooms. *In room:* A/C, TV, minibar, coffeemaker, hair dryer, safe.

Jinglun Hotel (Jinglun Fandian) ★★   The former Beijing-Toronto Hotel (*Jinglun* means Toronto) has maintained its high levels of service and upkeep under new management. This is a four-star hotel with many five-star facilities, a favorite of Western, Japanese, and Chinese guests, who stay here in equal numbers. Silk Alley and the Friendship Store are a few minutes' walk away. Rooms are modern, clean, and fairly spacious, with adequate counter space and thermoses (no coffeemakers); the compact bathrooms are well equipped. Deluxe rooms on floors 9 and 10 are larger and well worth the extra charge ($10). The restaurants are excellent here, and the service has received some high marks from foreign guests. The hotel runs an inexpensive airport shuttle bus (30RMB, $3.75).

3 Jianguomenwai Dajie, Beijing 100020. ⓒ 800/645-5687 in U.S., Canada, 0800/282-502 in U.K., or 010/6500-2266. Fax 010/6500-2022. www.jinglunhotel.com. 558 units (including 22 suites). $180 double; $190 deluxe. AE, DC, MC, V. Metro: Yonganli. **Amenities:** 5 restaurants (Beijing, Cantonese, Japanese, Western, French), bar; indoor heated pool; exercise room; Jacuzzi; sauna; bike rental; tour desk; business center; salon; 24-hr. room service; same-day laundry/dry cleaning; executive-level rooms. *In room:* A/C, TV, minibar, hair dryer.

Traders Hotel Beijing (Guomao Fandian) ★★★   This is one of the best four-star hotels in China, highly rated by foreign business travelers for its large rooms and efficient service. Plus, when you stay at Traders you have full guest privileges at its adjoining sister property—linked by a new underground shopping center—the five-star China World, including use of its superb fitness and health facilities. This hotel is in high demand most of the year. It opened with a west wing in 1990, added an east wing in 1996, and remodeled the west wing in 1999. Rooms in the west wing are the best, but all rooms are spacious, with writing desks, ample counter space, coffee table and chairs, firm beds, robe and slippers, and a handy desk drawer of office supplies (stapler, scissors, paper clips, ruler). The marble bathrooms have phones and packets of detergent. It is a luxurious yet practical hotel. The business center has one of the better-stocked English-language bookstores in Beijing. Most rooms and floors are nonsmoking; a room renovation program should be completed by 2002.

1 Jianguomenwai Dajie (1 block north of China World), Beijing 100004. C 800/942-5050 in U.S. and Canada, 1800/222-448 in Australia, 0800/442-179 in New Zealand, 4402/8747-8485 in London, or 010/6505-2277. Fax 010/6505-0818. www.shangri-la.com. 552 units (including 26 suites). $190–$210 double. Children under 18 stay free in parents' room. AE, DC, MC, V. Metro: Guomao. **Amenities:** 2 restaurants (Cantonese, International/Southeast Asian), lounge; access to nearby pool and health club; exercise room; Jacuzzi; sauna; concierge; tour desk; business center (with bookstore); attached shopping center; 24-hr. room service; babysitting; same-day laundry/dry cleaning; executive-level rooms. *In room:* A/C, TV, dataport, minibar, coffeemaker, hair dryer, iron, safe.

MODERATE

Gloria Plaza Hotel (Kailai Da Jiudian) ℱ   Renovated from top to bottom in 1997, this 18-story, four-star hotel has a good location and plenty of experience with international guests. The large lobby, decorated in red marble, is ostentatious, as are the facilities, which are capped by the biggest, brightest sports bar in Beijing. Rooms are sterling clean, of average size, with adequate counter space; bathrooms are well maintained with phones but no hair dryers. Services and facilities are better than at the nearby Scitech Hotel, and the views of downtown Beijing are superb from west- and north-facing rooms.

2 Jianguomenwai Nan Dajie (1 long block south of Jianguomenwai, east of Second Ring Road overpass, opposite Ancient Observatory), Beijing 100022. C 010/6515-8855. Fax 010/6515-8533. www.gphbeijing.com. 423 units. $155 double. AE, DC, MC, V. Metro: Jianguomen. **Amenities:** 4 restaurants (Cantonese, Vietnamese, Korean, International), massive sports bar; large heated indoor pool (with views of downtown); health club; Jacuzzi; sauna; bike rental; tour desk; 24-hr. business center; salon; 24-hr. room service; same-day laundry/dry cleaning; executive-level rooms. *In room:* A/C, TV, dataport, minibar, coffeemaker, hair dryer, safe.

Scitech Hotel (Saite Fandian)   Situated behind the Scitech Plaza shopping center and office complex, this 15-floor four-star hotel is good if other hotels in the area are full. It caters to Asians but also hosts Western guests, particularly business travelers. The rooms, last renovated in 1996, are bright and modern, with thermoses and in-house movies. Hotel guests get free use of the excellent health and fitness club in the attached Scitech Building. Although closer to the city center and slightly cheaper, this hotel lags well behind the international hotels farther along Jianguomenwai Dajie (such as the Jinglun and Jianguo) in amenities and service.

22 Jianguomenwai Dajie (1 block south of Jianguomenwai Dajie), Beijing 100004. C 010/6512-3388. Fax 010/6512-3537. sthotel1@sun.sw.co.cn. 324 units. $160 doubles. AE, MC, V. Metro: Jianguomen. **Amenities:** 3 restaurants (Cantonese, Korean, International), lobby bar; large indoor heated pool; indoor tennis court; attached health club; Jacuzzi; sauna; bike rental (at Scitech Plaza); table tennis; 5-lane bowling alley; 3 tour desks; business center; attached shopping center; salon; 24-hr. room service; same-day laundry/dry cleaning. *In room:* A/C, TV, minibar, hair dryer.

3 Chaoyang (Northeast)

VERY EXPENSIVE

Beijing Hilton Hotel (Xierdun Fandian) ℱℱℱ   This hotel is justifiably noted for its international atmosphere, efficient services, and fine restaurants. It's a favorite of many Western business travelers, perhaps because it is both a "familiar name" and a well-run establishment. The rooms are generally spacious but sparsely furnished. A complete room renovation started in 2001, with floors 18 to 25 scheduled for remodeling; the new design will jazz up the rooms, the best of which have views of the Third Ring Road. All rooms have writing desks, robes and slippers, and umbrellas; all bathrooms are equipped with separate showers and tubs. The health club is a private membership club, but its facilities are open to hotel guests for a small daily fee. A jazz theme is woven through the hotel's fine restaurants—try their European-style breads—and bars. A free downtown shuttle runs once a day.

1 Dongfang Lu, Dongsanhuan Bei Lu (west side of Third Ring Road North, north of Xinyuan Nan Lu), Beijing 100027. ⓒ **800/445-8667** in U.S. and Canada, 800/222-555 in Australia, or 010/6466-2288 in Beijing. Fax 010/6465-3052. www.hilton.com. 340 units. $235–$260 double. AE, DC, MC, V. No subway station. **Amenities:** 4 restaurants (Cajun/American, Cantonese, Japanese, International), deli, lobby jazz bar; large indoor heated pool; lighted outdoor tennis court; 2 indoor squash courts; health club (with a fee); exercise room; Jacuzzi; sauna; bike rental; concierge; tour desk; business center; salon; 24-hr. room service; in-room massage; babysitting; same-day laundry/dry cleaning; executive-level rooms. *In room:* A/C, TV, dataport, minibar, coffeemaker, hair dryer, safe.

Great Wall Sheraton (Changcheng Fandian) ★★
The Great Wall was the first five-star hotel to open (in 1984) on the Third Ring Road North, and it has set a high standard for the nearby hotels to match. This is a massive hotel, popular among American travelers, with plenty of services and facilities. The huge lobby has been remodeled, as have many of the rooms—but not the smaller standard rooms that tour groups use, so be sure to ask for a "deluxe" room. Remodeled rooms are spacious, gold-trimmed, with duvets on the beds and tile in the compact bathrooms. Public areas are elegant, with lighted exterior elevators and a large garden and fountains in the rear courtyard.

10 Dongsanhuan Bei Lu (east side of Third Ring Road North, south of Liangma River), Beijing 100026. ⓒ **800/325-3535** in U.S. and Canada, 1800/07 3535 in Australia, 0800/44-3535 in New Zealand, 1800/53-53-53 in Ireland, 0800/3253-5353 in U.K., or 010/6590-5566. Fax 010/6590-5222. 1,007 units. $250–$300 double. No subway station. **Amenities:** 4 restaurants (French, Italian, Sichuan, International), lobby brunch (Sun), 2 bars; disco; indoor heated pool; 2 outdoor lighted tennis courts; exercise room; Jacuzzi; sauna; bike rental; concierge; tour desk; business center; shopping arcade; salon; 24-hr. room service; same-day laundry/dry cleaning; executive-level rooms. *In room:* A/C, TV, dataport, minibar, coffeemaker, hair dryer, safe.

Kempinski Hotel (Kaibinsiji Fandian) ★★★
A favorite of Germans and other Europeans, this 18-story hotel, built in 1992, has extremely high levels of service and maintenance, meriting its five-star rating. The hotel is attached to the You Yi shopping center, which has modern shops, restaurants, and a department store. The red-marbled public spaces have an efficient, high-tech atmosphere. Rooms are of above-average size with sufficient counter space; the bathrooms sparkle. The Kempinski complex has a considerable range of facilities, from airline offices to numerous restaurants; it is one of the few hotels in Beijing with frequent shuttle bus service to both the airport and downtown locations.

50 Liangmaqiao Lu, Lufthansa Centre (1 block southwest of the Third Ring Road North), Beijing 100016. ⓒ **800/426-3135** or 010/6465-3388. Fax 010/6465-3366. www.kempinski-bj.com. 529 units. $270 double. Children 12 and under stay free in parents' room. AE, DC, MC, V. No subway station. **Amenities:** 10 restaurants (including German, French, Cajun, Italian, Sichuan, Cantonese), large deli, 3 bars; large indoor heated pool; 2 outdoor lighted tennis courts; indoor squash court; 2 health clubs; Jacuzzi; sauna; concierge; tour desk; 24-hr. business center; shopping arcade (attached shopping center); salon; 24-hr. room service; in-room massage; babysitting; same-day laundry/dry cleaning; executive-level rooms. *In room:* A/C, TV, dataport, minibar, coffeemaker, hair dryer, safe.

Kunlun Hotel (Kunlun Fandian) ★
This massive five-star, 28-story, Chinese-owned and -managed glass-and-steel tower has nearly every conceivable

perk and facility under the sun, but the old joke still has some truth: It's a Chinese copy of the Great Wall Sheraton across the road. Although it's a good copy, the atmosphere is cold rather than warm, and the service level, while good, is not great. The Kunlun is popular with some Western travelers, and its facilities are modern and Western: CNN and in-house movies; a large, well-stocked bookstore; a golf equipment store; karaoke and disco; even a post office and a tea ware shop. It's also within walking distance of the Sanlitun nightlife area. Despite its amenities, the nearby five-star competitors (Hilton, Sheraton, Kempinski) are favored by Western travelers, largely for their service and familiarity with foreign guests.

2 Xinyuan Nan Lu (1 block west of the Third Ring Road North), Beijing 100004. © **800/810-0018** or 010/6590-3388. Fax 010/6590-3228. www.hotelkunlun.com. 900 units. $270 double. Children 12 and under stay free in parents' room. AE, DC, MC, V. No subway station. **Amenities:** 10 restaurants (includes Shanghai, Cantonese, Japanese, Vietnamese, Continental, International), lounge, 2 bars, disco; indoor heated pool; outdoor lighted tennis court; health club; Jacuzzi; sauna; concierge; tour desk; business center; shopping arcade; salon; 24-hr. room service; in-room massage; babysitting; same-day laundry/dry cleaning; executive-level rooms. *In room:* A/C, TV, dataport, minibar, coffeemaker, hair dryer, safe.

EXPENSIVE

Radisson SAS Hotel (Huangjia Da Jiudian) ★★   This 15-story international hotel is the best (and most expensive) four-star hotel in northeast Beijing. Its stylish rooms are undergoing remodeling. Presently, the three decor choices are Oriental (red carpets, carved wood trim, floors 3–6), high-tech (glass and chrome detailing, floors 7–9), and Art Deco (1920s touches, pastels, floors 10–12). All rooms are large with clean, compact bathrooms (tub/shower combos). The hotel is spotless throughout, and it maintains a modern European atmosphere, highly efficient service, and facilities that are worthy of a five-star rating. An SAS shuttle bus links the hotel and airport (80RMB, $10 each way).

6A Beisanhuan Dong Lu (south side of the Third Ring Road East, 1 block from Airport Expressway overpass), Beijing 100028. © **800/333-3333** in U.S. and Canada, 1800/333-333 in Australia, 0800/44-3333 in New Zealand, 1800/55-7474 in Ireland, 0800/374411 in U.K., or 010/6466-3388. Fax 010/6465-3186. www. radisson.com. 362 units. $225 double. Children 12 and under stay free in parents' room. AE, DC, MC, V. No subway station. **Amenities:** 3 restaurants (Scandinavian, Sichuan/Cantonese, Continental grill), rooftop barbecue (in summer), lounge; large indoor heated pool; outdoor tennis court; 2 indoor squash courts; health club; Jacuzzi; sauna; concierge; tour desk; business center; salon; 24-hr. room service; babysitting; same-day laundry/dry cleaning; executive-level rooms. *In room:* A/C, TV, minibar, coffeemaker, hair dryer, safe.

MODERATE

Beijing Continental Grand Hotel (Wuzhou Da Jiudian)   This immense double-winged complex, 5 miles north of the city center, was opened in 1989, and had China won the bid for the 2000 Summer Olympics, it would have boomed because it is attached to the International Olympic Sports Centre. These days, it is rather distant and forlorn. It has four-star rooms and facilities, but its staff is not terribly experienced with Western guests. Nevertheless, if you're willing to take long taxi rides into the city, this hotel delivers good value for the money. The rooms are clean, modern, and spacious. Given the service level, however, it may be worth waiting until the 2008 Olympics before checking in here.

8 Beichen Dong Lu (Third Ring Road North, Asian Games Village), Beijing 100101. © **010/6491-5588.** Fax 010/6491-0106. www.chinatour.com/bcgh. 1,259 units. $120 double. AE, MC, V. No nearby subway station. **Amenities:** 12 restaurants (including Cantonese, Japanese, Western); heated indoor pool; health club; Jacuzzi, sauna; tour desk; air ticket office; business center; shopping arcade; salon; 24-hr. room service; in-room massage; same-day laundry/dry cleaning. *In room:* A/C, TV, minibar, hair dryer.

China Travel Service Tower (Zhonglu Dasha)   China Travel Service (CTS) opened its own hotel tower in 1995, with four-star facilities and an adequate service level. It has stiff competitors nearby, including the Radisson SAS Hotel (quite superior, but more expensive) and the Landmark (same quality, fewer services, but cheaper). Perhaps the main drawback is the tower's location on a difficult-to-reach island where freeways converge. Still, the staff is attentive, and the rooms are clean and modern. The CTS Travel Desk has excellent tours, but it is somewhat geared to Chinese-speaking clients If you book this hotel through CTS, you can get a good room rate, especially in winter.

2 Beisanhuan Dong Lu (intersection of Third Ring Road East, airport freeway), Beijing 100028. ✆ 010/6462-2288. Fax 010/6461-2502. ctstsale@public3.bta.net.cn. 185 units. $150 doubles. AE, MC, V. No subway station. **Amenities:** 5 restaurants (Western, Chaozhou, Cantonese, Huaiyang, Sichuan), jazz bar; heated indoor pool; 2 outdoor tennis courts; exercise room; Jacuzzi; sauna; game room; tour desk; business center; 24-hr. room service; same-day laundry/dry cleaning. *In room:* A/C, TV, minibar, hair dryer.

Landmark Hotel (Liangmahe Dasha) 🏆 *Kids*   Lost among the other hotel towers on the Third Ring Road North, this 15-story tower offers four-star facilities at a good price. Rooms are modern, bright, and of average size. There's a Chinese garden in the back and a children's playground off the mezzanine, as well as plenty of shops, two tour desks, a post office, and a branch of the Bank of China. There's even an entrance inside the hotel to the Hard Rock Cafe. If you want to stay in comfort in the vicinity of the Hilton, Kempinski, Kunlun, and Sheraton at a lower price, this is the spot. There's no airport shuttle, but the hotel runs a free bus to downtown sites.

8 Dongsanhuan Bei Lu (Third Ring Road North, across from Great Wall Sheraton), Beijing 100004. ✆ 010/6590-6688. Fax 010/6590-6513. www.chinatour.com/lmt/intro.htm. 450 units. $125 double. AE, MC, V. No subway station. **Amenities:** 5 restaurants (International, Korean, Shanghai, Cantonese, Sichuan), tea lounge, pub; indoor heated pool; 2 outdoor lighted tennis courts; exercise room; Jacuzzi; sauna; children's playground; concierge; 2 tour desks; business center; 24-hr. room service; babysitting; same-day laundry/dry cleaning; Bank of China; post office. *In room:* A/C, TV, minibar, coffeemaker, hair dryer, safe.

4 Xuanwu (Southwest) & Chongwen (Southeast)

EXPENSIVE

New World Courtyard Beijing (Beijing Xinshi Jie Wan Yi Jiudian) 🏆 *Kids*
Opened in 1998, this hotel is a "Courtyard by Marriott," although the Marriott connection seems to be downplayed. The 15-story hotel tower is connected to a larger complex, the Beijing New World Centre, which includes office high-rises, apartments, a large shopping plaza, and the New World department store. The hotel's rooms are bright and spacious; all come with a sofa and writing desk. The 10th floor is for nonsmoking guests. There is an extensive children's play area with playground, video games, and a rooftop park. The four-star facilities, combined with Marriott management and a convenient location, make this hotel a good value. Tiananmen Square and the Temple of Heaven are both within walking distance (about a mile), and the subway is within a block. The hotel also provides a downtown shuttle and a twice-daily free airport bus.

3C Chongwenmenwai Dajie, Chongwen District (1 block south of Qianmen Dong Dajie, 1 mile east of Tiananmen Square), Beijing 100062. ✆ 800/228-9290 in U.S. and Canada, 0800/441-035 in New Zealand, 1800/251-259 in Australia, 0800/221-222 in U.K., or 010/6708-1188. Fax 010/6708-1808. www.marriott.com or www.courtyard.com/BJSCY. 293 units. $180 double. Children under 17 stay free in parents' room. AE, DC, MC, V. Metro: Chongwenmen. **Amenities:** 2 restaurants (Western/Southeast Asian, Cantonese), lobby high tea, English pub; heated indoor pool; health club; Jacuzzi; sauna; children's playground; video arcade; concierge; tour desk; business center; shopping center and department store (via skybridge); tea shop; 24-hr. room service; babysitting; same-day laundry/dry cleaning. *In room:* A/C, TV, dataport, minibar, coffeemaker, hair dryer, safe.

MODERATE

Grand View Garden Hotel (Daguan Yuan Jiudian) ⭐ Many m...
the city center and even farther from most other attractions, the Gran...
Garden Hotel does have its charms. The architecture is stunning: This is a 1...
story hotel that really looks Chinese, its soaring tiled roofs and garden pavili...
layout fully in keeping with the famous Grand View classical garden nearby. On...
the inside, it's a quiet (if distant) retreat, kept fresh and up-to-date. The average-
sized rooms are bright (rich wooden trim and a white, gold, and red color
scheme), with a writing desk and comfortable chairs. The hotel has three internal courtyard gardens. The service, like the facilities, merits the hotel's four-star
rating. More than half the guests are tour group members, many of them from
Europe and the U.S. A taxi ride downtown takes about 30 minutes, and the
hotel provides a free shuttle bus to city center locations (but not to the airport).

88 Nancaiyuan Jie, Xuanwu District (Second Ring Road, west of Grand View Garden), Beijing 100054.
🕐 010/6353-8899. Fax 010/6353-9189. www.gvghotel.com. 384 units. $140 double. AE, DC, MC, V. No sub-
way station. **Amenities:** 3 restaurants (Western, Cantonese, hot pot), 2 lounges, karaoke/disco; heated indoor
pool; exercise room; Jacuzzi; sauna; billiards; video arcade; 8-lane bowling alley; tour desk; business center;
24-hr. room service; babysitting; same-day laundry/dry cleaning. *In room:* A/C, TV, minibar, coffeemaker, hair
dryer, safe.

5 Xicheng (West) & Haidian (Northwest)

VERY EXPENSIVE

Beijing New Century Hotel (Xin Shiji Fandian) ⭐⭐ This 32-story white
tower, well managed by ANA, a Japanese hotel group, welcomes many Japanese
guests (40%), but receives Europeans and Americans as well. The glittering
lobby reflects its five-star status, with a waterfall encircled by two mezzanines
with gold railings. Rooms have a window nook with good views of the zoo to
the northeast, the Western Hills to the northwest, and downtown Beijing to the
southeast. The New Century has three levels of rooms. Standard rooms (Floor
24 and below) are of average size, clean, modern, and bright and are in line for
renovations. Business level rooms (floors 25–28), the most recently remodeled,
are larger and better equipped. Executive-level rooms (floors 29–31) are also
newly remodeled, spacious, and variously shaped (they're not all rectangular);
fax machines and separate tubs and showers are standard features at this altitude.
The hotel has excellent restaurants and exercise facilities, and it is within an easy
walk (or bike ride) from the zoo, aquarium, and other northwest Beijing
attractions.

6 Shoudu Tiyuguan Nan Lu (4 blocks west of Beijing Zoo), Beijing 100044. 🕐 **800/ANA-HOTEL** in U.S.,
Canada; 212/332-1500 in New York City; or 010/6849-2001. Fax 010/6849-1103. www.newcenturyhotel.
com.cn. 720 units. $170–$250 double. AE, DC, MC, V. Metro: Xizhimen (25 min. east). **Amenities:** 4 restaurants (Sichuan/Hunan, Cantonese/Shanghai, Japanese, Continental), bar, lounge; large indoor heated pool;
2 outdoor lighted tennis courts; health club; table tennis; Jacuzzi; sauna; bike rental; 12-lane bowling alley;
concierge; tour desk; business center; salon; 24-hr. room service; in-room massage; babysitting; same-day
laundry/dry cleaning; business-level and executive-level rooms. *In room:* A/C, TV, dataport, minibar, hair dryer,
safe.

Shangri-La Beijing Hotel (Xiangge Lila Fandian) ⭐⭐⭐ The number-
one luxury hotel in northwest Beijing, this 24-story hotel has been noted for its
high service levels and elegance since it opened in 1986, receiving *Condé Nast
Traveler's* award for "Best Hotel in China" three times and a nod from the Beijing Tourism Association in 2000 for the best doormen, front office, restaurant,
and maintenance in the capital. The Shangri-La often hosts world dignitaries

including President Clinton in 1998) at its press center and provides catering for major events in the city. The superb traditional garden, with its arched bridges, pavilions, bunnies, and ducks, is a serene focal point for the lobby lounge and its two-story wall of glass. Rooms are equally elegant and among the largest in Beijing, with views of the Western Hills, plenty of counter space, writing desks, large closets, and marble bathrooms with phones. There are two guest rooms for travelers with disabilities. Fitness facilities are housed in the basement and in a separate complex behind the courtyard garden. The service is worthy of the five-star rating. There's a free shuttle service to downtown locations, and the Zhongguancun technology zone (Beijing's silicon valley) is nearby.

29 Zizhuyuan Lu (northwest corner of Third Ring Road), Beijing 100089. © 800/942-5050 in U.S. and Canada, 1800/222-448 in Australia, 0800/442-179 in New Zealand, 4402/8747-8485 in London, or 010/6841-2211. Fax 010/6841-8002. www.shangri-la.com. 640 units. $250 double. Children under 18 stay free in parents' room. AE, DC, MC, V. No subway station. **Amenities:** 4 restaurants (Cantonese, Italian, Japanese Robatayaki, International), deli, lounge, bar, large heated indoor pool; recreation center (2 indoor tennis courts, squash court, etc.); health club (basement); Jacuzzi; sauna; concierge; tour desk; large 24-hr. business center; salon; 24-hr. room service; in-room massage; babysitting; same-day laundry/dry; executive-level rooms. *In room:* A/C, TV, dataport, minibar, coffeemaker, hair dryer, safe.

EXPENSIVE

Friendship Hotel (Youyi Binguan) 🛪
One of the largest garden-style hotels in Asia, the Friendship complex is immense, with over 1,900 rooms, counting its apartments and offices. Since 1954, it has been the choice of many foreign delegations, experts, and academics. (Beijing University and other major universities are nearby to the north.) Over the years, it has upgraded its rooms and facilities to a four-star level. For the ordinary visitor, however, its location, near the Summer Palace but quite distant from city center, is a drawback. The various buildings are a bit bewildering, interlinked by walkways and large garden areas. The main lobby area, with red columns and gold filigree, is surprisingly compact. Rooms are somewhat compact as well, but clean and modern, with electric hot pots and safes. The higher-priced rooms ($210) in Building 1 are larger, with more amenities. This hotel has 26 restaurants, bars, and dining halls, and a wide range of facilities, from the driving range and bowling alley to the hotel's own branch of the Friendship Store. Many of the restaurants are quite elegant. This is a self-contained home-away-from-home for many foreign visitors who have taken up short-term residency in Beijing for teaching or high-tech, business-related assignments; ordinary visitors may use this as a base for exploring the capital as well, but for the money, the New Century Hotel is in the same district, nearer to the city and other attractions, and not such a huge labyrinth.

3 Baishiqiao Lu, Haidian District (intersection of Haidian Lu and Third Ring Road northwest), Beijing 100873. © 010/6849-8888. Fax 010/6849-8866. 800 units. $160–$210 double. AE, DC, MC, V. No subway station. **Amenities:** 26 restaurants (mostly Chinese and Western), coffee shop, ice cream stand, deli, bar; 2 heated indoor pools; golf driving range; 2 outdoor tennis courts; health club; Jacuzzi; sauna; bowling alley; concierge; tour desk; business center; shopping arcade; salon; 24-hr. room service; babysitting; same-day laundry/dry cleaning.

Radisson Plaza State Guest House (Guobin Jiudian) 🛪
Just opened in 2001, this Radisson is not a government-run guesthouse, as its foreboding name suggests, but rather Beijing's newest contender for a five-star international luxury hotel ranking. The lobby is a stunner; with three stories of marble draped in glass chandeliers, potted palms, a baby grand piano, plush sofas, and white columns ringed in gold trim, it rivals the St. Regis for over-the-top European elegance. The gold trim continues in the rooms, which are bright, light-filled,

and crammed with all the amenities. It's too soon to judge this hotel on its performance—the staff is just learning the ropes—but the facilities are certainly first rate. The entrance is a little out of the way, down an alley north of the big main street; just look for the fully bearded bellman in a great coat out front.

9 Fuchengmenwai Dajie (2 blocks west of Second Ring Road), Beijing 100037. ℭ **800/333-3333** in U.S. and Canada, 1800/333-333 in Australia, 0800/44-3333 in New Zealand, 1800/55-7474 in Ireland, 0800/374411 in U.K., or 010/6800-5588. Fax 010/6800-5888. www.radisson.com. 500 units. $220 double. AE, DC, MC, V. Metro: Fuchengmen. **Amenities:** 3 restaurants (Cantonese, International, American), 2 lounges; heated indoor pool; health club; Jacuzzi; sauna; concierge; tour desk; business center; salon; 24-hr. room service; babysitting; same-day laundry/dry cleaning; executive-level rooms. *In room:* A/C, TV, dataport, minibar, coffeemaker, hair dryer, safe.

MODERATE

Holiday Inn Downtown (Jindu Jiari Fandian) ★★ Though a good distance from downtown (Tiananmen Square is many miles to the southeast), this Holiday Inn is favored by many foreign businessmen (25% Westerners) for its efficient service and reasonable price, and is located within steps of the subway and the Vantone New World shopping plaza. It is an easy walk to Baita Temple and Temple of the Moon Park. Rooms are large, clean, and well equipped with satellite TV (CNN, CNBC, in-house movies) and king-sized beds. The bathrooms are small but spotless. This is an American-style hotel with good services and restaurants; nothing fancy, but not much lacking, either.

98 Beilishi Lu, Xicheng District (1 block north of Fuchengmenwai Dajie, west of Second Ring Road West), Beijing 100006. ℭ **800/465-4329** in U.S. and Canada, 1800/221-066 in Australia, 0800/442-222 in New Zealand, 1800/553-155 in Ireland, 0800/897-121 in U.K., or 010/6833-8822. Fax 010/6834-0696.

⸤Kids⸥ Family-Friendly Hotels

Beijing's hotels have plenty of amusements and amenities for adults, but what can they offer kids? These hotels have special facilities designed for the young traveler:

Sino-Swiss Hotel *(see p. 79)* runs organized children's programs all summer, using its excellent outdoor facilities, which include a playground, tennis courts, and a volleyball court with beach sand. There's also an indoor/outdoor swimming pool and a thermal hot springs pool, with horseback riding stables nearby.

Holiday Inn Lido *(see p. 77)* has plenty of foreign resident kids hanging about and a wider range of activities to keep children amused than any other hotel in Beijing, including an ice cream parlor, a 20-lane bowling alley, video games, a big swimming pool, and a large public park at its doorstep.

Kerry Centre Hotel *(see p. 66)* has a big new 25-meter pool, two indoor tennis courts, and a special splash pool, a play area for kids, and an outdoor track for in-line skating on its fourth-floor roof garden.

New World Courtyard by Marriott *(see p. 72)*, with a large swimming pool and rooftop garden area, has a special playground just for children and an amusement hall that houses an extensive collection of high-tech games for kids.

Backpackers' Specials

Beijing offers few cheap choices for lodging. Hotels rated at two-stars and below that are allowed to accept foreigners—many of Beijing's cheapest spots legally cannot accept them—are no-frills affairs situated in neighborhoods far from the city center. The best of them offer modern, if well-worn rooms, with private bathrooms. Don't expect too many amenities (or elevators, for that matter). Some bathrooms will have shower heads on the wall but no stalls or tubs—and little hot water. (Don't expect the plumbing to function perfectly, either.) The cleaning staff may try to get into your room at dawn. If you are willing to deal with a staff that speaks little or no English and are in search of a place only to sleep, the following shoestring operations may fit the bill (barely).

The two most popular backpackers' inns in Beijing are the Jinghua Hotel and the Qiaoyuan Hotel. The **Jinghua Hotel (Jinghua Fandian)** is located on Yongwai Xiluoyuan Nanli in the Fengtai District, about 1 mile west of the intersection of the Third Ring Road South and Yongdingmenwai Dajie, 6 miles due south of Tiananmen Square (*(℃* **010/6722-2211;** fax 010/6721-1455; 168 units; $25 double; no credit cards). The Jinghua hotel has some double rooms with private baths in addition to dormitories. The rooms are fairly clean but small, rundown, and quite spartan. The staff speaks some English; there's a tour office and bike rental; and a few nearby cafes cater to foreigners.

The **Qiaoyuan Hotel (Qiaoyuan Fandian)** is located at 135 Dong Binhe Lu in the Xuanwu District, on the south side of the Third Ring Road South (Youanmen Dong Binhe Lu), 1 mile west of the Yongdimen Bus Terminal (*(℃* **010/6303-8861;** fax 010/6318-4709; 440 units; $40 double; AE, DC, MC, V). Formerly a bleak but popular backpackers' mecca, the Qiaoyuan has been remodeled to achieve a two-star rating. It is 5 miles south of the city center, but within walking distance of Grand View Garden. The double rooms are modern, but don't expect any luxuries. The staff speaks little English.

www.holiday-inn.com. 346 units. $140 double. Children under 19 stay free in parents' room. AE, DC, MC, V. Metro: Fuchengmen. **Amenities:** 3 restaurants (Cantonese, Indian, International), deli, bar, karaoke; small indoor heated pool; health club; Jacuzzi; sauna; tour desk; air ticket office; business center; salon; 24-hr. room service; in-room massage; babysitting; same-day laundry/dry cleaning; executive-level rooms. *In room:* A/C, TV, minibar, coffeemaker; hair dryer; safe.

Xiyuan Hotel (Xiyuan Fandian)   This 23-story tower epitomized the inefficiency of a large, locally managed hotel in China during the 1980s, but with the dawn of the new century, the Xiyuan has taken on a new image. Extensive remodeling and upgrading of staff services (with the arrival of fresh international management) have put the Xiyuan firmly in the four-star category (although recent staff changes have slowed improvements down). Rooms are spacious, with sufficient counter space, adequate writing desks, and electric hot pots (no coffeemakers). Bathrooms are clean and equipped with phones and hair dryers. There are several rooms for travelers with disabilities, two new executive floors, and one floor dedicated to Islamic guests (no liquor permitted; directions to Mecca posted). In the past, most of the guests have been Chinese and Asian, but the hotel has been actively seeking Western visitors; its staff is knowledgeable about the requirements of foreigners. With a large shopping arcade, a vast three-story lobby, and 11 restaurants and bars, the Xiyuan is a full-service hotel, although guests must depend on taxis (or a mile-long walk to the subway) to get downtown. Not the equal of the nearby New Century or Shangri-La, but cheaper.

1 Sanlihe Lu, Xicheng District (south of Xizhimenwai Dajie, across from Beijing Zoo), Beijing 100044. ℭ 800/821-0900 in U.S. and Canada, 1800/655-147 in Australia, 0800/442-519 in New Zealand, 1800/553-225 in Ireland, 0800/894-351 in U.K., or 010/6831-3388. Fax 010/6831-4577. xyhotel@public3.bta.net.cn. 707 units. $150 double. Children under 12 stay free in parents' room. AE, MC, V. No nearby subway station. **Amenities:** 6 restaurants (Asian, Shandong, Sichuan, Xijiang, Asian fast food, Western), brewpub, lounge; heated indoor pool; health club; Jacuzzi; sauna; tour desk; business center; shopping arcade; salon; 24-hr. room service; babysitting; same-day laundry/dry cleaning; executive-level rooms. *In room:* A/C, TV, minibar, hair dryer, safe.

INEXPENSIVE

Exhibition Centre Hotel (Zhanian Guan Binguan) ✦ This inexpensive, three-star complex resembles the Russian-inspired Exhibition Centre next door. A KFC restaurant stands on Xizhimenwai Dajie, the main street, next to the entry lane. The marble lobby with mirrored ceiling is showing a bit of wear, as is the hotel, which bills itself as "the world's friendliest hotel." The staff does speak some English, but you should expect only basic help and service. Still, for the price, it's a reasonable choice in a pinch. The rooms are modern, compact, with views of a courtyard garden fountain or the lake to the north. Although Westerners do stay here, some in tour groups, most guests are Asian. There is no hotel shuttle bus, but the subway is within walking distance, as are restaurants along the main road west to the zoo.

135 Xizhimenwai Dajie (east side of Exhibition Centre, 2 blocks north of Xizhimenwai Dajie), Beijing 100044. ℭ 010/6831-6633. Fax 010/6834-7450. www.c-b-w.com/hotel/exhibition. 250 units. $60 double. AE, MC, V. Metro: Xizhimen (6 blocks east). **Amenities:** 3 restaurants (Shandong, Chaozhou, American), summer beer garden; exercise room; sauna; billiards; tour desk; small business center; salon; 24-hr. room service; next-day laundry/dry cleaning. *In room:* A/C, TV, hair dryer.

6 Near the Airport

EXPENSIVE

Holiday Inn Lido (Lidu Jiari Fandian) ★★★ *Kids* The world's largest Holiday Inn hardly resembles the ones back in the U.S. This is a city within a city. Because it lies near the expressway to the airport and offers airport shuttle bus service roughly every hour from 6am to 9:30pm (20RMB, $2.50), business travelers find it handy. It is one of the best four-star hotels in China, and its facilities—ranging from a bank and shoe repair to a drugstore and a supermarket—exceed those of most five-star hotels. The rooms are large, with writing desks, king-size beds, chairs, coffee tables, robes, modem links, and tidy bathrooms. Rooms for travelers with disabilities are available. The lobby underwent an extensive restoration in 2001. Western travelers often outnumber Asian guests. The Lido's apartment complex, which includes a kindergarten and an international school, has a fitness club that hotel guests can use for a fee during off-hours (Mon–Fri 7am–5pm). In addition to the airport shuttle, the Lido provides a free downtown shuttle bus with four stops daily.

Jichang Lu, Jiangtai Lu, Chaoyang District (east side of Airport Expressway, 10 miles southwest of airport), Beijing 100004. ℭ 800/465-4329 in U.S. and Canada, 1800/221-066 in Australia, 0800/442-222 in

Courtyard Hotels

For an alternative to the standard international hotels, Beijing offers a handful of locally run traditional courtyard hotels. These spots don't offer the convenient services and perks of a big hotel, but they do offer classic decors: tiled roofs, Chinese lanterns, carved wooden window frames, and intimate gardens. The 38-unit **Lusongyuan Hotel (Lusongyuan Binguan),** 22 Banchang Hutong (an alley 2 blocks north of Di'anmen Dong Dajie), Dongcheng District (*©* **010/6401/1116; fax** 010/6403-0418), offers a friendly staff, a series of tiny courtyard gardens, traditional architecture, a restaurant, a bar, and a few double rooms with private bathrooms for 450RMB ($54). The larger, 40-unit **Bamboo Garden Hotel (Zhuyuan Binguan),** 24 Xiao Shiqiao Jie (west off Jiugulou Dajie, south of the Gulou subway station), Dongcheng District (*©* **010/6403-2229,** ext. 252; fax 010/6401-2633), offers spacious, Imperial-style rooms, gardens, and an outdoor restaurant. Double rooms at the Bamboo Garden—once the estate of one of the Empress Dowager Cixi's chief eunuchs during the last dynasty—are priced at 450RMB ($54) and up. Neither of these courtyard hotels offers much in the way of deluxe facilities or international services, although the Bamboo Garden accepts major credit cards and does have a restaurant, bar, salon, and bike rental. Both courtyard hotels are located within old neighborhoods north of downtown, where the surviving courtyard houses and *hutongs* (alleys) beg exploration.

New Zealand, 1800/553-155 in Ireland, 0800/897-121 in U.K., or 010/6437-6688. Fax 010/6437-6237. www.holiday-inn.com. 726 units. $210 superior double. Children under 19 stay free in parents' room. No subway station. **Amenities:** 8 restaurants (Thai, Mexican, Shanghai, Cantonese, Beijing, German, Italian, International), ice cream parlor, deli, English-style pub, lounge, sports bar, disco; heated indoor pool; 4 indoor tennis courts; health club; Jacuzzi; sauna; bike rental; video arcade; 20-lane bowling alley; concierge; tour desk; 24-hr. business center; air ticket office; shopping arcade; salon; 24-hr. room service; in-room massage; babysitting; same-day laundry/dry cleaning; executive-level rooms; medical clinic. *In room:* A/C, TV, dataport, minibar, coffeemaker, hair dryer, safe.

MODERATE

Harbour Plaza (Hai Yi Fandian) *✦*   Remodeled in 1998, this 19-story, four-star hotel near the Holiday Inn Lido offers good staff services and sparkling, spacious modern rooms. It is situated between Lido Park and a large, newly opened public park (once intended for use as a golf course). If the Holiday Inn Lido is full (or if it just won't fit in your budget), this is a nice alternative, far from the urban center but just 5 minutes by taxi from the Third Ring Road North area and 10 minutes from Sanlitun. Although the recreational facilities are spare, the restaurants and other facilities are deluxe. There are plans to institute a hotel shuttle bus service to the airport and downtown sites. Taxis are readily available.

8 Jiangtai Xi Lu (Chaoyang District, east side of Airport Expressway, 1 block southeast Holiday Inn Lido, 10.5 miles southwest of Capital Airport), Beijing 100004. *©* **010/6436-2288.** Fax 010/6436-1818. www.harbour-plaza.com. 370 units. $160 double. No subway station. **Amenities:** 4 restaurants (Cantonese, International, Japanese, Shanghai), English-style pub, sports bar/disco; health club; Jacuzzi; sauna; business center; salon; 24-hr. room service; in-room massage; same-day laundry/dry cleaning.

Sino-Swiss Hotel Beijing (Guodu Da Fandian) ⊛ *Kids*   A true airport hotel, this former Movenpick Hotel is just a 10-minute drive from the airport via the free shuttle. This is also Beijing's only hotel with a resort atmosphere and outdoor recreational facilities. The service is efficient, and the facilities are worthy of the four-star rating. Rooms (renovated in 1996) are spacious with generous counter space, two closets, and a writing desk with accessories. Bathrooms have phones and hair dryers. (For $10 more, the business superior rooms come with modem plugs, robes, express checkout, and free breakfast.) There's a comfortable, European atmosphere at this airport hotel–cum–resort, which has the capital's only natural thermal hot springs pool, interconnected indoor and outdoor swimming pools, a courtyard chess board with resident master, children's programs all summer, beach volleyball with white sands, and even a resident camel. The free airport shuttle (airport location: Carpark D109 opposite arrival gate 5) runs every half hour from 6am to 11pm (there's a hotel desk in the airport arrival hall) and the free downtown shuttle bus makes 10 runs daily from 8am to 10pm. (The trip is 30–45 min., depending on traffic.) This is the nearest major hotel to the airport, located well beyond the urban smog belt.

Xiao Tianzhu Village, Capital Airport (Shunyi County, within 1.5 miles of airport), Beijing 100621. ℂ 010/6456-5588. Fax 010/6456-5678. www.sino-swisshotel.com. 408 units. $140 double. Children under 16 stay free in parents' room. No subway station. **Amenities:** 6 restaurants (includes Mongolian, Italian, Chinese, Japanese, International), bar, disco; indoor/outdoor pool; hot springs pool; 2 lighted outdoor tennis courts; indoor squash court; health club; Jacuzzi; sauna; bike rental; children's programs (in summer); playground; tour desk; 24-hr. business center; shopping arcade; salon; 24-hr. room service; babysitting; same-day laundry/dry cleaning. *In room:* A/C, TV, minibar, coffeemaker, hair dryer.

5

Dining

In a nation where the most popular greeting heard in the streets translates as "Have you eaten?" it's little wonder that dining ranks as a chief concern; it's nearly as important as family or fortune. The average Beijinger spends more on food than on housing. As incomes rose in the 1990s, the number of cafes in the capital mushroomed, and foreign visitors have benefited from this dining explosion. Just a decade ago, Beijing travelers had to choose between a few dozen expensive hotel restaurants and a few dozen cheaper, but less appetizing, private cafes. Now there are scores of fine restaurants for foreign guests located inside and outside of the big hotels, covering a wide range of prices and cuisines.

Eating is almost reason enough to visit Beijing because no other city in China offers such a range of Chinese dishes prepared at such a consistently high level. You can sample all of China through its regional specialties, from Cantonese to Sichuan. The emphasis in Beijing, of course, is on Northern Chinese cuisine. Beijing duck is a must, and there are restaurants that serve little else. The capital is also celebrated for its version of dim sum (*jiaozi*), the steamed dumplings with meat or vegetable fillings. Unique to Beijing cuisine are its Imperial dishes, which are derived from the lavish banquets enjoyed by the last emperors of the Qing Dynasty. Beijing has several restaurants that serve food of the Imperial courts using the ingredients, style, and sometimes even the actual recipes of the last chefs who worked in the Forbidden City. Recently, the dishes of the masses that were the hearty staple for millions during the Cultural Revolution (1966–76) under Chairman Mao have enjoyed a revival, spawning several popular, ever-so-humble eating places dedicated to Mao nostalgia.

The Mongolians from north of the Great Wall and the Muslim peoples from China's far northwest have supplied Beijing with excellent barbecues and hot pots, while the dishes of Canton, Sichuan, and lately Shanghai are particularly well represented in Beijing's restaurants. Visitors can spend weeks in Beijing these days eating nothing but the dishes of China's great cuisines.

In reality, however, most foreign visitors quickly become homesick for home cooking—or for something other than another Chinese meal, no matter how tasty it is. The boom in Beijing eating establishments has brought with it a dramatic increase in foreign restaurants, particularly Western ones—American, French, German, Russian, Scandinavian, and even Mexican. There are also esteemed dining places serving Indian, Thai, Korean, and Japanese fare. Plus, you can have your fill of fast food in Beijing; in fact, the sheer number of McDonald's, KFC, and Pizza Hut restaurants will astonish, and perhaps depress, visitors from the West. It is possible to visit Beijing for 2 weeks and eat well without once using a pair of chopsticks on a single Chinese dish.

> ### Tips   Hotel Versus Non-Hotel Dining
>
> For the visitor, the most pronounced dividing line in Beijing dining is between the hotel and the street. Beijing's hotels boast many of the very best restaurants in China. The quality of the food, the skill of the chefs, the hygiene of the kitchen, and the service of the waiters is high caliber. Outside of the hotels, these standards have generally taken a fierce beating—until recently. Today, there are several dozen private restaurants that rival those in the best hotels, and these upstarts consistently offer lower prices (as well as quite hygienic establishments, good service, and English-language menus). In addition, there are scores of smaller cafes outside the hotels that offer quite tasty Western dishes at economical rates. The international hotels now find themselves quite literally surrounded by private competitors, so that even a gourmet visitor's dining experience in Beijing need no longer be confined to the hotel.

Beijing consistently ranks high among the world's most costly cities in which to eat. The most recent Corporate Travel Index (with data supplied by Organization Resources Counselors, Inc., of N.Y.) rates Beijing food costs for business travelers as the second highest in the world (behind only Hong Kong) at $130 per day per person ($22 for breakfast, $28 for lunch, $80 for dinner)—but I find these estimates excessive. In my experience, you can have an inexpensive dinner (without drinks) for under 80RMB ($10) per person; a moderate dinner for between 80 to 120RMB (about $10–$15); and an expensive dinner for between 120 and 240RMB ($15–$30). You can splurge at a very expensive place for between 240 and 400RMB ($30–$50), although it's easy to spend over a $100 on a single entree at some restaurants—even cheap and dingy ones—if you so choose. Lunches are considerably cheaper (often half the price of a dinner). Hotels routinely add a 15% service charge to dining bills, although this practice is beginning to lessen as competition heats up with outside restaurants (many of which levy no service charges). Hotel restaurants accept major credit cards, and although a growing number of outside restaurants are beginning to do so as well, diners should always carry enough RMB to pay for a meal.

The restaurants listed below are arranged first by location, then by price. The most popular locations for restaurants catering to visitors, regardless of cuisine, are in the neighborhoods where many international hotels are clustered: in the city center (Dongcheng), east along Jianguomenwai Dajie (Chaoyang), and in the Sanlitun and Third Ring Road areas northeast of downtown (Chaoyang Northeast).

1 Restaurants by Cuisine

AMERICAN

Bella's (Chaoyang Northeast, $, p. 106)

Big Easy ✿✿ (Chaoyang NE, $$$, p. 101)

Häagen-Dazs ✿ (Chaoyang, $$, p. 95)

Henry J. Bean's ✿✿ (Chaoyang, $$, p. 95)

Louisiana ✿✿✿ (Chaoyang Northeast, $$$$, p. 98)

T.G.I. Fridays (Chaoyang Northeast, $$, p. 105)

Key to Abbreviations: $$$$ = Very Expensive $$$ = Expensive $$ = Moderate $ = Inexpensive

BEIJING/SHANXI

Beijing Express (Xicheng, $, p. 112)

Fangshan Restaurant ✹✹✹ (Xicheng, $$$, p. 110)

Gold Cat Jiaozi City ✹ (Chaoyang Northeast, $, p. 106)

Jinghua Shiyuan (Chongwen, $, p. 109)

Jinyang Fanzhuang ✹ (Xuanwu, $$$, p. 106)

Li Family Restaurant ✹✹ (Xicheng, $$$$, p. 109)

Quanjude Hepingmen (Xuanwu, $$, p. 108)

Quanjude Kaoyadian ✹✹ (Chongwen, $$$, p. 107)

Red Capital Club ✹✹ (Dongcheng, $$$$, p. 88)

Sihexuan ✹✹✹ (Chaoyang, $$, p. 97)

BRITISH

John Bull Pub ✹ (Chaoyang, $$, p. 95)

CANTONESE

Fortune Garden ✹✹ (Dongcheng, $$$$, p. 88)

Four Seasons ✹✹ (Chaoyang, $$$, p. 92)

Hong Kong Food City ✹ (Dongcheng, $$$, p. 90)

Horizon ✹✹ (Dongcheng, $$$, p. 92)

Oriental ✹✹ (Chaoyang Northeast, $$$, p. 93)

Sampan Restaurant ✹ (Chaoyang, $$, p. 96)

Sheng ✹ (Chaoyang, $$, p. 96)

Summer Palace ✹✹ (Chaoyang, $$$, p. 93)

Xihe Yaju ✹✹ (Chaoyang, $$, p. 98)

FRENCH

Bleu Marine ✹ (Chaoyang, $$$, p. 92)

Le Bistrot des Chateaux (Chaoyang, $$, p. 95)

La Scene ✹ (Chaoyang, $$$, p. 93)

Justine's ✹✹ (Chaoyang, $$$$, p. 91)

Plaza Grill ✹✹ (Dongcheng, $$$$, p. 88)

FUSION

Aria ✹✹✹ (Chaoyang, $$$, p. 91)

The Courtyard ✹✹✹ (Dongcheng, $$$$, p. 83)

GERMAN

Bavaria Bierstube ✹ (Chaoyang Northeast, $$$, p. 89)

Kebab Kafe ✹✹ (Chaoyang Northeast, $$, p. 104)

Paulaner Brauhaus ✹ (Chaoyang Northeast, $$$, p. 102)

INDIAN

Omar Khayyam (Chaoyang, $$, p. 105)

Shamiana ✹✹ (Xicheng, $$, p. 112)

ITALIAN

Danieli's ✹✹ (Chaoyang, $$$$, p. 91)

Metro Cafe ✹✹ (Chaoyang Northeast, $$$, p. 102)

Peppino's ✹✹ (Xicheng, $$, p. 112)

Roma Ristorante Italiano ✹ (Dongcheng, $$$$, p. 89)

Trattoria La Gondola (Chaoyang Northeast, $$, p. 106)

JAPANESE

Nadaman ✹✹ (Chaoyang, $$$$, p. 91)

Nishimura ✹✹ (Haidian, $$$$, p. 110)

San Si Lang ✹ (Chaoyang Northeast, $$, p. 105)

MEXICAN

Texan Bar & Grill ✹ (Chaoyang Northeast, $$$, p. 103)

Mexican Wave (Chaoyang, $$, p. 96)

MUSLIM
Afunti ✦ (Dongcheng, $$, p. 90)
Mongolian Gher ✦✦ (Chaoyang Northeast, $$$, p. 102)

RUSSIAN
Baikal ✦ (Chaoyang Northeast, $$$, p. 100)

SCANDINAVIAN
LaxenOxen ✦✦ (Chaoyang Northeast, $$$$, p. 98)

SHANGHAI
Lao Shanghai ✦ (Chaoyang Northeast, $$$, p. 101)
Moon Shanghai ✦ (Chaoyang Northeast, $$$, p. 102)
Shanghai Cuisine ✦ (Chaoyang Northeast, $$$, p. 103)

SICHUAN
Berena's Bistro ✦✦✦ (Chaoyang Northeast, $$$, p. 100)
Sheng Restaurant ✦ (Chaoyang, $$, p. 96)

Sichuan Restaurant ✦ (Xicheng, $$$, p. 110)
Xihe Yaju ✦✦ (Chaoyang, $$, p. 98)

SPANISH
Ashanti Restaurant & Wine Bar ✦ (Chaoyang Northeast, $$$, p. 100)

THAI
Borom Piman ✦✦ (Chaoyang Northeast, $$$, p. 101)
Red Basil ✦✦ (Chaoyang Northeast, $$$, p. 103)
Serve the People ✦ (Chaoyang Northeast, $$, p. 105)

VEGETARIAN
Gongdelin ✦ (Chongwen, $$, p. 107)
Green Tian Shi ✦✦ (Dongcheng, $$$, p. 89)

2 Dongcheng (City Center)

VERY EXPENSIVE

The Courtyard (Siheyuan) ✦✦✦ FUSION The hottest independent restaurant in town, The Courtyard frequently shows up on international lists of the best restaurants in the world. The owner, Handel Lee, is an American lawyer with Beijing ancestors; the chef, Rey Lin, loves to experiment with East–West fusions. Fresh salads blend Western and Chinese ingredients, as do the appetizers. The menu changes frequently. Recent main courses included a sumptuous ginger balsamic glazed black cod with baby bok choy and taro potato mash, lemon-lime prawns, Beijing duck spring rolls, marinated pork mignon, and lemongrass-coconut marinated lamb chops. The "black-and-blue chicken," made with a local low-fat, dark-skinned bird, is the chef's signature dish. Vegetables are always seasonal and fresh. The desserts range from chocolate mousse to steamed dumplings stuffed with fruit. The decor, with wooden floors and a glass roof, is that of a contemporary bistro. There's a neon-lit bar on the dining floor, a gallery in the basement featuring contemporary Chinese artists, and a living room–sized cigar divan upstairs, where the view of the Forbidden City and the moat is exceptional. The very upscale Courtyard has a smart, casual air—the perfect place to relax with a flute of Moët & Chandon and a Cuban cigar.

95 Donghuamen Lu (east side of Forbidden City moat; look for lions and glass doors). ☎ 010/6526-8883. Reservations required. Main courses 95–195RMB ($11–$23). AE, MC, V. Daily 6–10pm; until 1am for drinks and cigars.

Beijing Dining

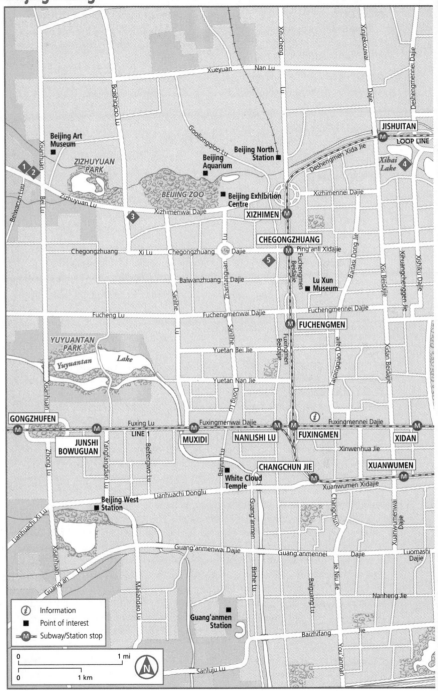

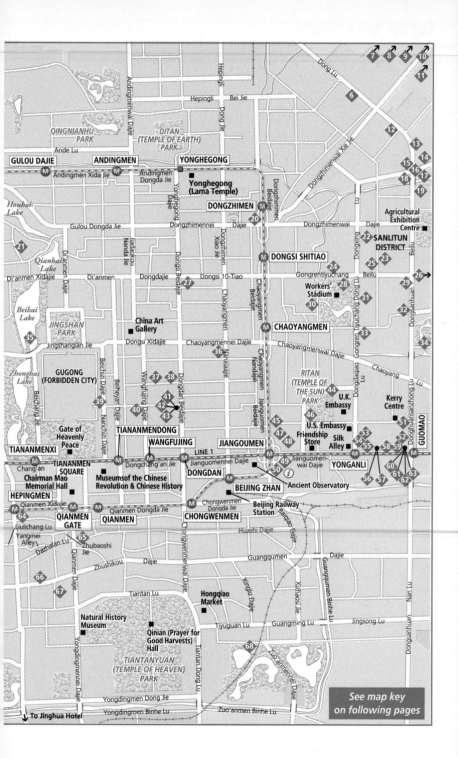

QINGNIANHU PARK

DITAN (TEMPLE OF EARTH) PARK

Hepingli Bei Jie

Dong Lu

Ande Lu

Hepingli

7 **8** **9** **10**

11

6

12

13

GULOU DAJIE Ⓜ

ANDINGMEN Ⓜ

YONGHEGONG ■

Andingmen Xida Jie   Andingmen Dongda Jie

15
16 **17**
18
19

14

Houhai Lake

Andingmenwai Dajie

Yonghegong (Lama Temple)

Dongzhimenwai Xie Jie

21

Qianhai Lake

Di'anmen Xidajie

Gulou Dongda Jie

Dongzhimennei Dajie

20

DONGZHIMEN Ⓜ

Dongzhimenwai   Dajie

Agricultural Exhibition Centre ■

Jiadaokou Nanda Jie

Di'anmen

Dongsi Beidajie

Dongsi 10-Tiao

DONGSI SHITIAO Ⓜ

22 SANLITUN DISTRICT

24

25 **23**

Beilu

Beihai Lake

JINGSHAN PARK

Jingshanqian Jie

Dongsi Beidajie

27

Dongsi 10-Tiao

Gongrentiyuchang

Workers' Stadium ■

28

30

29 **26**

31

32

Gongren Tiyuchang Dong Lu

Zhonghai Lake

GUGONG (FORBIDDEN CITY)

Beichizi Dajie

Beichang Jie

Beiheyan Dajie

China Art Gallery ■

Dongsi Xidajie

CHAOYANGMEN Ⓜ

Chaoyangmennei Dajie

Chaoyangmenwai Dajie

Chaoyang   Lu

33

34

35

36

RITAN (TEMPLE OF THE SUN) PARK

44

Dongdaqiao Lu

Kerry Centre ■

Gate of Heavenly Peace

TIANANMENDONG Ⓜ

Nanchizi Dajie

Wangfujing Dajie

Dongdan Beidajie

37 **38**

41
42
43

40
39

Chaoyangmen Nandajie

Jianguomen Beidajie

U.K. Embassy ■

46

U.S. Embassy ■   Friendship Store ■

Silk Alley

45

47
48

Dongdansanzhong Lu

51

52

53
54 **55**

58 **59**

GUOMAO Ⓜ

TIANANMENXI Ⓜ

Chang'an Lu

TIANANMEN SQUARE

Chairman Mao Memorial Hall ■

HEPINGMEN Ⓜ

Dongchang'an Jie

WANGFUJING Ⓜ

LINE 1

Jianguomennei Dajie

Museums of the Chinese Revolution & Chinese History ■

DONGDAN Ⓜ

JIANGUOMEN Ⓜ

49
50

Jianguomenwai Dajie

YONGANLI Ⓜ

56 **57**

60

61 **62**
63

ⓘ Ancient Observatory ■

Qianmen Xidajie Ⓜ

64

QIANMEN GATE Ⓜ

QIANMEN Ⓜ

Qianmen Dongda Jie

CHONGWENMEN Ⓜ

Chongwenmennei Dajie

BEIJING ZHAN Ⓜ

Chongwenmen Dongda Jie

Beijing Railway Station ■

Beijing Railway Station

Liulichang Lu

Yangmei Alley

Dazhalan Lu

Zhubaoshi Jie

65

Zhushikou   Dajie

Huashi Dajie

Chongwenmenwai Dajie

Guangqumen

Guangqumen Binhe Lu

66

67

Qianmen Dajie

Tiantan Lu

Hongqiao Market ■

Kingdu Dajie

Xihaosi Jie

Dajie

Jingsong Lu

Natural History Museum ■

Qinian (Prayer for Good Harvests) Hall ■

Tiyuguan Lu

Guangming Lu

Yongdingmennei Dajie

TIANTANYUAN (TEMPLE OF HEAVEN) PARK

Tiantan Dong Lu

68

Zuo'anmen Dajie

Dongsanhuan

↓ To Jinghua Hotel

Yongdingmen Dong Jie

Yongdingmen Binhe Lu

Zuo'anmen Binhe Lu

See map key on following pages

85

Key for Beijing Dining

Fortune Garden (Yuexiu Ting) ★★ CANTONESE   This wonderful restaurant, brightly decorated in Chinese motifs, features traditional music played by a trio of local musicians in the evenings. It's an elegant spot for enjoying fine southern Chinese dishes that are on par with the city's best Cantonese restaurants. If possible, request seating on the raised platform in the rear. Among the best dishes, prepared by three Hong Kong chefs, are the baked scallops in cheese sauce and the braised pigeon with black mushrooms. Fortune Garden also crosses regional lines and offers a Beijing duck that is less greasy than those in most duck restaurants. The lunchtime specialty is dim sum Cantonese style—at 18RMB ($2.16) a plate or steamer, these pastries are well worth sampling. Service is attentive.

Lower Lobby 2, Palace Hotel, 8 Jinyu Hutong, Wangfujing Dajie (2 blocks east of Wangfujing). ℂ **010/6559-8899**, ext. 7900. Reservations recommended on weekends. Main courses 150–300RMB ($18–$38) and up. AE, DC, MC, V. Daily 11:30am–2:30pm and 6–10pm.

Plaza Grill (Zimen) ★★ FRENCH   Reserve a table near the atrium railing on the mezzanine and prepare yourself for good service, beautiful presentations, and some eclectic dishes, dubbed *cuisine moderne* by chef Armin Wolfgang Lang. Traditional French cooking underlies many of the Asian-flavored entrees. From the open kitchen to the white tablecloths, the setting is elegant but not formal, and the live music below (usually Western classical) makes for a romantic evening. Start with a fresh salad (the Caesar is prepared tableside) or perhaps the borscht (with shredded duck and Harbin caviar), then select from a range of entrees including rainbow trout, Scottish salmon, and tiger prawns. With the imported sirloins and lamb chops from the grill, guests select their own sauce (herb butter, mushroom, béarnaise). Breast of duckling in a morel mango cream represents one of the chef's best fusion inventions. To top off a gourmet evening, consider an ice-cream creation, cherries jubilee, or a crêpe Suzette flamed with brandy.

In the Crowne Plaza Beijing, mezzanine, 48 Wangfujing Dajie. ℂ **010/6513-3388**, ext. 1132. Reservations recommended on weekends. Main courses 180–320RMB ($22–$38). AE, DC, MC, V. Mon–Sat noon–2pm and 6–10pm; Sun 6–10pm.

Red Capital Club (Xinhongzi Julebu) ★★ CHINESE   One of Beijing's trendiest new restaurants is part nostalgia, part storytelling, part fine Chinese food. The Red Capital Club is a tastefully remodeled courtyard mansion north of the city center with a lounge decorated in Mao memorabilia of the 1950s. The heyday of the Chinese Communist Party and the "innocent" 1950s of Mao's Great Leap Forward are evoked everywhere. The menu is not from those bleak and hearty days, however; it is a series of skillfully prepared dishes from the spectrum of Chinese cuisine. Each entree has its own long story, which the waiter recites. The Mandarin fish steamed in bamboo shoots and the sesame-toasted venison are typical and tasty offerings, as is the "Monkey's Hand" (eggplant and garlic). Lawrence Brahm, the American owner, is himself a collector of Mao relics and kitsch, to the point that he has purchased the Red Flag limousine used to transport the Chairman and his revolutionary cadre through the streets of the capital.

66 Dongsi Jiutiao (alley no. 9 off Dongsi Bei Dajie, halfway between the Lama Temple and Chang'an Ave.), Dongcheng District. ℂ **010/6402-7150** (days); 010/8401-8886 (evenings, weekends). Reservations required. Main courses 150–230RMB ($18–$28). AE, DC, MC, V. Daily 6–11pm.

Roma Ristorante Italiano (Luoma) ⍟ NORTHERN ITALIAN   This formal restaurant is a member of the Chaines des Rotisseurs, a group of international hotel gourmets; the service and dishes are of the highest standards. The top entrees are the veal medallions, the pan-fried sea bass, and the rack of lamb with a black-olive crust. There is a score of northern Italian choices too, featuring fresh pastas, herbs, and seafood. The black olives and tomatoes with mozzarella is a superb appetizer, and the large European wine list complements the stylish dining. Top off the evening with a heavenly tiramisu for dessert. This is a fine spot for a splurge. Roma's "bargain" day is Sunday, when the big buffet goes for about $20 per person.

In the Palace Hotel, first floor, 8 Jinyu Hutong, Wangfujing Dajie (2 blocks east of Wangfujing). ⓒ 010/6559-2888, ext. 7492. Reservations required. Main courses 160–240RMB ($19–$29). AE, DC, MC, V. Daily 11:30–2:30pm and 6:30–11pm.

EXPENSIVE

Bavaria Bierstube (Bafaliya) ⍟ BAVARIAN   Follow the lobby waterfall down the escalator, past the upscale boutiques in the basement, to what looks like a German inn, complete with polished floors and paneling, sculpted country chairs, and checkered tablecloths. This could be Bavaria—the menu certainly is. The sausages are made here, and so is the apple strudel. Top entrees include the cheese fondues and the sliced veal tenderloin in a mushroom sauce. This is the monthly meeting place of the "Beijing Wine and Cheese Club," and the cheeses are worth savoring. The Chinese staff, outfitted in Bavarian dress, is even versed in a bit of German (as well as English).

In the Palace Hotel, Lower Level 2, 8 Jinyu Hutong, Wangfujing Dajie (2 blocks east of Wangfujing). ⓒ 010/6559-2888, ext. 7410. Main courses 80–180RMB ($10–$22). AE, DC, MC, V. Daily noon–3pm and 6–11pm.

Why Chopsticks Aren't "Green"

Chopsticks have been the dining utensils of choice in China for at least 3,500 years, but only recently, with the dramatic rise in incomes, have the snap-apart, disposable wooden chopsticks become a staple. China produces—and tosses out—45 billion pairs of chopsticks each year, and it must chop down 25 million trees annually to supply consumers. At this rate, in just 10 years, the demand for disposable chopsticks will consume all the forests of China.

A grassroots movement that opposes the continued use of these throwaway wooden utensils is making waves in Beijing. Students at Beijing's Qinghua University have persuaded school officials to replace disposable chopsticks with reusable plastic spoons in the cafeteria, more than 100 state-owned restaurants in Beijing have promised to wash and reuse their chopsticks, and China's Finance Ministry is studying whether or not to impose a tax on disposable chopsticks. Meanwhile, environmentally minded diners can often be seen discreetly removing their own pair of reusable chopsticks from a bag in restaurants across the capital.

Green Tian Shi (Luse Tianshi) ★★ VEGETARIAN   There's a vegetarian grocery at the entrance and a gaudy dining room upstairs serving Beijing's tastiest and trendiest vegetarian fare. The menu (in English) is filled with Chinese dishes that are made entirely without meat or dairy products (although there are some egg and milk dishes available). The dishes employ legumes, grains, and tuber stalks, along with artfully disguised chunks of *doufu* (bean curd) to achieve the appearance, texture, and sometimes the taste of fish, flesh, and fowl. There's a whole steamed "fish," a Gong Bao "chicken," an assortment of "lamb kebabs," and even the old Cantonese delicacy, "Monkey Brains." Perhaps the best treat on the menu is a faux braised eel (*hangshao shanyu*). Fruit juices and green teas are the drinks of choice here. This Buddhist-run cafe has a more New Age atmosphere than the bigger, state-run vegetarian emporium, Gongdelin, which uses a heavier hand (and more oil) in preparing its more extensive menu. Green Tian Shi's lunches are also smaller and much more economical, costing less than 100RMB ($12) per person.

57 Dengshi Xikou Lu (east of the Crowne Plaza Beijing, 1 block off Wangfujing Dajie). ✆ 010/6524-2349. Main courses 50–200RMB ($6–$25). AE, MC, V. Daily 10am–9pm; 8am–midnight for drinks and snacks.

Hong Kong Food City (Xiang Gang Meishicheng) ★ CANTONESE   One of the first big, independent restaurants to hit downtown Beijing, its name says it all: This is a multilevel "hash house" with basic to extravagant Cantonese fare, from Hong Kong dim sum to shark's fin and bird's nest delicacies. The emphasis is on the business of eating, with large dining rooms and quick service. The seafood is fresh. Crab dishes cost from $8 to $35, depending on how elaborately they are prepared. Fortunately, there's an English menu to sort out all the possibilities, especially since the energetic staff seldom slows down enough to practice its English with customers. This is a rousing place to eat in the company of Chinese-speaking travelers from all over Southeast Asia.

18 Dong'anmen Dajie (southwest corner of Wangfujing Dajie). ✆ 010/6513-6668, ext. 3102. Main courses 80–140RMB ($10–$17). AE, MC, V. Daily 11am–2:30am.

MODERATE
Afunti (Afanti) ★ MUSLIM (XINJIANG)   The most rousing and popular of Beijing's Muslim restaurants, Afunti is as well known for its after-dinner performances as its actual dinners. In 1996, when it opened as Uncle Afanti, it was one among many dives specializing in cheap Uighur dishes. (The Uighurs are the minority Muslim people who constitute a near majority in the far west Chinese province of Xinjiang.) It then went "upscale," opening up a large dining hall and stage, although decorations are still minimal. Among traditional Uighur dishes not to miss are the *yang rou chuanr* (barbecued lamb skewers), *lamian* (long noodles with tomato sauce), and *nan* (flatbread with garlic). Set dinners are the best deal and usually cost about 100RMB ($12). If you're in the mood for a true Uighur celebration, order ahead for the all-from-one-sheep banquet (about $100). Between courses, resident Uighur women belly dance (inviting diners to join in), musicians pound on long-neck guitars and snakeskin drums, and Uighur dancers in provincial dress kick up a storm. This is a perfect place if you're in the mood for barbecue and spices and a night spent dancing on the tables.

2A Houguaibang Hutong, Chaoyangmennei Dajie (in alley south off Chaoyangmennei, 2 big blocks east of Wangfujing Dajie) ✆ 010/6525-1071 or 010/6527-2288. Reservations recommended on weekends. Meals 75–100RMB ($9–$12). AE, MC, V. Daily 11am–2:30pm and 4:30–11:30pm.

3 Chaoyang (East)

VERY EXPENSIVE

Danieli's (Dan Ni Ailisi) ✿✿ SOUTHERN ITALIAN   The entrance is stylish—via the sweeping marble stairway from the grand lobby of the St. Regis Hotel—and so is the restaurant, with windows on the tree-lined diplomatic compounds. The regional dishes are superb, and the Italian wine list is long. There are also some surprises, perhaps the best of which is a lobster and saffron-flavored risotto with Australian yabbies (mini-lobsters). The pastas are fresh, many of the ingredients imported, and the European wine list is extensive. Desserts are headlined by a cheesecake delicately flavored with nuts. You won't find a more elegant place to appreciate fine Italian dining in China.

In the St. Regis Hotel, 2nd floor, 21 Jianguomenwai Dajie (1 block north of Jianguomenwai Dajie on Xiushui Jie). ✆ **010/6460-6688**, ext. 2440. Reservations recommended on weekends. Main courses 145–225RMB ($17–$27). AE, DC, MC, V. Daily 11:30am–2:30pm and 6–10pm.

Justine's (Ouluxi Canting) ✿✿ FRENCH   This is the perfect place for a romantic European evening in China's capital. With the dark, wood-trimmed decor, the chandeliers, the linen tablecloths, the silverware, the crystal setting, and the string quartet, Justine's continues its long tradition of fine Continental dining. The focus these days is on seafood (fine filets and prawns) and steaks. The oysters are fresh, the goose liver the best in town, and the rack of lamb and the duck are hallmarks of Justine's, as is its excellent wine list. The crêpes Suzettes flambées are not to be skipped.

In the Jianguo Hotel, 5 Jianguomenwai Dajie. ✆ **010/6500-2233**, ext. 8039. Reservations required. Main courses 178–398RMB ($21–$48). AE, DC, MC, V. Daily noon–2:30pm and 6–10:30pm; Sun brunch noon–3pm.

Nadaman (Tanwan) ✿✿ JAPANESE   This is the first outlet in China of the Osaka family restaurant founded in Japan in 1830. Nadaman is celebrated for its Kansairyori cuisine. Ingredients are flown in from Japan, and several of the chefs are Japanese. The teppan dishes, cooked at table, are a favorite, as is the fresh Nadaman salad. There are separate teppanyaki, sushi, and tatami rooms. The decor is modern Japanese; everything is kept spotless. For a variation on the Mongolian cook-it-yourself hot pots that are a feature of many Beijing restaurants, Nadaman offers a *shabu shabu* hot pot, well worth trying. Nadaman has first-rate cuisine and a serene atmosphere, with high prices to match, making it one of the top Japanese restaurants in Beijing.

In the China World Hotel, 3rd floor, 1 Jianguomenwai Dajie (at the Third Ring Road East). ✆ **010/6505-2266**, ext. 39. Main courses 150–600RMB ($18–$72). AE, DC, MC, V. Daily 11:30am–2pm and 5:30–9:30pm.

EXPENSIVE

Aria (Aliya) ✿✿✿ FUSION   This plush but informal grill, with its open kitchen and rotisserie where the chefs love to perform for their customers, is one of Beijing's trendiest nightspots. Jazz is the focus, especially at the piano bar where featured performers play amid eclectic surroundings that include European masterwork reproductions, Chinese opera masks, and Thai musical instruments. Beyond the long bar on the first floor is a stunning centerpiece, a massive spiral staircase of polished wood honeycombed with shelves for storing bottles of wine. The wine bar features an extensive international wine list and serves up a special wine tasting. There's a snappy East–West menu with starters ranging from lobster pot stickers to raw New Zealand oysters, entrees emphasizing grilled fish and imported steaks, and desserts that begin with a ginger crème brûlée. A decidedly uptown, "smart casual" wine bar and grill, Aria has a romantic nook on the top floor, an intimate box for one or two couples that overlooks the hotel lobby.

In the China World Hotel, 2nd and 3rd floors, 1 Jianguomenwai Dajie (at Third Ring Road East). ② 010/6505-2266, ext. 36. Main courses 80–200RMB ($10–$24). AE, DC, MC, V. Daily 11am–midnight.

Bleu Marine ⊛ SOUTHERN FRENCH   This was one of Beijing's trendiest cafes when it opened in 1998, and it's still a nice little spot for lunch or dinner, even though the original chefs have left the restaurant. Sidewalk dining is available under the blue awning. Inside, the decor is Mediterranean: bright and informal, with white canvas director's chairs complementing the sea-blue-and-white interior. French melodies are piped in. The emphasis is on seafood. The set dinners are four-course affairs (700RMB, $88, for two, including house wine) that change with the season and whatever is freshest at local markets. The menu may include a prosciutto-and-melon salad, flamed tiger prawns with a cream sauce, Provençal-style frogs' legs, grilled salmon with dill and sea urchin sauce, mussels a la marnière, and grilled rump steak in a triple pepper sauce. The white and dark chocolate mousse is a perfect dessert. Set lunches are far more modest and less costly (80RMB, $10, per person, including one glass of wine or fruit juice). During the summer, the patio (facing west) is a fine place to enjoy a Mediterranean repast in Beijing.

5 Guanghua Xi Lu (2 blocks north of Jianguomenwai Dajie, up Dongdaqiao Lu). ② 010/6500-6704. Main courses 80–350RMB ($10–$44). AE, MC, V. Daily 11:30am–2:30pm and 6:30–10:30pm.

Four Seasons (Siji) ⊛⊛ CANTONESE   One of Beijing's most popular upscale Chinese restaurants, the Four Seasons serves a varied menu. Most of the dishes are Cantonese, with fine versions of rice and seafood dishes, including the expensive shark's fin, bird's nest, and abalone entrees, but you'll also find a complete Beijing duck menu for two people (260RMB, $31) that is as good as anything prepared at the specialty restaurants. The setting is as much European as Chinese, with linen tablecloths and fine china table settings. In the evenings, there are live performances of traditional Chinese music by local musicians. The atmosphere is one of elegance, making this a top choice for a stylish evening celebration with Chinese cuisine. Plates start at as low as 45RMB ($5), but you'll want several. Weekends provide the best deal, however, with an excellent set lunch of Cantonese dim sum for just 88RMB ($11).

In the Jianguo Hotel, 5 Jianguomenwai Dajie. ② 010/6500-2233, ext. 8041. Reservations required. Main courses 160–1,280RMB ($19–$154). AE, DC, MC, V. Daily 11:30am–2pm and 6–10pm.

Horizon (Haitian Ge) ⊛⊛ CANTONESE   Yet another elegant signature restaurant for the Shangri-La Hotel chain, the Horizon is quite popular, especially at lunch. Its main entrance is actually outside the hotel, in the Kerry Centre Shopping Plaza. The interior is an elegant version of traditional Chinese decor; the interior is bright and open. This is an excellent spot to enjoy upscale Cantonese dining. The menu runs the gamut, from simple noodle and rice dishes to elaborate shark's fin and bird's nest entrees. You can enjoy the most dishes by sharing several dishes among everyone at the table in true Chinese style. Try the chef's special XO sauce (it comes on a small plate in spicy vegetable strands), and if possible, order some dim sum (pastries). The chefs are from Hong Kong, and they know how to prepare the best of Cantonese cuisine. This is one of Beijing's top upscale Cantonese restaurants, on par with Summer Palace and Four Seasons.

In the Kerry Centre Hotel, 1st floor, 1 Guanghua Lu. ℂ **010/6561-8833**, ext. 41. Reservations recommended. 100–300RMB ($12–$36). AE, DC, MC, V. Daily 11:30am–2:30pm and 5:30–10pm.

La Scene (Saina Fengqing) ✿ FRENCH

Bleu Marine was such a success that the owners of La Scene decided to open their cafe right next door and serve up their own high-quality French dishes. The prices are roughly the same at each cafe, although La Scene is as bit less expensive overall. Its decor is a bit plusher than that of the bistro next door, too. Top appetizers are the soups, the goose liver paté, and the escargot casserole. For dinner, linguine and seafood stew are among the best. The set lunches are a deal at about $10. They include an appetizer and entree of your choice; add a dessert for about $2.50 more. With the recent departure of Bleu Marine's original chefs, La Scene is well worth a try.

5 Guanghua Xi Lu (2 blocks north of Jianguomenwai Dajie, up Dongdaqiao Lu). ℂ **010/6593-5650**. Main courses 100–250RMB ($12–$30). AE, MC, V. Daily 11:30am–2pm and 6–11pm.

Oriental (Dongfang Canting) ✿✿ CANTONESE

Another elegant gem for the Shangri-La Hotel chain, the Oriental offers not only fine Cantonese dishes prepared by Hong Kong chefs, but also some Beijing specialties. This is a good choice for an evening to savor; the setting is that of a traditional and romantic Chinese pavilion. The best seating is along the back wall, where a wall of glass affords a view of the extensive forested garden and the skylights of the underground ice rink and shopping mall just south of the restaurant. The menu has Cantonese standards, from vegetable and rice dishes to shark's fin and abalone. The dim sum are among the best in Beijing, making this a top choice for lunch or a weekend brunch. The food, the service, and the formal yet intimate atmosphere put this Cantonese restaurant on par with Summer Palace, Horizon, and Four Seasons.

In the Traders Hotel, 1 Jianguomenwai Dajie (1 block north of China World). ℂ **010/6505-2777**, ext. 34. Reservations recommended on weekends. 40–300RMB ($5–$36). AE, DC, MC, V. Daily 11:30am–2pm and 6–10pm.

Summer Palace ✿ CANTONESE

Sleekly decorated in the modern Chinese style, with tall wooden doors, marble walkways, and pale green and salmon walls trimmed in gold, newly remodeled Summer Palace has good service and even better Southern Chinese cuisine. Though some readers have encountered poor service and substandard dishes here, these problems appear to have been corrected with the arrival of new management. Expect a gracious dining experience with generous portions prepared by Hong Kong chefs. About 70% of the menu is Cantonese, with local Beijing favorites added on, including a delicious version of Beijing duck. Fresh seafood is a staple of Cantonese fare, and Summer Palace has fish tanks full of living specimens from which you can select your catch of the day. The menu is copious, but several surefire choices are the sautéed diced beef with black pepper sauce, the sweet and sour pork, and the deep-fried Mandarin fish with pine nuts. If you want to splurge, try the shark's fin. Traditional Chinese music performed by local musicians provides a serene background. The dim sum lunches aren't the cheapest in town ($10–$15), but the Cantonese dumplings are among the best in the capital. This is a restaurant in which you'll want to savor the evening.

In the China World Hotel, 2nd floor, 1 Jianguomenwai Dajie (at Third Ring Road East). ℂ **010/6505-2266**, ext. 34. Reservations recommended on weekends. Main courses 160–300RMB ($19–$36). AE, DC, MC, V. Daily 11:30am–2:30pm and 6–10:30pm.

New Tastes in Beijing

Three of the hottest dining trends in Beijing draw on culinary and cultural resources from near and far:

Bubble Tea (Zhenzhu Nai Cha), also known as Pearl Milk Tea, is a Taiwan import. The "pearls" in this tea are tapioca pearls; the "bubbles" are produced by a special shaking canister. Bubble teas are sometimes further enhanced with a variety of ingredients, from fruits to nuts and from sugar to coffee. Locals favor the sweeter versions of bubble tea; foreigners often favor the mild milk tea. Bubble tea houses have sprouted all over the capital. They're like coffee houses: You go there to drink tea, relax, and people-watch. A cup of this brew can run from 30¢ to $3 and up, depending on the place and the ingredients. A typical upscale bubble tea shop will have swinging chairs and benches suspended by ropes from the ceiling, false vines and trees, and floors of rock or stone as in a garden courtyard. Local snacks and pastries are also available. Two popular spots are **Fairyland (Xianzonglin)** at 69 Dongdan Bei Dajie, Dongcheng District, ✆ **010/6527-7896**, on the big shopping street east of Wangfujing (daily 10am–1am), and **Green Spring Tea (Lu Quan Cha)** at 233 Wangfujing Dajie, across from Sun Dong An Plaza, no phone (daily 8:30am–9pm).

Bagels (Beigu), that Jewish-American favorite, were brought to Beijing in 1996 by Taiwan-born Lejen Chen (known professionally as Mrs. Shanen), who grew up in New York City. That year, Chen and her husband opened a tiny factory. Even today, the factory is not a mass producer, cranking out no more than 2,000 bagels a day for a city of millions. But these bagels have made a big splash with the expatriate population, embassies, hotels, Western groceries, and adventurous locals. You can sample Beijing's best bagels (with lox and cream cheese, if you wish) at the factory outlet of **Mrs. Shanen's Bagels (Shan Tai Tai Beigu Mianbaofang)**, A3 Zhaojiu Lu, Jiuxianqiao, Chaoyang District, ✆ **010/6435-9561**. This neat little nook is open 8am–5pm (closing at 4pm on weekends).

Salsa, as in the South American food and dance craze, has swept the world; it entrenched itself in the capital of China at the beginning of the new millennium. The most upscale of these new lively bar and grills is **Salsa Cabana (Ka Ba Na Canting)**, Lufthansa Center/Kempinski Hotel, 50 Liangmaqiao, Chaoyang Northeast (✆ **010/6465-3388**, ext. 5700). Open from noon to 2am weekdays, until 3am on weekends, Salsa Cabana serves fairly pricey South American dishes and drinks, with live music and salsa dancing until the wee hours. Other new spots with a Latin beat in Beijing include the **Havana Cafe (Hawana Kafei)**, North Gate, Workers Stadium, Chaoyang (✆ **010/6586-6166**), open from 11am to 2am daily, a less upscale Cuban-style club fashioned out of the stadium ticket booth, with a lively patio in the back for summer dancing and rum-drinking (with signature mojito cocktails) and the classier Cuban-themed **Linda Habana Restaurant (Linda Hawana Canting)** in the Sheraton Great Wall Hotel, Chaoyang Northeast, ✆ **010/6590-5881**, open daily from 11am to 2am.

MODERATE

Häagen-Dazs ✪ AMERICAN   This purveyor of premium ice creams opened here in 1998, aimed at the upscale local market and foreigners looking for a special treat. The ice cream parlor is outfitted in bold Art-Deco splashes, with French doors and granite tabletops spread across two levels, all with a view of a tree-lined diplomatic avenue. There are Western cakes, pastries, and snacks; specialty coffees and fruity summer drinks (some with alcohol); and even frozen yogurts, but the focus is on fancy ice cream desserts. Although a single scoop of ice cream costs 25RMB ($3), the larger desserts are costly for Beijing. The "coffee break" concoction of layered ice creams and sauces in a tall fluted glass is priced at 68RMB ($8), but the idea here is to nurse a dessert well into the afternoon while reading the paper and people-watching (international diplomats, rich Beijing kids, health clubbers) in a suitably bright, upscale emporium.

21 Jianguomenwai Dajie, Room 196 (Beijing International Club complex, next. to St. Regis Hotel on Xiushi Lu). ✆ **010/6532-6661**. Items 50–100RMB ($6–$12). AE, DC, MC, V. Daily 11am–11pm.

Henry J. Bean's (Hengli Jiuba) ✪✪ AMERICAN   This bar and grill will satisfy anyone's desire for well-prepared American standards. The hamburger with all the trimmings is about the best you'll taste in China. The chicken Caesar salads and soups are delicious, too. The fajitas, nachos, and potato skins are all loaded with goodies. The polished wood decor resembles a spiffy family restaurant more than a bar, with kitschy American advertising posters and license plates on the walls, but there are enough TV monitors to give the feel of a sports bar. This is a good place to pull in at any hour to recharge one's American identity after it has been shredded a bit in China's capital.

In the China World Trade Center, west wing, 1 Jianguomenwai Dajie (near the Third Ring Road East). ✆ **010/6505-2266**, ext. 6334. Main courses 58–120RMB ($7–$14). AE, DC, MC, V. Sun–Thurs 11:30am–1:30am; Fri–Sat 11:30am–2:30am.

John Bull Pub (Zunbo Yinshi Jiuba) ✪ ENGLISH   This is a fully English pub in decor and cuisine, classy down to its dark wood panels. There's a billiards room, dartboard, full bar with bitters on draught, and tables on two floors in wood-paneled dining rooms. An American/British breakfast is served all day for about $8. This is the place to get Beijing's best banger and mash (75RMB, $9), steak and kidney pie (90RMB, $11), and fish and chips with Scottish cod (90RMB, $11). A large cheeseburger with chips and a pint of ale is 55RMB ($7). There are several Chinese dishes on the menu, as well as lasagna, grilled sirloin, and a fresh chef's salad. Food, service, and atmosphere are in the British mold, but not stuffy, making this a nice place in the diplomatic district to step out of Beijing and into London.

44 Guanghua Lu (1 block east of Second Ring Road East). ✆ **010/6532-5906**. Main courses 50–160RMB ($6–$19). Daily 9am–midnight; Fri–Sat until 1am.

Le Bistrot des Chateaux (Gubao Canting) FRENCH   It looks elegant and expensive from the outside—a series of cavernous archways front Beijing's main street, each a window for a private dining room with white tablecloths—but the prices are surprisingly inexpensive. In fact, the complete lunch specials are just 50 and 60RMB ($6 and $7), a fine price for decent Bordeaux cooking. You pay more for the poached egg and flan or the curly lettuce with lardon, but not as much as at comparable bistros in Beijing. This is an especially nice place to stop for a generous lunch while strolling or shopping the east end of Chang'an Avenue. The wine list, as you may imagine, is strong on Bordeaux, and there's an extremely long bar, said to be the capital's longest, in the main dining room (where live music starts at 9pm). A children's menu is available.

In the Jinglun Hotel, 3 Jianguomenwai Dajie. ℭ **010/6500-2266**, ext. 53. 50–130RMB ($6–$16). AE, DC, MC, V. Daily 11:30am–2pm and 6:30pm–2am.

Mexican Wave (Moxige Jiuba) MEXICAN

The fajitas and salads are good, but the burritos and enchiladas are unintentional fusion foods, as much Chinese as Mexican, and the pizzas are of the frozen variety. Still, Mexican Wave is an institution, one of the first private restaurants outside of the Beijing hotels that prepared something different at good prices for the expatriate crowd; it is still a favorite bar, with plenty of celebrating until midnight. Tacos and burritos cost about $7. The menu is in English, the waiters speak English, and about 80% of the patrons are foreign travelers. In the summer, it's worth a stop for lunch on the patio with a beer and a Mexican burger (topped with a runny egg; 40RMB, $5) or, in the evening, for the delicious margaritas. If you have a yen for authentic Mexican or Tex-Mex dinners, try the Texan Bar & Grill in the Holiday Inn Lido Hotel, but for a quick lunch or nighttime fun with bar food, catch the wave here.

Dongdaqiao Lu (1 block south of Guanghua Lu). ℭ **010/6506-3961**. Main courses 50–100RMB ($6–$12). MC, V. Daily 10am–midnight.

Sheng Restaurant (Sheng Fan Zhuang) ⋆ SICHUAN/CANTONESE

Formerly known as Ritan Park Restaurant, Sheng is almost a carbon copy of the Xihe Yaju restaurant at the opposite end of Ritan Park. Set in a pretty, Imperial courtyard, it tends to catch more tourists (and tour groups) and charge a bit more than Xihe Yaju. Still, it is a good choice for Sichuan dishes in an Imperial park setting when you want a break for lunch or a dinner with a garden atmosphere. The most fetching attraction, apart from the Imperial decor in the large dining hall inside, is the view from the courtyard of the park's pond and rockery. The menu has meat and tofu dishes, seasoned with a bit of red pepper (not too hot). The chili pepper chicken plate costs just 30RMB ($3.60), but the restaurant is best known for its noodles and Beijing dim sum. The Zhongcha duck is a bit greasy, but crispy enough to be authentic, and costs about 80RMB ($10) per person.

Ritan Park, southwest gate (off Guanghua Lu). ℭ **010/6500-5939** and 6500-5883. Main courses 30–150RMB ($3.60–$18). V. Daily 11am–2pm and 5–9pm.

Sampan Restaurant (Chuan Canting) ⋆ CANTONESE/DIM SUM

This is one of the best choices for Cantonese-style dim sum in Beijing, particularly on Sundays. The modern decor sparkles with Chinese touches: bamboo curtains, a model sampan boat as centerpiece, waitresses in costume serving from wicker market baskets. It's a place to have fun. Diners frequently leave their tables to watch the dishes and dim sum being prepared by the chefs at their cooking stations. The head chefs are from Hong Kong and know how to create fine standard Southern Chinese steamed pastries. Each little dumpling runs from 5 to 15RMB (under $2), but it's easy to pig out. Best treats: *char siu bao* (pork-filled dumplings), *shao mai* (seafood in tofu wrapper), and *har gau* (shrimp dumplings).

In the Gloria Plaza Hotel, 2 Jianguomenwai Dajie (on Second Ring Road, south of Jianguomen subway stop). ℭ **010/6515-8855**, ext. 3155. Meals 50–100RMB ($6–$10). Reservations accepted only for parties of 5 or more. AE, DC, MC, V. Daily 11:30am–2pm and 5:30–10pm; Sun dim sum brunch 10:30am–2pm.

Night Market Nosh

Street food can be tempting, especially in the midst of a long stroll through the capital's packed streets, but the hygiene of vendors and their carts and stands is unregulated, meaning that they are off-limits to visitors who are worried about the health consequences. Nevertheless, scores of foreigners can't resist sampling the culinary delights of the streets and alleyways.

Night markets, which are government-sanctioned but still far from safe on the stomach, line the streets after dark, stall by stall. The fried snacks and noodles are dirt cheap, costing from a few *mao* to a few *kwai* (2¢–24¢). There are popular night markets west of the Beijing Zoo (**Dongyuan Yeshi**) and near the north entrance to Beihai Park (called **Shichahai Yeshi,** the Lotus Bloom market), but the most celebrated snack strip of all is the **Donghuamen Night Market (Donghuamen Yeshi)** 🟊🟊, which runs up and down Donganmen Dajie between Wangfujing Dajie and the Forbidden City's east gate.

In an era when all of Beijing is undergoing fundamental cosmetic surgery, even the Donghuamen Night Market has had a face-lift. This food vendors' street has a history dating back to 1655; it was closed during the Cultural Revolution, beginning in 1966; reopened in 1984; then reorganized and rebuilt in 2000. The rebuilding included the installation of more than 80 stainless-steel carts, each with two gas burners and spiffy red-and-white striped awnings. It's almost hygienic. The menu below describes some of the street foods served here and at other night markets:

Baozi: Steamed buns with stuffings from cabbage to pork (under 1RMB, 12¢)

Huntun: Local version of wonton soup (3RMB, 36¢ a bowl)

Xianr bing: Tiny flat pancakes stuffed with vegetables and eggs (under 1RMB, 12¢)

Jing bing guozi: A large crepe the size of a pizza with egg, cilantro, and plum and hot sauces (about 2RMB, 24¢)

Miantiao: Noodles in various forms, fried, boiled, or in soup (1–5RMB, 12¢–60¢)

Youtiao: Deep-fried wands of dough, a breakfast favorite (under 1RMB, 12¢)

Yams: Yes, there are sweet potatoes in those oil drums (2RMB, 24¢).

Yang rou chuan: Lamb shish kebab roasted over an open flame (two for 1RMB, 12¢)

Sihexuan (Si He Xuan) 🟊🟊🟊 BEIJING   This is the best place in town to sample authentic Beijing specialties in a fine setting, amid red lanterns, long-spouted teapots, and photographs of old Beijing streets and pavilions. Many middle-class Beijingers come here looking for upscale versions of the authentic delicacies hawked at night markets. There's a fascinating open kitchen at the entrance where the dumplings and other treats are prepared. Trolley carts thread their way between tables; point at your choice or ask help (and translations) from the waiters. Start with a cold dish or two, such as celery with shreds of tofu. Then order some traditional snacks off the bilingual menu. The spring roll (12RMB, $1.40) is done in an almost Vietnamese style and the pan-fried *guan* sausage is good. The main courses come from the Sihexuan house specials. Try the *wu si tong* (five shredded buckets), which consist of a thin egg pancake filled with duck, pork, celery, ginger, scallions, and plum sauce. The noodles Shaanxi-style (18RMB, $2.20), served in a light soup, are bracing. The showstopper is the Spring Pie (35RMB, $4.20), a roll-your-own pancake with onion strips and pork. A plate of fruit wedges is a simple and traditional dessert.

In the Jinglun Hotel, 4th floor, 3 Jianguomenwai Dajie. ✆ 010/6500-2266, ext. 8116. Meals 50–120RMB ($6–$14). AE, MC, V. Daily 11:30am–2pm and 5:30pm–2am.

Xihe Yaju ★★ *Kids* SICHUAN/CANTONESE   Set in a beautifully reconstructed Qing-Dynasty mansion with red doors, carved beams, columns decorated in gold leaf, and a sweeping tile roof, Xihe Yaju is an ideal courtyard retreat for a reasonably priced selection of Chinese dishes. In the summer, diners can sit outside on wire patio chairs and small tables covered in blue-and-white tablecloths and enjoy the park setting. There are two separate menus (both in English), one with Sichuan dishes (which foreign travelers favor), one with Cantonese dishes (which locals favor). The Sichuan dishes can be quite spicy. The *gong bao jiding* (chicken with peanuts) is a great buy at 18RMB ($2.16) and not too hot. Other Sichuan dishes are in the same low price range. The *tie ban niu rou*, a sizzling plate of sliced beef with onions is tangy, but the *shiu zhurou pianr* (pork with peppers) is red hot. Cantonese choices range from steamed grass carp (starting at 28RMB, $3.36) to snake dishes at 120RMB ($14) and up. This is a very pleasant place for Chinese lunch or dinner, with an old Imperial park at the doorstep to walk off the feast.

Ritan Park, northeast gate (off Ritan Dong Lu). ✆ 010/6501-0385, 6594-1915. Meals 50–150RMB ($6–$18). No credit cards. Daily 11am–2pm and 5–10pm.

4 Chaoyang (Northeast)
VERY EXPENSIVE

LaxenOxen (Beiou Pafang) ★★ SCANDINAVIAN   Beijing's premier Scandinavian restaurant is an elegant affair, although the decor is not ornate nor is formal attire required. Nevertheless, this is a place worth dressing up for to enjoy an evening of fine dining and quiet celebration. The European wine list is extensive and the menu is strictly Scandinavian, headlined by Atlantic salmon, herring, lobster, and a superb blue-mussel soup. The grilled steaks are a delight, as are the open-faced sandwiches at lunchtime. Even the hearty, chewy breads have a European flavor. No less than three chefs from the northern reaches of Europe have found their way to these Beijing tables.

In the Radisson SAS Hotel, 2nd floor, 6A Beisanhuan Dong Lu (Third Ring Road East, near the China International Exhibition Centre). ✆ 010/6466-3388, ext. 3430. Main courses 150–250RMB ($18–$30). Reservations required for dinner. AE, DC, MC, V. Daily noon–2:30pm and 6–10:30pm.

Louisiana (Luyisi Anna) ★★★ AMERICAN/CAJUN   Frequently named the best American restaurant in Beijing, Louisiana has altered its purely Cajun and Creole menu to incorporate some of the recent trends in new American cuisine and Pacific Rim fusions. The result is still at the top of the Beijing scale for

Offbeat Eats

The southern regions of China are renowned for their bizarre edibles, but the northern Chinese of Beijing also cultivate tastes that would turn most Westerners green (and not with envy). From among the restaurants in the capital catering to whims for consumable fish heads, pig faces, and fried ants, perhaps you're brave enough to sample one of these:

Steaming Eyes. The **Tan Fish Head Hot Pot Restaurant (Tanyutou),** 32 Bei Zhong Dajie, Dongzhimennei Dajie, Dongcheng District (© 010/6401-8807) combines two of Beijing's culinary obsessions: the hot pot and the fish head. Fish heads, especially the eyes, are delicacies here, widely considered the most succulent part of the fish, and at this restaurant you can start from scratch to create your own gourmet treat, boiling an uncooked head, eyes intact, in your own pot of hot oil.

Bugs and Trees. The nostalgic cafe with the incredible name, **Recall Past Sufferings and Contemplate the Present Happiness Restaurant (Yiku Sitian Dazayuan Fanzhuang),** 17 Pichai Hutong, Xicheng District (1 mile west of the Forbidden City in an alley off Xidan Bei Dajie; © 010/6602-2640) is a courtyard restaurant with a sense of history. Its menu of the Bitter Past features tree leaves and fried black ants; its menu of the Sweet Present features chicken and mushrooms. Most items cost $1 to $3 and can be shared, making this an inexpensive meal for those who want to dwell in the past without abandoning the present.

Hog's Face. **Bazhulian (Jin San Yuan Pa Zhu Lian),** 2 Dongsanhuan Bei Lu (Third Ring Road Northeast), Chaoyang District (© 010/6467-6707) is a member of a chain of restaurants specializing in an underappreciated aspect of Northeast Chinese cuisine: the face of swine. The restaurant chain is headed by the man who invented a state-of-the-art process for cooking a hog's face to perfection. This dish is served to customers like Beijing duck, with slices of meat wrapped in pancakes. The highlight of this meal is when your order first comes to the table, a whole pig's face on a silver platter.

Western cuisine, whatever its label. The wine list, which remains the city's best, is quite extensive and includes a fine selection of cognacs (with a qualified sommelier at your service). Among the leading dishes to consider while bathing in the restaurant's elegance, soothed by its low lights and padded dining chairs, are the Creole salad (with tender prawns, smoked corn, tomato, grilled eggplant, and roasted garlic vinaigrette) and the Cajun gumbo (with seafood, sausage, and rice) for starters and the pan-seared filet of salmon with wild rice Napoleon and pecan-crabmeat sauce (168RMB, $20) or the "Dirty Pasta," orichiette with andouille sauce, tiger prawns, scallops, and calamari (148RMB, $18), for your entree. The smoked rack of lamb is a long-time favorite here, as are the grilled U.S. steaks (about $25). For dessert, try the pecan pie with vanilla ice cream or the Louisiana Mud Pie and admire the surroundings once again, particularly the wall posters of Louisiana and the statuettes of leading jazz, blues, and Dixie performers.

In the Beijing Hilton Hotel, 2nd floor, 1 Dongfang Lu (at Third Ring Road East). ℂ **010/6466-2288**, ext. 7420. Main courses 130–200RMB ($16–$24). Reservations recommended on weekends. AE, DC, MC, V. Daily 11:30am–2pm and 6–10pm.

EXPENSIVE

Ashanti Restaurant & Wine Bar (A Xian Di) ⍟ SPANISH Chef Carlos Chordi's native Spanish fare, heavy on tapas, has been influenced by where he lived (in Pamplona, Spain, near the French border) and by where he traveled (frequently in Portugal). The result is one of the most unusual dining choices in Beijing. The interior resembles a Mediterranean gallery, with white plaster walls and soft lights—in fact it *is* a gallery for avant-garde Chinese artists—but with Chinese furniture (late-Qing-dynasty designs). This is a dinner and late-night spot for many Beijing artists and musicians, as well as expatriates. Chef Chordi prepares tapas, raciones, and paella in the skillets himself, as much as possible. To get a complete taste, the stuffed mushrooms (*champiñones rellenos*) is a typical starter (12RMB, $1.44). A fine ración selection is the *gambas al ajillo* (65RMB, $8), boiled shrimp in garlic and olive oil, served with French bread. Paellas are brought straight to the table still in the skillet where large chunks of seafood, game (such as rabbit), and beans and peas top a layer of saffron rice. Paellas are priced at about $10 per portion. Flan and cheesecake are on the dessert menu. In the late evenings, this becomes a cigar and sangría kind of place, with the South African sangría at 35RMB ($4.20) per glass, 175RMB ($21) per pitcher.

168 Xin Zhong Jie (across from north entrance of Workers' Stadium). ℂ **010/6416-6231**. Main courses 65–130RMB ($8–$16). No credit cards. Daily 11:30am–2:30pm and 6pm–midnight.

Baikal (Beijia'er) ⍟ RUSSIAN More upscale than the aging Moscow Restaurant, with better food and more entertainment, Baikal gets its name from Russia's deepest lake, which is also the source of the restaurant's fish and sturgeon caviar, flown in weekly from Siberia. The chef, the food, and the atmosphere are all Russian, albeit a stagy version of authentic Russian, and a number of Russian diplomats are regulars here. The kebabs and the borsht (only 25RMB, $3) are excellent, and the fried and grilled fish are fair, but the real emphasis is on the lounge show. Strolling singers perform Russian folk songs during dinner, and come show time, 7:30 to 11:30pm nightly, the stage and sometimes portions of the vodka-fueled audience explode with Russian bands, dancers, and singers who alternately belt out Western favorites and more northern pop melodies. This is the closest thing in Beijing to a Western supper show. (Gourmands prefer the food at The Elephant, 17 Ritan Bei Lu, on the north side of Ritan Park, but I like Baikal—it's more fun.)

2 Beizhong Jie, Dongzhimennei Dajie (across the street from the Russian Embassy, near the Second Ring Road East). ℂ **010/6405-2380** or 010/6405-4902. Reservations recommended on weekends. Main courses 50–150RMB ($6–$18). V. Daily 11am–midnight.

Berena's Bistro (Bo Rui Na) ⍟⍟⍟ SICHUAN Long a favorite of the foreign community in Beijing, Berena's serves an extensive array of Sichuan dishes in a relaxed, romantic atmosphere. The lights are low, almost too low, and the marble floors are also dark, but there's enough candlelight to make out the colorful surroundings: Chinese and Western posters tacked to the walls, orange tablecloths, red napkins, and attentive waiters dressed in green. Most items on the menu are under $10. The Sichuan food is not as hot and spicy as in Sichuan, which pleases the mostly foreign crowd. The sweet and sour soup (20RMB, $2.40) is too vinegary, but full of good red chilies. The chicken with almonds (40RMB, $4.80) is a tasty, safe choice, and the *doufu* (tofu) dishes are also good. The *gong bao* chicken comes on a sizzling plate, and the sweet and sour pork is among the most popular dishes here, as is the Chengdu roast duck (80RMB, $10 per person), which some prefer to the greasy Beijing duck. One of Beijing's top Sichuan restaurants, with high standards in preparation and service, Berena's knows how to please foreign travelers looking for a good Chinese meal at a moderate price.

6 Gongrentiyuchang Dong Lu (across from east entrance of Workers' Stadium). ℂ 010/6592-2628. Main courses 60–120RMB ($7–$14). AE, MC, V. Daily 11:30am–2pm and 5–11:30pm.

Big Easy (Kuailezhan) ★★ AMERICAN/CAJUN

This upscale restaurant and bar took Beijing by storm, and it's easy to see why. Big Easy's depiction of Bourbon Street is posh through and thorough, and the Creole and Cajun cuisine is first rate. Unlike Louisiana, the superb American and mildly Cajun restaurant in the Hilton Hotel, Big Easy is relaxed and rollicking. From the red beans to the Bananas Foster to the late-night Hurricane cocktails and live blues and jazz, it has become the place to be for a weekend splash (or the all-day happy hour on Sun). The unexpected death of Big Easy's founder in January 2001, left the direction of his restaurant in some doubt, but it seems to be carrying on in style.

Chaoyang Park (south gate, at Jintai Lu intersection). ℂ 010/6508-6776. 100–300RMB ($12–$36). AE, DC, MC, V. Sun–Thurs 5pm–2am; Fri–Sat 5pm–3am.

Borom Piman (Lidou Tai) ★★ THAI

Beijing's first major Thai restaurant, Borom Thai is still one of the best in the capital. Part of the reason is the terrific cuisine, and part is the traditional and elegant setting—silk cushions, wood paneling, and a section of recessed-in-the-floor tables (with upright chairs). A third ingredient is the prompt and unobtrusive service. The Borom Piman is known by locals for its economical set lunches (88RMB, $11) and set dinners, although the a la carte menu is extensive. Typical, popular dishes include spring prawn soup and curry chicken. For a celebration or fine dinner, Borom Piman does not disappoint.

In the Holiday Inn Lido, 2nd floor, Jichang Lu, Jiangtai Lu (east side of Airport Expwy.). ℂ 010/6437-6688, ext. 2899. Reservations recommended on weekends. Main courses 80–160RMB ($10–$19). AE, DC, MC, V. Daily 11am–2pm and 5–10pm.

Lao Shanghai ★ SHANGHAI

Shanghai restaurants were all the rage in Beijing a few years ago, and among the hotels that introduced new venues, the Holiday Inn Lido presented the best new entry. The dining room is upscale, with crystal and silver settings and photographs of old Shanghai on the walls, but the feeling is quite relaxed. This restaurant is a cooperative effort with the original Lao Shanghai (established in old Shanghai in 1875) and the cooks know how to prepare light, flavorful standards. The dishes are beautifully presented with large portions of bamboo shoots and cucumbers setting off the fish and shellfish. The white eel and river shrimp are fresh. An excellent starter is the clear soup with shredded pork, chicken, and bamboo shoots. The showstopper is the liquefied hairy crab, extremely flavorful here. This is a fine place for a long, quiet evening, with a good European wine list. In the evenings, a three-piece jazz band recalls colonial days.

In the Holiday Inn Lido, 2nd floor, Jichang Road, Jiangtai Road (east side of Airport Expwy.) ℂ 010/6437-6688, ext. 1548. Reservations recommended on weekends. Main courses 80–150RMB ($10–$18). AE, DC, MC, V. Daily 11:30am–2pm and 6–10pm.

Metro Cafe (Mei Te Rou) ★★ ITALIAN   Within a relaxed, modern decor
of subdued light and soft music, the Metro serves up some of the finest fresh pasta dinners in town. You can create your own pasta and sauce combinations from the English-language menu, which includes freshly made fettuccine, tortellini, and ravioli. The spinach ravioli (100RMB, $12) is served in large, delicious portions, and the marble cheesecake is a good choice for dessert. The kitchen closes for dinner at about 10pm, when the Metro becomes a lively bar. In the summers, the outdoor courtyard seating is usually jammed with expats.

5 Gongrentiyuchang Xi Lu (across from west entrance of Workers' Stadium). ℂ 010/6552-7828. Main courses 80–160RMB ($10–$20). AE, MC, V. Mon–Fri 11:30am–2pm and 5:30–10pm; Sat–Sun 11:30am–10pm.

Mongolian Gher ★★ MONGOLIAN   The setting and the Mongolian food
here make for quite an extraordinary evening, one that is fully worth the extra journey back and forth from the airport. This is easily the best tent food—served in a traditional round fur tent, or *yurt* (*gher* in Mongolian)—in Beijing. These yurts, however, are far from basic itinerant affairs; they're richly carpeted and decorated in northern and Muslim patterns. Dinner becomes an adventurous affair, but also an elegant one. The gher is spacious enough for exceptional after-dinner performances by Mongolian dancers in costume. Two Mongolian cooks do all the kitchen labors, specializing in barbecues in the summer and Mongolian hot pots in the winter, but you can try either here, whatever the season. The two set menus vary but slightly, both consisting of four starters, five hot dishes, and dessert.

In the Sino-Swiss Hotel, Xiao Tianzhu Village, Shunyi (near the Beijing International Capital Airport). ℂ 010/6456-5588, ext. 1409. Reservations required. Set dinners 158RMB and 188RMB ($19 and $23). AE, DC, MC, V. Daily 6–11pm.

Moon Shanghai (Ye Shanghai) ★ SHANGHAI   A bit more modestly
priced than Shanghai Cuisine (see below) and the current favorite of Beijing's foreign community for Shanghai dishes, Moon Shanghai is located in a former jazz club. Here, too, the staff dresses up to evoke the notorious days of 1930s Shanghai, and the decor of polished dark woods underscores the nostalgia. Many of the ingredients are flown in from Shanghai, making any dish with vegetables and crab worth ordering. The English-language menu also features pictures of the dishes. The third floor is given over to karaoke, snacks, and drinks in the evening, so the place does have a noisy, slightly notorious feel. The Shanghai food itself is good and quite satisfying here, but it is better at Shanghai Cuisine in the Kunlun Hotel and Lao Shanghai in the Holiday Inn Lido. Moon Shanghai comes out ahead, however, on price and atmosphere.

4 Gongrentiyuchang Bei Lu (down the alley on the west side of Pacific Century Plaza). ℂ 010/6506-9988, ext. 203. Main courses 80–160RMB ($10–$19). AE, MC, V. Daily 11am–2pm and 5–10pm.

Paulaner Brauhaus (Pulana Pijiu Fang) ★ GERMAN   This is the best
brew house in town, with the beer brewed right here in the tanks according to the pure "Paulaner" methods of Germany; the Paulaner also serves some of the finest German cuisine. The tile floors, black wood trim, and the country tables

are all polished to a shine (even the bathrooms are first rate). The atmosphere is upscale, but casual and warm. Crispy fresh salad plates start at 25RMB ($3). The breads, in the northern European tradition, are superb. If you like schnitzels, you've found their home in Beijing. This is a fine stop for lunch and one of the cheapest (but most bracing) choices on the lunch menu is the country bacon potatoes with wild mushrooms (plenty of them) and a fried egg with melted cheese (75RMB, $9). Full German dinners are also available. Sausage plates with sauerkraut and mashed potatoes are 110 to 125RMB ($13–$15) per person (minimum two persons). Later in the evening, German performers dance and sing (Tues–Sun). The homemade beers are expensive, but quite tasty.

In the Kempinski Hotel (south side of Youyi Center), 50 Liangmaqiao (at Third Ring Road East). ℂ 010/6465-3388, ext. 5732. Main courses 95–220RMB ($11–$26). AE, DC, MC, V. Daily 11am–1am.

Red Basil (Zitian Jiao) ☆☆ THAI

Opened in 1996 by a Thai businessman and employing chefs from his native land, Red Basil is a stylish Asian restaurant noted for efficient service, real Thai dishes, and modern decor. The floors are a rich, polished wood, and mirrors stretch to the ceilings; there's mezzanine dining as well. The menu has many of the Thai classics, from *phad thai* (rice noodles in peanut sauce) to a variety of curries, fine soups, beef salads, shrimp cakes (very tasty), and delicate fish filets. Most dishes are in the $5 to $8 range—the fine Yellow Curry with chicken and potato, for example, is 60RMB ($7)—but it's easy to spend as much here as at Beijing's other expensive Thai restaurant, Borom Piman. The *tom yum koong soup* (with coconut milk) draws many raves. The food is hotly spiced, as it should be, but guests can request the cook to hold back on the fiery chilies. This is a pleasant, quite upscale spot in which to savor authentic Thai cooking.

Building 8, Nanxiao Jie, (south side of Third Ring Road North, opposite Jing Xin Plaza; northwest of Hilton Hotel). ℂ 010/6460-2339, ext. 44. Reservations required. Main courses 50–140RMB ($6–$17). AE, MC, V. Daily 11:30am–2pm and 5:30–10pm.

Shanghai Cuisine (Shanghai Canting) ☆ SHANGHAI

The Kunlun Hotel's Shanghai restaurant offers the most extensive and authentic Shanghai dishes in Beijing, not surprising since the hotel's management group is based in Shanghai. As a result, the chefs are not only Shanghai natives, but deeply experienced with preparing the dishes in a large setting. To enhance that setting within a great, rather garishly decorated hall, the wait staff is outfitted in 1930s Old Shanghai costumes. The staff is knowledgeable about the food it is serving, but service itself can be abrupt. The Wuxi spareribs are among a raft of excellent dishes, as are the braised pork patties with oyster sauce and the shredded eel. The flavors are light and delicate, the goose liver is rich, and the poached trout has become a signature dish, but watch out for the chili-laden entrees—they are quite hot.

In the Kunlun Hotel, 2 Xinyuan Nan Lu (west side of Third Ring Road East). ℂ 010/6500-3388, ext. 5394. Main courses 100–200RMB ($12–$24). AE, MC, V. Daily 11:30am–2:30pm and 5:30–9:30pm.

Texan Bar & Grill (Dekesasi Bafang) ☆ *Kids* MEXICAN

Despite its over-the-top Mexican decor (silly, tacky, but actually quite typical of the real Tex-Mex family eateries it emulates), the Texan delivers the best Mexican-American fare in Beijing. The Chinese staff in cowboy gear promenade from the grill to the tables toting genuine American steaks (rib-eye and T-bone) and solid Australian beef—never mind that neither has a whit to do with Mexico. What does come from Mexico are the sizzling fajitas (80RMB, $10), enchiladas, quesadillas

(Kids) Family-Friendly Restaurants

Almost any Beijing eatery is used to serving children, but for foreign families there are several (excluding the hundreds of familiar fast-food outlets) that stand out:

Texan Bar & Grill ♠ *(see p. 103).* Chinese cowboys and cowgirls serve up the best Tex-Mex in town to tourists and residents alike in a hotel complex (Holiday Inn Lido) where Western children will feel right at home.

Xihe Yaju *(see p. 98).* This Cantonese courtyard restaurant is located in a beautiful park and even has *ayis* (babysitting aunties) on hand to mind younger children while dining outside.

Hard Rock Cafe (near the Sheraton Great Wall Hotel on the Third Ring Road, 8 Dongsanhuan Bei Lu; ℃ 010/6590-6688, ext. 2571). The music, decor, and food (American hamburgers, french fries, and fajitas) should keep any Western teenager happy. This is just what Hard Rock Cafes look like the world over (and the fast food is quite good). Open daily from 11:30am to 1am, 100RMB ($12) cover charge after 10pm.

Holiday Inn Lido ♠♠ (Jichang Lu, Jiangtai Lu, Chaoyang District; ℃ 010/6437-6688, ext. 1971). This restaurant puts on a full international Sunday champagne buffet from 11:30am to 3pm with live entertainment on stage. This is a long-standing favorite of families, priced at 150RMB ($18); children under 10 eat free. This is the brunch to go for if you're in Beijing, with or without kids.

Cafe California (in the lobby of the Harbour Plaza Hotel, 8 Jiang Tai Lu, northeast Beijing; ℃ 010/6436-2288). This eatery has an inexpensive Sunday brunch (about $12 adults, $6 kids) from 11am to 2:30pm that is geared to children with balloons, cartoon figures, and entertainers.

(68RMB, $8), tacos, and margaritas, all rated passable to good—just don't expect the flare and spice of true Mexican cuisine. Worth a sombrero dance is the salad bar, a self-serve affair located in the chuck wagon.

In the Holiday Inn Lido, Jichang Lu, Jiangtai Lu (east side of Airport Expwy.). ℃ 010/6437-6688, ext. 1849. Main courses 70–150RMB ($8–$18). AE, DC, MC, V. Daily 11:30am–2pm and 5:30–10pm.

MODERATE

Kebab Kafe (Lianyi) ♠♠ GERMAN Not just another Sanlitun bar with a smattering of Western-style food, the Kebab is a serious restaurant serving some of the best German and Continental cuisine in Beijing, and it's one of the best cafes in this part of the city. The Chinese chef spent 20 years in Europe, training much of the time in German cooking, and the results show, from the humble kebabs that give the place its name (these are sandwich-style kebabs) to the salmon steak with dill cream. All 34 main courses on the menu come with fresh salads, including the chicken breast Cordon Bleu and Hungarian beef goulash. Desserts include Italian ice cream, lemon tart, and apple strudel with vanilla sauce. Lunchtime favorites, such as the vegetarian pizza, ratatouille, and spaghetti with pesto, are under $8. In the winter, the Kebab comes up with excellent Swiss cheese fondues and raclettes. The interior is that of a run-down bistro, seating about 60, with red cloths on the tables and oil paintings (for sale) on the wall. In the summer, the large patio opening on Sanlitun fills with Europeans and other Westerners eating sandwiches and pastries and drinking imported German beers.

On Sanlitun Bei Lu, west side. ℂ 010/6415-5812. Main courses 40–170RMB ($5–$20). AE, MC, V. Daily 8:30am–11pm.

Omar Khayyam (Weimeijia Yindu Canting) INDIAN

Slightly cheaper than Beijing's best Indian restaurant (Shamiana in the Holiday Inn Downtown, see later in this chapter) and boasting excellent dishes of its own, Omar Khayyam is a very popular lunch and dinner spot for foreigners living and working in the diplomatic district north of Chang'an Avenue east. Dishes here are mildly spiced, and the portions are adequate, but not heaped on. There are scores of vegetarian choices here, and the best reviews go to the *dahl* (with spinach, lentils, and cheese). The chicken, lamb, and fish dishes are roasted tandoori-style (over hot charcoals). An efficient, congenial staff and weekend set menu specials keep this one of Beijing's most popular and reliable Indian restaurants

Asia Pacific Building, 8 Yabao Lu (1 block north of Guanghua Lu, east of Second Ring Road). ℂ 010/6513-9988, ext. 20188. Reservations recommended on weekends. 70–100RMB ($8–$12). AE, MC, V. Daily 11:30am–2pm and 6–10pm.

San Si Lang (Sansilang) ⭐ *Finds* JAPANESE

The original location of this favorite of the international community—lauded for inexpensive and delicious Japanese food—couldn't withstand the wrath of the wrecking ball early in 2001, but San Si Lang's second location is still the place to go for inexpensive sushi and tempura. A multilingual, illustrated menu boasts prices several times lower than those in the leading Japanese restaurants in Beijing's hotels. The sushi bar has a variety of items, including an excellent shrimp sushi on sticky rice. The tuna or cucumber rolls, six to a plate, are just 15RMB (less than $2), the same price as the soba (cold noodles). At the "pricier" end are the tempura prawns (60RMB, $7), still a relative bargain. Sashimi is also a specialty here. With plenty of reasonably priced dishes to try, warm sake, and even steamed cloths for hands and face, this is Beijing's best economy Japanese restaurant, a good late lunch stop in graceful surroundings off the Third Ring Road East.

Tuanjiehu Park (north of the park's west gate). ℂ 010/6506-9625. 60–100RMB ($7–$12). AE, MC, V. Daily 11am–11pm.

Serve the People (Wei Renmin Fuwu) ⭐ *Finds* THAI

Beijing's newest entry in the growing field of good Thai restaurants, this cafe on the crowded Sanlitun bar strip is winning customers with its sparkling white-walled, wooden-floored interior, friendly waiters, and a moderately priced menu of well-prepared Thai favorites. Those favorites include a salad with rice noodles and seafood, a fish salad with mango, stir-fried vegetables with shrimp sauce, and a stewed roast duck with pineapple. This is a comfortable bistro with finely prepared, not overly spiced (hot) dishes.

Sanlitun Bar Street North (in an east-running alley). ℂ 010/6415-3242. Meals 50–100RMB ($6–$12). No credit cards. Daily 11am–11pm.

T.G.I. Fridays (Xingqiwu Canting) AMERICAN

This American chain does a fairly authentic imitation of American food, service, and atmosphere in Beijing, with a menu that is quite close to the original, too. In addition to its New Orleans burgers, fries, and stuffed potato skins, Beijing's T.G.I. Fridays branch has spicy Thai noodles, seafood pastas, and excellent fajitas. The salads are generous and fresh and can be a lunch in themselves at about $6. The interior is gaudy and dazzling. Lately it has become a favorite of younger Beijingers. It's also an excellent choice for foreign family meals with a Chinese touch.

Huapeng Dasha, 19 Dongsanhuan Bei Lu (west side of Third Ring Road East). ☎ **010/6597-5037** or 010/6597-5314. 50–100RMB ($6–$12). AE, MC, V. Daily 11:30am–11pm.

Trattoria La Gondola (Wei Ni Si) ITALIAN This bright, open, upscale country-style Italian restaurant is both elegant and casual. It can be the scene of a fine, romantic dinner, complete with musical performers, or a relaxing (and filling) lunch. Not as formal or expensive as some of its hotel-based competition (Danieli's, Roma Ristorante), Trattoria La Gondola offers excellent cuisine, casual but modern decor, and moderate prices. At lunch, when the prices are even lower, you can choose your own pasta and sauce for 68RMB ($8), try a large pizza for 75RMB ($9), and select from among the antipastos, salads, and soups.

In the Kempinski Hotel, 50 Liangmaqiao Lu (You Yi Shopping Center). ☎ **010/6465-3388**, ext. 5707. 70–160RMB ($8–$19). AE, DC, MC, V. Daily 11:30am–2:30pm and 5:30–11pm.

INEXPENSIVE

Bella's (Beila) AMERICAN This popular coffee and sandwich shop has four locations, the best being on the Sanlitun bar street. It's basically a deli, with fresh baked muffins, sandwiches, salads, and coffees—a casual place to hang out that has become an institution among Beijing's expats and independent travelers.

44 Sanlitun Bei Jie. ☎ **010/6416-8929**. 25RMB–60RMB ($3–$7). No credit cards. 7:30am–10pm. Other locations: behind Silk Alley, at Kylin Plaza on Gongrentiyuchang Bei Lu, and near the west gate of Chaoyang Park.

Gold Cat Jiaozi City (Jin Mao Jiaozi Cheng) BEIJING For an economical introduction to Beijing's famous *jiaozi* (steamed, filled dumplings), try this courtyard emporium, guarded by two stone lions. This is a no-frills restaurant dedicated to churning out 20 to 40 assorted varieties of the city's pastries, stuffed with pork, seafood, or vegetables in season. Summertime sees dining in the open courtyard, the best time and the best seating (inside seating is serviceable but stark). My favorite *jiaozi* is the standard *zhurou jiucai* (a steamed bun stuffed with shreds of pork and local chives) that families all over Northern China spend hours making at home together. They are juicy and strongly flavored, and locals can eat them by the dozens. In fact, the Gold Cat *jiaozi* come four or five to a plate, each plate costing just 50¢ or so. For an authentic flavor of Beijing, this is the place for an adventurous lunch break. There is an English menu that helps narrow the choices. Avoid the late evenings and wee hours, when Gold Cat becomes a noisy karaoke palace.

Tuanjiehu Park, East Gate (on the Third Ring Road East). ☎ **010/8598-5011**. A full meal of snacks 40–100RMB ($4.80–$12). AE, MC, V. Daily 24 hr.

5 Xuanwu (Southwest) & Chongwen (Southeast)

EXPENSIVE

Jinyang Fanzhuang SHANXI (NORTHERN CHINESE) Situated in the courtyard estate of Imperial scholar Ji Xiaolan, who lived here 2 centuries ago during the reign of the great Qing Emperor Qianlong, the Jinyang Restaurant broadcasts an ideal, if fading, image of Old Cathay. The Jinyang actually opened its doors in this scholar's house a bit more recently, in 1956, but that makes it old in the new China. The food here is that of the rough, tough north of China, of hardscrabble Shanxi Province, where long noodles in vinegar (*dao xiao mian*) are the staple. Another regional noodle found here is known as *mao er duo* (cat's ear noodle) and has the shape and texture to go with vegetables and vinegary meats. The twice-fried pork with black fungus mushroom and vinegar (*guo you rou*) is yet another standard, offered here as an appetizer. Perhaps the most popular Shanxi dish served here is the *xiang suya*, the crispy duck that's less greasy than the Beijing duck, priced at 80RMB ($10) per person.

241 Zhushikou Xi Dajie, Xuanwu District (north side of the street, 1 block east of Nanxinhua Jie, southwest of Tiananmen Square). *C* 010/6303-1669. Main courses 60–120RMB ($7–$14). No credit cards. Daily 11am–2pm and 5–8:30pm.

Quanjude Kaoyadian ✦✦ BEIJING DUCK   The first Quanjude roast duck restaurant opened its doors during the Qing Dynasty in 1864 and has been the foremost purveyor of crispy duck ever since. Quanjude is now a local chain. This particular restaurant is the most elegant (and expensive) and it enjoys a reputation as the best Beijing duck restaurant in the world. It may very well be, for outside of the capital there are few restaurants that are so specialized. The interiors of this large restaurant, which includes dining rooms and halls on several floors, are uniformly Imperial, ornate, garish, and somewhat worn (as all truly royal halls are). This spot is great for groups—reserve a private room if possible. Think of it as a small, relaxed banquet, one that goes to the heart of Beijing cuisine.

32 Qianmen Dajie, Chongwen District (a few blocks straight south of Tiananmen Square, east side). *C* 010/6511-2418. Reservations required. Main courses 110–200RMB ($13–$24). AE, MC, V. Daily 10:30am–1:30pm and 4:30–8:30pm.

MODERATE

Gongdelin ✦ VEGETARIAN   Until Green Tian Shi Restaurant came along (see review earlier in this chapter), Gongdelin was by far Beijing's best vegetarian eatery. It still has the most extensive menu, and some of its dishes remain at the top. Inside, it's institutional and run-down, but the staff is efficient. The second floor dining room is a bit more inviting. The central notion in Chinese vegetarian cooking is to create dishes that look, taste, and smell like what they are presumed to be replacing in the animal world: the flesh of the duck, chicken, fish, or pig so favored by most Chinese. Gongdelin, for example, has a "jellyfish" on its menu, but the *huase zijin* (many-colored gems) is better, with its use of almonds, tofu, and various vegetables to suggest a duck-based appetizer. The *su yazi* resembles and even tastes vaguely like Beijing duck. Some of the dishes merely have the appearance of meat dishes, but tastes all their own. Simple vegetable dishes here are superb. If you can get together six or more diners, consider arranging a small banquet (naming a price per person, usually about 100RMB, $12 each). Gongdelin is worth trying even if you're not a vegetarian.

158 Qianmen Nan Dajie, Chongwen District (directly south of Tiananmen Square, 2 blocks south of Zhushikuo Ave.). *C* 010/6511-2542. Main courses 50–120RMB ($6–$14). AE, MC, V. Daily 11:30am–2:30pm and 5:30–9pm.

Tips How to Eat Beijing Duck

Beijing duck is roasted in such a way that the skin is terribly crispy and the meat is quite juicy. And although some would describe it as fat and oily, true Beijing duck is supposed to be on the greasy side. The duck will be carved at your table. Smear a thin pancake with plum sauce, sprinkle it with spring onion shreds, add bits of the carved duck, then roll up the whole package, and eat it with your hands.

Fast-Food Invaders

One of the last of the world's major capitals to experience the phenomenon, Beijing is now in the throes of a full-scale "Mac-Attack," with American fast-food chains slithering across this ancient Chinese city like a dragon run amok in french fries and milk shakes. At last count, there were more than 55 McDonald's restaurants in Beijing alone, one every few blocks or so in the main shopping districts and some setting up shop where few foreign tourists ever venture. These McDonald's are fairly faithful copies of the American model, with prices about on par and picture menus for non-Chinese speakers. Beijing yuppies, well-to-do teens, middle-class families, and anyone else able to scrape together the money for a truly American experience are slowly making burgers as popular as Beijing's own steamed dumplings.

In addition to scores of **McDonald's** (near the Friendship Store, in most shopping plazas, and almost everywhere), you can find **A&W** (across from the Lufthansa Centre), **Baskin-Robbins** (at the Friendship Store, one of five outlets), **Häagen-Dazs** (*see p. 95*), **Dairy Queen** (with all the ice cream flavors), **Dominos** (Third Ring Road West), **Dunkin' Donuts** (at least seven outlets, including 219 Wangfujing Dajie), **KFC** (over 20 of the Colonel's favorites, including the world's largest franchise at the south end of Tiananmen Square), **Pizza Hut** (eight huts and counting, including two on Jianguomenwai Dajie), and **Subway** (at least four branches now, with one just west of the China World Hotel). This list just scratches the surface of the invasion and doesn't include slightly more restaurant-like troops, such as **Kenny Rogers Roasters,** already with three locations, or coffee cafes, such as **Starbucks.**

Ordering by pointing is usually no problem for foreigners in a foreign fast-food emporium in Beijing, but here are the essential translations:

Pizza	*Bisa bing*
Bagel	*Beigu*
Hamburger	*Han bao-bao*
French fries	*Shu Tiao*
Coffee	*Kafei*
Sprite	*Xuebi*
Coca-Cola	*Kekou-Kele*
Diet cola	*Jianyi kele*
McDonald's	*MaiDanglao*
Big Mac	*Juwuba*
McChicken	*Maixiang Ji*
Do you take credit cards?	*Ni shuo xinyongka ma?*

Quanjude Hepingmen BEIJING DUCK A more modern (still rather garish) member of the venerable Quanjude roast duck restaurant chain, the Hepingmen branch serves the same side dishes and roasted duck as the more elegant Kaoyadian outlet (see above), but at a lower price. The Hepingmen looks like a big hotel, marble lobby and all, with seven floors and over 40 dining rooms, all pretty much dedicated to duck. It can handle 2,000 diners at a time without blinking. The side dishes are kept in the freezer section up front, supermarket style, for your perusal before ordering, but the main concern here is the duck. For two to three diners, order one duck, but for four or five diners, split two ducks. Each roasted duck costs 180RMB ($21.60). The duck will be expertly carved at your table, the pieces to be incorporated as the final ingredient in the pancake you're about to roll. (Before filling the pancake with duck meat, you will coat it with plum sauce and sprinkle it with onion slices.) This is one of the few big Chinese dishes where chopsticks do not come into play. What this bright, uninspired cavern of a roast duck restaurant lacks in charm, it really makes up for with its main course.

14 Qianmen Xi Dajie, Xuanwu District (southeast corner at the intersection with Nanxinhua Jie, within sight of the Hepingmen subway station). (✆ 010/6301-8833. Main courses 75–120RMB ($9–$14). AE, MC, V. Daily 10:30am–1:30pm and 4:30–8:30pm.

INEXPENSIVE

Jinghua Shiyuan BEIJING DIM SUM   The ambience is that of old Beijing, the setting is an ornate courtyard compound on the shores of Longtan Lake, and the food is the simple snack food (*xiao chi*) that is native to the capital and North China, including *jiaozi*, the steamed dumpling with a meat or vegetable filling. In Beijing's hutongs, the most common snack consists of a deep-fried breadstick (*you tiao*) and soy milk (*dou jiang*), which Jinghua provides in a traditional (and more hygienic) setting. Jinghua is known for its basic little cakes (*bing*), filled with meat or tofu (*doufu*), and its bean soup (*dou zhi*) made from fermented ming berries. Most foreigners stick with the *jiaozi* and tea, enjoy the lake views in summer from the outdoor round wooden tables and benches, and watch the tea ceremonies performed at Jinghua's own teahouse. Tea is synonymous with this restaurant. Jinghua's shop sign is a 9-foot-tall dragon-mouthed teapot on a pedestal, cocked to pour into an enormous tea bowl, and it is the largest copper teapot in the world.

8 Longtan Lu, Chongwen District (at Big Teapot sign beside the north entrance to the Beijing Amusement Park). (✆ 010/6711-5331. Snacks 10–30RMB ($1.20–$3.60). No credit cards. Daily 8am–7pm.

6 Xicheng (West) & Haidian (Northwest)

VERY EXPENSIVE

Li Family Restaurant (Li Jia Cai) ★★ *Overrated* IMPERIAL BEIJING Located in a traditional hutong courtyard complex near the historic Back Lakes, the Li Family Restaurant, founded by Ms. Li Li, has taken Beijing by storm. Here you can enjoy the very recipes that were created for the Qing Dynasty Empress Dowager herself during the twilight of the Forbidden City. Ms. Li Li's great grandfather commanded the Palace Guard before the fall of the last dynasty, and he was able to walk away with a number of the royal recipes. Li Family is one of the most difficult restaurants to book in Beijing, with the waiting list sometimes stretching 3 weeks. It is a great experience, but don't expect an "Imperial" evening. Imperial cuisine is plain, rustic stuff, with interesting but hardly delicate flavors. Order by set menus ranging from 200 to 560RMB ($24–$67). The 300RMB ($36) version, for example, consists of nine appetizers and four main courses (sweet and sour ribs, lobster on a broken shell, fluffy shrimp balls on shredded rape seed leaves, and Beijing duck). The Beijing duck is not oily, but not crispy either, with a dull taste. Although the Li Family Restaurant receives little but unqualified raves from all quarters and is surely a top Beijing experience, you may come away wondering what the fuss was about, with its high prices, plain decor, and rough cuisine. Nevertheless, it is wildly successful, and Ms. Li Li long ago moved to Australia to open another branch, with plans in the works to export the concept worldwide.

11 Yangfang Hutong, Deshengmennei Dajie, Xicheng District (south of Xihai and Houhai lakes). 𝄞 010/6618-0107. Reservations required. Set menus 200, 300, 360, 480, and 560RMB ($24–$67). No credit cards. Daily 6–10pm.

Nishimura (Xicun) 𝄞𝄞 JAPANESE Beijing's first *robatayaki* (grill) opened in May 1998 and has been turning out delectable fare ever since. This clean, spacious restaurant consists of a standard dining room, two tatami mat rooms, a takeout counter, a large and small teppanyaki grill, and the long robatayaki grill. Go for the robatayaki, where the chef grills whatever you point out. There are two Japanese chefs here and a manager also from Japan, with everyone trained at one of the many Nishimura restaurants overseas. The food is presented on a show-grill, then slow cooked on the spot and served by the chef with large wooden paddles. A typical robatayaki meal might consist of miso soup, chicken, a bacon roll with asparagus, a bit of potato with butter, and a giant prawn. The prawn is heavenly and the potato is superb, simply prepared and delectably sweetened. Depending on your selections, this can serve as a modestly priced lunch or a very expensive and satisfying dinner.

In the Shangri-La Beijing Hotel, 2nd floor, 29 Zizhuyuan Lu, Haidian District (northwest corner of the Third Ring Road). 𝄞 010/6841-2211, ext. 6719. Main courses 90–350RMB ($11–$42). AE, DC, MC, V. Daily 11:30am–2:30pm and 6–10pm.

EXPENSIVE

Fangshan Restaurant (Fangshan Fandian) 𝄞𝄞𝄞 IMPERIAL Beijing's first Imperial restaurant, opened before the Revolution (1949), Fangshan serves dishes dating from the Qing Dynasty's reign in the Forbidden City. The setting couldn't be more appropriate: a courthouse mansion looking out on the long covered corridor along the northern shores of an Imperial pleasure park, a stone's throw from an old temple and its white *dagoba*. The staff is in Forbidden City dress, and the dining room is decorated in red, gold, and yellow with Imperial motifs and wooden carvings. This is a bit of tourist trap, but the set lunches, at 100RMB ($12) and 150 RMB ($18), give a good sampling of what's meant by Imperial cuisine. Small steamed pastries, peas from the wok, and roast duck and chicken are the standard fare of the hearty, plain food of North China. More flavorful are the bean-curd cakes, the spicy squid soup, and the duck baked in a walnut batter. One of the more expensive royal treats is the steamed lake fish (*tian xiang bao yu*), a challenge for the chopsticks at 250RMB ($30). This is a prime stop for tourists looking for a taste of China's past glories, which Fangshan does deliver.

1 Wenjing Jie, inside Beihai Park, north shore of Beihai Island, Xicheng District. 𝄞 010/6401-1879. Reservations required. Set meals 100–500RMB ($12–$60). AE, MC, V. Mon–Fri 11am–1:30pm and 5–7:30pm; Sat–Sun 10:30am–1:30 and 4:30–8pm.

Sichuan Restaurant (Sichuan Fandian) 𝄞 SICHUAN Located in an old courtyard mansion amidst a scholar's gardens in one of Beijing's major tourist sites, the Sichuan is synonymous with good Sichuan dishes. The decor is classical Qing Dynasty Chinese, and the friendly staff knows some English, since this is a popular stop for tour groups, foreign travelers, and expatriates. This was the capital's most famous Sichuan restaurant at its former location (the estate of Yuan Shikai, President of the Republic of China, 1912–16), opening with Premier Zhou Enlai's blessing there in 1959, but now that native

The Food of the People: Nostalgia for the Bad Old Days

As unlikely as it seems to anyone who has read about or lived through the horrific, chaotic days of the Cultural Revolution (1966–76)—when China shut down and its Mao-inspired Red Guards ransacked the nation's intellectual and cultural heritage—there is nevertheless a certain nostalgia for the simpler days of the Chairman Mao dynasty. If you want to see what the people ate before the economic reforms launched China into the modern world in the 1980s and '90s, there are now a few "novelty" restaurants that create that milieu and serve sanitized versions of the harsh and simple fare of the people. The food tends to be quite salty, with such items as fried dough (*su hung cai*), vinegary cucumber sticks, and "Earth's Three Freshnesses" (*disanxian*), which is potatoes, eggplants, and green peppers mixed and fried together. The Cultural Revolution cafes are run-down, plain storefronts or courtyard houses with cement and brick walls, floors, benches, and tables—and Mao posters and memorabilia for decoration. Here's a list of the most interesting re-creations of Communist China's recent past, the favorites of many a foreign visitor:

Sunflower Village Food Street Restaurant (Xiang Yang Tun), 26 Wanquanhe Lu, Haidian District (© 010/6256-2967), a courtyard cafe on the way to the Summer Palace, has red painted rooms, hard wooden benches, mural-laden concrete walls, and clay dishes and bowls. Lunch and dinner, featuring silkworms and ant soup, is served from 10am to 2pm and 4:30 to 9pm; cost is under 100RMB ($12).

Black Earth Restaurant (Heitudi), 9 Heplingli Dong Dajie, Chaoyang Northeast (east of the Lama Temple near the northeast corner of the Second Ring Road; © 010/6427-1415), also serves Red Guard lunches and dinners (11am–2pm and 5–11pm), has an English-language menu, and is noted for its walls, where locals, including many Chinese leaders and celebrities, pin notes seeking to regain contact with comrades lost in the bad old days.

Chairman Mao's Family Restaurant (Mao Jiacai), 30 Yonghegong Lu (near the south gate of the Lama Temple), Dongcheng, (© 010/6421-9340), is a culinary shrine to the god of Chinese communism, complete with a large bust of the Great Helmsman, bamboo booths for dining, and faded photos of Mao himself on the walls. The cuisine here is a surprisingly refined rendition of Hunan cuisine from Mao's home province; the braised pork, at about $10 a plate, is succulent. Eat, worship, and recall the better days before the Cultural Revolution, daily from 11am to 2pm and 5 to 10pm.

Sichuan Deng Xiaoping is no longer China's supreme ruler, that restaurant has been removed in favor of the new exclusive China Club. Its new site here, in the home of a court Mandarin who served under Emperor Qianlong, is still elegant. Beyond the set menus, choices include such Sichuan classics as *dan dan mian* (long noodles), *mala douhua* (soft tofu soup), *guoba roupian* (pork and vegetables over a sizzling rice cake), *zhangcha yazi* (tea-drenched duck smoked in camphor wood), and *mapo doufu* (a numbing plate of chili-infused bean chunks).

14 Liuyin Jie, Prince Gong Mansion (Gongwangfu), Xicheng District (north of Beihai Lake). *C* 010/ 6615-6924. Reservations recommended on weekends. Main courses 100–150RMB ($12–$18). AE, MC, V. Daily 11am–2pm and 5–9pm.

MODERATE

Peppino's (Babinuo) ★★ *finds* ITALIAN
Beijing has plenty of good Italian eateries, but one of the least heralded is the Shangri-La hotel's own Peppino's. The setting is bright and upscale, with attentive service; the dishes are uniformly tasty, from the bread, soups, and salads to the pizzas and cannelloni. My favorites are the *bruschette assortite* (grilled country breads with marinated vegetables, smoked salmon, olive paté, and basil tomatoes) for a starter; the *minestra diverdura*, a vegetable soup with pasta and bacon; the *cannelloni di ricotta e spinaci*, an entree of homemade pasta in a pepper and cheese sauce; and the tiramisu for dessert. Try these dishes after a few days away from Western food and it will all taste like heaven. The cooking is first-rate and the setting is smart but casual, making for an enjoyable evening out.

In the Shangri-La Beijing Hotel, Level B1, 29 Zizhuyuan Lu, Haidian District (northwest corner of the Third Ring Road). *C* 010/6841-6727. Main courses 65–85RMB ($8–$10). AE, DC, MC, V. Mon–Sat noon–2:30pm and 6–10:30pm; Sunday 6–10:30pm.

Shamiana (Xiangweilang) ★★ INDIAN
Beijing's premier Indian restaurant imports both its chef and its fresh ingredients from India. The decor is bright and fresh, with wood-paneled walls and Indian motifs, and in the evenings it is a busy place with live music and dancers. The set menus (starting at 80RMB, $10) change often, but include such popular items as the vegetable somosa (crunchy fried pastries), chicken or lamb curry, cottage cheese in tomato gravy, *ajwaini naan* (bread with carrom seed), *kadhi* (chickpea flour in yogurt gravy), *chawal* (plain rice), mango chutney, and *phirni* (rice pudding). Vegetable dishes, such as *saag paneer* (spinach and homemade cottage cheese with garlic and cumin), can be a main course or split as a side dish. The *tandoori murgh* is a good choice from the grill (leg and breast of chicken) and the *nosh jehangiri* (clear mutton soup) is a house specialty. Shamiana also produces one of the best snacks in Beijing, its *kheema patti somosa* (minced lamb in a deep-fried triangular crust); at dinner, you can partake of an entire plate of its mixed kebabs for 112RMB ($13).

In the Holiday Inn Downtown, 98 Beilishi Lu, Xicheng District (1 block northwest of Fuchengmen subway station). *C* 010/6833-8822, ext. 7107. Reservations recommended on weekends. Main courses 80–150RMB ($10–$18). AE, DC, MC, V. Daily 11:30am–2:30pm and 6–10:30pm.

INEXPENSIVE

Beijing Express BEIJING
This is Beijing fast food served with flair in a comfortable, modern setting at reasonable prices. The polished wood floors, carved block chairs, decorative roof tiles, Chinese lanterns, and new food stalls give a suggestion of the cuisine's origins: the streets of Beijing. Snacks, priced from 6 to 10RMB (72¢–$1.20), include pancakes filled with vegetables, fried pork buns, rice cakes, and spring rolls. Noodles (12–21 RMB, $1.44–$2.52) feature shredded pork, Korean vegetables, or sliced eel in soup. Cold dishes run a similarly priced gamut from salty duck to deep-fried scorpions. Hot dishes include deep-fried chicken with chilies on a skewer to sautéed kale with chopped garlic.

In the Beijing New Century Hotel, 6 Shoudu Tiyuan Nan Lu, 3rd floor, Xicheng District (southwest of the Beijing Zoo). *C* 010/6849-2001, ext. 1157. Main courses 20–50RMB ($2.40–$6). AE, DC, MC, V. Daily 11:30am–2:30pm and 5:30–9:30pm.

Exploring Beijing

B eijing is packed with sights, ancient and modern, and it is China's most popular city for tourists, the majority of them from China itself. If your time is quite short, it is wise to book a day tour of the highlights through your hotel tour desk because getting around on your own, even via taxi or the subway, can be time-consuming at first. The city is flat, but the blocks are extremely long—and what looks like a 10-minute walk on the map can turn into a much longer march. If time allows, however, it is certainly worthwhile to explore parts of the city on foot or by bicycle, immersing yourself in a place that is both familiar and alien. (See chapter 7, "Beijing Strolls," for four recommended walking tours.) This is how I like to explore the city.

Again, your hotel staff can be helpful in showing you on a map how to reach some of the best sites.

Beijing's most famous attraction, the **Great Wall,** is well out of the city and requires a day trip. It and the **Qing Tombs,** the **Ming Tombs,** the **Western Hills,** and several other sites require excursions from Beijing, and these are covered in chapter 10, "The Great Wall & Other Side Trips from Beijing." The many treasures of the city itself—its temples, historic houses, museums, and parks— are described in this chapter, with a special focus on Beijing's four top attractions: **Tiananmen Square,** the **Forbidden City,** the **Temple of Heaven,** and the **Summer Palace.**

HOW TO SEE BEIJING

There are three basic ways to see the sights: by organized tour, by hired car, and on your own. The organized tours offered at hotel tour desks give quick, superficial views of major sights in the company of English-speaking guides. Costs start at about 250RMB ($30) for a half-day tour and 500RMB ($60) and up for a full-day tour that includes lunch. This is a good way to cover ground in a hurry, with a minimum of hassles. **China International Travel Service (CITS),** with headquarters at 28 Jianguomenwai Dajie, Chaoyang District (© **010/ 6515-8566;** www.cits.net), can also arrange private group tours with a guide and transportation at a much higher fee. CITS maintains convenient branches in many hotels throughout the city.

A second option is to hire a car for the day (through your hotel) to take you to as many sights as you can fit in. You won't have a guide, but the taxi will wait so that you can take the time to see the sights at your own pace. This is a fairly expensive option when arranged at your hotel, costing from 800 to 1,200RMB ($96–$144), but it can be done cheaper if you hire a taxi on your own for the day (a task that requires some "street smarts" and bargaining savvy).

The last option is to strike out on your own with a map and a plan, using taxis, the subway, perhaps a rented bicycle, and certainly your own two feet. This allows you to see the sights at your own pace at relatively little expense, but you do have to make your own arrangements and pay your own entrance fees.

Beijing Attractions

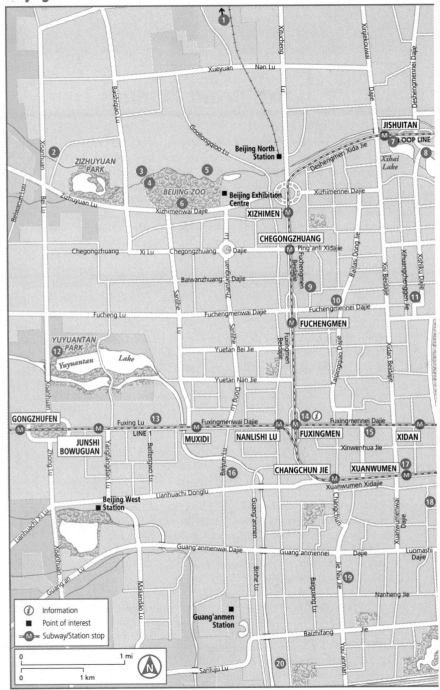

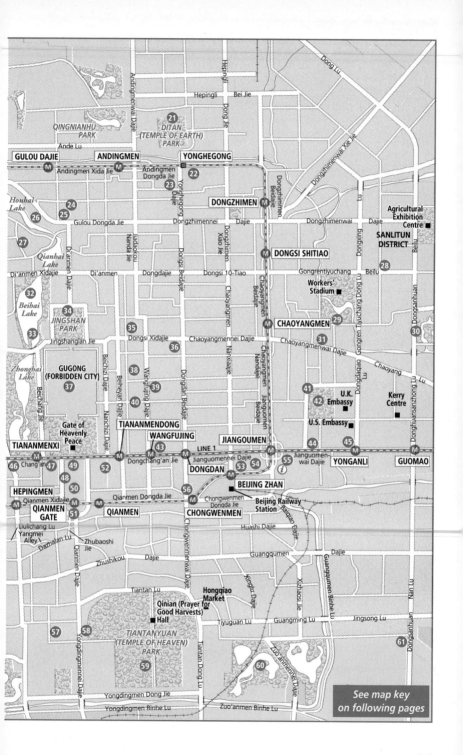

Key for Beijing Attractions

SUGGESTED ITINERARIES

The top attraction, the **Great Wall**, isn't in Beijing but about 2 hours away, so a group tour there is almost mandatory. Most day tours stop for an hour or so at the Great Wall and swing by one or two of Beijing's other top attractions, with a stop for lunch along the way.

If You Have 1 Day

Spend your only day in the capital playing tourist by booking a tour to the **Great Wall** through your hotel. This is the one sight you shouldn't miss, and it will use up most of your daylight hours. Such a tour usually includes a stop at one or two more major sights, but it doesn't leave much free time.

If you want to skip a walk on the Wall, I recommend that you begin with an early breakfast in your hotel, take a taxi to the **Temple of Heaven,** and survey its main attractions (allowing about an hour). Next, take another quick taxi ride north to **Tiananmen Square,** the world's largest square, which you can traverse in about 20 minutes, taking a glance at **Mao's Mausoleum,** the **Great Hall of the People,** and the **Monument to the People's Heroes.** Then cross Chang'an Avenue, pass under the Gate of Heavenly Peace, and proceed into the vast **Forbidden City.** You'll emerge at the northern moat around lunchtime. Grab yet another taxi for the **Summer Palace,** relax, have lunch there, and stroll its Long Corridor. Return downtown via taxi; you will still have time to walk up and down Beijing's number one shopping street, **Wangfujing.**

With either option, there's still time for dinner. Treat yourself to Beijing duck or try the city's top restaurant, The Courtyard, located on the Forbidden City's moat. Either way, you won't have trouble sleeping.

If You Have 2 Days

Spend your first day with excursions to the **Great Wall** and the **Summer Palace.** Finish up with a real Beijing dinner at the Sihexuan Restaurant in the Jinglun Hotel. The next Day, concentrate on city center attractions: **Tiananmen Square,** the **Forbidden City,** and the **Temple of Heaven.** Two days should also give you time to take in **Silk Alley,** the **Friendship Store,** and the **Hongqiao Market** (which you can reach from your hotel by taxi) for shopping. A spare 2 hours also offers a chance to visit Beijing's most popular religious site, the **Lama Temple.**

If You Have 3 Days

Three days is the minimum to do much in the way of Beijing sightseeing. It requires 2 days just to take in the top sights listed in the 1- and 2-day itineraries. On the third day, take a stroll on the historic antique avenue of **Liulichang** (see Walking Tour 1 in chapter 7, "Beijing Strolls"); if you're here on a Sunday, start very early with the **Dirt Market (Panjiayuan).** It's worthwhile to book a **Hutong** tour of the Back Lakes area in the afternoon—or tour it yourself on a rented bicycle. If there's a sunset, don't miss it from the top of the **Ancient Observatory.**

If You Have 4 Days or More

Four days will give you enough time to take a look at most of Beijing's best attractions, although a week would be better. You'll be able to sift through all the big sights and begin to explore those that are off the beaten track. Return to Tiananmen Square to tour Mao's Mausoleum, the Great Hall of the People, and the Museum of Chinese History. From the north gate of the Forbidden City, strike out for the views from **Jingshan Hill** and **Beihai Park.** Plan to visit some ancient temples, poke around the Soong Ching-Ling Residence

Jugglers, dancers and an assortment of acrobats fill the street.

She shoots you a wide-eyed look as a seven-foot cartoon character approaches.

What brought you here was wanting the kids

to see something magical while they still believed in magic.

America Online Keyword: Travel

With 700 airlines, 50,000 hotels and over 5,000 cruise and vaca-

tion getaways, you can now go places you've always dreamed of.

Travelocity.com
A Sabre Company
Go Virtually Anywhere.

"WORLD'S LEADING TRAVEL WEB SITE, 5 YEARS IN A ROW" WORLD TRAVEL AWARDS

and Rear Lakes neighborhood, enjoy lunch or late-night fun in the Sanlitun district, browse the shops and new department stores on Wangfujing Dajie, and stroll through some of the open-air markets around town. Don't be afraid to take a walking or bike tour on your own. If there's time left over, book an excursion to one of the less-visited sections of the Great Wall, to the Western Hills, or to the Qing Tombs. Actually, even a week isn't enough time to do more than take a glance at everything worth seeing in the capital, but it will give you a broad picture of China, old and new.

1 Tiananmen Square (Tiananmen Guangchang)

This is the world's largest public square, the size of 90 football fields (covering 99 acres) with standing room for 300,000 people. It is the heart of Beijing and of the Chinese nation. The square received a face-lift over the winter of 1998–99; its old paving blocks were replaced with granite stepping stones, which were laid just in time to celebrate the 50th anniversary of the founding of the People's Republic of China, on October 1, 1949. Chairman Mao Zedong stood that day on the Gate of Heavenly Peace at the entrance to the Forbidden City, across Chang'an Avenue from the square, and announced the founding of a new China to the masses. Mao's portrait now hangs from that reviewing stand, where a new generation of leaders gathers every October 1 to face the citizens of China. Tiananmen Square served as China's open-air forum through much of the 20th century, the scene of both historic ceremonies and protest demonstrations. It is best known to the outside world (via live international television coverage) as the arena for the democracy demonstrations that culminated in the crackdown on June 4, 1989. When foreigners stroll across Tiananmen Square, as most visitors do at least once, it is this specter that still seems to haunt the stony expanses and its monuments.

Tiananmen Square stands on the central north–south axis of the old Imperial city. In fact, there was no square here during the time of the emperors, only a wide boulevard, the Imperial Way, lined with state offices. The Imperial Way ran from the Gate of Heavenly Peace south to **Qianmen** (Front Gate), which still stands guard at the southern end of Tiananmen Square. Qianmen was one of the nine great gates when Beijing possessed its city walls. (They were removed in 1958.) The Imperial Way was the southern axis of the city, stretching from the Forbidden City all the way to the Temple of Heaven. Qianmen, which dates back nearly 500 years, remains a city landmark. Its northern passage is known as the Main Gate, and its southern passage is the Arrow Tower. Just beyond the square stands the world's largest KFC.

Today, Tiananmen Square contains fresh monuments to the new city. Located on the square itself are the Monument to the People's Heroes and the Mao Zedong Mausoleum. To the west is the Great Hall of the People and on the east flank are the Museum of Chinese History and the Museum of the Chinese Revolution. Each site is open to the public. The square itself is open daily from dawn to dusk. At twilight each day, there is a ceremonial lowering of the Chinese flag by a detachment of the People's Liberation Army, a popular photo opportunity among visitors. And those contraptions that look like video cameras on the speaker poles encompassing the square are just what you supposed—surveillance devices to record what happens in China's most sensitive and venerated public forum.

Fun Fact **A Man & a Tank**

The man who stood alone on Chang'an Avenue in Beijing at the height of the Tiananmen democracy protests in 1989 and lifted his hand to prevent its advance, blocking the tank this way and that, is an indelible image that is recognized worldwide—but what became of him? The lone protestor was quickly identified as Wang Weilin, and reports at the time had him being arrested, executed, or killed during the siege of Tiananmen Square. However, President Jiang Zemin reportedly said in 1990 that no one named Wang Weilin had been arrested or killed during the turmoil, and a computerized search by police, which turned up 400 men named Wang Weilin, placed none of them in central Beijing at the time. The widespread feeling is that he disappeared into the underground and remains undiscovered, at large, his whereabouts and true identity unknown. He remains the most mysterious figure of modern history, one of only two Chinese who made *Time* magazine's list of the major figures of the 20th century, along with Chairman Mao.

The **Museum of Chinese History** and the adjacent **Museum of the Chinese Revolution,** both located on the east side of Tiananmen Square, are described in detail in the "Museums & Mansions" section, later in this chapter.

Mao Zedong Mausoleum (Mao Zhuxi Jinian Bei) *⚐*   Mao has received more than 5 million visitors a year since this memorial opened in 1977, a year after his death. Check your cameras and handbags at the kiosk on the east side (8RMB, 96¢ fee) and join the lines forming in front of the north entrance. You'll be quickly ushered into the northern reception hall, where a large white marble statue of a seated Mao awaits, then into the central chamber where the Great Helmsman lies in state in his crystal sarcophagus. He has a rather ghoulish patina. Onlookers maintain complete silence for a few seconds before they are ushered out. The poem inscribed in gold in the south hall on your way out is by Mao, who left behind hundreds of poems in public places (as some of the old emperors did). Upstairs, there's a commemorative hall to three of Mao's political cohorts (Zhou Enlai, Liu Shaoqi, and Zhu De), but it's not worth viewing (and a lame attempt to counterweight Mao's importance). Obviously, the Mao memorabilia for sale in the counters on the way out of the mausoleum is overpriced. Shop in the markets for such prizes.

South end of Tiananmen Square. Free admission. Mon–Sat 8:30–11:30am. (Also sometimes open Mon, Wed, Fri 2–4pm.) Subway: Qianmen.

Monument to the People's Heroes (Renmin Yingxiong Jinian Bei) *⚐⚐*
This 124-foot granite obelisk, erected in 1958, is carved with tableaus of revolutionary martyrdom and victory, from a popular uprising in 1851 to the Communist Revolution of 1949. More recently it became the combat post of the young democracy protestors during the 1989 occupation of Tiananmen Square. On the front of this cenotaph, in Mao's calligraphy, is an inscription: THE PEOPLE'S HEROES ARE IMMORTAL. Until the recent renovation of the square, locals said they could still see bloodstains and bullet impressions from 1989 in the stone stairway.

Southwest section of Tiananmen Square. Free admission. Subway: Tiananmen Dong or Qianmen.

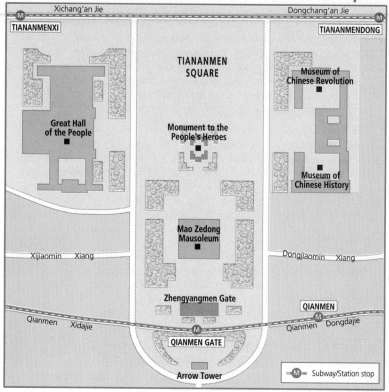

Great Hall of the People (Renmin Dahui Tang)   Whenever the National People's Congress is not in session, the Great Hall is usually open for tours. (It's worth having your hotel desk check ahead of time.) The hall is immense, more than half a mile long, and the main auditorium, with the great big red star on the ceiling (outlined by 500 light bulbs), seats 10,000 and is in fact called the 10,000 People Hall (Wanren Dalitang). The chief interest in seeing China's legislative center from the inside is the decorative elements that make up its 32 ostentatious reception rooms (each done in the style and motif of a separate province, autonomous region, or municipality). The scale of the banquet and assembly rooms is also impressive, especially since this whole complex was a patriotic rush job that required just 10 months to complete (opening in 1959).

West side of Tiananmen Square. ✆ 010/6608-1181. Admission 15RMB ($1.80). Daily 8:30am–3pm (but sometimes closes earlier; go in the morning). Subway: Tiananmen Xi.

2 The Forbidden City (Palace Museum)

Westerners call it the Forbidden City (Zijin Cheng); the Chinese prefer Palace Museum (Gu Gong). By any name, it is simply the most magnificent Imperial palace in China. Its vast courtyards and palaces cover an area the size of 166 football fields (183 acres), dwarfing Tiananmen Square. This ancient royal city, stuck in the heart of the modern city of Beijing like a life-size time capsule, is nearly a half-mile wide (east–west) and more than a half-mile long (north–south). Its palaces, pavilions, and halls are divided into 9,000 rooms; the whole complex is enclosed in thick walls more than 30 feet tall and is outlined by a moat 170 feet across. Twenty-four emperors and empresses of the Ming and Qing (Manchu) dynasties made this their home, holding court here across a span of 5 centuries. The first of the emperors to reside in the Forbidden City moved in in 1421, several generations before Columbus set sail and 200 years before the Pilgrims landed at Plymouth; the last emperor departed in 1923.

ESSENTIALS

The Forbidden City, located north of Chang'an Avenue (© **010/6513-2255,** ext. 615), is open daily from 8:30am to 5pm, but the ticket window closes at 3:30pm. Admission is 30RMB ($3.60); a ticket that includes admission to special displays in side halls, which are worth seeing, is 55RMB ($7). The main entrance is via the Gate of Heaven (Tiananmen), the massive archway with Chairman Mao's portrait on it facing Tiananmen Square to the south. The ticket booth is several blocks straight north at another massive gate (*Wumen,* Meridian Gate) in an open area that also contains the east entrance to the Forbidden City. The ticket window is to the right (east) of Meridian Gate.

It usually takes from 90 minutes (on an organized tour) to 4 hours (lingering on your own) to make the procession through the Forbidden City. The complex can be overwhelming and confusing, so try to take your time, imagining what this city-within-a-city was like for members of China's Imperial courts stretching back over 6 centuries.

SEEING THE HIGHLIGHTS

There are five main segments of the Forbidden City from south to north. In order, they are (1) the entrance gates, (2) the outer court, (3) the eastern exhibit halls, (4) the inner court, and (5) the Imperial gardens.

Walk north from the Gate of Heavenly Peace along the great central axis of old China until you reach the entrance gate at Wumen (Meridian Gate). Buy your ticket there and enter the outer court of the Forbidden City, which contains the three great ceremonial halls and their wide courtyards. Next you'll arrive at the inner court, which consists of the palaces and halls that served as royal residences. Before exploring the inner court, however, you can turn right and visit the smaller eastern exhibit halls, pavilions that now house special collections of Imperial treasures. At the northern end of the Forbidden City are the Imperial Gardens and a Daoist shrine.

THE ENTRANCE GATES

Gate of Heavenly Peace (Tiananmen)   Used as a reviewing stand by government officials, it is now open to the public (entrance inside, to the west; admission 30RMB, $3.60). There's not much reason to make this detour unless you want a panoramic view or picture of Tiananmen Square. The long corridor between Tiananmen and the entrance to the Forbidden City was once used for staging troops. It now contains food and souvenir stands, a yard for commercial photographers who pose tourists in Imperial costumes (east side), and a sideshow (west side) where two female mummies (entombed in 1274 and 1482) are on display (admission 4RMB, 48¢). Keep trudging northward.

Meridian Gate (Wumen)   This now serves as the southern and eastern entrance to the Forbidden City; the ticket booth and audio rental hall are also here. The gate was built in 1420 and renovated in 1647 and 1801. The emperors

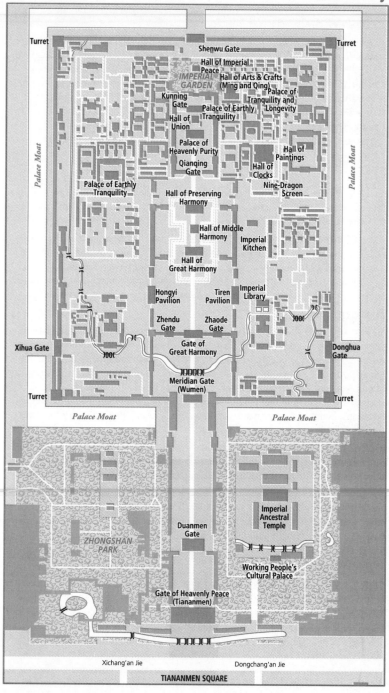

reviewed their armies at this location. Also called the Five Phoenix Tower, this gate once maintained separate entrances for court officials (on the left) and for the Imperial family (on the right).

Gate of Great Harmony (Tai He Dian)   Immediately inside the Meridian Gate entrance is a wide courtyard with five marble bridges spanning the Golden River, followed by yet another gate. This is the Gate of Great Harmony, erected in 1420 and rebuilt after a fire in 1889. It stands on the central axis of the Forbidden City. This is where the emperor listened to reports from his ministers.

THE OUTER COURT

Hall of Great Harmony (Tai He Dian) 🛪   Immediately inside the Gate of Great Harmony is a courtyard, flanked by closed halls on both sides, that is stunningly vast; this courtyard leads to the first great ceremonial hall, Tai He Dian, popularly known as the Hall of the Imperial Throne. From this throne (which you can see but not touch because the major halls are all closed to foot traffic), the emperor marked the new year, important birthdays, and other grand occasions. There are gorgeous carved columns within this pavilion, which was the tallest edifice in Beijing for centuries.

Hall of Middle Harmony (Zhong He Dian)   The second great hall of the outer court, built in 1420 and rebuilt in 1627, is where the emperor received ministers of the Imperial rites before he performed official ceremonies. There is a smaller Imperial throne here.

Hall of Preserving Harmony (Bao He Dian)   The final hall of the outer court is the site that, under the Qing emperors, was used for the Palace examinations that selected the nation's best students for the civil service. It was also where truly Imperial banquets, sometimes consisting of over a hundred courses, were served.

THE EASTERN EXHIBITION HALLS

Hall of Clocks 🛪   The royal collection of timepieces is located in the Hall of Worshipping Ancestors (Feng Xian Dian), which requires a detour to the east (right) before entering the inner court. Follow the signs, which will be in English and Chinese. There's a separate admission (5RMB, 60¢) unless you carry the all-inclusive admission ticket. You may also be charged 2RMB (24¢) for plastic slippers to pull over your shoes. The overshoes, designed to preserve the marble floors, quickly disintegrate. The collection of watches and clocks is fascinating, although the exhibit hall is poorly lit. Most of the foreign timepieces here came from England and Europe in the 18th century.

Nine Dragon Screen (Jiu Long Bi)   Southeast of the clock museum is a courtyard with this much-prized mosaic, fashioned in 1773 of shining ceramic tiles; it is 96 feet wide and nearly 12 feet high. Although highly regarded by art historians, it will probably strike you as pretty but overrated. The dragon is a symbol of Imperial rule, and this dragon mosaic is considered the best artistic rendering of that symbol.

Hall of Jewelry   Northeast of the Hall of Clocks is a second collection, housed in the Palace of Tranquility and Longevity (Ning Shou Gong) complex. Separate admission is again 5RMB (60¢), and protective slippers may be required. Within these eastern halls running northward is an extensive collection of ornaments, gold figurines, ceremonial plates, jewelry, and royal robes and jades. The fabled Empress Dowager of the final dynasty, Cixi, celebrated her 70th birthday (in 1904) in one of these halls and, in 1903, received the wives of foreign envoys in another (Yang Xing Dian), where her throne can still be seen. Through the Belvedere of Flowing Music (Changyinge), a three-tiered theater supported by Empress Dowager Cixi, is Zhen Fei Well, where the Empress Dowager was alleged to have drowned her nephew's favorite concubine.

From here, it is easily possible to wander off the beaten path into **Qianlong Garden,** a tranquil rockery where the Qing emperor enjoyed drinking games. (This is often a good place to escape the crowds for a bit before meeting up with them again at the Inner Court.)

THE INNER COURT

Gate of Heavenly Purity (Qian Qing Men)   If you resume your course on the main north–south axis, you come to this gate, which marks the entrance to the inner court of the Forbidden City. Only the Emperor, his family, his concubines, and the Palace eunuchs (who numbered 1,500 at the end of the final dynasty) could enter here. The view of golden roof upon golden roof is breathtaking. While the three palaces of the inner court are not as splendid nor as fully decorated as the great palaces of the outer court, they do give one some idea of the life enjoyed by China's Mandarins and royalty.

Palace of Heavenly Purity (Qian Qing Gong)   The first palace of the inner court is where emperors lived up to the time of Kangxi in the 18th century.

Hall of Union (Jiao Tai Dian)   This residence contains the throne of the empress.

Two Emperors & a Notorious Empress Dowager

Much of the surviving Imperial legacy of Beijing has the imprint of three notable sovereigns who ruled during the Qing Dynasty (1644–1911). Emperor **Kangxi** (1654–1722) and his grandson **Qianlong** (1711–99), two of the longest-reigning rulers in Chinese history, were responsible for maintaining and renovating the palaces of the Forbidden City as well as the royal parks and temples that we see today. Empress Dowager **Cixi** (1835–1908), reviled as the power behind the throne who plotted and poisoned her way to power, is blamed for the decline of the final dynasty. Her treasures are scattered throughout Beijing, in the halls of the Forbidden City, in her massive tomb outside the city, and most of all at the Summer Palace, which she rebuilt during her reign.

Palace of Earthly Tranquility (Kun Ning Gong)   Bedchamber of a Ming Dynasty empress, this is where Qing Emperor Kangxi was married and where China's last emperor, Pu Yi, married as a child in 1922.

THE IMPERIAL GARDENS

Near the northern gate is an elaborate garden of fantastic rockeries and pavilions, Yu Hua Yuan, which was created during the Ming Dynasty. Many of its cypress trees are ancient. There are several kiosks nearby selling refreshments and snacks. The northern exit is through the gate behind the last large structure, the **Hall of Imperial Peace** (Jin An Dian), a shrine to the god of fire, Xuanwu. You are, however, free to walk back to the southern gate (against the human tide) if you have time to extend your stroll and savor the days of the dynasty.

3 The Summer Palace (Yi He Yuan)

China's grand Imperial garden has been the site of Imperial palaces for 8 centuries, but its present outlines were created under Emperor Qianlong from 1749 to 1764. He enlarged both the pretty lake and the hills on its shore, adding numerous pavilions. In 1860, French and British troops destroyed most of the park. It was rebuilt by the Empress Dowager Cixi in 1886 but was again leveled by foreign armies. What we see today is the Empress Dowager's second re-creation of a Summer Palace, completed in 1903. This became her summer retreat and, increasingly, her full-time residence. Once the site of her lavish birthday parties, the park remained a countryside version of the Forbidden City until it was declared a public park in 1924 and spruced up in 1949. It is the most beautiful of Beijing's parks—the lake, hills, and groves, enhanced by Qing Dynasty pavilions, all bear the Empress Dowager's imprint.

ESSENTIALS

The Summer Palace (known in Chinese as Yi He Yuan, or Garden for Cultivating Harmony; ✆ **010/6288-1144**) is located 7 miles northwest of Beijing in Haidian District, a 20- to 30-minute taxi ride from the city center (60RMB, $7). There is no nearby subway stop. The gates open daily at 6:30am; no tickets are sold after 5pm. Admission is 10RMB ($1.20) for entry to the grounds or 30RMB ($3.60) for entry and access to most halls and exhibits. The main entrance is at the east gate (Donggongmen). The least-crowded time to visit is in the morning, as early as possible. Allow 4 hours to tour the major sites on your own, with a stop for lunch. Organized day tours often include the Summer Palace as a major stop, but they seldom allow you more than an hour to tour the grounds.

EXPLORING THE SUMMER PALACE

This spacious park (about 700 acres) consists of Kunming Lake to the south and Longevity Hill to the north. Kunming Lake takes up most of the parklands. It is transected by several long dikes, creating smaller portions known as West Lake and South Lake. There are many beautiful bridges and islands in Kunming Lake. The north side of Longevity Hill has its own Back Lakes, but the northern shore of Kunming Lake is the most popular strolling area. There, the Long Corridor (beginning at the eastern gate of the Summer Palace) links the pavilions, halls, and courtyards with the Marble Boat located on the west side of the park.

Organized tours usually allow time only for a stroll along the shores of Kunming Lake under the Long Corridor, a look at the Marble Boat, and sometimes a boat ride back to the east gate. These tours cover several striking sites, but they ignore some of China's very finest Qing Dynasty halls and pavilions.

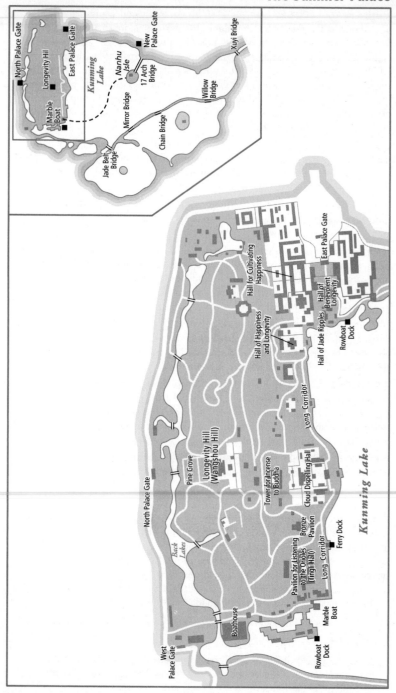

Long Corridor (Chang Lang) ✿✿   This covered wooden promenade, running about half a mile (2,550 ft.) along the northern shore of Kunming Lake, from the Eastern Halls to the Marble Boat, is a pure treasure out of dreamy old China. Its crossbeams, ceiling roof panels, and pillars are painted with more than 10,000 scenes from Chinese geography, history, literature, and myth. The promenade is a picture encyclopedia of China. The paintings are crude but bright. Built in 1750 (and rebuilt and restored many times since), the Long Corridor consists of 273 crossbeam sections and four pavilions which lead to cafes, boat docks, or sites on Longevity Hill.

Hall of Benevolent Longevity (Renshou Dian)   Located directly across the courtyard from the east gate entrance, this hall is where the Empress Dowager Cixi and her nephew (who was appointed emperor but placed under her protection) received members of the court. Cixi occupied the dragon throne.

Hall of Jade Ripples (Yulan Tang)   This is the lakeside residence of the Empress Dowager's nephew, Emperor Guangxu, where he was kept from the throne, a prisoner to his aunt.

Hall for Cultivating Happiness (Yile Dian)   Here, ensconced on her gold lacquer throne, the Empress Dowager enjoyed performances in her private three-stage theater that was built for her 60th birthday. Now a theater museum, this hall contains some of Cixi's own garments, her perfumes, and the first car imported into China (a Mercedes-Benz).

Hall of Happiness and Longevity (Leshou Tang)   This complex on the northeast tip of the lake was the Empress Dowager's private residence. Most of the furniture, the bed curtains, and the glass lamps (China's first electric lamps) are original. The Long Corridor begins here.

Hall of Dispelling Clouds (Pai Yun Dian) ✿   Located halfway along the Long Corridor on the foot of Longevity Hill, this hall served the Empress Dowager for her birthday parties and now contains some of the presents she received, including her most famous portrait, painted by Dutch artist Hubert Vos in 1905 for her 70th birthday.

Pavilion for Listening to the Orioles (Tingli Guan)   Situated at the west end of the Long Corridor, this complex is now the location of an Imperial restaurant where the menu is based on recipes from Forbidden City days.

Marble Boat (Boat of Purity and Ease) ✿   Outfitted with a paddlewheel, stained glass, and mirrors in 1893, the Marble Boat has become a symbol to Beijingers of the extravagance and cruelty of the Qing Dynasty. The funds that were to have strengthened the Chinese Navy instead funded the building of a stone boat in Cixi's private pleasure garden; China soon paid the price when Japan and other aggressors invaded. Although this story probably is not true, it does enhance the Empress Dowager's image as an Imperial villain. The Marble Boat (118 ft. long) can be photographed, but visitors are no longer allowed to board it.

Fun Fact **Tunnel of Love**

The Long Corridor is such a lovely spot for a stroll that locals say that any unmarried couple that enters at one end will emerge at the other engaged to be married.

Moments **Row Your Boat through Old Cathay**

A pleasant exit from the Summer Palace is aboard one of the pleasure barges that depart from the wharf near the Marble Boat and meanders along the shore back to the main east gate. Even nicer is to rent a rowboat and drift at your own pace, perhaps enjoying a picnic on Kunming Lake with all the ancient beauty of Longevity Hill and its halls and pavilions as poetic background. Barge seats usually go for about 25RMB ($3); rowboats rent for about 30RMB ($3.60) per hour and require a deposit (usually 100RMB, $12).

Seventeen-Arch Bridge (Shiqi Kong Qiao) ⭐ This quintessential arched bridge, 492 feet long and fashioned of marble, connects South Lake Isle (Nanhu Dao) to the east shore. It's wonderful to view and photograph. If time allows, you can either walk to it or pass under it aboard a rowboat.

4 The Temple of Heaven (Tiantan)

At the same time that Ming Emperor Yongle laid out and built the Forbidden City (1406–20), he oversaw the construction of an enormous park and altar to heaven directly south of the Imperial palaces. Each winter solstice, the emperor would lead a procession out of the Forbidden City, across what is today Tiananmen Square, and southward down the Imperial Way to Tiantan, the Temple of Heaven, where he would perform rites and make sacrifices to the cosmos on behalf of China. Much of the architecture of these ancient rites survives in Tiantan Park (Tiantan Gongyuan), but what makes this park rank so high among attractions in China is a single remarkable building, the magnificent tower known as the Hall of Prayer for Good Harvests (Qinian Dian).

If you are on an organized tour, you may have time only to view the Hall of Prayer, which is grand indeed, but Tiantan Park has several other architectural marvels, and it is also a fine public park to poke around in for glimpses of how ordinary Beijingers enjoy themselves.

ESSENTIALS

Temple of Heaven Park (Tiantan Gongyuan; ✆ **010/6702-2617** or 010/6702-8866) is open daily from 5am to 9:30pm in summer and from 8am to 5:30pm in winter. Tour buses and taxis favor the west entrance because it is nearest Qianmen Dajie, the major thoroughfare to the city center. Admission is 14RMB ($1.68) for the park and all the cultural sites, and 4RMB (48¢) just for the park.

SEEING THE HIGHLIGHTS

Located south of Tiananmen Square on the east side of Qianmen Dajie, Tiantan Park is rounded like heaven on the north and squared like the Earth to the south, following ancient Chinese cosmology. There are four entrances at the four cardinal points on the compass. The west entrance is used most often. The major halls and vaults all lie on a north–south axis, which runs roughly through the center of the park.

There are four major sights:

Hall of Prayer for Good Harvests (Qinian Dian) *★★* This circular wooden hall with its three soaring blue-tiled roofs, capped with a golden ball, has become an emblem of China's Imperial architecture. The red, blue, green, and gold colors, used inside and out, are bold and rich. The entire edifice was constructed without a single nail, its pieces artfully fitted and snapped into place without cross beams. The 28 massive pillars take much of the load, particularly the four massive central columns, called the Dragon Well Pillars. The Hall of Prayer stands 125 feet high and 98 feet across. Here, the emperors of China performed the ancient rites intended to bring the dynasty and the nation into harmony with the will and course of the heavens.

Unfortunately, there's little you can do here but stand and admire this great altar from the outside. Visitors are no longer allowed within, although you can still peek inside. This tower was finished in 1420 and remained in place until 1889, when lightning set it ablaze. What we see now is a meticulous reconstruction of the original. The tall, straight timbers used to rebuild it were imported from Oregon by a U.S. shipping owner, Robert Dollar, although official Chinese sources claim the lumber is from Yunnan Province; no doubt, some of it is.

Circular Altar (Yuan Qiu) This three-tiered marble terrace is an open altar, built in 1530 and enlarged in 1749 by Emperor Qianlong. It is located at the southern end of the park. Bundles of silk were once burned here as gifts to Heaven. The emperors communed with the cosmos from this platform, which is also said to possess strange acoustical properties, magnifying the sound of the voices of orators who stand at its center (but diminishing it for their immediate audience). Follow the lead of many Chinese visitors here, if you dare, and try delivering your own oratory from this hallowed stage.

Imperial Vault of Heaven (Huang Qiong Yu) *★* Due south of the Hall of Prayer via the Bridge of Vermilion Stairs, this pavilion with the blue-tiled roof, a smaller version of the Hall of Prayer, was built of wood in 1530 to store ceremonial stone tablets. The Vault is encircled by Echo Wall. On a quiet day, it is still possible to experience its remarkable acoustics, which work like a walkie-talkie, enabling two people to conduct a conversation in whispers along the wall no matter how spread out the two communicants become. Give it a try; my own experiments here suggest that the wall does indeed have some amazing properties. The three Echo Stones at the base of the main staircase are also fun to try. Clap your hands sharply while standing on the first stone and a single echo is returned; one clap on the second stone step produces two echoes; and a clap on the third step is echoed three times—or so says the tradition.

Hall of Abstinence (Zhai Gong) Located at the west entrance, these halls and the Bell Tower are where the emperor would cleanse himself by fasting before making his report and conducting the sacrifices to Heaven. The interior is spartan, with some pieces of 18th- and 19th-century Imperial furniture; the bell in the tower, which once signaled an emperor in residence, can now be struck for a mere 1RMB (12¢). This hall is seldom visited, but nearby in the early mornings many locals gather to perform their morning exercises (*tai ji quan*) and students claim benches to cram for exams. It's a nice place to sneak a peek at locals preparing for the rigors of the day.

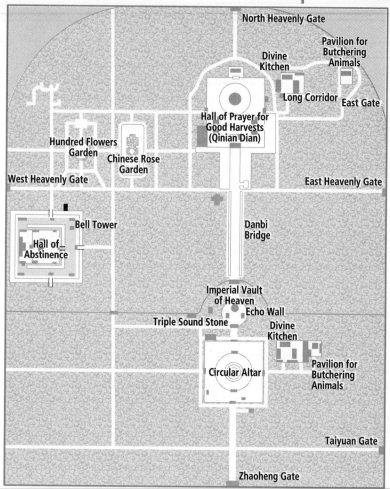

Map labels: North Heavenly Gate, Divine Kitchen, Pavilion for Butchering Animals, Long Corridor, East Gate, Hall of Prayer for Good Harvests (Qinian Dian), Hundred Flowers Garden, Chinese Rose Garden, West Heavenly Gate, East Heavenly Gate, Bell Tower, Danbi Bridge, Hall of Abstinence, Imperial Vault of Heaven, Echo Wall, Triple Sound Stone, Divine Kitchen, Circular Altar, Pavilion for Butchering Animals, Taiyuan Gate, Zhaoheng Gate

5 Temples, Mosques & Churches

Beijing's most popular Buddhist shrine is the Lama Temple. It is situated a few blocks from another major temple complex, the Confucius Temple. The most interesting place of worship in Beijing is the less-touristy White Cloud Temple (Bai Yun Guan), an active Daoist complex. The recently reopened, largely undiscovered Eastern Peak Temple (Dong Yue Miao) is also a splendid find. The White Pagoda Temple (Bai Ta Si) and the Five-Pagoda Temple (Wu Ta Si) are among several notable Buddhist complexes located off the beaten track, but highly recommended if time allows for a visit. In addition, Beijing has active Christian churches and Islamic mosques with services that foreign visitors may view or attend.

TEMPLES

Confucius Temple (Kong Miao) 🏛   Built in 1306, the temple honors China's great philosopher and is a part of the Imperial College (Guozijian). It is China's second largest Confucian shrine (next to the temple in his hometown, Qu Fu) and a quiet refuge from the crowded Lama Temple nearby. In the first courtyard are 198 steles (carved stone tablets) bearing the names of successful candidates in the national civil service examinations during the Yuan, Ming, and Qing dynasties. There are also many ancient trees, including a 700-year-old cypress in the main courtyard. The Hall of Great Achievements (Da Cheng Dian) stands at the north end of the complex, fronted by a statue of Confucius in the center and a group of 18th-century ceremonial stone drums on the right. Side halls sell antiques and inexpensive rubbings of the steles (about 50RMB, $6 each). Running along the east wall is a museum of Beijing history, chronologically arranged and with signs in English, that is quite worth strolling. The grounds also contain the complete text of the Confucian Classics carved on 189 stone tablets, as well as the Sir Donald Sussman Center for Chinese Antiques, established in 1995. Qing Dynasty emperors once came to this temple to expound on the teachings of Confucius, and students competed here in the highest national examinations for the title of Jinshi.

13 Guozijian Jie, Dongcheng District. ℂ 010/6407-3593. Admission 10RMB ($1.20). Tues–Sun 9am–5pm. West from the Lama Temple, across Yonghegong Dajie, on the old archway-lined street. Subway: Yonghegong.

Eastern Peak Temple (Dong Yue Miao) 🏛🏛 *(Finds*   Rarely visited and only recently opened to the public, this Daoist temple is among the most fascinating in the city. It was originally devoted to a cult founded by a mystic healer, Zhang Daoling, in the second century, and it retains many touches of the truly superstitious and miraculous. Above all, it is a veritable discount warehouse of bureaucratic Daoism, its main courtyard surrounded by stalls that are presided over by divine specialists who can address every known concern and ill. Worshippers purchase paper placards, locate the desired stall, and petition for divine intervention. The stalls run the gauntlet of human desire, whether for wealth or fame, health or longevity, marriage or offspring, justice or revenge. Each of the 76 stalls, fronted by a picket fence, contains white statues depicting a divine judge and his attendants. Much of the fun is in seeing which stall attracts the most devotion (easily determined by the number of placards left dangling from the fence posts). Stalls devoted to various forms of Wealth and Longevity usually lead the pack, but there is a myriad of departments, each with a sign in English. If you have been betrayed, if you wish to preserve the wilderness, if you are seeking to overturn the decision of a petty bureaucrat (and wish to consign that corrupt official to his or her politically correct level of Hell), this is your courtyard, with a pipeline to the Highest Court of Old China.

Built in 1322, the temple was renovated in 1761 under Emperor Qianlong. In the courtyard, a stele, one of over 100 carved monuments, records the patronage of both Qianlong and his grandfather, Emperor Kangxi (1704). The complex also has two major halls: Daiyuedian, which is divided into the 76 departments that oversee the 18 layers of Daoist Hell, and Yudedian, where the temple's main god (the god of Tai Shan) once slept. Dong Yue Miao is especially lively during the temple fairs of Chinese New Year.

North side of Chaoyangmenwai Dajie, Chaoyang District (opposite Full Link Plaza and Landao Shopping Centre). ℂ 010/6553-2184. Admission 1RMB (12¢). Tue–Sun 6am–7pm. Subway: Chaoyangmen.

Five-Pagoda Temple (Wu Ta Si) ★★   One of the most striking and unusual of Beijing's temples, the Five-Pagoda Temple is located on the grounds of Zhenjue Temple and the Beijing Stone Engraving Art Museum, an outdoor collection of over 1,000 fascinating stone pillars, shrines, statues, and carvings from the Han, Tang, and Song dynasties, as well as many gravestones commemorating Jesuit missionaries who died in Beijing. The most famous stone relic is the Statue of the Northern Wei Tai He Dynasty, a Buddhist memorial carved over 1,500 years ago and recently repaired (after thieves had broken it into five parts in 1998). The Five-Pagoda tower at the center consists of a square hall whose walls are engraved with the niches of 1,000 Buddhas and topped by 5 magnificent pagodas (each about 25 ft. high and built in 1473) that are more Indian than Chinese in style. For an extra 5RMB (60¢), you can climb the stairs into the central pagoda. The pagoda tower is one of Beijing's less-visited visual treasures; the stele collection will be more interesting and more accessible to foreign visitors once it is re-housed in new quarters at the rear of the temple sometime, it is said, in 2002. Meanwhile, the temple is closed for construction; call ahead to be sure that it's reopened.

24 Wutasicun, Haidian District. ℂ 010/6217-3836. Admission 3RMB (36¢), but will probably increase due to current renovations. Daily 8:30am–4pm. Located across the Nanchang River directly north of the Beijing Zoo; or a 10-min. walk east of Baishiqiao Lu. No subway.

Guanghua Temple (Guanghua Si)   This lovely little temple, the only one to survive on the eastern shores of the Back Lakes, is called the "Great Transformation" temple after a wandering monk who ate only half the rice he received from the people and used the other portion to help to pay for (or be "transformed" into) this temple. The four engraved stone tablets in the main courtyard show great damage, probably by the marauding Red Guards during the Cultural Revolution (1966–76). There are just two small temples on the grounds, which enshrine statues of the 3 Buddhas (past, present, and future) and have paintings of the 18 lohans, Buddha's semi-divine followers. The temple receives few tourists, but at least 20 monks are in residence here.

On the southeast shore of Houhai Lake along Ya'er Hutong, 5 blocks west of the Drum Tower, Dongcheng District. ℂ 010/6403-5032. Admission 5RMB (75¢). Daily 8am–5pm.

Huifeng Temple (Huifeng Si) *Finds*   This temple is far off the beaten track, although its location could hardly be more picturesque: on a rocky island just offshore in the most western of the Back Lakes, with a view south over the water towards central Beijing. A rocky crag presents a short but steep climb to the temple on the summit. Formerly thought to be a site for worshipping Guanyin, the goddess of Mercy, Huifeng today is not an active shrine, but its halls have been recently renovated with fresh brick, cement, and statuary. There is a small museum with astronomical charts, displays, and celestial instruments related to the Yuan Dynasty (1215–1368). The real draw is its romantic location, the island rockery, and the fine views.

On an island on the northern tip of Xihai Lake, south side of the Second Ring Road, east of Jishuita subway station, Dongcheng District. Admission 50 mao (6¢). Daily 8am–8pm. Subway: Jishuita.

Lama Temple (Yong He Gong) ★★★   The one temple everyone must see in Beijing is quite crowded except in the early morning and late afternoon, but it is a gorgeous complex and well worth investigating anytime. Built in 1694 as the residence for the prince who became Emperor Yongzheng, it was converted to a temple in 1744. Later, during the rule of Emperor Qianlong, it became the major center (outside of Lhasa) of the dominant Yellow Hat sect of Tibetan Buddhism. Even today, it has a strong hand in determining the next Dalai Lama, the "living Buddha;" about 200 monks, many from Mongolia, live, pray, and study here.

A long walkway leads to the temple gate, through which there is a courtyard with a bell tower, a drum tower, and a collection of 108 carved stone tablets. In the first of five magnificent worship halls, there is a large statue of the future Buddha, Maitreya, also known as the laughing Buddha. In the courtyard beyond the first hall is a large copper cauldron, Beijing's oldest incense burner, dated 1747, and a pavilion containing an immense stone tablet bearing the words of Emperor Qianlong carved in Tibetan, Mongolian, Manchu, and Chinese.

The Hall of Harmony, crowded with prayer wheels, contains Buddhas of the past, present, and future flanked by the 18 *luohan* (disciples who have achieved transcendence but elected to return to Earth to help others). The Hall of Eternal Blessing is a few steps to the north.

In the fourth great hall (Falun Dian, or Wheel of the Law), there is a 40-foot bronze statue of the founder of this sect (in the yellow hat). The Dalai Lama's throne is on the left. Here the monks pray and study on raised platforms equipped with electric brass reading lamps.

The final of the five central halls contains an immense image of the Buddha carved from a single Tibetan sandalwood tree. It is over 75 feet tall, with Buddha's head beaming out from the third floor above. This must have been a showstopper in past centuries when monks and followers made pilgrimages here by the thousands.

Seldom pointed out by local tour guides are the displays of esoteric Buddhist figures in the side halls lining the east wall, particularly near the temple entrance. Many of these entangled Tantric figures (some life-size, most smaller) are discretely draped in scarves to conceal their true activities. This aspect of Tibetan Buddhism takes a Kama Sutra approach to matters of body and spirit, and the religious statuary in these side halls, while quite inventive, is not for the easily offended. To appreciate the Lama Temple, allot at least 2 hours for a tour.

12 Yonghegong Dajie, Dongcheng District. © 010/6404-3769. Tue–Sun 9am–4pm. Admission 20RMB ($2.40). The temple entrance is located on the east side of the street, a block south of the subway station. Subway: Yonghegong.

Wanshou Temple (Wanshou Si) ⭐ The Wanshou Temple (Temple of Longevity), which dates from the Ming Dynasty (1577), is a lovely Buddhist complex of halls and pavilions that now houses the Beijing Art Museum (Zhongguo Meishuguan). It was renovated in 1761 by Qing Emperor Qianlong. The Empress Dowager Cixi stayed overnight here on her way to the Summer Palace aboard the royal barge from the Forbidden City. The entrance gate, capped by a painted carving of blue sky, clouds, and 100 red bats (signifying good fortune), leads to a courtyard with a drum tower on the left and bell tower (with a small store) on the right, both built in 1577. The first central hall is devoted to the worship of the laughing Buddha and the four heavenly kings. The second shrine, the Precious Hall of the Buddha (Dayanshou) contains lovely statuary and is intended for the worship of the "Medicinal Buddha of the Pure Glazed World." A long courtyard leads to a large meditation hall (50 ft. wide by 75 ft. deep) that now serves as a gallery of modern paintings. Behind the meditation hall is a rock garden with three halls devoted to the divinities presiding over three sacred Chinese peaks (Mt. Wutai and Wenshu to the left, Mt. Emei and Puxian to the right, and Mt. Putuo and Guanyin, goddess of Mercy, in the center). At the rear of the temple behind the rock garden are two pavilions built in 1761 (one housing a stone tablet recounting the rebuilding of this temple, signed by Emperor Qianlong in several languages), as well as two interesting arched gates, built under Qianlong in 1761, in a Western style reminiscent of the gates destroyed in 1860 at the Old Summer Palace.

Xisanhuan Lu, Haidian District. ✆ 010/6841-3380. Admission 10RMB ($1.20). Tue–Sun 9am–5:30pm. On the Changhe River, east side of the Third Ring Road West, 4 blocks from the Shangri-La Hotel. No subway.

White Cloud Temple (Bai Yun Guan) ★★★

Beijing's leading Daoist temple, and the most fascinating temple complex in the capital, is a highly active place of worship among locals. The clouds of incense are thick inside its walls. The Wind Containing Bridge in the first courtyard is surrounded by worshippers trying to strike a golden coin (suspended from a large 17th-century copper bell) with small modern coins, a feat that ensures good luck. Beyond the first hall, which enshrines the temple's god, Wang Shan, lies the Spring Hall for the Jade Emperor, a major Daoist deity. Inside, you will see the faithful rubbing their hands over engravings and the golden feet of the statues (as these are gods of wealth). There are several similar shrines on the central axis (with signs on the stairways reading "Do Not Spit Everywhere!") leading north to an unusual two-story hall dedicated to the Four Celestial Emperors. At the very rear (north) is a rockery (Cloud Gathering Garden) where I have seen dozens of novice monks receiving training. The side halls on the west side are particularly intriguing, with shrines dedicated to solving eye problems, increasing fertility, ensuring wealth, getting a good job, passing exams, and guaranteeing good fortune and longevity (once you locate your place on the zodiac). At every stop, the crowds burn incense and touch the powerful deities, praying that their wishes be granted, demonstrating a remarkable return to ancient Daoist beliefs. Festivals, which present a great time to visit and mingle, occur here on the first and fifteenth day of every lunar month.

Baiyunguan Jie, Xuanwu District. ✆ 010/6346-3531 or 010/6346-3887. Admission 8RMB (96¢). Daily 8:30am–4:30pm. South down Baiyun Lu (a major market street), across the city moat, then east 1 block on Baiyunguan Jie. Subway: Nanlishi Lu.

White Pagoda Temple (Bai Ta Si)

Renovated in 1998, this temple features the largest Tibetan pagoda (usually called a *dagoba* or *stupa*) in China, built over 700 years ago (1279) by order of Kublai Khan. The main gate and museum in the first courtyard are new. The museum contains Buddhist statuary and Emperor Qianlong's hand-copied sutra (1753, unearthed in 1978). The Hall of the Great Enlightened Ones, the first building, contains thousands of little Buddhas in glass cases, which are set into the columns. There are two more beautifully renovated halls and then the White Pagoda itself, an immense structure 167 feet high.

171 Fuchengmennei Dajie, Xicheng District (a 10-min. walk east from the subway stop). ✆ 010/6616-0023. Admission 10RMB ($1.20). Daily 9am–5pm. Subway: Fuchengmen.

MOSQUES & CHURCHES

In addition to the places listed below, there are many other cathedrals, churches, and places of worship in Beijing. For the locations and times of Catholic, Protestant, and Jewish services in Beijing, inquire at your hotel.

Chongwenmen Protestant Church (Chongwenmen Tang)   Methodists from the U.S. built the first church here in 1876. Razed during the Boxer Rebellion (1900), it was rebuilt in 1904. Closed during the Cultural Revolution (1966–76), it reopened in 1982. Now served by three ministers, the church attracts overflowing crowds (2,500 worshippers) on Sundays. This church has been visited by the Archbishop of Canterbury (George Carey) and U.S. President Bill Clinton. The American evangelist Reverend Billy Graham has preached in this church on two occasions.

D2 Hougou Hutong (northeast of the subway station, behind the Jinlang Hotel), Chongwen District. ✆ 010/6524-2193. Services: Sun 9:30am (in Chinese). Subway: Chongwenmen.

Ox Street Mosque (Niu Jie Qingzhen Shi)   The spiritual center of Beijing's 200,000 Islamic followers, this is also the capital's largest mosque, dating from 996. Its main prayer hall (facing Mecca to the west) can hold 2,000. (Non-Muslims are not permitted to enter.) The courtyard is surrounded by a Tower for Viewing the Moon, a minaret (for calls to prayer), a hall of inscribed clay tablets, and the tombs of Muslim leaders from the Yuan Dynasty (1271–1368). Beijing's other mosque that welcomes foreign visitors is the Dongsi Mosque (Dongsi Qingzhen Si), located at 13 Dongsi Nan Dajie (daily 10am–5pm; admission 10RMB, $1.20), a short walk northeast from the Wangfujing shopping area.

88 Niu Jie, Xuanwu District. ✆ 010/6353-2564. Admission 10RMB ($1.20). Daily 9am–sunset. No subway.

South Cathedral (Nan Tang)   Beijing's main Catholic cathedral was built on the site of Jesuit missionary Matteo Ricci's house in 1650 and rebuilt for the last time in 1904. It is known in English as the Cathedral of the Immaculate Conception of the Blessed Virgin Mary, or Mary's Church by expatriates who worship here. The cathedral is quite large and active, but it is not ornate (no stained glass). There is a "Holy Things Handicraft Department" that sells small items at the southern gate and a pretty rock garden that's dedicated to the Virgin on the southwest corner. The South Cathedral's counterpart is the North Cathedral (Bei Tang), built in 1887 and located at 33 Xishiku Dajie, Xicheng District (✆ 010/6617-5198); services here are usually conducted in Chinese only. *Note:* Catholic churches in Beijing are under government control and are not recognized or sanctioned by the Roman Catholic Church.

141 Qianmenxi Dajie, Xuanwu District (1 block east of the subway stop). ✆ 010/6602-5221. Services Mon–Fri 6am (Latin), 7am (Chinese); Sat 6:30am (Latin); Sun 6am and 7am (Latin), 8am (Chinese), 10am (English). Subway: Xuanwumen.

St. Joseph's Cathedral (Dong Tang)   This imposing structure was secreted away in the heart of the Wangfujing central shopping district until the avenue was renovated in 2000. Now it has a wide raised plaza, open to the street, where many shoppers take a break. Its towering spires add a touch of the spiritual past to the otherwise thoroughly secular, modern avenue. This church was founded by the Jesuits in Beijing after the death of one of their earliest missionaries to China in 1666. It was rebuilt 2 centuries ago (when it was said to be the most beautiful church in the capital), then burned to the ground during the Boxer Rebellion in 1900. The present structure is "only" a century old.

74 Wangfujing Dajie, Dongcheng District. ✆ 010/6524-0634. Sun services in Chinese and Latin; check for times. Subway: Wangfujing.

6 Parks & Gardens

Beijing's parks are splendid places for a stroll. The best, such as Beihai, combine scenic beauty and people-watching with historic monuments, Imperial court-yard restaurants, and Buddhist temples. All are particularly lively in the hours just after dawn, when people gather for their morning exercises (ranging from *tai ji quan* to ballroom dancing). All are gated, with a ticket booth charging a small admission at the entrance.

Beihai Park (Beihai Gongyuan) ★★★   Containing the city's largest lake and a landmark white pagoda, this is the capital's oldest Imperial garden, with an 800-year history. It is the best single park to visit—and a wonderful place to stroll—especially since it is within walking distance of the Forbidden City. It was not opened to the public until 1925, instead serving only the Emperor and his court. The **Round City** (Tuan Cheng), located just outside the south entrance of the park, contains a massive jade bowl that was once the prized possession of Kublai Khan; the **Light Receiving Hall** within houses a 10-foot Buddha of white jade sent to Emperor Qianlong as a gift from Burma.

Qionghua Isle, constructed of the materials excavated to create the sur-rounding Beihai Lake, contains the most spectacular sights in Beihai Park, start-ing with the nicely maintained halls of the **Yongan Temple** (Yongan Si) and leading up Jade Hill to the White Pagoda. The towering Tibetan-style **White Pagoda** (Bai Ta), 118 feet tall and dating from 1651, commemorates a visit by the Dalai Lama; it is believed to contain precious Lama relics. The views from the peak, across the lake, and toward the Forbidden City, are dazzling. If you look due south, between Zhonghai Lake and the Forbidden City, you will see the compound where China's Communist government is sequestered. The northern shore of the islet is rimmed by a covered walkway with painted scenes in the fashion of the Long Corridor at the Summer Palace. The cluster of build-ings here, known as the Hall of Rippling Waters (Yilantang), is a former palace (as well as the site of an Imperial restaurant, Fangshan).

The northwest shore is the site of a glazed-tile **Nine Dragon Screen** (1417), smaller than the one in the Forbidden City, and a botanical garden. The eastern shore contains halls and pavilions known as the "Gardens Within Gardens" where emperors and empresses once enjoyed the lakeshore. Today's commoners take to the waters in paddleboats and rowboats (rented at 20RMB, $2.40 per hr.) during the summer and on a type of ice sled (made up of crates on skis) in the winter. Beihai Lake was drained and cleaned and its shoreline renovated in the late fall of 1998, making it an even more beautiful spot to tour. For a walk-ing tour that includes Beihai Park and describes its sights in fuller detail, see Walking Tour 3 in chapter 7, "Beijing Strolls."

1 Wenjin Jie, Xicheng District. © 010/6404-0610 or 6407-1415. Admission 5RMB (60¢) for the park; 10RMB ($1.20) for the park, temple, and pagoda; 5RMB (60¢) extra for Round City. Daily 6am–dusk. Subway: Tianan-men Dong (1 mile south). South entrance is just northwest of the Forbidden City; east entrance is 2 blocks west of Jingshan Park.

Grand View Park (Daguan Yuan)   A newly built park, opened in 1986 on the site of the Imperial Vegetable Garden, Grand View is a reproduction of the classic family garden described in one of China's most famous novels, *The Dream of the Red Chamber,* an elaborate soap opera written by Beijing resident Cao Xueqin (1715–63). The park has already served as the set for a Hong Kong TV movie of the book. Complete with a central pond, bamboo lodges, pavilions, arched bridges, towers, and halls, Grand View is a faithful modern version of the classic Chinese garden, a pleasant diversion if you are in the neighborhood.

Southwest corner of lower Second Ring Road and the city moat, Guang'anmen Beibinhe Lu, Xuanwu District. Admission 10RMB ($1.20). Daily 9am–5pm. No subway.

Jingshan Park (Jingshan Gongyuan)   Also called Meishan (Coal Hill), this promontory overlooking the Forbidden City was created from the excavations of the Imperial moat in 1420. According to the principle of *feng shui* (Chinese geomancy), this hill would protect the Forbidden City from the evil spirits swooping in from the north. It was on this hill, however, that the last Ming emperor, Chongzhen, hanged himself from a tree before the Manchu conquerors could arrive (from the north, of course). Today, Jingshan is a pretty park, which requires a steep walk from the Beautiful View Tower (Qiwang Lou), an exhibition hall at the southern foot, to the viewing pavilion (Pavilion of Everlasting Spring, *wan chun ting*) on its middle summit. The view over the golden-tiled roofs of the immense Forbidden City and Tiananmen Square to the south is justifiably a celebrated one, but there are also superb vistas of the Drum and Bell towers and the Back Lakes to the north. The pavilion's balcony fills up with locals enjoying the view; its aging interior has been taken over by a souvenir and snack outlet.

Directly across from the north gate of the Forbidden City, on Jinshan Qian Jie, Dongcheng District. ✆ 010/6404-4071. Admission 2RMB (24¢). Daily 7am–8pm. Subway: Tiananmen Dong (1 mile walk).

Old Summer Palace (Yuan Ming Yuan) 🕸   China's largest Imperial park when Qing Emperor Kangxi built it in the 18th century, Yuan Ming Yuan was smashed and burned to the ground by French and British troops during the Second Opium War in 1860 and never restored. It is today a haunting picnic spot, with a few ruins of its hundreds of original pavilions, gazebos, and goldfish ponds still visible. The most evocative remains of this Chinese Versailles are located in the Garden of Eternal Spring (Changchun Yuan), where the emperor oversaw the creation of European-style mazes, marble fountains, an aviary, and a concert chamber. The broken and fallen columns and arches of the Hall of Tranquility form an ideal setting for a picnic in the suburbs of Beijing, with a hint of Old Cathay and the disappearance of dynasties.

Qinghua Xi Lu, Haidian District. ✆ 010/6255-1488. Daily 6:30am–7pm. Admission 10RMB ($1.20). No subway. Located north of Beijing University, a short taxi ride east of the "new" Summer Palace.

Ritan Park (Ritan Gongyuan)   Like its more famous sister, the Temple of Heaven (Tiantan), the Temple of the Sun (Ritan) served as an altar where the emperor conducted annual cosmic rites. Built in 1530, Ritan today is an exceptionally pleasant park in the heart of a tree-lined diplomatic quarter, its northwest corner surrounded by Russian restaurants. The altar is on the southern summit of the park, where a new pavilion has been erected. The parklands are encompassed by high-rise buildings now, giving it the feel of a small version of New York's Central Park. There is a pleasant rock garden and pond on the southwest side, where fishing poles can be rented (10RMB, $1.20) and the catch (mostly grass carp) is priced by weight (including an additional 10RMB if you catch nothing).

The other two Imperial altars, also built in the early 16th century, are located in similar city parks. The Temple of the Earth Park (Ditan Gongyuan) is north of the Lama Temple, just across the Second Ring Road North, and the Temple of the Moon Park (Yuetan Gongyuan), where stamp collectors swap and sell their wares, is just west of the Second Ring Road West. In the old days, these four altars encircled the city walls of Beijing and roughly corresponded to the four cardinal points of the compass.

Ritan Lu, Chaoyang District. ✆ 010/6502-1743. Admission 5RMB (60¢). Daily 6:30am–8:30pm. Subway: Yonganli. Located 3 blocks north of the Friendship Store and Silk Alley.

7 Museums & Mansions

Many of Beijing's outstanding museums are housed in ancient temples, towers, and historic garden residences throughout the capital. In many instances, the setting is one of the chief attractions. Although lighting and display is seldom state-of-the-art—and English signage can be spotty or nonexistent—simply viewing the objects in these fine storehouses can be fascinating.

Ancient Observatory (Guguan Xiang Tai) 🖈 The Imperial Observatory has been here, atop the Jianguomen gate in the city wall, since 1442; it is now surrounded by expressways, skyscrapers, and the city's busiest avenue. On a fine day, it offers one of Beijing's finest views. Inside, is a collection of some of the world's rarest astronomical instruments, most them originally fashioned by Jesuit missionaries who took up residence in Beijing in the 17th century and charmed the emperor with their scientific knowledge of the heavens. The observatory has a wonderful gold foil map of the stars as they were plotted in the Ming Dynasty and fine copies (for the most part) of the old instruments that were used to plot the heavens. On the roof, with its superb views of the Forbidden City, are copies of the Jesuit-designed armillary sphere, bronze gnomons, and other large ornate bronze devices that the Son of Heaven depended on 3 centuries ago.

2 Dongbiaobei Hutong, Chaoyang District. ✆ 010/6524-2202. Admission 10RMB ($1.20). Wed–Sun 9–11:30am and 1–4:30pm. Subway: Jianguomen. Located 1 block south of Jianguomenwai Dajie, west side of the Second Ring Road overpass.

Beijing Art Museum (Zhongguo Meishuguan) 🖈 The newest of Beijing's art museums occupies the grounds of the Wanshou Temple (Temple of Longevity), a small Buddhist complex of Ming halls and pavilions that dates from 1577 and was restored in the 18th century. The entrance gate, capped by a painted carving of blue sky, clouds, and 100 red bats (signifying good fortune), leads to a courtyard with a drum tower on the left and a bell tower (with a small store) on the right, both built in 1577. The first central hall is devoted to the worship of the laughing Buddha and the four heavenly kings. The second shrine, the Precious Hall of the Buddha (Dayanshou), contains lovely statuary and is intended for the worship of the "Medicinal Buddha of the Pure Glazed World." The meditation hall (50 ft. wide by 75 ft. deep) in the center of the grounds serves as a gallery of modern oil paintings, with prices in the $2,000 range. The halls on the west side display paintings, scrolls, textiles, ceramics, furniture, and artifacts from the Ming and Qing dynasties, as well as Japanese artworks created during the occupation of Manchuria in the 1930s and '40s.

In the Wanshou Temple, Xisihuan Lu (Third Ring Road West), Haidian District. ✆ 010/6841-3380. Admission 10RMB ($1.20). Tues–Sun 9am–5:30pm.. No subway. On the Changhe River, east side of the Third Ring Road West, 4 blocks from the Shangri-La Hotel

Big Bell Temple and Museum (Da Zhong Si) ⭐ The temple was built in
1733 and received its present name in 1743 when an enormous bronze bell, the
largest in China, was brought here (on ice sleds). This Big Bell is thought to have
been cast in 1420 when Yongle, builder of the Forbidden City, was emperor.
Weighing in at 46 tons and standing 23 feet high, it is displayed in its own tower
in a rear courtyard. Emperor Qianlong lit incense and prayed for rain before it.
For fun and good fortune, you can climb the spiral stairs to the top of tower and,
like Buddhist pilgrims of old, cast coins into the bell's opening, which makes a
pleasing sound. (This ritual was once the major source of income for the temple monks.) Other halls in the former Juesheng (Awakening) Temple house
4,000 years of Chinese bells, including a set of stone chimes from the Warring
States Period (475–221 B.C.) that visitors are invited to ring (for 2RMB, 24¢).
Among its 700 relics are friendship bells from New Zealand and Italy and newly
cast Chinese bells marking great occasions (such as the resumption of sover-
eignty over Hong Kong in 1997). Before this temple reopened as the Bell
Museum in 1985, it served as the Beijing No. 2 Food Factory.

31A Beisanhuan Xi Lu, Haidian District. ✆ **010/6255-0843** or 010/6255-0790. Admission 10RMB ($1.20).
Daily 8:30am–4:30pm. No subway. Located on the north side of the Third Ring Road between Haidian Lu and
Xizhimen Bei Dajie.

China Millennium Monument (Zhonghua Shiji Tan) Finished in late
1999 as China's gift to the new century, this monument has as many formal features as an ancient temple or modern mausoleum to a national hero—and
enough world records to keep the ambassador from Guinness pretty busy. The
complex faces south, following *feng shui* prescriptions; and the world's largest
block of white marble marks the entrance, carved with an inscription by President Jiang Zemin. A block-long square (Holy Fire Square) runs north to a raised
round rotunda at the head of the monument grounds. The square is festooned
with Chinese symbols, including an eternal flame at the center, streams representing the Yangzi and Yellow rivers flowing on the east and west flanks, and a
300-yard-long, 40-foot-wide causeway connecting the square to the northern
rotunda. The causeway is lined with bronze reliefs picturing the history of China
from 3000 B.C. to A.D. 2000. Finally, rising like a shield above the square, is the
massive, revolving rotunda (154 ft. in diameter), which is pitched at a 19-degree
angle and punctuated with a rod 90 feet high, resembling a sundial. Officially,
the rod is a "universal probe" symbolizing the "infinity of time and space." As
monuments go, this one is memorable, if a bit pretentious and abstract. Inside
the rotunda, which rotates once every 12 hours, are two galleries of statues representing 40 outstanding characters in Chinese history. To the east is the China
Millennium Bell, a newly cast 50-ton, 22-foot-tall monster—yes, it's the largest
bell in the world. Also deep inside the northern head of the monument is the
Century Art Museum, which sometimes hosts major exhibitions of Chinese art
and archaeology.

Fuxing Lu at Yangfangdian Lu (between the National Military Museum and Yuyuantan Park), Xicheng District.
No telephone. Admission 10RMB ($1.20). Daily 10am–5pm. Subway: Junshi Bowuguan.

China National Art Gallery (Zhongguo Meishuguan) Housed in a
monumental Chinese-style edifice (built in 1959 and renovated 1991), the
14 galleries of China's national gallery includes traditional artworks as well as the
work of emerging Chinese artists, some of whom are at work in studios here.
Contemporary works can be purchased at the gift shop (west wing), as can
woodcuts and traditional papercuts.

1 Wusi Dajie, Dongcheng District. ℭ **010/6401-9833** or 010/6401-2252. Admission 15RMB ($1.80). Tues–Sun 9am–5pm. Subway: Tiananmen Dong (³/₄ mile). Entrance on north side of Wusi Dajie, 1 block west of intersection with Wangfujing Dajie.

Drum Tower (Gulou)

Beijing's original Drum Tower, which sounded the hours with the beating of drums, was built here by Kublai Khan in 1272 and rebuilt by the Ming rulers in 1420. It's worth climbing the 69 steps in the narrow stairwell for the view from the open balconies above. Only one of the 24 watch drums once in use has survived. Its cowhide head was slashed in 1900. What is said to be the world's largest drum (8.5 ft. in diameter, constructed in 1990) is on display here, but the chief attraction is the view over the lakes and hutong neighborhoods of old Beijing. The Bell Tower (Zhonglou), rebuilt in 1747, is just a few blocks directly north up an alley from here and affords similar views.

Intersection of Gulou Dajie and Dianmenwai Dajie, Dongcheng District. Admission 6RMB (72¢). Daily 9am–4:30pm. Subway: Gulou.

Great View Tower (Chang Guan Lou) *Finds*

Empress Dowager Cixi frequently journeyed to her pet project, the Summer Palace, from the Forbidden City aboard the royal barge. Always in need of a correspondingly royal stopover, she had the Great View Tower built for that purpose in 1908. The tower, located at the northwest corner of the Beijing Zoo, is a 2-story European mansion in the baroque style consisting of 2 towers, 88 windows, and 66 doors. It is the only baroque Imperial residence left in Beijing and was recently reopened, after a $17 million renovation, as the Beijing Royal International Club, a club and catering restaurant. For a peek into the lives of old China's dynastic rulers, guided tours of the splendid interiors are available for a nominal charge. Many of the rooms are furnished as they were in the Empress Dowager's day, including her bedchamber, where the Imperial bed is still in place (and where the club guide would be happy to snap your photo).

137 Xizhimenwai Dajie (west gate of Beijing Zoo, over an arched bridge), Xicheng District. ℭ **010/6833-8888**. Admission 10RMB ($1.20). Daily 10am–6pm. No subway.

Lao She Museum (Lao She Bowuguan) ✮ *Finds*

This is more a home than a museum, the very house in which one of China's greatest writers of the 20th century lived before his life ended tragically at the beginning of the Cultural Revolution in 1966. Lao She's widow persisted for over 30 years before her home could be opened as a museum and memorial; now it is one of the most serene courtyard houses open to visitors in Beijing.

Born in 1899, Lao She achieved international success as a novelist and playwright for such works as *The Rickshaw Boy (Luotuo Xiangzi)* and *Teahouse.* He committed suicide at age 67 in nearby Taiping Lake, just before the Red Guard was to try him for political incorrectness. Today, his courtyard home is a tasteful, unsealed time capsule. Visitors may see his personal library and mementos of his days as a successful writer. His den is a study in solitude, down to a game of Solitaire on his bed and a photograph of the place where, according to the caption, "the patriotic writer, literary master, and artist of the people's culture jumped into the lake at midnight."

19 Fengfu Hutong (from Wangfujing Dajie, go west from the Crowne Plaza Beijing along Dengshikou Xi Jie several blocks and turn right up the Fengfu alley), Dongcheng District. ℭ **010/6514-2612**. Admission 5RMB (60¢). Tue–Sun 9am–4pm. Subway: Wangfujing (½ mile).

Lu Xun Museum (Lu Xun Bowuguan)   Heralded as China's greatest 20th-century writer, Lu Xun (1881–1936) is best known for *The True Story of Ah Q*. His museum contains letters, diaries, manuscripts, and even the author's clothing, as well as English translations of his work for sale. Well off the beaten track, this museum is seldom crowded.

19 Gongmenkou Ertiao, Xicheng District. ⓒ 010/6616-4080. Admission 5RMB (60¢). Tues–Sun 9am–3:30pm. Subway: Fuchengmen. Located 3 blocks north off Fuchengmennei Dajie, east of the subway station.

Museum of Chinese History (Zhongguo Lishi Bowuguan) ⓐⓐ   The southern wing of the massive building that also houses the Museum of the Chinese Revolution, this museum contains China's largest collection of historical artifacts, a fine complement to the holdings in the Forbidden City. It consists of two large courtyard floors. The exhibits are arranged chronologically, starting on the ground floor and moving clockwise. The first gallery, "Primitive Society," has skeletons and pottery from the Stone Age site at Banpo. The "Slave Society" gallery has artifacts from the Xia and Shang dynasties (21st–11th century B.C.). The "Feudal Society" gallery has shoes from the Warring States Period, two terra-cotta warriors and a horse from the Qin Dynasty, and an outstanding sampling of silks and pottery from the Tang Dynasty. On the second floor, there are many objects from the Qing (the last dynasty), concluding with two Western printing presses dated 1895. The displays grow more remarkable as one advances on the timeline, although there are no signs in English. Many of China's true national treasures are stored here among the 300,000 relics, and they should not be missed. Cameras and handbags must be checked before entry.

East side of Tiananmen Square, Chongwen District. ⓒ **010/6512-9381**. Admission 5RMB (60¢). Tues–Sun 8:30am–3:30pm. Ticket booth on the first flight of outside stairs to the right (south). Subway: Tiananmen Dong.

Museum of the Chinese Revolution (Zhongguo Gemin Lishi Bowuguan)   The north wing of this massive building (that also houses the Museum of Chinese History) is not nearly as interesting as its sister museum (see above). The exhibition of over 100,000 items focuses on the history of the Chinese Communist Party, 1919–49. The photographic record is its best display, but there are a few signs in English to help. Check cameras and handbags before entry.

East side of Tiananmen Square, Chongwen District. ⓒ **010/6512-3355**. Admission 3RMB (36¢). Tues–Sun 8:30am–3:30pm. Subway: Tiananmen Dong.

Natural History Museum (Ziran Bowuguan)   This spacious gallery contains some fine specimens of primitive man and of dinosaur skeletons and eggs excavated in China. It's big but stale as natural science displays go.

126 Tianqiao Nan Dajie, Chongwen District. ⓒ 010/6702-4431. Daily Tues–Sun 8:30am–5pm. Admission 15RMB ($1.80). Subway: Qianmen (½ mile). Entrance north of the west gate to Temple of Heaven Park (Tiantan).

Prince Gong's Mansion (Gong Wang Fu) ⓐ   Prince Gong's estate is Beijing's best-preserved example of how the upper class lived during the Qing Dynasty. It consists of 31 pavilions, halls, and residential buildings, 9 courtyards, several arched bridges, large ponds with islands and swans, an immense rock garden in the classical style, and even its own private pagoda for gazing at the moon. Yet the estate, except on the sunniest of days, seems gray and rundown. Prince Gong's brother was China's emperor from 1851 to 1861 and Gong served as regent for the next emperor along with Cixi, who would become the

Empress Dowager. Gong's son, Pu Yi, became China's last emperor. Prince Gong moved into this palace estate in 1852, but its design originated more than a century earlier. The mansion has its own stage for outdoor performances of Peking Opera, a teahouse open to hutong tour groups, and a Sichuan restaurant open to the public.

17 Qianhai Xi Lu, Xicheng District. © 010/6616-8149. Admission 5RMB (60¢). Daily 9am–5pm. No subway. Located west of Qianhai Lake and east of Liuyin Jie.

Soong Qing-ling Residence (Song Ching Ling Guzhu) 🏵🏵

Wife to the founder of the Republic of China, Sun Yat-sen, and sister-in-law of Chiang Kai-shek, Soong Qing-ling lived her life as if it were a Chinese opera played out at the highest levels. After the communists triumphed in 1949 and Chiang Kai-shek fled to Taiwan, Qing-ling stayed. Her sister, Soong Mei-ling, became famous in America as the great defender of Taiwan against Mao's China, while Soong Qing-ling, who supported the other side, served as vice-president of the People's Republic. Soong's Beijing residence has been preserved both as a family museum and a fine example of a courtyard estate. Soong lived here from 1963 to 1981, the year of her death. A large red sign in Chinese is all that identifies the entrance to her villa these days, but inside there are many signs in English identifying not only objects in the museum, but also the various pavilions and plants that make up the impressive garden grounds. This was originally the garden of a Dr. Mingzhu, a scholar during the rein of Emperor Kangxi, and there are trees here that he planted more than 200 years ago. A fine view of the landscaping—its winding lanes, pavilions, flowers, and pine trees girding a pond and stream fed by Imperial Jade Spring—can be seen from the Fan Pavilion (Shan Ting). The Soong museum is housed in the large former residences, where there is a chronology of her life in pictures, letters, newspaper articles, and memorabilia, such as a radio with a golden case (a gift from her brother, T.V. Soong) and X-ray equipment airlifted into China during World War II.

46 Houhai Beiyan, Xicheng District. © **010/6404-4205** or 010/6403-5858. Admission 8RMB (96¢). Daily 9am–4:30pm. Subway: Jishuitan. Located on the northeast shore of Houhai Lake.

8 Hutongs & Siheyuans (Lanes & Courtyard Compounds)

Hutongs are the narrow, twisting, east–west lanes and alleyways of old Beijing; much of the city's history during the Ming and Qing dynasties is preserved in their layout and colorful names. *Siheyuans* are the small courtyard dwellings behind the hutong walls. These rectangular complexes usually have an arched entry gate facing south and an outer courtyard with side halls surrounding an inner courtyard. In the old days, such a courtyard house would be owned by a single family with servants. In modern times, these siheyuans have often been divided up among many families. Roughly half of Beijing's population lives in some form of hutong, although these neighborhoods are rapidly disappearing under the bulldozer of urban renewal.

The Back Lakes area of Beijing (north of Beihai Park and the Forbidden City, on either side of Qianhai Lake) is the most popular area for touring the hutongs. Here you'll find the city's shortest hutong, **Yichi Dajie** (about 30 ft. long), and the narrowest, **Qianshi Hutong**, which squeezes down to just 15 inches.

Although there are pedicabs everywhere offering tours in this area, English-language communication and fare-bargaining can be problems when you're on your own. That's why the **Beijing Hutong Tourist Agency** 🏵, 26 Dianmen Xi

The Last Hutong in China

The courtyard houses of old Beijing's narrow lanes (hutongs) are fast disappearing. "Given the city's bad traffic and residents' difficult living conditions," explains one senior city planner, Fan Yaobang, "we have no choice but to renovate the old districts." Many, perhaps most, Beijingers agree. The question is how many hutongs will be preserved. In the past 50 years, 2 of every 3 alleys have disappeared (of 1,339 hutongs in the 1950s, 459 remain today). Presently, 260 hutongs with 2,000 siheyuans (courtyard dwellings) are in cultural protection zones.

There have been protests, including a rare sit-down demonstration by about 50 middle-aged and elderly residents who gathered at city government headquarters near Tiananmen Square in April 1998, declaring that they did not want their homes demolished to make way for a new subway line. Nor did they want to be forced, as thousands have, into tall modern apartment complexes in the far suburbs. The protests were to no avail.

One man much in the news recently, octogenarian Zhao Jingxin, had simply refused to budge from his 400-year-old courtyard house that stood on a hutong slated to become a shopping plaza. He ignored eviction notices and refused extravagant offers to evacuate (6 apartments for $330,000). All his neighbors had given in and the demolishers closed in. Like a few others in Beijing, Zhao was arguing that Beijing should end the wholesale eradication of its historic architecture and begin preserving what's left, exiling the new commercial buildings instead of the old downtown residents to the suburbs; but his position found few converts in the boomtown that is modern Beijing, and his house was razed in October 2000. Preservation of Beijing's historic neighborhoods is still often on the lips of politicians but, as the official *People's Daily* put it, that may be "like strengthening the sheep pen after all the sheep are dead."

Lu, Xicheng District (a block northwest of the north gate to Beihai Park; ✆ **010/6615-9097,** 010/6400-2787, or 010/6612-3236), has been so successful with its organized pedicab (bicycle-driven rickshaws) tours.

Beijing Hutong Tourist Agency, the city's largest hutong tour company, employs a fleet of pedicabs that can carry one or two passengers each. One English-speaking guide leads the procession. Most tourists purchase their tickets 1 day in advance at their hotel tour desks. Tours cost between 180 and 240RMB ($22–$29) and are offered daily from 9 to 11:30am and 2 to 4:30pm. A hotel taxi to and from the rendezvous point is sometimes included in the service (at about three times the cost of taking your own taxi, which is usually 25–40RMB, $3–$4.80). Directions to the departure point (corner of Dianmenxi Lu and Shishahai Tixiao) are furnished by the hotel ticket agent. Plan to arrive 20 to 30 minutes early.

The pedicabs with the red canopies snake through the alleys and streets, usually visiting such sights as the Drum Tower, the Shisha Lakes, and Guanghau

Temple. The highlight is a walking tour of several hutongs and a chance to go inside a siheyuan, see its courtyard rooms, and talk with the family that lives there today. The tour usually ends with a stroll and tea at Prince Gong's Mansion, which is an immense and stately version of the courtyard house. The same company also offers extended hutong tours that enable visitors to stay longer with the residents and enjoy a family meal with them. Groups of at least 10 visitors are required. Some travelers find these organized hutong tours rather tedious and overrated, but this is the easiest way to get a quick look behind the scenes at Old Beijing.

9 Especially for Kids

In a country known for the emphasis it places on the family—known, too, for the lengths a family can go to to spoil its "only child"—attractions for children are commonplace. The following are some that appeal particularly to younger foreign travelers in Beijing.

Automobile Forum Beijing *Finds* This automobile showroom for kids and the kids-in-adults, is strictly a showroom (sales are not permitted) where Volkswagen, manufacturer of a line of sedans in China known as the Santana, displays its newest, jazziest models and invites anyone and everyone to kick the tires, look under the hood, and sit at the steering wheel. Kids have fun jumping in and out of the cars.

Wonderful World Mall, 1 Dong Chang'an Jie, Oriental Plaza (Shop AA50, upper ground floor), Dongcheng District. © 010/8518-6000, ext. 101. Daily 10:30am–7pm. Subway: Wangfujing or Dongdan.

Beijing Amusement Park (Beijing Youle Yuan) ✹ This rather old-fashioned (1970s) amusement park with a Ferris wheel, water slide, looping roller coaster, and teacup rides has added an animal park, go-cart track, and Imax theater. It's a great place to join local families having fun.

West entrance of Longtan Lake Park, 1 Zuoanmennei Dajie, Chongwen District. © 010/6714-6909 or 010/6711-1155, ext. 221. Admission by height: above 140cm, 57RMB ($7); 100–140cm, 37RMB ($4.44); under 100cm, free. Mon–Fri 8:30am–dusk; Sat–Sun 8am–dusk. No subway.

Beijing Aquarium (Beijing Shuizuguan) ✹ Billing itself as "the world's largest inland aquarium," this new attraction, located on the northeast side of the Beijing Zoo, has elaborate displays with ecological themes and a popular performance by its porpoises—but admission is pricey.

18 Gaoliangqiao Xiejie (north of Xizhimenwai and the zoo), Haidian District. © 010/6217-6655. Admission 120RMB ($14) includes admission to Beijing Zoo; students half price; 2 children free with 1 paid adult ticket. Daily 9am–5pm.

Beijing Zoo (Beijing Dongwu Yuan) Once a private garden estate, the zoo was created here by Empress Dowager Cixi, who imported hundreds of exotic animals from Germany in the late 19th century. The main gate and many of the animal exhibition halls and outdoor pens seem to have changed little after a century. Most Western visitors abhor the conditions here, with the emphasis on cages for most of the 6,000 animals. The new Panda Garden, with its six adults and baby twins, is an improvement over the general facilities, with outdoor as well as indoor spaces.

Xizhimenwai Dajie (6 long blocks west of subway station), Xicheng District. © 010/6831-4411. Admission (including Panda Garden) 10RMB ($1.20) adults, 3RMB (36¢) children. Daily 7:30am–6pm. Subway: Xizhimen.

Blue Zoo Aquarium (Lan Dongwu Shuizuguan) Highlighted by a 100-yard-long underwater tunnel, the longest in Asia, that's surrounded by baby sharks and piranhas, this water park has tanks, classrooms, and educational galleries and is the favorite among expatriate kids and their families.

South gate of Workers' Stadium, Chaoyang District. ℭ **010/6591-3397** or 010/6591-3398, ext. 1177. Admission 50RMB ($6) children, 75RMB ($9) adults. Daily 8am–8pm. Subway: Chaoyangmen (¾ mile).

Chinese Ethnic Culture Park (Zhonghua Minzu Yuan) In this ethnic theme park, costumed representatives of China's 55 minorities re-enact their customs in reconstructed model houses and villages. Song and dance performances occur regularly on the grounds, and ethnic food is served at small restaurants.

Southwest corner of Fourth Ring Road and Beichen Lu, Chaoyang District. ℭ **010/6206-3640.** Admission 60RMB ($7). Daily 8am–7pm summer, 8:30am–5:30pm winter. No subway.

Dynasty Wax Works Palace Billed as the world's largest wax museum, this palace of effigies is home to the famous and infamous from the Chinese world.

Xiguan Traffic Circle, Changping, on the highway to the Ming Tombs and Great Wall at Badaling, Changping County. ℭ **010/6974-8675.** Admission 60RMB ($7). Daily 9am–6pm. No subway.

Five-Color Earth Craft Center (Wu Setu Gongyifang) Try your hand here at some do-it-yourself arts and crafts in ceramics, plate-painting, paper-making, tie-dying, and embroidery.

East Children's Palace, 10 Dongzhimen Nan Lu (Second Ring Road East, north of Poly Plaza, across from subway station), Dongcheng District. ℭ **010/6415-3839.** Admission 50RMB ($6) 1 hr., 80RMB ($10) 2 hr. Daily 9am–6pm. Subway: Dongsishitiao.

Fundazzle (Fandoule) This indoor playground—with slides, a pool of balls, games, and a climbing wall—is a place for kids to work off excess energy while their parents watch from above.

Workers' Stadium, Gongrentiyuchang Lu, Chaoyang District. ℭ **010/6593-6207** or 010/6441-2208. Admission 30RMB ($3.60) for 2 hours. Daily 9am–5pm. Subway: Dongsishitiao.

Kaite Mini-Golf Arched bridges, walls, gates, pavilions, and other maddening obstacles—all in miniature—pose a pleasant challenge in the park.

At north entrance to Ritan Park, Chaoyang District. ℭ **010/6415-1047.** Admission 25RMB ($3). Daily 8am–10:30pm, summers only. Subway: Jianguomen or Yonganli.

Lido Park This large park offers plenty of summer arts and crafts classes for kids, rents fishing poles, and has outdoor swimming (30RMB, $3.60 for children under 17).

East of the Holiday Inn Lido Hotel, Jichang Lu and Jiangtai Lu, off the Airport Expressway, Chaoyang District. ℭ **010/6438-0882.** 5RMB (60¢). Daily 6am–11pm summers; dawn to dusk winters. No subway.

Putt-Putt Golf This place offers good, clean, all-American fun and is favored by expatriate families.

Beijing Dongdan Sports Center, Dongdan Park, 108 Chongwenmennei Dajie District. ℭ **010/6528-8495.** Admission 25RMB ($3). Daily 8am–10pm, summers only. Subway: Chongwenmen.

Sony ExploraScience Museum 🌟 This interactive science and technology museum is a favorite of local and expatriate kids. The new exhibit features four zones employing digital technology to amuse and educate, including exhibits from the Exploratorium in San Francisco and gadgets from Japan.

1 Chang'an Dong Lu, Oriental Plaza (Shop A201, Upper Ground Floor, The Malls), Dongcheng District. ℭ **010/8518-2255.** Admission 60RMB ($7) adults, 40RMB ($4.80) students, under 6 free. Daily 10:30am–7pm (closed 2nd Mon and Tues of the month). Subway: Wangfujing or Dongdan.

Taipingyang Underwater World   Penguins and sharks cavort as visitors watch from a conveyor belt.

11 Xisanhuan Zhong Lu (Central Third Ring Road West), Haidian District. ☎ **010/6846-1172.** Admission 60RMB ($7.20). Daily 9am–5:30pm. No subway.

Tuanjiehu Manmade Seashore   The artificial beach is a great place for hot-weather swimming in the park pool.

Tuanjiehu Park (east side of Third Ring Road East), Chaoyang District. ☎ **010/6507-3603.** Park only admission 2RMB (24¢). Admission to swim 20RMB ($2.40) adults, 15RMB ($1.80) children. Daily 7am–9pm, June–Sept only. No subway.

Universal Studios Experience (Huanqiu Yincheng Didai)   Special effects and behind-the-scenes peeks at Hollywood moviemaking are presented with sets, scenes, and characters from *Waterworld* and *Jurassic Park.*

Basement, Henderson Center, 18 Jianguomennei Dajie, Chaoyang District. ☎ **010/6518-3260,** ext. 301, or 010/6518-3404. Admission 30RMB ($3.60) weekdays and 35RMB ($4.20) weekends for adults, 25RMB ($3) weekdays and 30RMB ($3.60) weekends for children; 85RMB ($10) for 2 parents, 1 child. Mon–Fri noon–8pm; Sat–Sun 10am–9pm. Subway: Dongdan or Jianguomen.

World Park (Shijie Gongyuan)   China's largest theme park (116 acres) and an extreme, but fun, curiosity, World Park consists of miniaturized reproductions of over 100 of the world's great sites, skylines, monuments, and landmarks, include an Eiffel Tower, Statue of Liberty, and Sphinx, each standing 30 feet tall.

Fourth Ring Road South, Fengtai District. ☎ **010/6382-3344.** Admission Mon–Thurs 40RMB ($4.80), Fri–Sun 48RMB ($6). Daily 8:30am–5pm. No subway.

Yuyuantan Water World   Beijing's largest water park has plenty of slides, sluices, and swimming pools and is next to the Soong Ching-Ling Children's Science Park and the Diaoyutai Guest House, where world leaders stay.

Yuyuantan Park, Fourth Ring Road West, Haidian District. ☎ **010/6851-4447.** Admission 15RMB ($1.80). Daily 9am–6pm, June–Aug only. Subway: Gongzhufen.

10 Organized Tours

Most Beijing hotels have tour desks that can arrange a variety of day tours for guests. These tour desks are often extensions of **China International Travel Service** (CITS), with offices at 28 Jianguomenwai Dajie (☎ **010/6515-8562**) and 103 Fuxingmennei Dajie (☎ **010/6601-1122;** www.cits.net). CITS operates most of the English-language group tours in Beijing, even if you buy your ticket in your hotel. The only reason to go directly to the CITS office is to arrange a special tour, perhaps of sites not offered on the regular group tour list or for a private tour with guide, driver, and car.

The ordinary group tours are usually inexpensive, seldom have more than 20 people, and all are conducted by local English-speaking guides (of varying quality). Each tour costs from 300 to 500RMB ($36–$60) per person. A typical full-day coach tour may consist of one of the following: (1) the Great Wall and the Ming Tombs; (2) the Forbidden City, Tiananmen Square, and the Temple of Heaven; or (3) the Summer Palace, Lama Temple, and Panda Garden at the Beijing Zoo. Lunch at a local restaurant of reasonable quality is included (as is a stop at the guide's favorite jade factory outlet). Hotel tour desks sometimes feature entertainment packages for an evening at the Beijing Opera or a dinner show with the acrobats, but these seldom include a guide or transportation.

Specialized tours within Beijing can be arranged by CITS, although smaller private travel agencies may be able to do a more efficient job. One proven

---

Fun Fact **Michael Jordan in China**

He is worshipped by sports fans the world over—even in China, where he is known as *Fei Ren,* the Flying Man. When he retired in 1999, Michael Jordan made the front pages across the Middle Kingdom, the *Beijing Morning Post* mourning his departure as "touching the hearts of hundreds of millions." The Chinese admire Jordan for his athleticism and easygoing style. Air Jordan sneakers and Chicago Bulls caps and jerseys are still hot items; black market version are sold at street stalls from Kashgar to Beijing. Some 50 million Chinese play basketball regularly (20 million of these play in a total of more than 1 million amateur leagues), and the NBA Game of the Week is broadcast on Saturdays by China Central Television (CCTV) across the nation.

---

private travel agency providing tours, tickets, and hotels to international clients is **Sunshine Express** at Jing Ding Commercial Building, 2 Dongsanhuan Lu (Third Ring Road), Chaoyang District, Beijing 100020 (✆ **010/6586-8069;** fax 010/6586-8077; sunpress@public.bta.net.cn). Another reliable agency is **Panda Tour,** located at 36 Nanli Shi Lu, Xicheng District, Beijing 100037 (✆ **010/6803-6963;** fax 010/6803-7044; bjpanda@public.bta.net.cn).

11 Staying Active

Most visitors to Beijing do not come to pursue outdoor recreation or sports, but China's capital offers a surprisingly wide range of such activities. Hotels routinely offer exercise machines, weights, aerobics, and workout areas, as well as swimming pools and locker rooms, and, less often, tennis and squash courts, all at little or no charge to their guests. It is possible to use the fitness facilities and courts of most hotels and private health clubs on a daily basis, too, even if you are not a guest (although the fees can be steep).

Some exercises, such as jogging, require little in the way of facilities. Joggers in Beijing can always take to the early morning streets (before the crowds block them), but the large public parks are much nicer places for a run. No one bats an eye at runners these days; Beijing, after all, has its own international marathon every October.

Golf, bowling, and billiards have become the three most popular recreational sports in Beijing, pursued by well-to-do locals, foreign residents, and overseas visitors, but horseback riding, ice-skating, and traditional *tai ji quan* can also be enjoyed in the capital, if time and energy allow. Beijing even boasts paintball emporiums, shooting ranges, rock-climbing walls, and China's first bungee-jumping venue.

Spectator sports, on the other hand, are more limited and less to Western tastes, although professional basketball, interleague soccer, and international badminton, volleyball, and tennis matches draw large crowds in the capital.

ACTIVITIES A TO Z

BOWLING   Bowling experienced a boom in China during the 1990s, when more than 15,000 alleys were built, many of them in Beijing. You can find alleys in the **Holiday Inn Lido** (✆ **010/6437-6688,** ext. 3801; 11am–2pm, 10RMB [$1.20] per game; 2–7pm, 15RMB [$1.80] per game; 7pm–1am, 20RMB

[$2.40] per game), the **Beijing International Hotel** (℮ **010/6512-6688,** ext. 6173; 10am–2pm, 5RMB [60¢] per game; 2–6pm, 10RMB [$1.20] per game; 6pm–midnight, 25RMB [$3] per game), the **Beijing New Century Hotel** (℮ **010/6849-2001,** ext. 88; 10am–2pm, 6RMB [72¢] per game; 2–7pm, 15RMB [$1.80] per game; 7pm–midnight, 25RMB [$3] per game), and the **China World Hotel** (℮ **010/6505-2266;** 11:30am–2pm, 10RMB [$1.20] per game; 2–7pm, 15RMB [$1.80] per game; 7pm–1am, 25RMB [$3] per game; slightly higher rates Fri–Sun; shoe rental 5RMB [65¢]).

BUNGEE JUMPING   China's first venture into elastic cord excitement is the **Shidu Bungee Jumping Facility,** Shidu Scenic Area, Fangshan District, 55 miles southwest of Beijing (℮ **010/6134-0841**). Open daily from 8am to 6pm on the bridge over the Juma River. The charge is 180RMB ($22) for a high jump, 150RMB ($18) for a low jump.

GOLF   Greens fees at Beijing's handful of golf courses run from $80 to $100 on weekdays, $100 to $150 on weekends. Caddies cost $10 to $20 and club rental is $30 to $40. All courses require advance reservations; summer weekends are particularly crowded. The 18-hole **Beijing International Golf Club,** also known as the Ming Tombs Golf Course, northwest of Beijing in Changping County (℮ **010/6974-5678** or 010/6974-6388) is still the capital's top links. The **Beijing Country Golf Club,** northeast of Beijing on the airport road (Mapo Village, Shunyi County; ℮ **010/6944-1005**) has 36 holes. The **Beijing Grand Canal Golf Club,** on the Grand Canal in the Tongzhou District (east of Beijing; ℮ **010/8958-3058**) is a new 18-hole course with night golf. **Chaoyang Golf Club,** Tuanjiehu Xiaoqu, Shangsi Lu (near the Zhaolong Hotel), Chaoyang District (℮ **010/6500-1149**), has just nine holes and a driving range, but is close to downtown Beijing, and its greens fees are low: 240RMB ($29) weekdays, 350RMB ($42) weekends, with the driving range costing 30RMB ($3.60) plus 25RMB ($3) per bucket of balls. The **Huatang International Golf Club,** located in the Sanhe Yanjiao Development Zone (15 miles from airport, free shuttle bus from Traders Hotel; ℮ **010/6159-3930**), is opening Beijing's newest 18-hole championship course, designed by Graham Marsh. Also new on the Beijing links scene is the **Graneronel Golf Club,** southwest of Beijing near Liulihe Town (℮ **010/6500-1188,** ext. 3480), an 18-hole layout charging 600RMB ($72) weekdays, 900RMB ($108) weekends, although guests at Traders Hotel can play for as little as 200RMB ($24) on Tuesdays, 690RMB ($83) on weekends; shuttle bus and caddie are included.

HEALTH CLUBS   Some hotels offer day rates to outsiders. The **Gloria Plaza Hotel** has stair machines, exercise bikes, treadmills, weights, an indoor pool, and locker rooms (120RMB, $14 per day). The **Great Wall Sheraton** has two outdoor tennis courts, locker rooms, exercise bikes, stair machines, rowing machines, Ping-Pong, and indoor swimming (150RMB/$18 per day). The **Holiday Inn Lido** has a gym, exercise machines, weights, and an indoor pool (120RMB, $14 per day). The **Kempinski Hotel** provides a weight room, lockers, machines, indoor pool, exercise area, and squash and tennis courts (200RMB, $24 per day). The **Shangri-La Hotel** has exercise machines, locker rooms, an indoor pool, Ping-Pong, aerobics, volleyball, basketball, bowling, squash courts (60RMB, $7 per hour), tennis courts (160RMB, $19 per hour), most located in a separate fitness building, for which there is a fee of 150RMB ($18) per day. **Traders Hotel** has Nautilus equipment, stair machines,

Happy Feet

After a hard day walking the hard streets of Beijing, nothing is more satisfying than a massage that gets to the sole of your aches and pains. Foot massage (reflexology) has swept the capital, where crumbling sidewalks, busy streets, and endless flights of stairs are all too common. The most delightful treat you can bestow on your feet at the end of the day is readily available at the foot massage studio of **Beijing Tianhe Liangzi Refreshing Company, Ltd** ★★★. Located a block west of China World, on the second floor at the back of the Jin Zhi Qiao Mansion, 1 Jianguomenwai Dajie, Dongcheng District (② **010/ 6506-4466,** ext. 6087), the Liangzi foot-massage studio has seen its share of tired feet (of visitors and locals alike). Massaging the foot is part of long traditional Chinese medical practice related to acupuncture, the theory being that by working with the meridians in the foot, a skilled masseuse can also cure the ailments in other parts of the body that share the same internal energy (*qi*) channels. Be that as it may, a foot massage is an unforgettable experience and one that's sure to ease some cramps. Sessions begin by soaking the feet in a tub of heated medicinal herbs as young reflexologists massage pressure points in your hands and arms. Leaning back in a comfortable chair, feet raised on an ottoman, the real work begins, a vigorous 30-minute foot rub that begins in pain and ends in bliss. The final phase is a shoulder rub topped off with a knee in the lower back and a final snap of the sacroiliac. The young attendants are happy to practice a little English as they work. A 90-minute foot massage costs about 140RMB ($17), longer but cheaper than the full-body massage also offered here (60 min. for about 170RMB, $20). Open daily from 11am to 2am.

Another popular massage experience in Beijing is the traditional full-body variety conducted by blind masseuses at the **Axin Massage Keep-Fit Centre,** opposite the southeast corner of Workers' Stadium at 2A Baijiazhuang Lu, Chaoyang District (② **010/6595-0997).** The friendly staff here is professionally trained. Open daily from 9am to 10pm; the 60-minute Axin blind massage costs just 60RMB ($7).

treadmills, exercise bikes, and a locker room (100RMB, $12 per day). The newest, and in some ways the most impressive, health club in town is at the **Kerry Centre Hotel,** where there are over 70 exercise machines, free weights, an NBA regulation-size basketball court, a 35 meter pool, and a 235 meter outdoor jogging/roller-blading court. Call ② **010/6561-8833** for day rates.

ICE-SKATING   Beijing has superb outdoor ice-skating in the winter at **Beihai Park** and the **Summer Palace.** Skate rental concessions on the shore charge about 10RMB ($1.10) per day. Even more popular in winter are the ice cars (*bing che*), boxy sleds propelled by ski poles that rent at 5RMB (60¢) per hour. Indoor skating is available at the **Ditan Ice Arena,** Zilongxiang Liubing Chang, near the Ditan Park north gate, 14A Hepingli Zhong Jie, Dongcheng District (② **010/6429-1618**), open daily from 10am to 10pm (from 9am on weekends).

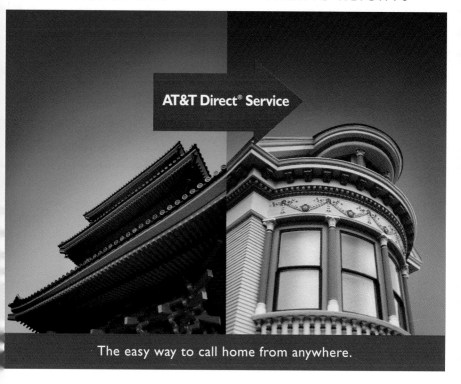

AT&T Direct® Service

The easy way to call home from anywhere.

Global
connection
with the AT&T
Network

AT&T
direct
service

For the easy way to call home, take the attached wallet guide.

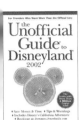
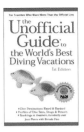
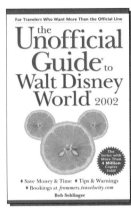
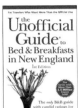

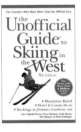
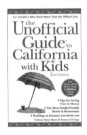

Admission is 10RMB ($1.20) per hour for kids, 20RMB ($2.40) per hour for adults. Beijing's newest skate rink is the upscale **Le Cool,** Guomao Liubing Chang (© **010/6505-5776**), in the new underground shopping center that connects Traders Hotel to China World Hotel. Open Sunday through Friday from 10am to 10pm and Saturday until midnight, this ritzy rink charges 30RMB ($3.60) for 90 minutes from 10am to 6pm, 40RMB ($4.80) from 6 to 10pm, and 50RMB ($6) after 6pm on Saturdays.

KITE-FLYING   The Chinese have been flying their invention for over 2,000 years. The best places to buy and fly local kites are at the **Summer Palace, Tiananmen Square,** or in the parks, particularly **Tiantan** (Temple of Heaven).

PAINTBALL   Helmets, paintball guns, camouflage uniforms, thick forests, and towers are all available at **Color Me Purple** (Wanfangting Paintball Shooting Range), located in Wanfangting Park, Yangqiao Xili, Nansanhuan Zhonglu, Fengtai District (© **010/6729-7320**). Admission is 100RMB ($12) including rental equipment and 30 rounds. Reservations are required in summer. Hours vary, and night games are available.

ROCK CLIMBING   It's only 15RMB ($1.80) per hour to climb the indoor walls at the **Qidagudu (Seven Ancient Cities) Climbing Club,** 183 Xuanwumen Dajie, Xicheng District (© **010/6605-3563**). It's open daily from 10am to 9pm.

SHOOTING RANGES   Take your choice of imported or Chinese rifles, even a machine gun, at the **China North Shooting Range,** Nankou Village, Changping County (toward the Great Wall at Badaling; © **010/6977-1368**). Open daily from 9am to 5pm, prices are by the bullet (2–7RMB, 25¢–85¢, depending on the gun).

SWIMMING WITH THE SHARKS   Depending on your profession, you may have already spent years "swimming with the sharks," but in Beijing you can do it for real, in the company of an instructor, at **Taipingyang Underwater World,** 11 Third Ring Main Road West, Xisanhuan Zhong Lu (© **010/6846-1172**), open daily from 8:30am to 5:30pm. The price is 60RMB ($7.20), and the instructors say that, as far as they know, there's not much to fear. (*Remember:* In China, no one sues for negligence, and liability laws don't extend very far.)

TAI CHI (TAI JI QUAN)   These venerable and graceful "shadow-boxing" exercises practiced by tens of thousands of Beijingers every morning can be learned at classes held in the Lido Club in the **Holiday Inn Lido Hotel,** Jichang Lu, Jiangtai Lu, Chaoyang District (© **010/6437-6688,** ext. 1603) on Tuesday and Thursday from 9 to 10am.

SPECTATOR SPORTS

The **Chinese National Basketball League** (CNBL) has been building a strong following across China since its inception in 1994. Each team is allowed to hire two foreign players (usually Americans). The **Beijing Ducks** play their home games at Workers' Stadium, as does Beijing's popular **Guo An** (National Guardians) professional soccer team. Tickets for either home team can be purchased at the Workers' Stadium north gate or from Li Sheng Selection, 74A Wangfujing Dajie, Dongcheng District (© **010/6525-0581**), open daily from 9am to 8:30pm. The soccer season runs April through November; the basketball season, November through April.

7

Beijing Strolls

Few world capitals are as frustrating, yet as fascinating, to walk as Beijing. The frustration comes first from the fact that much of the city is not meant for strolls: Although flat, Beijing is quite sprawling, and many of its long blocks are monotonous, ugly, and uninteresting. Yet there are fascinating walks, utterly unlike any of those in the West. Some of these walks, however, are embedded with their own frustrations. Street signs are difficult to spot and interpret, addresses are omitted from buildings, and the sidewalks are crowded not only with other pedestrians, but also with bicycle parking lots, construction sites, vendors and their carts, card players, laundry strung between doors and trees, and even a brazenly parked car or two. More than once, you may find yourself walking in the streets and gutters just to get around these obstacles. But in looking back, it is often just these obstacles that added to the fascination of a stroll in Beijing. Crowded, dusty, odoriferous—these are city streets that still have character, where barbers with a chair, a water pan, and a straight razor line up at park entrances, where itinerant vendors from Tibet sell yak skulls for mounting, where foot masseurs work the sidewalks.

Strolling Beijing is exhilarating, but also strangely tiring. Half a day's walk is usually plenty. You may return to your room feeling not so much exhausted as bruised—by the polluted air and dust, the raw odors, the jarring sounds, the slamming crowds, the grinding obstacle course. The strolls described in this chapter are the most fascinating and least grueling possible. Each of them also lends itself to bicycling. Renting a bike from your hotel is not necessarily the suicidal act that it appears to be at first. Bike traffic is quite orderly in Beijing, the basic rule being that cars have the right of way even when they shouldn't; this is the basic rule of survival on foot as well. *Cars always have the right of way, even when you have a green light, so look both ways and always be prepared to yield.* Whether you walk or ride a bike in Beijing, adjust to the flow of the Beijingers themselves. They know how and when to proceed across the intersections. Follow, don't lead, and slow down: Savor these walks through the capital of China.

WALKING TOUR 1	LIULICHANG CULTURE & ANTIQUES STREET

Start:	Intersection of Liulichang Xi Jie and Nanxinhua Jie (subway: Hepingmen).
Finish:	Qianmen Gate, south end of Tiananmen Square (subway: Qianmen).
Time:	2 to 3 hours.
Best times:	Any weekday starting at about 10am or 2:30pm.
Worst times:	Sundays are unbearably crowded, and Saturdays aren't much better. Avoid early mornings (before 10am) and from noon to 2pm (lunch hour). Most shops close about 8:30pm.

Walking Tour—The Liulichang Antiques Street

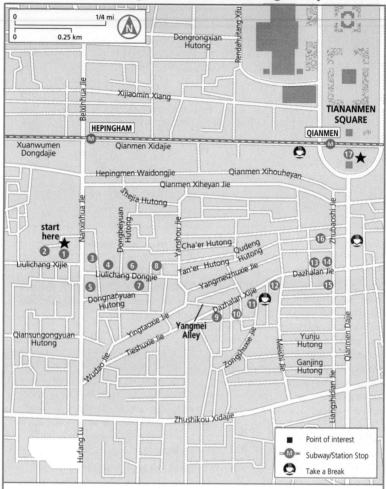

1 Liulichang Culture Street West

2 Rongbaozhai

3 China Bookstore

4 Liulichang Culture Street East

5 Jiguge

6 Zhongguo

7 Wenshenzhai

8 Diayuexuan

9 Dazhalan pedestrian shopping street

10 Neiliansheng Shoe Store

11 Tongrentang Traditional Medicine Shop

12 Underground City

13 Ruifuxiang Silk and Cotton Store

14 Qianmen Women's Clothing Store

15 Liubiju Pickle Shop

16 Zhubaoshi Jie

17 Qianmen (Front Gate)

The Dazhalan neighborhood southwest of Tiananmen Square contains several of old Beijing's most historic streets. **Liulichang Street,** with a 500-year legacy dating back to the Ming Dynasty, was renovated in the 1980s to capture the look and atmosphere of Qing Dynasty Beijing with its finely decorated tile-roofed shop houses. Scholars and art connoisseurs frequented Liulichang in the old days. Now it is noted for its shops selling scrolls, rubbings, handmade paper, paintbrushes, ink sticks, jade carvings, and, above all, antiques. Liulichang runs about 6 blocks east; just south of it begins **Dazhalan,** another old shopping street that has been converted into a cobblestoned pedestrian-only mall. Dazhalan terminates at **Zhubaoshi Street,** which runs north, parallel with Qianmen Dajie, into Qianmen (Front Gate) at Tiananmen Square. There are many pre-Revolutionary shops on Zhubaoshi and Dazhalan streets, including apothecaries selling traditional medicines. This stroll should give you the feel of Old Beijing's bustling commercial districts at a time when the emperor still ruled China from the nearby Forbidden City.

To begin, take a taxi or walk straight south from the Hepingmen subway station down Nanxinhua Jie to:

❶ Liulichang Culture Street West (Liulichang Xijie)

This street presently occupies 3 blocks and is pushing ever westward. This end of Liulichang Jie (Glazed-Tile Factory Street) has plenty of tiny storefronts and vendors' stalls selling collectibles and art supplies, including the renowned:

❷ Rongbaozhai

The most prominent shop on the west section of Liulichang (no. 19, north side; open daily 9am–6pm), Rongbaozhai sells woodblock prints, copies of famous calligraphy, historic paintings (reproductions), and art supplies. It is one of Beijing's top art shops and well worth browsing. The shop at no. 34 (south side) carries old books and the store next door (no. 36) has an interesting selection of Chinese musical instruments.

Backtrack to Nanxinhua Jie where you began, cross it, and enter:

❸ The China Bookstore (No. 115)

This shop carries a hodgepodge of classical Chinese books and piles of foreign-language books on Chinese culture. It's a good place for book lovers to "get lost" in the stacks.

You've now crossed over to:

❹ Liulichang Culture Street East (Liulichang Dong Jie)

This street, which runs for about a half-mile, has interesting old shops on either side, including

❺ Jiguge (Nos. 132–136)

Stop here for reproductions of famous Chinese paintings and scrolls, clay tomb figures, rubbings from stone tablets, and fine jade carvings. Jiguge also carries a wide range of Yixing teapots and teas, which you can sip at a table in its teahouse daily from 9am to 11pm.

❻ Zhongguo (No. 115)

This place is worth a stop to look at antiquarian books.

❼ Wenshenzhai (No. 92)

This shop was once the chief supplier of fans and paper lanterns to the Forbidden City.

❽ Diayuexuan (No. 73)

This store has been in the artist brush business for over 80 years.

Liulichang east ends at Yanshou Jie. Make a southward jog until you come to a gate and the start of a pedestrian-only cobblestoned street. This is:

⑨ Dazhalan Pedestrian Shopping Street (Dazhalan Jie, also called Dashilan Jie)

Though a bit more modern than Liulichang, Dazhalan is still quite interesting. Relax and enjoy the window-shopping.

In the first block on the right side there are, in order:

⑩ Neiliansheng Shoe Store (No. 34)

Established in 1853, this is still the place to buy footwear.

⑪ Tongrentang Traditional Medicine Shop (No. 24)

Established in 1669, this was once Beijing's most celebrated pharmacy.

Just down the street is a real curiosity, the:

TAKE A BREAK for a cup of tea and a Chinese steamed pastry right next door to the traditional medicine store at the **Zhang Yi Yuan Tea Shop**, 22 Dazhalan Jie, open daily 8am to 7pm.

⑫ Underground City

At no. 18 Dazhalan there's an arrow pointing down to the Underground City, a vast labyrinth of tunnels built in the late 1950s as Beijing's underground air-raid shelter. It was built by hand. Take a peek. There are dozens of little shops and stands in the tunnel, as well as an entire hotel.

When you re-emerge, you're nearly at the east end of Dazhalan. Don't miss its most famous store:

⑬ Ruifuxiang Silk and Cotton Store

Established in 1893 on the north side of Dazhalan, Ruifuxiang was once the prime outlet for Qing Dynasty royalty and rich merchants. Within its gaudy marble entrance is a vast selection of silks and clothing. (Open daily 8:30am–9:30pm.)

Next door is the:

⑭ Qianmen Women's Clothing Store

This shop offers suits, blouses, and a selection of wool and silk fabrics that can be custom-tailored. (Open daily 8:30am–9pm.)

On the south side of the street is:

⑮ Liubiju Pickle Shop

Still going quite strong after 400 years.

This marks the end of the Dazhalan pedestrian mall. Make an immediate left turn (north) up the side street known as:

⑯ Zhubaoshi Jie

Its name means "Jewelry Street." This was the gateway to a major brothel and theater district up until Liberation (1949). Today it is a major outdoor bazaar of stands and carts selling inexpensive clothing, collectibles, and edibles.

Ahead, looms:

⑰ Qianmen (Front Gate)

North of the Zhubaoshi bazaar is the traffic arc that leads to the south end of Tiananmen Square. To the northeast is the old Front Gate (Qianmen, officially Zhengyangmen), a towering remnant of the city wall, through which the emperors passed on their annual procession from the Forbidden City to the Temple of Heaven. You can ascend the tower at two points for excellent views of Tiananmen Square to the north and the Dazhalan District to the southwest. There's also a fine photographic exhibition of the streets and walls of old Beijing.

WINDING DOWN From Qianmen Gate you can go in any direction. The world's largest **KFC** is a block west on Qianmen Xi Dajie, and a few blocks south, at 32 Qianmen Dajie (the old Imperial Way), is the city's most famous Beijing duck restaurant, **Quanjude Kaoyadian**, open daily 10:30am to 1:30pm for lunch and 4:30 to 8:30pm for dinner, the perfect ending to a day on foot in old Beijing.

Start:	Huifeng Temple, Xihai Lake (subway: Jishuitan).
Finish:	Prince Gong's Mansion.
Time:	4 to 6 hours.
Best times:	Sunday mornings (for the street markets), but any nice morning will do.
Worst times:	Mondays, when some of the museums and sites are closed. Don't start later than noon, in order to enjoy the lake scenery.

The three Back Lakes (*Shi Sha Hai*)—Xihai, Houhai, and Qianhai—were once the exclusive beachfront property of China's Qing Dynasty royalty, who alone could own and maintain houses here. The three Back Lakes were connected in turn to three lakes immediately to the south—Beihai, Zhonghai, and Nanhai—adjacent to the Forbidden City. Barges once used this string of lakes to transport grain from the Great Canal to the Imperial Court. Today, the Back Lakes neighborhoods teem with old Beijing's quickly disappearing, colorful *hutongs* (alleyways) and *siheyuans* (courtyard houses). The shores of these lakes are gorgeous in the summer and dazzling when frozen over in the winter, making this a prime spot for strolling and exploring by bicycle.

This Back Lakes ramble takes in the beautiful lake shores, a seldom-visited island temple, one of the nine ancient gates to the city, the former residence of Soong Ching-ling, a Buddhist shrine, two exceptional outdoor markets, and the garden estate of a Qing Dynasty prince, with other options along the way if you want to keep rambling.

Begin a few blocks east of the Jishuita subway station along the south side of the busy Second Ring Road at:

❶ Huifeng Temple (Hifeng Si)

Located on the northern tip of the northernmost Back Lake, Xihai, this forgotten temple has recently been restored. Located on a steep, rocky islet, it's the ideal place to survey the lake scenery to the south.

Resume walking east on the Second Ring Road until you spot:

❷ Deshengmen Arrow Tower

This is an impressive fragment of the city wall. The towering gate and guardhouse (with archers' windows) of Deshengmen is one of Beijing's nine Ming gates. Cross over at the overpass to the tower where a courtyard house contains an ancient coin museum (Gudai Qianbi Zhanlanguan) open daily from 9am to 5pm (admission 4RMB, 48¢). There's a coin and open-air antiques market here, too. Upstairs in the tower are exhibits on the history of Beijing's architecture and balcony views of the Back Lakes (open Tues–Sun 9am–4pm).

Cross the Second Ring Road directly south and follow:

❸ Deshengmen Street (Deshengmennei Dajie)

The main street leading to the bridge between the two northernmost Back Lakes, it's an interesting old street to stroll. Keep to the right where it soon branches off (Gulou Xi Dajie is the big street heading west). Deshengmen is a street with plenty of local flavor. Cross to the east side and walk south to the bridge dividing Xihai Lake from Houhai Lake.

To your left is a fascinating outdoor market, the:

❹ Deshengmen Market

Running along both sides of the narrow passage between these two lakes, this market can be hopelessly crowded, particularly on a Sunday

Walking Tour—Back Lakes Ramble

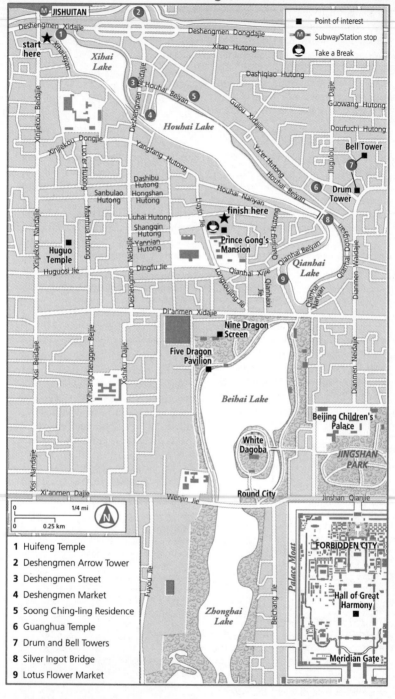

Legend:
- ■ Point of interest
- Ⓜ Subway/Station stop
- ☯ Take a Break

1 Huifeng Temple
2 Deshengmen Arrow Tower
3 Deshengmen Street
4 Deshengmen Market
5 Soong Ching-ling Residence
6 Guanghua Temple
7 Drum and Bell Towers
8 Silver Ingot Bridge
9 Lotus Flower Market

morning when the market is at its best. Fresh produce, spices, and meats are the main wares, but there's always an odd assortment here (including roving vendors hawking white toilet seats). Many of the vendors sell from cases or drums on the back of their bicycles. This is not a touristy market.

Work your way east, then north along the shore of Houhai Lake, heading toward:

5 Soong Ching-ling Residence (Song Ching Ling Guzhu)

The residence is located a few blocks down the northeast shore of Houhai Lake at 46 Houhai Beiyan. There's no sign at the entrance in English, just a big red sign in Chinese. The grounds consist of a lovely classical garden and a house filled with the photographs and belongings of this legendary Soong sister, who married Sun Yat-sen and stayed in communist China while her sister married Chiang Kai-shek and fled to Taiwan. Ching-ling resided in this palatial estate from 1963 to her death in 1981. Open daily from 9am to 4:30pm; admission is 8RMB, 96¢. (For a full description of the museum, see the entry in chapter 6, "Exploring Beijing.")

Continue south down the lakeshore to:

6 Guanghua Temple (Guanghua Si)

Located a half-mile from the Soong estate, this is an active temple now, with monks in residence, and worth a brief tour.

At this point you can make an optional detour eastward to:

7 Drum and Bell Towers (Gulou and Zhonglou)

The towers are visible on the horizon and just a few blocks from Houhai Lake via a convoluted *hutong* (at the intersection of Gulou Dong Dajie and Dianmenwai Dajie). The Drum Tower (described in chapter 6, "Exploring Beijing") can be climbed.

The Bell Tower is directly north; the alley between encloses an interesting market where you can purchase street snacks from vendors.

Retrace your path to the lakeshore and prepare to cross:

8 Silver Ingot Bridge (Yin Ding Qiao)

This white marble bridge, which separates Houhai (Back Lake) from Qianhui (Front Lake), has stood here for centuries, although the latest version is the work of modern masons (1984). If the day is clear and you can see as far as the Western Hills, you will be enjoying one of the Eight Grand Views of Beijing, as enumerated by Emperor Qianlong in the 18th century.

Cross the bridge and stick to the winding road along the west shore of Qianhai Lake until you come to:

9 Lotus Flower Market (Lianghua Shichang)

This lively market on the southwest shore of Qianhai Lake is one of the prettiest areas in the Back Lakes region. There's shade under the willows, summer lotus near the lakeshore, snack and souvenir vendors aplenty, and, in the evenings, a night market of hot foods and amateur opera singers.

 WINDING DOWN Northwest of the Lotus Flower Market is **Prince Gong's Mansion (Gong Wang Fu)**, 17 Qianhai Xi Lu, which is open daily from 9am to 5pm. It's the most lavish of the courtyard houses in the Back Lakes region and its pavilions and rockeries are a page out of Imperial Beijing, as are the Back Lakes themselves. Prince Gong's Mansion is described in chapter 6, "Exploring Beijing," and the charming courtyard restaurant adjacent to it, the Sichuan (14 Liuyin Jie), is reviewed in chapter 5, "Dining"—it's just the spot to conclude a Back Lakes ramble with a fiery lunch or dinner.

THE IMPERIAL PARKS, FROM BEIHAI TO COAL HILL

Start:	Round City, south entrance of Beihai Park.
Finish:	Prospect Hill, Jingshan Park.
Time:	3 to 4 hours.
Best times:	Weekday mornings or summer afternoons.
Worst times:	Weekends can be hideously crowded, particularly Sundays. Go early if weekends cannot be avoided.

Many visitors get no closer than the Forbidden City's northern gate to two of Beijing's loveliest parks, Beihai and Jingshan. It's a pity. If time allows for a half-day park stroll, these two are prime candidates. Jingshan (Prospect Hill) Park, also called Meishan (Coal Hill), is literally at the back door of the Forbidden City; it was created from the soil removed to fashion the Forbidden City moat. This man-made mountain offers a superb view of central Beijing.

Virtually next door to Jingshan Park is Beijing's most beautiful urban park, Beihai. Its lovely artificial lake, 8 centuries old, was the site of Kublai Khan's palace. Marco Polo walked its shores. Emperor Yongle, builder of the Forbidden City, enlarged Beihai; Qing Dynasty leaders elaborated on its beauty. The Empress Dowager Cixi kept a garden on its shore, where she presided over Epicurean picnics. These days, Beihai is a favorite of locals for year-round recreation.

Begin your walk at the south entrance to Beihai Park, within a block of the northwest corner of the Forbidden City, on the east side of the marble Rainbow Bridge, which dates from the Ming Dynasty. Buy your Beihai Park all-inclusive admission ticket (15RMB, $1.80) at the booth northeast of the big bridge and enter the:

❶ Round City (Tuan Cheng)

This is the site of the barracks of the royal troops during the reign of the Khans. Here, in the Hall of Receiving Light (Cheng Guang Dian), is a large Jade Buddha, a gift from Burma to Empress Dowager Cixi; in a pavilion in the courtyard is Beihai's oldest relic, an enormous Jade Jar (weighing over 3 tons), thought to have been used by Kublai Khan himself.

Proceed northward through the large ornate gate (*pailou*) and cross the marble bridge to:

❷ Hortensia Isle (Qiong Hua Dao)

On what is also known as Jade Isle, you see Beihai's famous landmark, the White Dagoba (Bai Ta), rising from its center. Explore it on your return to the island later after circling the lake.

Bear right along the eastern shore of the island and walk north to the eastern entrance of Beihai Park. At the large ornate gate known as Nirvana Pailou, turn right, cross the bridge to the east, and then follow the path north to a cluster of buildings on the right known as:

❸ Hao and Pu (Hao Pu Jian)

Built in 1757 by the emperor as a garden within a garden, the rockeries here are exquisite, as is the pond, pavilion, and seven-arched bridge at its center. Empress Dowager Cixi would come here to hear musical performances.

Pass the boathouses on the eastern lakeshore as you head another 400 yards to the:

❹ Studio of the Painted Boat (Hua Fang Zhai)

Also built by Qing Emperor Qianlong, the square stone pool here is lined with corridors where the French army bivouacked in its 1900 during the Boxer Rebellion and the siege of Beijing.

Proceed north past a large amusement park to the:

⑤ Altar of Silkworms (Can Tan)

This altar was created for performing rites to the goddess of silkworms. Once here, you have nearly reached the northeast tip of the lake.

Cross the bridge and turn left, heading south along the northwest shore to the:

⑥ Studio of the Serene Mind (Jing Xin Zhai)

This beautiful garden is where China's last emperor, Pu Yi, composed his memoirs. The halls, courtyards, pools, and rockeries are quiet and relaxing.

TAKE A BREAK
The Studio of the Serene Mind, a teahouse located in the **Room for Roasting Tea (Bei Cha Wu)** at the eastern edge of this garden complex, is perfectly named.

Return to the northwest lakeshore and follow it south to the:

⑦ Hall of the Heavenly Kings (Tian Wang Dian)

This was once a Ming-era studio for printing Buddhist sutras.

Behind this studio and to the east is the 83-foot-long:

⑧ Nine Dragon Screens (Jiu Long Bi)

Decorated on both sides with colorful glazed-tile dragons, the Nine Dragon Screens were built by Emperor Qianlong as a wall to ward off evil spirits heading to Beihai Lake.

Further south along the western shore are the:

⑨ Hall of Pleasant Snow (Kuai Xue Tang) and the Iron Spirit Screen (Tie Ying Bi)

This dark rock slab was carved on both sides with a mythological beast during the Yuan Dynasty.

Pleasure boats depart from the docks near here (on the north side of Five Dragon Pavilions) for the 5-minute voyage back to Hortensia Isle; but before you board, continue due east to inspect:

⑩ Little Western Heaven (Xiao Xi Tian)

This square pagoda with a moat and four guard towers was built in 1770 as shrine to Guanyin, goddess of mercy. It was restored in the 1980s, and it is magnificent, the largest pagoda complex of its kind in China.

Return to the lakeshore and buy a boat ticket (departures every 30 min.) for the trip to:

⑪ Fangshan Imperial Restaurant

Treat yourself to a set lunch or dinner at Fangshan, which was staffed by Forbidden City chefs when it first opened at Beihai in 1926 (see review in chapter 5, "Dining"). It is located in the complex of buildings known as the Hall of Rippling Waters (Yi Lan Tang), on the north shore of the isle at the foot of the White Dagoba.

After a royal repast, set out to explore the delights of Hortensia Isle itself by turning left (west) on the covered pathway known as the:

⑫ Pavilion of Shared Coolness (Fen Liang Ge)

This veranda along the northwest lakeshore was a favorite strolling place of the Empress Dowager Cixi. In winter, she could admire those skating on the icy lake.

Just beyond the western end of the Pavilion of Shared Coolness, a stone path leads up the steep hill toward the White Dagoba, first passing the:

⑬ Plate for Gathering Dew (Cheng Lu Pan)

This whimsical bronze statue depicts an old emperor gathering dew (which was thought to be an elixir of immortality).

Walking Tour—Imperial Parks, from Beihai to Coal Hill

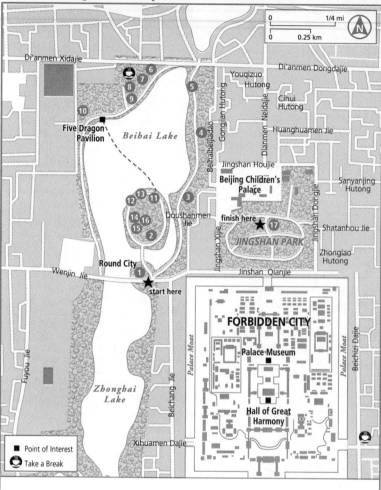

1 Round City
2 Hortensia Isle
3 Hao and Pu
4 Studio of the Painted Boat
5 Altar of Silkworms
6 Studio of the Serene Mind
7 Hall of the Heavenly Kings
8 Nine Dragon Screens
9 Hall of Pleasant Snow and the Iron Spirit Screen

10 Little Western Heaven
11 Fangshan Imperial Restaurant/ Hall of Rippling Waters
12 Pavilion of Shared Coolness
13 Plate for Gathering Dew
14 Tower for Reading the Classics
15 Temple of Eternal Peace
16 White Dagoba
17 Pavilion of Eternal Spring

Higher up still is the:

⑭ Tower for Reading the Classics (Yue Gu Lou)

The tower contains nearly 500 specimens of ancient calligraphy carved on stone tablets.

Turn to the south and enter the:

⑮ Temple of Eternal Peace (Yong An Si)

This Lama Buddhist complex has been nicely restored.

The temple courtyards lead due north to the summit, where you'll at last reach the:

⑯ White Dagoba (Bai Ta)

The crowning glory of Beihai Park was built in 1651 in honor of a visit by the Dalai Lama. It soars 118 feet above the man-made hilltop.

Retrace your steps southward or pick your way carefully northeastward down the maze of rock pillars. Your goal is to reach the east entrance, where you can exit Beihai Park and walk across to the western entrance of Jingshan Hill.

Enter Jingshan Park and climb to the:

⑰ Pavilion of Eternal Spring (Wan Chung Ting)

Located on the central peak of Jingshan's five peaks that overlook the Forbidden City (and shield it from evil spirits flying down from the north). Each peak once had a pavilion and a golden image of the Buddha, but the statues are gone and only this central pavilion is now visited. You'll see some extraordinary panoramas. Relax here after a day in the Imperial parks, sit on the balcony ledge with the locals, buy a soda from the concessionaire in the pavilion (which still has its dazzling painted ceiling), and enjoy the famous view.

WINDING DOWN
If you have any walking energy left, exit Jingshan Park to the south or east, skirt the Forbidden City at its northeast corner, and head south, following the moat down Beichzi Dajie to **The Courtyard** (95 Donghuamen Lu) for a fabulous dinner or a drink, taking in yet another exceptional view of the Forbidden City, this time from ground level. The Courtyard is reviewed in chapter 5, "Dining."

WALKING TOUR 4 | **WANGFUJING SHOPPING CIRCLE**

Start:	Beijing Hotel.
Finish:	Oriental Plaza.
Time:	2 to 4 hours.
Best times:	Weekday mornings or late afternoons.
Worst times:	Weekends and evenings are jammed with shoppers. Lunchtime any day (11:30am–2pm) is also crowded.

Wangfujing is the capital's number one shopping street, but it is worth strolling even if you aren't interested in buying a thing. The newest and literally the oldest human enterprises in China's capital are found right along Wangfujing. All of commercial China seems to be encapsulated within a few crowded blocks, with old silk shops and open-air markets competing shoulder-to-shoulder with ultramodern shopping plazas. Situated just a few blocks east of the Forbidden City, Wangfujing became a favorite residential neighborhood of the rich and the royals during the Ming and Qing dynasties; it was named for a well that supplied the mansions of ten Ming Dynasty princes. By the end of the 19th century, it was beginning to attract resident foreigners, including an influential correspondent

Walking Tour—Wangfujing Shopping Circle

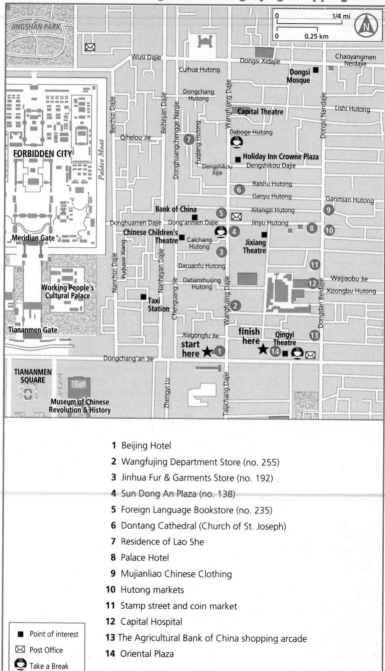

1 Beijing Hotel

2 Wangfujing Department Store (no. 255)

3 Jinhua Fur & Garments Store (no. 192)

4 Sun Dong An Plaza (no. 138)

5 Foreign Language Bookstore (no. 235)

6 Dontang Cathedral (Church of St. Joseph)

7 Residence of Lao She

8 Palace Hotel

9 Mujianliao Chinese Clothing

10 Hutong markets

11 Stamp street and coin market

12 Capital Hospital

13 The Agricultural Bank of China shopping arcade

14 Oriental Plaza

■ Point of interest

⊠ Post Office

☕ Take a Break

for the *London Times* named Morrison—and Morrison became the street's name for a time among Westerners. Tradesmen have set up their shops on this street and along the attached *hutongs* (alleys) for centuries, but it was not until 1928 that Wangfujing was paved.

These days, Wangfujing is not only paved, but it's also transformed. Much of the retail district outlined by Wangfujing and the parallel shopping street to the east, Dongdan, is being rapidly modernized. How long the small art galleries and brush stores, the optical shops and the silk stores will survive is anyone's guess. The past is surely being erased, as the southern section of the avenue has become, at least most of the time, a wide, spiffy new pedestrian mall with shiny facades. Wangfujing's pedestrian flow has reached 200 million per year, and the capital now boasts some 700,000 upper-income shoppers, most of them local Chinese.

Our walking tour is a circle—north up Wangfujing and south down Dongdan—beginning at the historic Beijing Hotel on Chang'an Avenue and ending in China's newest and largest megamall, Oriental Plaza. Along this route you'll take in shops old and new, cafes, open-air markets, a cathedral, a historic courtyard house, and even an archaeological site, the oldest in Beijing. Start with the:

❶ Beijing Hotel (Beijing Fandian)

In 1917, this hotel opened under French management as the **Grand Hotel de Pekin.** Wander through the lobby. Unfortunately, much of the hotel was remodeled in 2000 and 2001; although the lobby has lost its old-fashioned character, its historic grand piano, and the maze of tacky shops, you can still take a peek at the grand (very grand) old ballrooms at the top of the lobby staircases.

Outside, turn east and go up the first street on your left, Wangfujing Dajie. Oriental Plaza, where you'll finish this circular stroll, is straight across the street to the east along Chang'an Avenue, so stay on the west side of Wangfujing for now and head north. You'll come to a public lavatory at the first intersection (with a McDonald's on the opposite corner); this is where Wangfujing has been transformed into a wide, marvelous pedestrian mall. There are plenty of new shops on both sides of the pedestrian mall to explore, but start on the west side with the landmark:

❷ Wangfujing Department Store (No. 255)

Aging, sprawling, and rumored to be on the verge of a face-lift, this was once Beijing's big-time department store. It's now a fascinating throwback to the 1970s and '80s, chock-full of Chinese products for the Chinese consumer. It's worth browsing a floor or two (there are no escalators) to see what most of Beijing's consumers can actually afford to buy.

On the other side (the east side) of the Wangfujing pedestrian mall, you'll see a traditional painting and scroll-carving shop (Cheng Gu Zhai), a hat shop (Sheng Xi Fu), a toy and clothing shop for kids (the Store for New China Children, no. 168), and, next door, the newly-relocated but historic:

❸ Jinhua Fur & Garments Store (No. 192)

This is the city's oldest purveyor of furs. It may seem politically incorrect to some, but this store, moved a block over from Dongdan Street, has a steady customer base of northern Chinese and Russian buyers. Fur hats are a specialty. One floor up is a more modern, more foreign tenant: KFC.

The east side of the pedestrian mall is dominated by what was just a few years ago China's glitziest shopping center:

❹ Sun Dong An Plaza (Xin Dong An Shichang) (No. 138)

You can wander here for hours among its glass-elevatored, chrome-escalatored seven levels and multiple atriums. Bossini, London Fog, Burberrys, Flying Scotsmen? They're all here, along with a Mickey Mouse logo store (Toonsland), a Nike store, yet another

McDonald's (no. 241), and an espresso bar named Boodles. (There's a Bank of China branch on the first floor, open weekdays only.) The supermarket, electronics, and large appliances are in the basement, and deeper in the labyrinth are eight movie theaters. What you shouldn't miss is in the basement: **Old Beijing Street,** a free-admission re-creation of a typical commercial street in Qing Dynasty Beijing with wax models, period costumes, and reproductions of the shop-houses of earlier centuries. The basement also has the less expensive merchandise, from crafts to foodstuffs.

Back on Wangfujing, the pedestrian mall ends at the cross street (called Dong'anmen Dajie to the east, Jinyu Hutong to the right) in front of Sun Dong An Plaza. Directly across Wangfujing, on the west side, beyond the life-size bronze statues of a Qing Dynasty barber, musician, and rickshaw puller, is the:

⑤ Foreign Language Bookstore (No. 235)

This shop houses Beijing's largest selection of English-language materials on several floors; it's a must for anyone interested in books.

Heading north, the next major site is on the east side of Wangfujing, a testimony to the influence of Western missionaries on pre-revolutionary Beijing:

⑥ St. Joseph's Cathedral

Known locally as *Dong Tang,* the Eastern Church. Destroyed during the Boxer Rebellion, this Jesuit church, with roots in the 17th century, was rebuilt about a hundred years ago, but it was hardly visible from Wangfujing until the renovations of 1999–2000. The large, open courtyard is new and makes a nice place to rest, people-watch, or stare at the big store (Century Plaza) across the street (with the huge statue of the basketball star on one corner) where, at least recently, a massive, group bungee-jump apparatus has been in action.

Continuing north up Wangfujing, you'll notice the China Silk Shop (no. 133) and a tea ware shop (no. 119) on the west side of the street before you come to a second major intersection, Dengshikou Street, with the Crowne Plaza Beijing and the massive One World Department Store on opposite corners. Cross over and follow Dengshikou a long block west (toward the Forbidden City moat) to an alleyway, Fengfu Hutong, which you follow north (to your right) to the charming courtyard house that is the:

⑦ Residence of Lao She

This serene museum (open Tues–Sun; admission 5RMB, 60¢), which is dedicated to the great early 20th-century writer, is worth touring just to see how Beijingers lived in Old China. It's a few blocks, but seemingly centuries, away from modern Wangfujing.

Retrace your steps back down Wangfujing to the north end of the pedestrian mall at the intersection with Jinyu Hutong, where the Sun Dong An Plaza stands, and:

TAKE A BREAK
Wangfujing is filled with cafes and restaurants, inside and outside major hotels, but one bright new spot to pause at is on the southwest corner of pedestrian mall at the trendy **Green Spring Teahouse** (no. 233), with its bamboo screens and swing-seats, where "bubble tea" and snacks are served.

After Beijing-style tea and crumpets, abandon Wangfujing and walk east along Jinyu Hutong to the luxurious:

⑧ Palace Hotel

Located at 8 Jinyu Hutong, this hotel features a waterfall in its marble lobby, which looks like it was designed by Frank Lloyd Wright. The basement has the highest-end shopping in China, with the nation's first Armani, to go along with Cartier, Hermès, and others.

The lobby is a refreshing spot for tea, coffee, or a lavish lunch before continuing a few steps eastward to Dongdan Bei Dajie, a shopping street parallel to Wangfujing. Turn right southward down Dongdan Street, which is clogged with Beijing's latest in boutiques, bars, and bistros. The far (east) side of Dongdan is currently under construction, so you may find plenty of new shops I haven't seen yet. If you stick to the near (west) side of Dongdan, you'll find:

⑨ Mujianliao Chinese Clothing, (No. 46 Dongdan Bei Dajie)

Shop here for *qipao* (bright silk and satin dress with a side slit). This Manchu-inspired fashion was the rage in 1920s China, then banned in the politically correct Mao era, but it is now the basis for the new fashions in the new China.

Continuing down Dongdan toward Chang'an Avenue, in addition to an Audi dealership, you'll find:

⑩ Hutong Markets

The markets run eastward, with vendors selling collectibles and edibles from their carts or blankets spread out on the sidewalks. The east side of Dongdan also features a row of six portable pay toilets and a wedding shop where brides and grooms are coifed and outfitted for a Western-style ceremony.

Meanwhile, on the west side of the street there's a:

⑪ Stamp Street and Coin Market

Located in one *hutong*, next door to a tape and disc music store named **FUN.**

Of an entirely different nature is the entrance to:

⑫ Capital Hospital (Xiehe Yiyuan) (Peking Union Medical Hospital)

Part of this medical complex is in the mansion of Qing Dynasty prince, part in a modern high-rise. It has an emergency clinic for foreign patients on the sixth floor. This hospital was founded in 1915 and underwritten for decades by American millionaire John D. Rockefeller. The dynastic architecture of this complex is fascinating, especially along the western alley of Dongdan Santiao.

As you near Chang'an Avenue, you pass:

⑬ The Agricultural Bank of China Shopping Arcade

You'll find storefronts for Nelli, Baleno, Eland, Apple, Hush Puppies, and even Starbucks (at no. 9).

To close your shopping circle, enter Beijing's newest shopping plaza-cum-office complex:

⑭ Oriental Plaza

This blocks-long city-within-a-city shopping center, office complex, and five-star hotel consortium was built in 1999 on the site of the short-lived "world's largest McDonald's."

WINDING DOWN
Asia's largest commercial complex, **Oriental Plaza**, is, among other things, a $2 billion emporium of 5 themed malls, complete with its own unending series of upscale shops, restaurants (including 2 McDonald's and a Starbucks), drugstores, supermarkets, an interactive science museum, a VW showroom, and underground parking for 1,800 cars and 12,000 bicycles. On the lowest level to the south there's a direct entrance to the subway, and next to it is an archaeological site where the oldest human settlement in Beijing was discovered, a result of the construction dig. Even 20,000 years ago, there were residents of Wangfujing, perhaps lured here—as we are today—by the shopping.

8

Shopping

Until economic reforms took hold in China in the 1980s and kicked into high gear in the '90s, Beijing could not be described as a shopper's city. Now it can—it offers an interesting variety of goods, from local and regional specialties to international luxuries. The focus of most travelers is on uniquely Chinese products, and these are widely available at private as well as government-run department stores and shops, at sidewalk stalls as well as hotel kiosks, and in the indoor and outdoor street markets where bargaining and caution are the bywords. After decades of dreary and monotonous retailing, shopping has become fun in Beijing.

The Chinese enjoy shopping; they are known as careful buyers and masterful sellers. Expect to find elbow-to-elbow shopping at some sites, and be prepared to enter the fray with your commercial wits sharpened. Language won't be a problem. English may be the world's second language, but shopping is universal.

1 The Shopping Scene

Western-style shopping malls are flexing their muscles in Beijing, replacing the traditional storefronts, Chinese department stores, and alley markets. Even the new, privately run stores on major shopping streets tend to be versions of the boutiques and specialty outlets familiar to shoppers in the West. But there are still plenty of open-air markets and streetside vendors offering more traditional arts and crafts, collectibles, and clothing, usually at prices far below those in the big plazas and modern stores. If you're looking for souvenirs or Chinese treasures, check out the prices and selection at hotel shops, the Friendship Store, and modern shopping malls first; then see what's available in the streets and at markets.

BEIJING'S BEST BUYS

Beijing is known for selection and low prices in **cashmere** and **silk** (both off the bolt and in finished garments, such as sweaters). Markets also have incredibly good buys in brand name **athletic wear** (Gore-Tex jackets, outdoor clothing, and shoes) and **designer label clothing,** but these items can be seconds or fakes. Jewelry can also be a bargain, particularly **gold** and **pearls,** but bargaining and a critical eye are required.

Tips **Shopping Hours**

Most stores are open daily from about 9am to 8pm (even later in the summer). Weekends (especially Sun) are the most hectic days to shop, since most Beijingers make their purchases then and thousands of locals spend these days off window-shopping.

(*Tips*) **Buyer Beware**

A note of caution: The open-air markets that line the entrances to major tourist sites generally charge extravagant prices and offer mass-produced kitsch of shoddy quality, including outright fakes. **Jade** is particularly difficult to evaluate and prone to being faked, so buy only what you like and don't pay much.

One of the most popular gifts is a **chop** (also called a seal), a small stone that is a custom-engraved stamp with your name (in English, Chinese, or both) and used with an ink pad to print your ID on paper. Chops can be created the same day or overnight, sometimes even while you wait. Prices depend on the stone you select and the skill of the engraver. Among other popular crafts made in Beijing are **cloisonné, laquerware, porcelain,** and **carved jade.** Prices vary considerably. The best rule is to find something you truly like, then consider how much it is worth to you.

Artworks are also abundant, often in the form of a **hand-painted scroll** or **rubbing** taken from a carved stone tablet. Again, buy what you like because these works are priced across the spectrum, from 100RMB to 1,000RMB ($12–$120) and up. Shop around.

Antiques are plentiful. A **red wax seal** must be attached to any item created between 1795 and 1949 that is taken out of China; older items may not be exported. Many hotel shops specialize in antiques, and they can send purchases to your home. The Friendship Store, with a department devoted to antiques, has a highly efficient shipping department, too. Collectibles include **Mao buttons** and posters, old Chinese **coins,** small religious **statues,** old **woodcarvings,** and painted **plates**—all priced lowest at markets and stands. **Furniture** in traditional Chinese styles, both antiques and reproductions, can be purchased or custom-ordered at several factory outlets. Furniture prices are relatively low, but shipping can add considerably to the bill.

Tea is a good buy in Beijing, but **electronics** and other high-tech goods are not, although **small appliances** such as razors can be found in department stores for low prices.

Good **arts and crafts** buys may also be found, particularly in paper **kites,** hand-stitched **embroideries** (including sheets and pillow cases), **teapots, bamboo** items, **fans, chopsticks,** and decorative ornaments (excellent for small Christmas gifts). These are often sold in markets and on the sidewalks by itinerant vendors.

THE ART OF BARGAINING

It helps to know the going prices for items you're interested in. The Friendship Store is worth scoping out with prices in mind because it sets the standard price for most items. Also, check up on the prices in hotel shops and at the new megamalls. This will give you a notion of the high-end price. Then see if you can beat the price elsewhere.

Street markets sometimes have the lowest prices. For example, at the Lido Market (see below), I found porcelain chopstick rests starting at 5RMB (60¢), sandalwood fans at 10RMB ($1.20), silk shirts at 100RMB ($12), quilts at 150RMB ($18), and ecru tablecloths at 200RMB ($24). Similar products in an air-conditioned mall on Wangfujing Street or at Xidan are often sold at double or triple these prices.

One-Stop Gift Shopping at the Friendship Store

The Friendship Store carries most of the items that foreigners coming to China dream of buying—and it's easier to shop here for gifts, souvenirs, and Chinese treasures than anywhere else in Beijing. The merchandise is targeted to foreign travelers, the selection is wide, and the prices (no bargaining allowed) are high enough to ensure quality, while generally lower than in the high-end hotel shops and mega-malls. Start here to get an overview of what's available in Beijing at a fair price, shop the streets and malls, then return to make those last-minute purchases.

Friendship stores began as outlets exclusively for foreigners in China (at one time, no local Chinese were allowed inside), but they now compete freely with department stores, shopping plazas, private stores, and street vendors. Beyond its extensive selection, quality goods, and convenience, the Beijing Friendship Store provides a foreign-exchange counter and honors credit cards. It also has an overseas shipping department to handle those big purchases. One old-fashioned procedure remains: At most counters, the clerk hands you a slip for your purchase. You must take the slip to a cashier in a nearby kiosk, pay there, and take your receipt back to the clerk to claim your merchandise (a system that keeps many people employed, it seems).

The ground floor sells sundry items, from Chinese musical instruments to home appliances. There are Chinese kites, papercuts, teas, medicines, watches, and porcelains. Near the back is a section devoted to English-language books, magazines, and newspapers. To the east is a supermarket, carpet store, and Chinese furniture showroom (and even a Starbucks). The second floor has a large selection of clothing for adults and children (cottons, silks, brocades, and cashmeres). The third floor is crammed with gifts, including cloisonné, lacquerware, jade, silver, and freshwater pearls. The fourth floor handles artworks (scrolls and paintings), crafts (carved screens and opera masks), and antiques. On my most recent trip, I actually ended up buying freshwater pearls here, rather than at the stalls in the Pearl Market. I found the prices reasonable and the quality higher. Friendship doesn't sell goods at discount or rock-bottom prices, but the quality is assured.

Beijing Friendship Store, 17 Jianguomenwai Dajie (20–30 min. walk due west of the Forbidden City), Chaoyang District (℡ 010/6500-3311). Daily 9am–8:30pm. Subway: Yonganli.

Haggling is not done at government-run stores, most hotel shops, and mall outlets, but it is expected on the street, at market stalls, and in small private stores. A good rule of thumb is to offer no more than half the quoted price and not to accept the first counteroffer. Try to reach a compromise. Walking away with a firm but polite "no" often brings about a more favorable price. Remember that locals are demon shoppers who scrutinize each potential purchase and exercise mountains of patience before making a buy.

BEIJING'S TOP SHOPPING AREAS

Beijing's top shopping area is downtown on **Wangfujing** and **Dongdan** streets (see chapter 7, "Beijing Strolls"), where the most modern and the most traditional modes of retailing commingle. Here you'll find Beijing's two top megamalls, Sun Dong An Plaza and Oriental Plaza.

Equally popular among locals is **Xidan Street,** running north from Chang'an Avenue. Xidan is located about a mile west of Tiananmen Square (at the Xidan subway stop). In addition to a fascinating but aging mall, the **Xidan Shopping Center,** there are now several brand-new megamalls with large open plazas located at the intersection of Xidan (Xidan Bei Dajie) and Chang'an Avenue (Xichang'an Jie).

Another major shopping strip is along **Jianguomenwai Dajie,** east of the Forbidden City, stretching from the **Friendship Store** and **Silk Alley** to the **China World Trade Center.** Many of Beijing's top international hotels are situated here as well. The Friendship Store is Beijing's number one outlet for souvenir shoppers, while Silk Alley is the most popular open-air market among tourists.

A strong mix of modern malls, department stores, private storefronts, and open-air markets is located northeast of city center along the **Third Ring Road North** where the Hilton, Sheraton Great Wall, and Kempinski hotels are clustered. It is an easy walk from this sector of the Third Ring Road southwest to the adjoining **Sanlitun** neighborhood and **Gonrentiyuchang Bei Lu** (Workers' Stadium Rd. N.), a street with an excellent assortment of small shops and big stores.

Last but not least is the **Liulichang/Dazhalan** culture street and pedestrian mall southwest of Tiananmen Square off Qianmen Dajie (see chapter 7, "Beijing Strolls"), Beijing's best shopping district for antiques, arts and crafts, and traditional merchandise.

2 Markets & Bazaars

Beijing's most interesting shopping experiences are to be had in its street markets and alley bazaars. Curios, crafts, collectibles, antiques, jewelry, and coins are all here for those who are not afraid to bargain hard. Most of these markets are outdoor affairs where the vendors pitch their stalls and awnings on both sides of a narrow passageway (often a *hutong*) and customers squeeze their way through. Perhaps the most common item you'll find in the markets these days is not silk, souvenirs, or crafts, but designer-label clothing, much of it knockoffs, with the upscale labels sewn in, although some items are factory seconds or overruns (sometimes smuggled out of legitimate brand-name factories). Many of the markets also sell fresh produce, seafood, spices, and other consumables to residents, along with snacks and drinks. These markets and bazaars are quite colorful and the prices can be low, but they are also attractive to pickpockets, so don't bring a purse or wallet and keep all your valuables in a concealed pouch or money belt. And speaking of valuables, these market vendors are seldom if ever equipped to deal with credit cards. Cash is the sole means of exchange.

The most popular market is **Silk Alley;** the best for clothing and jewelry is **Hongqiao Market;** the most interesting is **Panjiayuan** (also known variously as "Dirt Market," "Sunday Market," or "Ghost Market"); but there are many others worth browsing.

SILK ALLEY *Overrated* ✦   The famous Silk Alley Market (Xiushui Shichang) is located at Jianguomenwai Dajie and Xiushui Jie (the first alley west of Dongdaqiao Lu), a half-mile east of the Friendship Store in the Chaoyang

District. The Yonganli subway stop is very near. The south entrance of this market looks to be nothing more than a hole in the wall where a storefront might have once stood, but this is the gate to Beijing's most popular clothing market. Hawkers barking "CD-ROM!" stalk the sidewalk outside, selling bootlegged music and movie discs (of dubious quality). Squeeze in through the main gate and then press along either of the two main passageways for a look at hundreds of booths. There's not much silk in Silk Alley these days, and the astonishingly low prices that once thrilled travelers are becoming harder to find, as the initial asking price seems to be about three times what it should be. Nevertheless, there are some good deals to be had here on "name-brand" sportswear, Gore-Tex jackets, silk apparel, fake Levi jeans, sweaters, and Nike-like footwear. Try them on—some of these items may even be the real McCoy. Logo luggage and handbags abound, as do Timberland shirts and designer-label shirts and blouses. (I've had mixed luck here: poor quality designer shirts for $10, The North Face copy-jackets and gloves for $25, a good duffel bag for $5, and reasonably decent faux silk ties for $1.) There's a fair amount of duplication among vendors, so keep browsing before you haggle. Silk Alley runs on for a few blocks due north, emptying out at the intersection of Xiushui Dong Jie and Xiushui Nan Jie near the embassies of Ireland, Bulgaria, and the U.S. in a pleasant diplomatic district. Open daily from 9am to sunset.

HONGQIAO MARKET ★★   Also called the **Pearl Market,** the Chongwenmen Market, and the Farmers' Market, Hongqiao Market is located at 16 Hongqiao Lu (© **010/6711-7429**), just northeast of the Temple of Heaven (Tiantan) near Tiyuguan Lu in Chongwen District. From the Chongmenwen subway station, it's an uninspiring walk south down Chongmenwai Dajie for nearly a mile to where the avenue bends eastward around the Temple of Heaven Park. This is Beijing's best market for clothing (particularly brand-name outdoor clothing), luggage, and pearl jewelry. Its thousands of stalls are jammed into a modern but run-down five-story building. There's an exceptional jewelry section on the third floor, notable for its freshwater pearls. This is where visiting heads of state are taken to do their pearl shopping. I have used it numerous times for buying Western-label Gore-Tex jackets (at a tenth of their U.S. price) and rolling duffel bags (very cheap), but it is a place where you have to bargain hard just to get vendors down to half their opening price. Open daily from 8:30am to 7pm.

⟨**Tips**⟩   **What You Need to Know About Knockoffs & Fakes**

The customs services of many nations frown on the importation of knock-off goods (copies). The U.S. Customs Service allows U.S. residents to return with one trademark-protected item of each type, that is, one counterfeit watch, one knockoff purse, one camera with a questionable trademark, and so on. This means that you are not permitted to bring back a dozen "Polo" shirts as gifts for friends. Even if the brand name is legitimate, you are not a licensed importer. In addition, copyrighted products, such as CD-ROMs and books, must have been manufactured under the copyright owner's authorization; otherwise, tourists may not import even one of these items—they are pirated. The U.S. Customs Service booklet *Know Before You Go* and the U.S. Customs website, www.customs.ustreas.gov, provide further guidelines.

PANJIAYUAN ANTIQUE & CURIO MARKET 🎯🎯🎯   Also called the Sunday Market, the Dirt Market, and the Ghost Market, Panjiayuan (© **010/ 6775-2405**) is located well south of downtown on Huaweiqiaoxi Nan Dajie, inside the Third Ring Road (Dongsanhuan). Some regard this as the best antiques market in China. The best time to go (the only time, according to locals) is Sunday morning at dawn or shortly after. Panjiayuan is open Saturdays, too, from dawn to about 3pm, but early Sunday morning is the hot time to look and buy. As many as 60,000 shoppers visit here each Sunday. Taxis from downtown hotels take about 25 minutes to reach this distant market (35RMB, $4.20 each way; no subway). The attractions are ceramics, furniture, antiques, and the exotic, with an emphasis on collectibles, many of which seem to have been family heirlooms. The vendors are as interesting to watch as the wares. The market is surprisingly well organized, divided into aisles beneath flowing, brightly striped canopies. As many as 3,000 vendors gather here (paying 300RMB, $36 a month for space). The aisles are even numbered and labeled, rather haphazardly, in English. There's an aisle for "Jade," another for "Folk Secondhand," and one for "Brone *[sic]* Teapot." Scrolls are displayed on one side wall. Among the more massive items are rusty cannons, Mao posters, Tibetan costumes, Qing dynasty furniture, sewing machines, large Buddhist statues, and even upright pianos. There are food stands just outside the marble aisles and an air-conditioned building serving fast food, apparently intended for foreigners and named "House of Guests."

> **Tips   Jackpots & Junk**
>
> In 1996, a farmer from Henan Province sold a piece of pottery at the Panjiayuan Sunday Market in Beijing for the hefty price of 800RMB (about $100). This purchase turned out to be a Qing Dynasty antique appraised at 250,000RMB (about $30,000). But be careful. Some vendors "age" newly minted porcelains by smearing them with clay and blackening the surface with smoke.

LIDO MARKET 🎯   Straight across from the main entrance to the Holiday Inn Lido on Jiangtai Lu (east of the Airport Expressway) in the Chaoyang District is one of Beijing's newest markets, with lower prices than Silk Alley for similar clothing. The market is entirely indoors, in a narrow, one-story white-tile building about 2 blocks long, next door to a tiny boutique called "Mystery Garments." Over 100 numbered stalls and adjacent tables line both sides of the long hall. There's a selection of brand-name outdoor attire, designer-label sportswear, silk blouses and scarves, scrolls, swords, stuffed animals, luggage, coins, and bric-a-brac. Some of the vendors can be too eager, latching on as you pass. It lacks the color and atmosphere of Silk Alley, but the prices are reasonable.

YABAOLU MARKET (RUSSIAN MARKET) 🎯   Formerly a massive outdoor market located on the northeast corner of Ritan Park on Ritan Lu in the Chaoyang District, this market favored by Russian clothing buyers has undergone several great moves. As a result of a city government initiative to upgrade and bring indoors the outdoor markets of the city center, the outdoor stalls that lined the northwest side of Ritan Park have disappeared. Some of the vendors reappeared in the brand-new, very spiffy **Ya Bao Lu Shopping Centre** that occupies the first block of Yabao Lu west of Ritan Park. This arcade (open daily 9am–7pm), like the neighborhood restaurants, still caters to Russian business

The Pearls of China

In the Chinese tradition, pearls are the gems of love. Ground into a powder, in fact, they are the essential ingredient in Nanzhung tablets, a Chinese aphrodisiac.

These days, China's oyster beds remain among the world's most fertile grounds for pearls, of both the saltwater and freshwater variety. On the third floor of the **Hongqiao Market,** for example, there are more than a hundred stalls and counters featuring pearls of varying quality, color, and setting. These are cultured (farmed) pearls. Most are sold in 40cm tassels. The only problem is how to determine quality and a fair price.

Seawater pearls are usually more expensive than the freshwater gems, but in both cases, look for roundness, luster, and size. The bigger, rounder, and shinier the pearl, the better (and the more expensive).

Fakes can be detected by knicking the surface of the pearl with a sharp blade (the color is uniform within and without); rubbing the pearl along your teeth (to feel or hear a grating sound, since a real pearl's surface is actually scored and minutely cratered); scraping the pearl on glass (pearls leave a mark); or passing the pearl through a flame (fakes turn black, real pearls don't). Careful shoppers may try all of these maneuvers, although few actually bother.

Try to pick a string of pearls that are of the same size, shape, and color. Here's a rough pricing guide, based on what's charged in the market:

- 10 to 20RMB ($1.20–$2.40) for a string of small rice-shaped pearls
- 20 to 40RMB ($2.40–$4.80) for a string of larger pearls of mixed or low luster
- 50 to 100RMB ($6–$12) for a string of larger pearls of different colors
- 150 to 400RMB ($18–$48) for interwoven, multiple strings of small freshwater pearls

A string of very large, perfectly round pearls of the same color sells for considerably more, 10,000 to 20,000RMB ($1,200–$2,400) and up. Tassels of odd-shaped pearls can also fetch higher prices, selling for 100 to 1,000RMB ($12–$120).

When U.S. President Bill Clinton stopped by a stall (#99) in the Hongqiao Market during a state visit in 1998, he established a benchmark for the shopper to go by, picking up ten strings for about 800RMB ($96). You should be able to do better if you bargain hard enough.

---

travelers shuttling back and forth across borders with furs, leather goods, wool coats, and other textiles in bulk. Speaking of leather, if shoes are your shopping fetish, the **Beijing Auterlima Shoe Market** (open daily 9:30am–6:30pm), a second indoor offshoot of the outdoor Russian Market, now flanks both sides of the north entrance gate to Ritan Park. The biggest move of all, however, was the creation of a mega-Yabaolu Russian Market in four buildings under a series of blue metal roofs at 16 Chaoyangmenwai Dajie (east of Full Link Plaza). This complex, containing 1,500 stalls that rent at about $450 a month each, is chock-full of winter and outdoor clothing, furs, fake designer fashions, household goods, and cheap bric-a-brac.

MORE MARKETS While the **Liangmaqiao Market,** opposite the Kempin-ski Hotel in northeast Beijing, has been leveled by bulldozers (to make way for a new embassy row), and the popular **Sanlitun** clothing and wicker markets have been shut down, too, there are still plenty of indoor and outdoor markets to explore. The Sanlitun version, for example, has moved a few blocks due west to a shabby, metal-roofed building at the Xindong Lu/Gongrentiyuchang Bei Lu intersection, although so far it is not thriving in its new location.

The **Bird Market** (also known as the Guanyuan Market), north of the Xizhimen subway stop along the east side of the Second Ring Road West, in the Xicheng District, is Beijing's best outdoor bird market. Here the delicate and ornate cages are as pretty as the larks, orioles, and other songbirds on display. There are also singing crickets for sale (as well as cats, dogs, turtles, rabbits, and mice). Antique, curio, and houseplant shoppers also have some stalls to cull here. This market is at its best on Saturdays and Sundays from 6am to dusk.

The **Chaowai Flea Market,** north of Ritan Park on Chaowei Shichang Jie (the northern extension of Ritan Lu) in the Chaoyang District, has a good selec-tion of furniture, woodcarvings, collectibles, and some antiques in the back section, all under an arching roof. This market, open daily from 10am to 5pm, is popular with the foreign diplomatic corps on the weekends.

The **Houhai Market** is located on the east side of the Deshengmen Bridge between Xihai and Houhai lakes, on the northwest shore of Houhai Lake, in the Xicheng District. It is a truly local market, jammed every Saturday and Sunday with itinerant vendors, some of whom display their wares from the back of their black one-speed bicycles. (See the Back Lakes section of chapter 7, "Beijing Strolls.")

The **Scroll and Goldfish Market,** 2 blocks north of the Chegongzhuang sub-way stop, just inside the Second Ring Road North, off Ping'anli Xi Dajie, in the Xicheng District, sells painted scrolls and artworks at bargain-basement prices. There are $3 scrolls here, there are $10 scrolls here, but the better sort sell for $25 to $100, with some costing three times that. Artists here will do scrolls to your design (but it could take 10 days). This is also an inexpensive place to buy chops (ink stamps). As a bonus, the market has a large section devoted to goldfish—heaven for a photographer on a sunny day.

3 Shopping A to Z

ANTIQUES & CURIOS

Beijing has surprisingly few good antique stores (nothing like you'd find in Hong Kong). The markets and bazaars (listed above) are a primary source of the antiques and collectibles Beijing offers. So are the small hotel antique shops, the shops along **Liulichang Antique Street,** and the **Beijing Friendship Store's** antique department. Here are some other antique stores worth checking out:

Beijing Curio City Dealers who formerly worked at the nearby Jinsong Porcelain Market have moved indoors here, where there are four floors of jew-elry (including diamonds and jade), old clocks, cloisonné, furniture, and porce-lain, as well as curios and genuine antiques. This establishment gets its share of tour groups, meaning that the prices start high, but bargaining is acceptable.

This is a good place to check out the porcelains. International shipping is provided. 21 Dongsanhuan Nan Lu (south of the Panjiayuan Market, west side of Huawei Bridge, on Third Ring Road), Chongwen District. ℭ **010/6774-7711** or 010/6773-6018. Daily 9:30am–6:30pm.

Century Art Center   Specialists in handmade Tibetan cabinets, chests, carpets, and religious artifacts, Century Art Center is located in a courtyard house. Many of the pieces here are genuine, centuries-old antiques. The Tibetan chests are the most popular pieces, wooden boxes for storage decorated in cloth, yak leather, and religious paintings. Small chests start at 5,000RMB ($600), about a third of the overseas price. Carved cabinets start at 7,000RMB ($850). There is also a wide selection of well-restored Qing Dynasty scholar's studio furniture, including hand-carved chairs and lacquered screens. West side of Ritan Park in Jufu Palace, Chaoyang District. ℭ **010/6502-1627.** Tues–Sun 10am–5pm.

Guang Han Tang Beijing Classical Furniture Company   A large dealer in antique furniture and furnishings, Guang Han Tang has opened a second showroom in the Kempinski Hotel (Unit S. 108; ℭ 010/6465-1030). East of the Third Ring Road and Jing Guang New World Center (Chaoyang Lu) on Qingnian Lu at Ganlu Yuan #3. ℭ **010/6557-4659.** Daily 10am–5pm.

Hua Yi Classical Furniture Company   This company specializes in restored furniture items from the late Qing Dynasty. Packaging and shipping are available. Showrooms at 89 Xiaodian Dongwei Lu and in Beijing Curio City, 3rd floor, #69, off the Third Ring Road South, Chaoyang District. ℭ **010/6773-5909.** Daily 9am–6pm.

ART SUPPLIES

The **Liulichang Cultural Street** (see chapter 7, "Beijing Strolls") has many small shops selling traditional artist brushes, ink stones, paper, and other art supplies. The largest art store in Beijing, however, is **Gongyi Meishu Fuwubu,** 200 Wangfujing Dajie, Dongcheng District (ℭ **010/6512-4160**). Daily from 8am to 6pm.

BOOKS

Hotel kiosks and shops are often the best place to find English-language guides to Beijing attractions and books about China, but there are several bookstores with decent selections.

China Bookstore   Located on the corner dividing east and west Liulichang Cultural Streets, China Bookstore focuses on old Chinese books and used foreign publications. 115 Liulichang Xi Jie, Xuanwu District. ℭ **010/6303-5759.** Daily 9am–6:30pm (until 6pm in winter).

Foreign Language Bookstore   Largest collection of English-language books and tapes in Beijing, starting on the third floor. The **Foreign Imports Bookstore** next door, on the ground floor, is also worth checking out. 235 Wangfujing Dajie, Dongcheng District. ℭ **010/6512-6911.** Daily 9am–8:30pm.

Friendship Store   The collection of English-language books and magazines is in its own room at the back of the store, first floor. 17 Jianguomenwai Dajie, Chaoyang District. ℭ **010/6500-3311.** Daily 9am–8:30pm.

Sanwei Bookstore   Upstairs is a traditional teahouse, downstairs a small bookstore with a few English-language titles and the friendliest staff in town. 60 Fuxingmennei Dajie (1 mile from the Forbidden City, south side of Chang'an Avenue), Xicheng District. ℭ **010/6601-3204.** Daily 9am–10:30pm.

Fun Fact **Mao's Little Red Disc**

Chairman Mao Zedong has entered the computer age, and his Little Red Book, a compilation of his sayings that became the Bible for thousands of devout and fanatical Red Guard followers during the Cultural Revolution (1966–76), has been released on CD-ROM. Along with 20 volumes of Mao's anti-Western political thought, the disk contains 120 film clips and 3,000 pictures from the Mao archives. So far, there have been no mass rallies of latter-day Red Guard Nerds at Tiananmen Square waving their Little Red Discs with the downloaded sayings of the late Great Helmsman.

World of Books   Take the elevator located between the Kempinski Hotel and Lufthansa Centre to the sixth floor for a good selection of coffee-table books, novels, and travel guides. 50 Liangmaqiao Lu, Chaoyang District. ✆ 010/6465-3388. Daily 9am–9pm.

CAMERAS & FILM

Kodak, Fuji, and other imported camera films can be purchased all over Beijing, at hotel kiosks, megamalls and shopping plazas, and camera stores. Prices are about on par with those in the West. There are 1-hour and next-day film processing outlets in hotels and shopping centers. For reliable camera repairs and film developing, try **Beijing Photography,** 263 Wangfujing Dajie, Dongcheng District (✆ **010/6525-7301**). Daily from 8:30am to 8pm.

CARPETS

Inspect carpets carefully, with an eye to faded colors. Colors should be bright and the threads fine. A 6-by-8-foot silk carpet, tightly woven (300–400 stitches/inch) can cost 50,000RMB ($6,000) or more. Carpets at the **Friendship Store's** showroom on the first floor start at about 2,000RMB ($240). You may be able to cut that price in half by shopping some of the outlets listed below.

Beijing Carpet Import and Export Corporation   Excellent choice of styles. Most carpets are new Chinese creations, but there are some Persian designs and antique rugs. Hong Kong Macau Center, 1st floor, Third Ring Road East, Dongsishitiao, Chaoyang District. ✆ 010/6523-5293. Daily 7:30am–11pm.

China Beijing Carpet Trade Center   One of China's biggest carpet stores, with thousands of hand-woven carpets in all styles. 90 Weizikeng, Liangjiazhuang, Fengtai District. ✆ 010/6761-6018. Daily 9:30am–4:30pm.

Qianmen Carpet Factory   Located in a former bomb shelter, Qianmen has a selection of older northwestern Chinese and Tibetan carpets. The antique rugs include Tibetan prayer rugs, Xinjiang yurt rugs, and Mongolian saddle rugs, all handmade using natural dyes. The factory also makes antique reproductions and Henan silk carpets. Bargaining is a must. Cleaning and repair services available. Chongwen Cultural Palace, Basement, 44 Xingfu Dajie, Chongwen District. ✆ **010/6715-1687.** Daily 9:30am–5:30pm.

Xu's Chinese Antique Carpet   Good selection of old camel-wool rugs from northwest China, Inner Mongolia, Tibet, and Samarkand. 404 Lujiaying Village, Shibalidian, (on 4th Ring Road South, west of the Jingjintang Fwy.), Chaoyang District. ✆ 010/8769-3331. Daily 10am–5pm.

CRAFTS

Beijing Arts and Crafts Factory Good selection of local arts and crafts. 5 Xinkang Jie, Xinjiekouwai Dajie, Xicheng District. ✆ 010/6201-2228. Daily 8am–6pm.

Huaxia Arts & Crafts Store The main store on Chongwen has a superb collection of Beijing opera masks, costumes, and Chinese collectibles, while the Wangfujing branch carries porcelains, folk art, and skilled handicrafts. Two locations: 12 Chongwenmennei Dajie, Chongwen District (✆ 010/6513-6204) and 293 Wangfujing Dajie, Dongcheng District (✆ 010/6525-1819). Daily 8:30am–6pm.

Ji Gu Ge The best arts and crafts shop on historic Liulichang Culture Street, this is a venerable outlet for fine reproductions of Chinese artworks. There is also a good selection of tea, scrolls, paintings, porcelain, and jewelry. 136 Liulichang Dong Jie, Hepingmenwai, Xuanwu District. ✆ 010/6301-2897. Daily 9am–8pm.

Liu Ren Papercut House *Finds* In 1999, Liu Ren, a Beijing artist, established the city's first papercut studio in this traditional courtyard villa. Liu has been fashioning art by cutting paper since 1990; in 1994, she demonstrated her art abroad (with stops in Holland, Finland, America, and Japan). Chinese papercuts are exhibited in the main building of the studio, where Liu's own work is also for sale. This is a chance to meet a traditional artist and see her at work. 16 Shou Shui He Hutong (from Xidan subway stop, walk west on Fuxingmennei Dajie to Tonglingge Lu, south past Xinwen Hua Lu to the Shou Shui alleyway on your left), Xicheng District. ✆ 010/ 6601-1946 or 6803-5915. Fri–Sun 9:30am–5pm.

White Peacock Art World Well known for its carpets, this store carries embroidered goods and a range of arts and crafts. Beibinhe Lu, Deshengmenwai Dajie, Haidian District. ✆ 010/6201-3008. Daily 9am–7:30pm.

DEPARTMENT STORES

Beijing's one-stop department stores are being eased aside by the onslaught of megamalls and shopping plazas (see below), but the single-owner department store is still worth a shopping visit, both in its traditional Chinese form (fast disappearing) and the new superstore format (17 big new department stores opened in 1996 alone). This listing includes the store that often matters most to most tourists, despite all the advances in retailing: Beijing's original **Friendship Store.**

Friendship Store For the foreign visitor to Beijing, this is the ultimate one-stop shop, containing a generous sampling of nearly everything worth hauling home: arts and crafts, jewelry, silk, books, souvenirs, antiques (see the box, "What You Need to Know About Knockoffs & Fakes," in the "Markets & Bazaars" section, earlier in this chapter). Should be your first and last shopping stop. 17 Jianguomenwai Dajie, Chaoyang District. ✆ 010/6500-3311. Daily 9am–8:30pm.

Parkson This ultramodern department store tower has high prices but superb clothing and fashions and an excellent arts and crafts department (5th floor) which complements an in-house gallery called the National Treasures Exhibition Centre. There are restaurants and a grocery on the top floor. 101 Fuxingmennei Dajie, Xicheng District. ✆ 010/6601-3377. Daily 9am–9pm.

PriceSmart Membership Shopping This wildly successful, American-based, membership bulk-shopping warehouse opened in Beijing in 1997. Offering everything under the sun in massive quantities at a discount (from cleaning supplies to movie tapes), PriceSmart just keeps growing in lock step with China's Westward-leaning economy. Three locations: 54 Third Ring Road South, Chaoyang District, ✆ 010/6779-1113; A18 Xueqing Lu, Haidian District, ✆ 010/6292-7011; and Yuquan Lu at Fuxing Lu, Fengtai District, ✆ 010/6818-2211. Daily 10am–10pm.

Wangfujing Department Store   A true-blue department store in the traditional mode, Beijing's leading Chinese emporium is considering a massive remodel. Too bad, because even without escalators, this is a store worth exploring, filled with goods the locals can actually afford to buy. The first-floor toy department is the best in Beijing. 255 Wangfujing Dajie, Dongcheng District. ✆ 010/6512-6677. Daily 8:30am–8:30pm. Subway: Wangfujing.

Xidan Shopping Center   Modern and Western-looking, but decidedly for the local Chinese shopper, this crowded and chaotic complex is stuffed with everything a department store should have: from food and toys in the basement to cosmetics and hearing aids on the first floor, with sports equipment, clothing, and appliances filling up three more floors. Xidan Bei Dajie (east side), Xicheng District. ✆ 010/6602-4695. Daily 9am–8pm. Subway: Xidan.

DRUGSTORES

Watson's   Watson's is a large, Western-style drugstore, the only such store in Beijing, with a fairly wide range of imported beauty and health aids, from cosmetics to toothpaste, tampons to Tylenol. Two locations: Holiday Inn Lido, Chaoyang District, ✆ 010/6436-7653, daily 9am–9pm; and Full Link Plaza, 18 Chaoyangmenwai Dajie, Chaoyang District, ✆ 010/6588-2145, daily 10am–9pm.

Wangfujing Drugstore   This convenient downtown emporium has a small selection of Western cosmetics and health needs, along with a large selection of traditional Chinese medicines. 267 Wangfujing, Dongcheng District. ✆ 010/6524-9932. Daily 9am–8pm.

JEWELRY

Beijing is a great city for jewelry buyers who are willing to search and bargain. The **Hongqiao Market,** also known as the Pearl Market, has dozens of jewelry stalls (mostly pearls and jade) on its third floor, as does the **Friendship Store** on its second floor; there are, however, a number of other outlets to shop.

Amy's Pearls & Jewellery Co.   This is one of the larger stalls in the Pearl Market. Stall no. 4311 (4th floor), Hongqiao Market, 16 Hongqiao Lu (east side of the Temple of Heaven), Chongwen District. ✆ 010/6715-2372. Daily 8:30am–7pm.

Beijing Arts & Crafts Central   Jade, jade, and more jade. 200 Wangfujing Dajie, Dongcheng District. ✆ 010/6523-8747. Daily 9:30am–8pm.

Beijing Wenli Pearls and Jewelry Co.   In addition to pearls, there are also plenty of gems and stones, including lapis, coral, onyx, and citrine. The necklaces are gorgeous. Stall no. 4326 (4th floor) and stall no. 101 (3rd floor), Hongqiao Market, 16 Hongqiao Lu (east side of the Temple of Heaven), Chongwen District. ✆ 010/6711-7497. Daily 8:30am–7pm.

Shard Box Store   A good selection of silver and jade creations, presided over by a delightful staff and highly recommended by several of our readers. The jewelry designs are inspired by what China's minorities wear in the more remote western provinces. 1 Ritan Bei Lu (across from northeast corner of Ritan Park), Chaoyang District. ✆ 010/6500-3712. Daily 8:30am–7:30pm.

Sharon's Stone   Part of the Yonghong Pearls and Jewelry Company, this branch in the Pearl Market has a good selection of freshwater, sea, south sea, and Tahitian pearls. Stall no. 4201 (4th floor), Hongqiao Market, 16 Hongqiao Lu (east side of the Temple of Heaven), Chongwen District. ✆ 010/6717-1888. Daily 8:30am–7pm.

Fast Food & Old Bones

In 1992, the world's largest **McDonald's** opened in Beijing. The location couldn't have been better: the intersection of Beijing's main east–west avenue (Chang'an) with the city's number-one downtown shopping street (Wangfujing). With a 20-year lease securely in hand, this modern landmark seemed secure, but it wasn't. When overseas developers with yet bigger plans, more money, and better connections arrived on the doorstep, Beijing caved in. McDonald's was stripped of its lease in 1996. Work began on the **Oriental Plaza,** a multiblock, multifunctional commercial complex just a stone's throw from Tiananmen Square and the Forbidden City.

Money talks in Beijing, but even Oriental Plaza had its problems. It was too vast and too tall, and city zoning regulations designed to prevent the old imperial palaces from being overshadowed by modern business palaces could not be stretched. Meanwhile, during excavations near the abandoned McDonald's site, a more ancient curse was unearthed. Shovels struck the remains of a Stone Age village 22,000 years old. A doctor at Beijing University, Yue Shengyang, whose hobby was combing building sites for old porcelains, happened by and put his hands not on clay, but on bones. For the first time, Beijingers could connect the heart of China's capital with truly ancient settlements, with stone tools, fragments of prehistoric buffalo and elephants, and above all the fossilized human bones of their ancient ancestors that were little short of sacred.

As archaeologists raised the cry for preservation and the Oriental Plaza architects fumed at an obstacle even more venerated than McDonald's or the Forbidden City, city officials struck an expedient compromise. Excavation and construction of the great plaza continued, impeded only by the necessity to place a 2,000-square-foot Stone Age museum down in the basement—thus implanting the capital's newest (and oldest) attraction in the belly of Beijing's newest shopping and commercial center.

The exiled McDonald's survived, too, by folding up its golden arches and moving a block up Wangfujing, 1 of over 50 McDonald's now doing turn-away business by bringing the locals a taste of daily life in the West.

MALLS & SHOPPING PLAZAS

Beijing's mammoth shopping plazas are multiplying. These glitzy indoor malls consist of scores of independent brand-name and designer-label outlets, most with international merchandise. The experience is much like shopping the malls of the West with its boutiques, high prices, fast-food and coffee outlets, basement supermarkets, entertainment, and exhibits.

China World Trade Center Shopping Center   This three-level mall caters to foreign business travelers and expatriate families, and its outlets have recently been expanded by the opening of the underground shopping mall (complete with "Le Cool" ice rink) that connects the China World Hotel with Traders

Hotel 1 block north. The ground level of China World contains airline offices, shops, cafes, and Beijing's first Starbucks. Upstairs, there's a large Sparkice Internet Cafe. On the lower level (down the escalator) lies most of the shopping. There are plenty of boutiques (from Louis Vuitton to Beijing's own Mystery Garments) featuring imported and domestic men's and women's clothing; shoe stores; an antique fabric store (Zhang's Textiles); and folk craft outlets and contemporary Chinese art galleries. The CRC Supermarket (daily 9am–9:30pm) is crammed with imported edibles. A number of small Chinese arts and crafts gazebos line the center lane of the wide passageways, and near the ice rink to the north there's a fenced-in children's play area next to an ice cream/sandwich outlet. 1 Jianguomenwai Dajie, Chaoyang District. 𝄢 010/6505-2288. Daily 10am–9:30pm. Subway: Guomao (direct basement level link).

COFCO Plaza Facing outward and flanking the entrance to this megamall are branches of both the Hongkong and Shanghai Bank (Mon–Fri 9am–12:30pm and 1:30–5pm) and a McDonald's (daily 7am–11pm). Inside, expensive clothing stores dominate the four floors and three basements that orbit around a flashy central atrium. On the first floor, one can find a branch of the China Silk Shop and a florist; outlets for Crocodile, Christian Dior, and Benetton; Copy Max and a Konika Photo Express (for fast developing); and a store selling nothing but cowboy boots. Park 'N Shop supermarket (daily 8am–10pm) is in basement one; a large furniture store and a Baskin-Robbins ice cream parlor are in basement two; and a bowling alley (Haiba Bowling Club) is in the third basement down. An underground walkway connects this mall to the north side of Chang'an Avenue. 8 Jianguomennei Dajie, Dongcheng District. 𝄢 **010/6526-6666.** Daily 9am–9pm. Subway: Jianguomen.

 Does Sex Sell in Beijing?

Beijing, like the rest of China, wears a puritanical face, despite a flourishing underground in prostitution and pornography (both punishable by death). The city is not besmirched by sex shops and adult entertainment districts, but some "sex health shops" are permitted. There's one basement store labeled "Adult Shop" with a bold sign proclaiming in Chinese and English "Love Goods" (on the small street connecting Traders Hotel to the Kerry Centre); there's Beijing's oldest such emporium, the Adam and Eve Sex Shop (on the north side of Fuchengmen Dajie); and there are several small sex shops in the Maizi Dian neighborhood (east of the Great Wall Sheraton Hotel). Each of these outlets turns out to be a tame version of its counterpart in the seedier districts of the West. In Beijing, these shops are stocked with dry academic texts on sexual behavior and an assortment of traditional love potions and devices. Taxi drivers know the way to these shops, which have lately been selling a Chinese counterpart to Viagra for the treatment of male impotency. Known in Beijing as *Weige,* or "Great Brother," these expensive pills (300RMB, $36 each) allegedly bolster the performance of "Little Brother." One of these shops has been displaying an unintentionally wishful sign in English reading: "Thank You For Your Coming." Few foreign shoppers, however, seem to venture in.

Full Link Plaza   Opened in 1997, this spacious, sophisticated, uncrowded mall has four floors and two basements of shops and restaurants. The first floor includes a Watson's Drug Store and a Nautica outlet, and the second floor has Esprit and MacGregor branches. There's a Kenny Roger's Roasters Restaurant on the fourth floor and a Park 'N Shop supermarket in the basement. On the main floor is Beijing's most lavish Starbucks, complete with a glass-walled meeting room for hire by the hour. 18 Chaoyangmenwai Dajie, Chaoyang District. ☎ 010/ 6588-1997. Daily 9am–9pm. Subway: Chaoyangmen.

Lufthansa You Yi Shopping Center   Located on the east side of the Third Ring Road and connected to the Kempinski Hotel, Lufthansa Center is the largest and most modern mall in northeast Beijing (site of a number of international chain luxury hotels). There's a department store in the thick of things, with a range of upscale specialty shops, boutiques, restaurants, and arts and crafts outlets on the upper floors. The basement has a busy supermarket. 50 Liangmaqiao Lu, (east side of Third Ring Road East), Chaoyang District. ☎ 010/6435-4930. Daily 9am–8:30pm. No subway.

Oriental Plaza   Asia's largest shopping, office, apartment, and hotel complex, Oriental Plaza covers about 4 city blocks (from Wangfujing to Dongdan) of the capital's top commercial real estate. Supplanting the world's biggest McDonald's (which was razed in 1999), the plaza cost $2 billion to build (largely provided by Hong Kong developers). The result for shoppers is a huge, upscale, international two-story arcade with 200 shops (divided into five themed malls). There's also a Watson's drugstore; a Volkswagen/Audi showroom; the Sony Explora Science museum for children; the obligatory McDonald's, Starbucks, and their ilk; and a major archaeological site next to the basement subway entrance. There's even a five-star, 595-room hotel tower in the center of the plaza (the Oriental Harbour Plaza), next to the large musical fountain. This is Beijing's first plaza for the 21st century, created on a grand scale in the heart of the city. Dong Chang'an Dajie, Dongcheng District. ☎ 010/6526-3366. Daily 9am–9:30pm. Subway: Wangfujing (direct basement link).

Palace Hotel Shopping Arcade   Shop the swank lobby and then take the escalator down behind the waterfall to Beijing's most upscale collection of designer-name outlets. There are about 40 shops on three lower levels, as well as a small newsstand and a Bank of China (Mon–Fri 8:30am–noon and 1–5pm). To its fine international lineup (Gucci, Royal Copenhagen, Cartier, Gianni Versace, Baccarat), the Palace recently added China's first Armani. Despite the high prices, local Chinese are the biggest customers by far. Lower lobby levels, Palace Hotel, 8 Jingyu Hutong (1 block east off Wangfujing Dajie), Dongcheng District. ☎ 010/ 6512-8899. Daily 9am–9pm. Subway: Wangfujing.

Sun Dong An Plaza   Beijing's second grandest, most up-to-date megamall (built on the site of a humble farmers' market and small business arcade in the heart of Wangfujing), Sun Dong An is a series of galleries and atriums rising six flights, higher than any temple in the Forbidden City. Basement levels contain a supermarket, several department stores, and a new Starbucks. The first floor has cosmetics and camera outlets; the second floor, menswear; the third floor, women's wear; the fourth floor, shoes and hats; the fifth floor, snacks (Chinese and Western); and the sixth floor, restaurants. Among boutiques and brand-name outlets are Bossini, Burberry, Esprit, London Fog, and Nike. McDonald's and DeliFrance have restaurants on the second floor, and Bank of China has a branch on the first floor (open Mon–Fri 9am–noon and 1:30–5pm). 138 Wangfujing Dajie, Dongcheng District. ☎ 010/6527-6688. Mon–Thurs 9am–9pm; Sat–Sun 9am–10pm.

MUSIC

Beijing Accordion & Piano School   Take a peek (and a picture) of this one-of-a-kind Western musical instrument store with the piano in the window, right next door to Beijing's first Heavy Metal shop (at #16) with all the punk accessories and plenty of Bob Marley posters. South side of Xi Chang'an Jie, between Xidan shopping street and Tonglingge Lu. No phone or hours posted.

Hongsheng Musical Instruments   Chinese musical instruments make fine gifts or souvenirs. 225 Wangfujing Dajie, Dongcheng District. ℂ 010/6513-5190. Daily 8:30am–7pm.

Youdai Records   A favorite record, tape, and disc store of Beijing's expatriates. Features modern Chinese and Western music. 78 Yude Hutong, Xinjekou, Xicheng District. ℂ 010/6618-1701. Daily noon–6pm.

SILK, EMBROIDERY & FABRIC

Baizhifang Embroidery Factory   Silk yardage and a good selection of embroidered tablecloths, sheets, and pillowcases. A44 Liren Jie, Xuanwu District. ℂ 010/6303-6577. Daily 8am–5pm.

Qianmen Women's Clothing Store   Silk and wool yardage, custom tailoring, blouses, suits, and dresses. Dazhalan pedestrian street, west off Qianmen Dajie, Chongwen District. No phone. Daily 8:30am–9pm.

Ruifuxiang Silk and Cotton Store   Plenty of silk fabrics and ready-made clothing. Dazhalan pedestrian street, west off Qianmen Dajie, Chongwen District. No phone. Daily 8:30am–9:30pm.

Yuanlong Embroidery and Silk Store   This store has Beijing's largest selection of fabrics in silk, brocades, and wool, with tailoring and shipping services right on site. At the south entrance to the Temple of Heaven (Tiantan), 15 Yongdingmenwai, Chongwen District. ℂ 010/6511-4635. Daily 9am–6:30pm.

SUPERMARKETS

Beijing's hotels often have a small shop in the lobby with some Western snacks and bottled water, but for a broad range of familiar groceries, try one of the large-scale supermarkets listed here.

CRC Market   Everything the Western heart yearns for in one convenient, very modern supermarket. Basement Level 1, China World Trade Center, 1 Jianguomenwai Dajie, Chaoyang District. ℂ 010/6505-2288. Daily 9am–9:30pm. Subway: Guomao (direct basement link).

Holiday Inn Lido Supermarket   Excellent selection of imported foods and drinks, from potato chips to frozen dinners. In the Holiday Inn Lido, Jichang Lu, Jiangtai Lu, Chaoyang District. ℂ 010/6437-6688, ext. 1541. Daily 8:30am–9pm. No subway.

Jenny Lou's   A popular grocer with expats, Jenny Lou's carries excellent fresh fruits and vegetables, some imported. The cheese and bread selections in the attached deli are also popular. 4 Ritan Gongyuan Bei Lu, Chaoyang District. ℂ 010/6586-0626. Daily 8am–9pm. No subway.

Lucky Chain   This new chain of tiny hole-in-the-wall groceries knows how to cater to Western tastes (and members of the diplomatic compounds), stocking a nice range of imports (soft drinks, juices, mineral water, beer, wine, milk, butter, cheese, bread, cookies) at reasonable prices. They're friendly and they make free deliveries. 2 locations: across from east gate of Workers' Stadium on Gongrentiyuchang Dong Lu (next to Frank's Place), Chaoyang District, ℂ 010/6500-1532, daily 11am–midnight; and 3211 Tayuan Diplomatic Compound, Chaoyang District, ℂ 010/6532-2832, daily 9am–9pm.

Park 'N Shop   Emphasis on Western imports (over 1,000 items), including cheese and dairy products, wines, and soft drinks. Features an in-store Western-style bakery and delicatessen. (There's also a Park 'N Shop in the basement of COFCO Plaza, 8 Jianguomennei Dajie, open daily 8am–10pm.) Basement Level 2, Full Link Plaza, 18 Chaoyangmenwai Dajie, Chaoyang District. ✆ **010/6588-1908**. Daily 8:30am–9:30pm. Subway: Chaoyangmen.

TAILORS

Although other cities in Asia offer more extensive tailoring of suits, shirts, blouses, and dresses, Beijing has several reliable and reasonably priced custom tailor shops. Some specialize in *qipao,* the high-necked Mandarin-collar silk dress with a side slit.

Cao Shi Fu Qipao Shop   Mr. Cao Senlin has been making *qipao* for 6 decades. One dress takes him a month to complete. He does all the work in his small house. A hand-tailored *qipao* costs about RMB400 ($48); have your hotel desk call for an appointment. 25 Shi Jie Hutong, off Dongsi Nan Dajie, Dongcheng District. ✆ **010/6526-4515**.

Dreamweavers   This tiny tailor shop with a selection of silk, wool, and cotton fabrics, is experienced and skilled at sewing up Western as well as Chinese garments to your specifications. Expect to pay $80 and up per dressy item. 51 Taiyuancun Lu (north of Friendship Supermarket, off Sanlitun Bei Lu), Chaoyang District. ✆ **010/6466-3449**. Call for hours. No subway.

Kanna Custom Clothing Specialty Store   Hundreds of fabrics are housed here, and they can be converted into clothing of your choice within 48 hours. Across from China World Trade Center, 2 Jianguomenwai Dajie, Chaoyang District. ✆ **010/ 6594-8997**. Daily 10am–6pm.

Kylin Plaza   The 4th floor of this Chinese department store is stuffed with fabrics (mostly silk). Tailors wait at every turn. Ask to see samples of their work. These tailors can turn out any style quickly and fairly cheaply (a traditional *qipao* dress for about $40 complete). Popular among foreigners living in Beijing. 58 Gongrentiyuchang Bei Lu, Chaoyang Distinct. ✆ **010/6415-4548**. Daily 9am–9pm.

Muzhenlao Chinese Fashions   This popular chain, with outlets in Sun Dong An Plaza and COFCO Plaza, features the latest styles on their racks and a tailoring service if you want something custom-made. This is not the cheapest place in town for tailored fashions, but the quality is high. 138 Wangfujing Dajie, Sun Dong An Plaza, Dongcheng District. ✆ **010/6528-1827**. Mon–Thurs 9am–9pm, Fri–Sun 9am–10pm. Subway: Wangfujing.

TEA

Bichun Tea Shop   Nice assortment of classic teapots and packaged Chinese teas. 233 Wangfujing Dajie, Dongcheng District. ✆ **010/6525-4722**. Daily 8:30am–8:30pm.

Ji Gu Ge Teahouse   Good selection of Yixing clay teapots, tea sets, and packaged Chinese teas. 132–136 Liulichang Dong Jie, Xuanwu District. ✆ **010/6301-7849**. Daily 9am–11pm.

QinglinchunTeaShop   Teas, teapots, and tea sets, all made in China. 9 Qianmen Dajie, Chongwen District. ✆ **010/6303-8512**. Daily 8am–8pm.

Xidan Tea Shop   The selection of teas and teapots is limited in this small shop, but the quality is very high. 209 Xidan Bei Dajie, Xicheng District. ✆ **010/ 6605-7640**. Daily 8am–8pm.

9

Beijing After Dark

Until the 1990s, Beijing provided its foreign visitors very few venues for nighttime entertainment. At sunset, the city closed down, and tourists were largely confined to their hotels, unless they were part of a group tour that had arranged an evening's outing at the Beijing Opera. Recently, however, the possibilities for an evening on the town have multiplied. Beijing is still not in the same late-night league as Hong Kong or Tokyo, but once the sun sets on the Forbidden City and the shopping plazas, foreign travelers in China's capital do not have to tuck themselves in.

Beijing still offers large-scale performances of opera, acrobatics, and music by China's premier artists. But the performing arts are no longer confined to the capital's theaters. Teahouses have opened their doors to foreign visitors with presentations of opera excerpts, dance, music, acrobatics, and comedy in intimate, traditional surroundings.

More recently, Beijing has experienced an explosion of Western-style entertainment. The number of small cafe/bars in Sanlitun and other districts that foreign residents frequent after hours is increasing. More than watering holes, these restaurants-by-day become music clubs by night, featuring recorded or live rock and jazz until the wee hours. There's even a Beijing branch of the Hard Rock Cafe. Discos are extremely popular, too, and, like the cafe/bars, have become mixing bowls for locals and foreigners. Sports bars and small international cinemas are also sprouting up.

Beijing will not be mistaken for Paris, London, or New York after dark, but it isn't sleeping anymore either.

1 The Performing Arts

Beijing opera and acrobatics are the two most popular theatrical events, but puppetry, drama, and classical music (both Eastern and Western) are regularly featured in the capital's theaters, hotel auditoriums, and concert halls.

BEIJING OPERA

Nearly extinguished in the early 1990s, Beijing's most famous performing art, the traditional Beijing Opera, is thriving, thanks to a resurgence in popularity among locals and the funding of several theaters. Beijing Opera (*Jing Ju*) is derived from 8 centuries of touring song-and-dance troupes, but it became institutionalized in its present form in the 1700s, under the Qing Dynasty. The stylized singing, costuming, acrobatics, music, and choreography set apart Chinese opera from Western opera. It usually strikes foreigners as garish, screechy, and incomprehensible. It helps to know the plot (usually a historical drama with a tragic outcome), and English subtitles are sometimes provided. Songs are performed on a five-note scale (not the eight-note scale familiar in the West). The gongs, cymbals, and string and wind instruments punctuate (often jarringly) the

Tips **How to Find Out What's On & Get Tickets**
Check the entertainment listings in *China Daily* or the free English-language newspapers, such as *Beijing This Month, City Weekend, Metro,* or *Beijing Journal.* Your hotel tour desk or concierge may be able to secure tickets. Some tickets are sold by WEBTIX at (✆) **800/810-0443,** 010/6588-1337, www.webtix.com.cn, or www.66cities.com. Otherwise, you can go to the ticket office yourself. Locations of theaters, concert halls, teahouses, cafes bars, cinemas, and other entertainment sites are listed below.

action on the stage. Faces are painted with colors symbolizing qualities such as valor or villainy, and masks and costumes announce the performer's role in society, from emperor to peasant. Most Beijing Opera these days consists of abridgements, lasting 2 hours or less (as opposed to 5 hr. or more in the old days), and with the martial arts choreography, the spirited acrobatics, and the brilliant costumes, these performances can be a delight even to the unaccustomed, untrained eye. With the closure of Beijing's oldest and most venerated opera house, the Zhengyici Theater (see box), the Liyuan Theater has become the leading opera house.

Hu Guang Guild Hall   This century-old hall has all the trappings of a traditional Chinese opera house, including carved and painted columns and hanging scrolls. Dinners before the opera are served inside the historic guild. They include such signature dishes as "Rainbow Bridge Pearl" and "Dragon and Phoenix Playing," which are served with carved vegetable flowers illustrating an operatic sequence.

3 Hufangqiao, Xuanwu District, (✆) **010/6351-8284** or 010/6355-3114. Admission 60–180RMB ($7–$22). Dinner extra. Nightly performance 7:15–9pm. No subway.

Liyuan Theater   The best bet for the foreign tourist, this theater puts on spirited Beijing Opera abridgements from at least three operas performed by the Beijing Opera Troupe. Simultaneous translations into English are flashed on subtitle screens. The price levels reflect the quality of the seating and the range of snacks provided while you listen.

In the Qianmen Hotel, 175 Yong'an Lu, Xuanwu District. (✆) **010/6301-6688,** ext. 8860. Admission 30–150RMB ($3.60–$18). Nightly performance 7:30–8:45pm. No subway.

Other opera venues include the **Chang'an Grand Theater,** 7 Jianguomennei Dajie, Chaoyang District ((✆) **010/6510-1155** or 010/6510-1309; admission 60–180RMB [$7–$22]; Fri–Sat 7:30–9:30pm; subway: Jianguomen), and **Grand View Garden Theater,** 12 Nancaiyun Jie, Xuanwu District ((✆) **010/ 6351-9025;** admission 40–150RMB [$5–$18]; nightly 7:30–8:45pm; no subway).

ACROBATICS

For 2,000 years, the Chinese have been perfecting their acrobatic performances. These days the juggling, contortionism, unicycling, chair-stacking, and plate-spinning have entered the age of modern staging. The Beijing Acrobatic Troupe (also known as the Tianqiao Acrobatics Troupe) spends most of the year outside Beijing touring the stages of the world, but the groups that are left home are superb. Acrobatic shows receive high marks from foreign tourists.

Chaoyang Theater   The China Acrobatics Troupe or the Sichuan Acrobatic Troupe usually perform here.

36 Dongsanhuan Bei Lu (Third Ring Road East), Chaoyang District. *C* **010/6507-2421.** Admission 80–120RMB ($10–$14). Nightly performance 7:15–8:20pm. No subway.

Poly Plaza International Theater   A Las Vegas–style acrobatics show is often staged in this state-of-the-art auditorium by the China Acrobatic Troupe. Tickets are sold through hotel tour desks or at the Poly Plaza ticket office, with prices determined by seating and dining options (from snacks to full dinners). This theater, which opened in 1990, has staged over 2,000 shows. After an extensive renovation, it reopened October 2000. With 1,400 seats (including eight VIP boxes), it is one of the most comfortable theaters in China to take in an evening of acrobatics, opera, or other performances.

In the Poly Plaza Hotel, 14 Dongzhimen Nan Dajie, Chaoyang District. *C* **010/6500-1188,** ext. 5127, or 010/6608-4160. Nightly performance 7:15–9pm. Admission 50–500RMB ($6–$60). Subway: Dongsishitiao.

Wansheng Theater   Home of the renowned Beijing Acrobatics Troupe, the most artistic of the capital's performers.

95 Tianqiao Market, Xuanwu District. *C* **010/6303-7449.** Admission 100–150RMB ($12–$18). Nightly performance 7:15–9pm. No subway.

PUPPETS

Puppet shows (*mu ou xi*) have been performed in China since the Han Dynasty (206 B.C.–A.D. 220). Shadow puppets, hand puppets, and string puppets (marionettes) all perform on an irregular basis, but they are sometimes featured in the variety shows at Beijing's teahouses. Most theatrical performances, including weekend matinees, are held at the **China Puppet Art Theater,** A1 Anhuaxili (near Third Ring Road North), Chaoyang District (*C* **010/6424-3698** or 010/6425-4798); admission is 20 to 25RMB ($2.40–$3).

OTHER PERFORMING ARTS VENUES

Beijing is the site of major national and international music, drama, and dance performances nearly every day of the year. Many of these concerts are held in the **Beijing Concert Hall** or the **Poly Plaza International Theater.** The Beijing Philharmonic and the Central Ballet (China's premier dance company) perform frequently in Beijing when not on tour, and an increasing number of major orchestras, symphonies, ensembles, and soloists from abroad have put Beijing on their itineraries. The capital has also spawned the Beijing Symphony Orchestra, the Beijing Chamber Quartet, the Beijing International Orchestra, and a number of ensembles playing traditional Chinese music.

Fun Fact **End of the Road for Beijing's Oldest Opera House**

The leading venue in Beijing (and in all of China) for traditional opera had long been the **Zhengyici Theater.** Originally a temple (built in 1620) that was constructed entirely of wood, it had served as a theater since 1713. Closed after Liberation (1949), it was restored and reopened in 1994 by a wealthy patron, but competition from karaoke parlors, cinemas, discos, television, and videos doomed its existence once again in October 1998. Beijing's Education Bureau now owns the building, located at 220 Xiheyan Dajie in the Xuanwu District, and it plans to convert the theater into a community center where children can study traditional arts and culture.

The most important formal performance hall in China is the **Beijing Concert Hall,** 1 Bei Xinhua Jie, Liubukou, Xuanwu District (℗ **010/6605-5812** or 010/6605-7006). The hall seats 1,000 and serves wine and sells CDs in the foyer. During a recent 2-week period, it presented a French pianist, the Hua Ying Women's Military Orchestra, the Beijing Chamber Ensemble, the Tibetan Lamas Ensemble, the China Singing and Dancing Ensemble, the Children's Philharmonic Orchestra, the Canadian True North Brass Group, and the Beijing Symphony Orchestra. Tickets for most performances are 30 to 120RMB ($3.60–$14), with prices for local performers lower and for international stars (such as Yo Yo Ma) considerably higher (150–750RMB, $18–$90).

Three other top concert venues attracting international performers are the **Beijing Exhibition Theater,** 135 Xizhimenwai Dajie, Xicheng District (℗ **010/6835-4455**); the **Century Theater,** 40 Liangmaqiao, Sino-Japanese Youth Center, Chaoyang District (℗ **010/6462-8470** or 010/6466-3311, ext. 3165); and the **Forbidden City Concert Hall,** on the west side of Tiananmen Square, inside Zhongshan Park, Dongcheng District (℗ **010/6559-8294**).

Many of Beijing's top classical and traditional musicians perform in hotel lobbies and hotel restaurants on a regular basis. One of the most popular such venues is in the **Crowne Plaza Beijing,** where the lobby atrium is often filled with song in the evening; small concerts are held at the International Art Palace on the second floor (48 Wangfujing, Dongcheng District, ℗ **010/6513-3388,** ext. 1209).

2 Teahouse Theater

For centuries, China's teahouses were the chief gathering places for artists and mandarins, intellectuals and dilettantes—places of leisure where traditional culture and the performing arts were appreciated and sustained. This tradition almost disappeared from modern China, but in Beijing teahouses, it is undergoing a revival. The teahouses that offer theater are especially attractive to foreign visitors. They are the Chinese version of the Western dinner theater, offering snacks or full meals while presenting, on intimate stages, a spectrum of traditional performing arts: highlights from Beijing Opera, acrobatics, magic, crosstalk (stand-up) comedy, puppetry, singing, dancing, and music played on ancient instruments. An understanding of the Chinese language isn't necessary to enjoy the fast-paced, highly dramatic, and visual selections. There's no better place to enjoy a full banquet of Chinese performing arts.

Beijing Teahouse (Beijing Chaguan)   An excellent break while shopping on Liulichang Culture Street, this teahouse is noted for its traditional storytellers who perform every afternoon. The teahouse itself is open for tea and snacks daily from 9am to 9pm.

8 Changdian, Liulichang Jie, Xuanwu District. ℗ 010/6303-3846. Free admission. Daily performances 2:30–4:30pm. Subway: Hepingmen.

Jingwei Teahouse (Jingwei Chaguan)   Another teahouse on Liulichang Culture Street with live performances, Jingwei features traditional comedy every Saturday and Sunday at 2:30pm. There's an English tea menu, too.

76 Liulichang Xi Jie, Xuanwu District. No phone available. Free admission. Comic performances Sat–Sun at 2:30pm. Subway: Hepingmen.

Lao She Teahouse (Laoshe Chaguan)   Every night's entertainment is different, but expect a sampling of opera, traditional music, acrobats, comedians, magicians, and storytellers. The higher admission fees provide better seating (closer to the front) and more snacks.

Dawancha Bldg., 3rd floor, 3 Qianmenxi Dajie, Chongwen District. ℂ **010/6303-6830**. Admission 40–130RMB ($5–$16). Performances Fri–Sun 7:50–9:20pm. Subway: Qianmen.

Sanwei Bookstore   Located a mile west of the Forbidden City, on the south side of Chang'an Avenue, Sanwei is a bookstore below and a traditional teahouse above. Decorated in dark carved woods, the attic teahouse provides a relaxed studio setting in which to take in jazz by local groups (Fri nights) and classical Chinese music (Sat nights) over tea and Beijing snacks.

60 Fuxingmennei Dajie, Xuanwu District. ℂ **010/6601-3204**. Admission 30RMB ($3.60). Performances Fri 9–11pm and Sat 8:30–10:30pm. Subway: Xidan.

Tian Hai Teahouse   A serene wooden and bamboo interior, a Qing Dynasty–attired wait staff, and musical and operatic performances every Friday and Saturday evening re-create the quiet feel of an old teahouse tucked away down a hutong in Beijing's busiest bar strip.

Sanlitun Lu (half a block north of Gonrentiyuchang Bei Lu), Chaoyang District. ℂ **010/6416-5676**. Daily 10am–1pm. Performances nightly at 7:30pm. No subway.

Tian Qiao Happy Teahouse   The Happy Teahouse has all the atmosphere of a Qing Dynasty Theater. Waiters are dressed in Imperial costumes, and they never stop serving tea. The opera excerpts are quite energetic. Acrobatics, music, and comedy can be sampled from tables in front of the stage or on the balcony.

A1 Beiwei Lu (#113 Tianqiao Market, west of the Temple of Heaven), Xuanwu District. ℂ **010/6304-0617**. Admission 180RMB ($22) for table and snacks, 330RMB ($40) for Beijing duck dinner. Performances Tues–Sun 6:30–8:30pm. No subway.

3 The Bar & Club Scene

Beijing today is undergoing an avalanche of bar openings, much of it centered on **Sanlitun,** a tree-lined neighborhood of foreign diplomatic compounds located in the Chaoyang District northwest of the city center between the Workers' Stadium and the Third Ring Road North. There are also plenty of nightlife venues opening along the adjacent **Gongrentiyuchang Street** all the way east to Chaoyang Park. Most of these small, privately owned cafe/bars serve Western cuisine by day and imported beer, wine, and spirits by night. They attract a large number of foreign residents, diplomats, and students, as well as young, moneyed Beijingers. In the summer, most of these cafe/bars offer outdoor seating, pleasant places to while away the sunlit hours. In the evenings, most become meccas for after-dinner drinks and live music, particularly rock.

The international hotels also have their own lounges and lobby bars that are popular with tourists and foreign business travelers. Recently, the city has added such Western venues as sports bars, jazz clubs, cinemas, and discos. There's no shortage of places for foreign travelers to relax and enjoy a drink or dance into the wee hours. The surroundings are those familiar in the West, as are the cover charges and prices for drinks and snacks.

SANLITUN & BEYOND

The liveliest and most compact nightlife district in Beijing is on Sanlitun Lu, officially designated as **Sanlitun Bar Street** (Sanlitun Jiuba Jie) in 1996. By the end of 1996, 25 bars had moved onto the street and its *hutongs*. A dozen more opened their doors the next year, and by 2000, the tally was over 60. The

Sanlitun outdoor wicker and clothing market was summarily eliminated, and the southern extension of Sanlitun was recently leveled, but Sanlitun still has plenty of steam. While some of its cafe/bars barely survive 6 months in business, others have been at Sanlitun for years. The scene is always changing rapidly, but at present, it is a great place to stroll by day and to barhop after the sun sets.

Most of the bars and cafes are situated chockablock on the east side of Sanlitun Lu running north from the intersection at Gongrentiyuchang Bei Lu (west of the Third Ring Road East). Here a green sign announces (in English) that you are at the gateway to Sanlitun Bar Street. The sidewalk is strung with bright pennants and table umbrellas. The cafes, bars, and clubs line the street and alleyways for the next 4 blocks, but the farther north you walk, the more likely it is that the bars will be interspersed with small boutiques, art galleries, and rattan furniture shops. Eventually you reach the north end of Sanlitun Lu, where the foreign embassies and consulates are located, but there are cafes and bars here, too. Along the southern shore of the Liangma River, 1 block west off Sanlitun Lu, is **Schiller's II** (1 Sanlitun Bei Lu; © **010/6507-1331**), a bar and restaurant long popular with local expats and open daily from 5pm to 1am. If you follow the river east, you'll come to the **Third Ring Road** area, the location of Beijing's own **Hard Rock Cafe** (see below).

If Sanlitun and the Third Ring Road don't do you in, there's now a barhopping street within easy walking distance west of Sanlitun (just off Gongrentiyuchang Bei Lu, toward the Workers' Stadium): **Dongdaqiao Xie Jie.** This little street curves south and west and is now popularly called "Sanlitun Bar Street South." Cafe/bar names run the gamut from Nashville to Dirty Nellie's Irish Pub, but the best-known spot is **Hidden Tree** (see below). Dondaqiao Xie Jie connects to Beijing's original expatriate bar, the ever-popular **Frank's Place** (see below), located directly across the street from the east entrance to Workers' Stadium—a most comfortable place to begin and end an extended barhop through Sanlitun.

The newest nightlife mecca is currently directly east of Sanlitun, also along Gongrentiyuchang Street, but rather farther: far across Third Ring Road at the entrance to Chaoyang Park. Here you'll find a "rock 'n' roll city" of bars, discos, and trendy restaurants (led by **Big Easy,** below); it's the newest gold-rush camp for those who dig after dark.

CAFE/BARS

Here's a list of some of the most popular late-night spots that foreigners (tourists and residents alike) frequent, along with locals. Most are in the Sanlitun, Dongdaqiao, and Workers' Stadium sectors described above.

Boys and Girls (Nanhai Nuhai)   A quintessential Sanlitun drinking spot, large, lively, and favored by young Chinese just having fun. The house band plays Western and Chinese pop. 52 Sanlitun Bei Jiuba Jie, Chaoyang District. © **010/6416-4697.** Daily 11am–6am.

Dirty Nellie's (Dubolin Xicanting)   One of Beijing's only bars with a vaguely Irish theme, this is a popular drinking bar (with Guinness on tap) that has foreign rock bands on weekends. Dongdaqiao Xie Jie, Chaoyang District. © **010/6502-2808.** Daily noon–2am.

Frank's Place (Wanlong Jiuba)   Founded in 1990 by Frank himself, this American grill and bar is Beijing's original expatriate hangout, comfortable as an old shoe, crowded and lively. The hamburgers, fries, and Philly cheese steaks, as well as the full dinners, are some of the best Western fare in the city. If home is

North America, this is the place to come home to in Beijing. Credit cards accepted. Across from the east gate of Workers' Stadium, Gongrentiyuchang Dong Lu, Chaoyang District. ✆ 010/6507-2617. Daily 9am–1:30am.

Henry J. Bean's (Hengli Jiuba)   Beijing's best American-style bar and grill, with plenty of fresh beer on tap, Henry's has live dance bands on its small stage every night but Sunday. (See restaurant review in chapter 5, "Dining.") Credit cards accepted. West Wing, China World Trade Center, 1 Jianguomenwai Dajie, Chaoyang District. ✆ 010/6505-2266, ext. 6334. Sun–Thurs 11:30am–1am, Fri–Sat 11:30am–2:30am.

Hidden Tree (Yinbi De Shu)   Beer from Belgium and live music by local bands on weekends are the hallmarks of this bar that started the rush that transformed Dongdaqiao Xie Jie into the unofficial Sanlitun Bar Street South. Good steaks are grilled here and served late into the night. Credit cards accepted. 12 Dongdaqiao Xie Jie, Chaoyang District. ✆ 010/6509-3642. Nightly 6pm–2am.

John Bull Pub (Zun Bo Jiuba)   Beijing's best English pub and English grub (see restaurant review in chapter 5, "Dining"), John Bull has pool, darts, and live music in the evenings. Credit cards accepted. 44 Guanghua Lu, Chaoyang District. ✆ 010/6532-5905. Daily 11am–1am.

Kebab Kafe (Lian Yi)   Excellent patio drinking and dining in the summer (see restaurant review in chapter 5, "Dining"), Kebab is renowned among European travelers for its imported beers. Credit cards accepted. Sanlitun Lu (west side), Chaoyang District. ✆ 010/6415-5812. Daily 10:30am–2am.

Mexican Wave (Moxige Canting)   One of Beijing's oldest expatriate hangouts, established in 1990. (See restaurant review in chapter 5, "Dining.") Dongdaqiao Lu, Chaoyang District. ✆ 010/6506-3961. Daily 11:30am–2am.

Minders Cafe (Minda Kafei Wu)   Located at the entrance to the southwest extension of Sanlitun Bar Street, Minders is an established drinking hole among area expatriates. There is live music (often rock or disco) most nights except Mondays. Dongdaqiao Xie Jie, Chaoyang District. ✆ 010/6500-6066. Daily 11am–2am (until 4am Fri–Sat).

Nashville (Xiangyao Jiuba)   This country-western bar—with an interior to match—attracts foreigners and Chinese yuppies. There's live music some nights; Tuesdays often feature a live country music performer. Shows start at 9pm. Dongdaqiao Xie Jie, Chaoyang District. ✆ 010/6502-4201. Nightly 6pm–2am.

P. J. O'Reilly's Irish Pub (Ai Er Lan Jiuba)   This swank pub looks Irish, but the name and the Guinness are the most Irish things about it. The house band plays pop and jazz on Wednesdays and weekends. 18 Jianguomennei Dajie (southwest side of Henderson Center), Dongcheng District. ✆ 010/6559-4238. Daily 11am–2am.

Press Club Bar (Jizhe Julebu)   The nearby Beijing International Club, renowned in days gone by as the meeting spot for foreign correspondents, inspired this elegant upscale creation, which seats just 55. Bookshelves with leather-bound tomes, a marble fireplace, a grand piano, leather armchairs, brocade sofas, and old prints and vintage photos of Beijing pundits and press correspondents line the long bar, where the happy-hour hors d'oeuvres (complimentary daily 4–6pm), served on silver platters by waiters in white jackets, change frequently and can't be beat. Credit cards accepted. In the St. Regis Beijing Hotel, 21 Jianguomenwai Dajie, Chaoyang District. ✆ 010/6460-6688. Daily 4:30pm–midnight.

Public Space (Bai Fang Zi)   One of the most subdued and elegant cafe/bars on Sanlitun, this is the place to relax after an afternoon of sightseeing or an evening of barhopping. The shakes, desserts, wines, and cocktails hit the spot, as

The Sexual Underground

A sexual as well as an economic revolution may be sweeping China these days, but the gay and lesbian scene is still far underground, even in "liberal" Beijing. Gay bars do pop up now and then, only to be closed. It's okay for people of the same sex to walk down the street hand in hand—many same-sex Chinese friends do so quite platonically—but no embraces or kisses are acceptable. China's puritanical approach to sexual expression will probably strike many homosexuals from the West as naïve rather than barbaric because anti-gay policies seldom ever surface and rarely, if ever, afflict foreign visitors, at least overtly.

On another sexually forbidden front, it is worth noting that at least one bar in the quiet southern end of the Sanlitun bar district (the **Golden Eye Pub** on Sanlitun Nan Lu, ✆ **010/6509-3267**) has been staging what it bills as transvestite stage shows recently. Moreover, Beijing's best-known transsexual, Jin Xing, who owns a Sanlitun cafe/bar herself (called the **Half Moon** in press reports, but otherwise unidentified), has been quoted on several occasions by foreign reporters. The former army colonel and men's dance champion, known for her flashy gowns and shiny nail polish, claims that the Clinton scandals would have never been an issue in China. At the same time, she admits that her own love life after a sex-change operation could be better. "I'm too much for Chinese men," she concludes, "But I'm able to lead a normal life in Beijing. No discrimination."

Currently, gay-friendly night spots include the **Half and Half Cafe** (15 Sanlitun Nan Lu, ✆ **010/6416-6919**), the **Drag-On** (also on Sanlitun Nan Lu, ✆ **010/6593-2360**), and the new **Hotline 1950** (4–5 Liangmaqiao Lu, ✆ **010/6461-1950**). Gays also favor **Rock 'n' Roll** and **Nightman** discos (see below).

does the "very cool" decor. 50 Sanlitun Bei Jiuba Lu, Chaoyang District. ✆ **010/6416-0759**. Daily 10am–2:30am.

Sgt. Pepper's (Shajin) _Finds_ One of many new cafe/bars surrounding Chaoyang Park, this one employs a cover band to play Beatles tunes and other rock classics while providing well-prepared Western snacks and meals. The decor is 1960s rock, too. With U.S. Black Angus steaks and a rooftop barbecue, Sgt. Pepper's a new favorite among many expatriates. 1 Nongzhanguan Nan Lu (Chaoyang Park), Chaoyang District. ✆ **010/6500-8088**. Nightly 6pm–2am.

SPORTS BARS

Goose and Duck (E He Ya) A well-established sports pub and restaurant with a British flair (where fish and chips is 50RMB, $6, and the Guinness is on draft), Goose and Duck has darts, pool, foosball, big-screen satellite TV, and patio seating. Happy hour is 4 to 8pm daily. Credit cards accepted. 1 Bihuju Nan Lu (west gate, Chaoyang Park), Chaoyang District. ✆ **010/6538-1691**. Daily 8am–2am.

Grandstand Sports Bar With billiards, darts, sports posters, and all-sports TV, the Grandstand is perched above the Freezer Disco. Credit cards accepted. In the Holiday Inn Lido, Jichang Lu, Jiang Tai Lu, Chaoyang District. ✆ **010/6437-6688**, ext. 1404. Sun–Wed 8pm–2am, Thurs–Sat 5–10pm.

Pit Stop (Kuaichehao) Pit Stop features American snacks from the open grill, a dance floor, and plenty of satellite TV monitors with the latest sports broadcasts, all with a Formula-One racing theme. From 9am to midnight, all you can drink is 120RMB ($14). Credit cards accepted. In the Harbour Plaza Hotel, 8 Jiang Tai Xi Lu, Chaoyang District. © 010/6436-2288, ext. 2617. Sun–Thurs 4pm–1am, Fri–Sat 4pm–2am.

Sports City Cafe (Yundongcheng) Beijing's biggest and brightest new sports bar, with half-court basketball, darts, a putting green, billiards, sports video games, large TV screens, a cigar room, and a dance floor. In the Gloria Plaza Hotel, 2nd floor, 2 Jianguomennei Dajie. © 010/6515-8855. Nightly 7pm–1am.

JAZZ CLUBS

Aria (Aliya) Live jazz by local and international soloists and groups is performed nightly at the piano bar in what remains Beijing's plushest, most sophisticated wine bar and grill. Credit cards accepted. In the China World Hotel, 2nd and 3rd floor, 1 Jianguomenwai Dajie, Chaoyang District. © 010/6505-2266, ext. 36. Daily 11am–midnight.

Big Easy (Kuaile Zhan) Renowned for its superb Cajun dining and decor (see restaurant review in chapter 5, "Dining"), Big Easy is Beijing's favorite new place to listen to live jazz and blues nightly. Features the best overseas jazz and blues artists to hit Beijing. Credit cards accepted. 1 Nongzhanguan Nan Lu (Chaoyang Park south gate). © 010/6508-6776. Daily 5pm–2am (Fri–Sat until 3am).

CD Cafe Jazz Club (Sendi Kafei) Long one of Beijing's premier night spots for jazz and blues performers, CD is under new management (by a local musician), and the emphasis is slated to change from mostly jazz to mostly pop. Sundays are still reserved for live jazz (or blues), starting at 9:30pm. This is an upscale club (with imported drinks, Western bar food, and varying cover charges), and the new managers aim to keep it that way. Dongsanhuan (Third Ring Road East, south of the Agriculture Exhibition Hall), Chaoyang District. © 010/6501-8877, ext. 3032. Daily 8pm–2am.

Jam House (Jiemo Fang) This popular live music bar (owned by a Beijing guitarist) lives up to its name on Thursdays, with its free jazz and blues jam. Weekends bring in a more serene crowd, with live flamenco bands. Dongdaqiao Xie Jie, Chaoyang District. © 010/6506-3845. Daily 5:30pm–2:30am.

Jazz Ya (Jue Shi Wu) The jazz is via CDs in this relatively quiet, long-established bar, which has a steady Japanese and European clientele. It's a sophisticated lounge weekdays; it's packed on weekends. The summer patio has good Japanese-style barbecues. 18 Sanlitun Bei Lu (alley 1 block west of the main bar street, near Bella's), Chaoyang District. © 010/6415-1227. Daily 10:30am–2am.

Sanwei Bookstore Local jazz performers often entertain upstairs in this traditional teahouse on Friday nights at 7:30pm (cover charge usually 30RMB, $3.60); Chinese classical musicians play Saturday nights at 8:30pm. 60 Fuxingmen-wai Dajie (west of Forbidden City, near Xidan intersection), Xicheng District. © 010/6601-3204. Daily 9:30am–10:30pm.

DANCE CLUBS & DISCOS

Club Banana (Ba Na Na Julebu) Once an exclusive night club with an MTV room and a dress code, this is now an aging strobe-lit disco with plenty of singles waiting to meet other singles. In the Sea Sky Shopping Center, 5th floor, 12 Chaoyangmen-wai Dajie (near Full Link Plaza), Chaoyang District. © 010/6599-3351. Cover 50RMB ($6). Nightly 9pm–2am.

The Den (Dunhuang)   A restaurant by day, this disco is decorated as an antique gambling den. The upstairs dance floor is almost claustrophobic, but young professionals, East and West, seem to like it that way. Dancing gets going around midnight. 4A Gongrentiyuchang Dong Lu (next to City Hotel), Chaoyang District. ✆ 010/6592-6290. Cover 30RMB ($3.60). Daily 10:30am–3am (until 6am weekends).

Freezer Disco Club   This place is everything you'd expect from a good hotel disco: It has a big bar, a small stage featuring live local bands or a DJ, a sunken dance floor, table-seating with karaoke—in summary, it's a dark, spacious, reverberating cavern. In the Holiday Inn Lido, Jichang Lu, Jiang Tai Lu, Chaoyang District. ✆ 010/6437-6688, ext. 1414. No cover for foreign patrons. Sun–Wed 8pm–2am, Thurs–Sat 8pm–3am.

Hard Rock Cafe   The music, live and loud, really kicks in at 10pm (as does the cover charge), except on Sundays. The American fast food is among the best served in China, and the beer and mixed drinks are fine, too, but quite expensive (up to $20 for some cocktails). The spacious dance floor is usually full. Credit cards accepted. 8 Dongsanhuan Bei Lu (Third Ring Road East), Chaoyang District. ✆ 010/6590-6688, ext. 2571. Cover 50RMB ($6). Sun–Thurs 11:30am–2am, Fri–Sat 11:30am–3am.

Hot Spot (Redian)   A few years ago, this was the hottest spot in Beijing for a disco evening; today, only the most adventurous are advised to venture inside, as the local crowd has grown rough, even dangerous. Located inside the grounds of the People's Liberation Army (PLA), Hot Spot does have atmosphere: PLA soldiers in uniform are on hand to greet customers. Break dancing, hip-hop, and rap are still performed on stage, while the lightly attired cage-dancers rise and fall overhead in their metal cages. This is about as wild as nightlife gets in Beijing. Third Ring Road East (just south of the Jingguang New World Hotel), Chaoyang District. ✆ 010/6501-9955. Cover 30RMB ($3.60). Nightly 7pm–1:30am.

 A Night at the Movies

China limits the release of new Hollywood films to just ten a year, all dubbed into Mandarin. The leading import seems to be Hong Kong kung fu action films. Chinese directors produced some of the best films in the world during the 1980s and 1990s, but even some of these can't be shown in China. Non-Chinese-speaking visitors hungering for a night at the pictures do have some outlets these days. Perhaps the most interesting venue is **Cherry Lane Cinema,** at the Sino-Japanese Youth Exchange Center, International Conference Hall, 40 Liangmaqiao Lu (about 1 mile east of the Lufthansa Center, off the Third Ring Road East), ✆ 010/6461-5318. Cherry Lane's focus is on screening contemporary Chinese films before foreign audiences, using English subtitles. These screenings are usually held on Friday evenings at 8pm, with an admission of 50RMB ($6).

Some of Beijing's cafe/bars show foreign films (in English) in a video format on large screens. The newest of the cinema cafes is **Sculpting In Time (Diaoke Shiguang),** 45 Chengfu Jie, Haidian District, ✆ 010/6252-1746, which shows classic foreign video releases (such as Bergman's *The Seventh Seal*) Tuesdays through Thursdays at 7:30pm, with an admission of 10RMB ($1.20).

The Loft (Cangku Jiuba) This spiffy, ultramodern, high-tech restaurant becomes a hot dance spot with disco DJs after dinner, attracting a well-to-do young Chinese crowd, along with plenty of foreigners. 4 Gongrentiyuchang Bei Lu (down west side alley at Pacific Century Plaza), Chaoyang District. ℂ 010/6501-7501. Cover 50RMB ($6). Sun–Thurs 11am–2am, Fri–Sat 11am–4am.

NASA (Na Sa) One of Beijing's oldest discos, NASA has a military theme, with an army jeep serving as the bar and a helicopter suspended from the balcony. This mainly attracts the nearby university crowd, local and foreign. 2 Xitucheng Lu (near Beijing film academy), Haidian District. ℂ 010/6203-2906. No cover for foreigner patrons. Sun–Thurs 9pm–1am, Fri–Sat 9pm–2am.

Nightman Disco (Laiteman) This is one of Beijing's older discos, its cavernous disco surrounded by large screens broadcasting music videos—but it's still going strong. 2 Xibahe Nanli (west side of International Exhibition Center), Chaoyang District. ℂ 010/6466-2562. No cover for foreign patrons. Nightly 8pm–3am.

Poachers Inn the Park Ensconced inside a Chinese-style mansion within a classic Chinese garden, Poachers consists of Smugglers Bar, an English-style pub, and a disco dance floor with walls and floor of stone. In the summer months, the dance and music sometimes move outdoors onto the more inviting Island Park stage. Tuanjiehu Park (west gate), Third Ring Road East, Chaoyang District. ℂ 010/ 6500-8390 or 010/6532-3063. Cover 50RMB ($6). Daily 3pm–3am or later.

Rock N Roll (Gun Shi) This huge disco anchors the newest nightlife station in Beijing, located at the south gate of Chaoyang Park. Its multilevel, hydraulic dance floors and outdoor extensions have attracted the city's youngest, wealthiest, and wildest, along with adventurous expats. (Older, more sedate dancers should swing by the just-opened, quite luxurious **Trendsetters** opposite this disco.) 1 Nongzhanguan Nan Lu, Chaoyang Park (south gate), Chaoyang District. ℂ 010/6592-9856. Cover 25RMB ($3). Nightly 8pm–5:30am.

Vogue (Shishang Fengge) Beijing's hottest dance spot when it opened in 2000, this is the place where celebrities and would-be celebrities make their appearances. The upstairs Art-Deco lounge serves high-priced drinks. Weekends, which often have theme parties, are extremely crowded. 88 Gongrentiyuchang Dong Lu (northeast of Workers' Stadium), Chaoyang District. ℂ 010/6416-5316. Cover 50RMB ($6). Nightly 7pm–3am.

10

The Great Wall & Other Side Trips from Beijing

The Great Wall is the number one site in the Beijing vicinity—the number-one site in all of China—and it should not be missed. There are four other places near Beijing that are worth an excursion as well: the legendary Western Hills, the famous archaeological site of Peking Man, and the tombs of the Ming and Qing dynasty emperors. From Beijing, each of these treasures requires just a day trip, but it can add up to a long day. Most travelers book a group tour with an English-speaking guide to smooth the way. The main drawback to such an arrangement is that you will have but a short time to explore the site itself, often 2 hours or less. Alternatives are to hire a car and driver yourself, with the assistance of your hotel concierge, or to use public buses (the cheapest, but most grueling means to make the trip). That way you set your own itinerary. Whatever means you choose, seeing these ancient remains outside Beijing is well worth a day's journey.

1 The Great Wall ★★★

The Chinese call it *Wan Li Chang Cheng,* the "Long Wall of Ten-Thousand Li." (with three *li* to the mile). Actually, the Great Wall is even longer than its poetic name claims, measuring about 6,200 miles from east to west, counting all its serpentine sections. The Wall's origins go back at least to the 5th century B.C., when the rival kingdoms of the Warring States Period (453–221 B.C.) built defensive ramparts against their enemies. The First Emperor of unified China, Qin Shi Huang Di, fortified the barriers in the 3rd century B.C. Over a 10-year period, 300,000 conscripted laborers, many of them slaves, knit the walls into a continuous rampart to protect the western frontier. New sections extended the Wall east to the Yellow Sea.

The Great Wall was constantly repositioned along new routes as successive dynasties rose and fell. In the year A.D. 607, more than a million workers toiled on this line of defense, but soon after, the Great Wall was abandoned. The Mongols eventually broke through from the north and established the Yuan Dynasty (A.D. 1271–1368), making Beijing their capital. Their successors, the emperors of the Ming Dynasty (A.D. 1368–1644), set in motion the last great phase of wall-building, which created the Great Wall as we see it today north of Beijing.

You can visit the Great Wall most easily at four dramatic points near Beijing. The Great Wall at **Badaling, Mutianyu, Simatai,** and **Juyongguan** are all appealing. Badaling is where most tourists walk the Great Wall. Mutianyu is a fine alternative, beautifully restored and less crowded with visitors. Simatai is a wild, nearly unrestored segment, farther from Beijing and, as a consequence, far less inundated with tour buses. Juyongguan is the newest section to be opened to tourists and the nearest to Beijing. All four sections are 300 to 500 years old,

Side Trips from Beijing

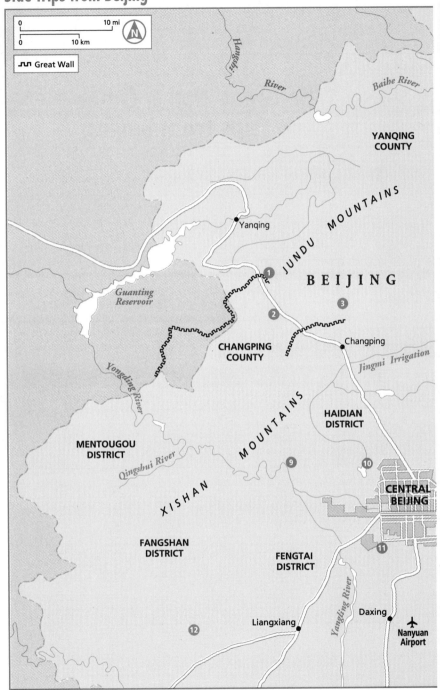

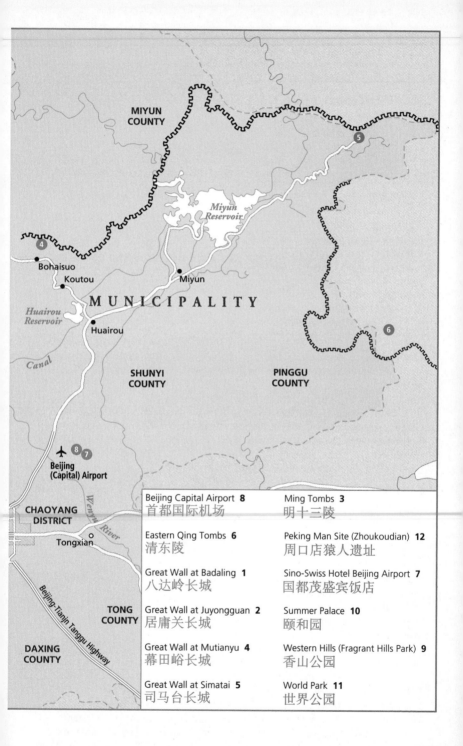

MIYUN
COUNTY

*Miyun
Reservoir*

5

4

Bohaisuo
Koutou
• Miyun

*Huairou
Reservoir*

M U N I C I P A L I T Y

• Huairou

Canal

SHUNYI
COUNTY

PINGGU
COUNTY

6

✈ 8 7
**Beijing
(Capital) Airport**

CHAOYANG
DISTRICT

Wenyu River

Tongxian

TONG
COUNTY

DAXING
COUNTY

Beijing–Tianjin Tanggu Highway

Beijing Capital Airport 8 首都国际机场	**Ming Tombs 3** 明十三陵
Eastern Qing Tombs 6 清东陵	**Peking Man Site (Zhoukoudian) 12** 周口店猿人遗址
Great Wall at Badaling 1 八达岭长城	**Sino-Swiss Hotel Beijing Airport 7** 国都茂盛宾饭店
Great Wall at Juyongguan 2 居庸关长城	**Summer Palace 10** 颐和园
Great Wall at Mutianyu 4 幕田峪长城	**Western Hills (Fragrant Hills Park) 9** 香山公园
Great Wall at Simatai 5 司马台长城	**World Park 11** 世界公园

dating from the Ming Dynasty, and all four are beautiful sections of the Great Wall, coiling up and down impossibly steep terrain. They are each a fitting representative of the greatest wall ever built by man—what one 19th-century traveler called a "fantastic serpent of stone."

THE GREAT WALL AT BADALING ★★
42 miles NW of Beijing

Almost everyone who pays a call on the Great Wall, from heads of state to adventurers crossing China with backpacks, visits Badaling. This is a grand section of the Wall, set in a steep, forested mountain range. Here, the Wall, its stairs, and the magnificent watchtowers were carefully restored beginning in 1957. Although many a traveler pooh-poohs Badaling as a deplorable tourist trap, crowded beyond all endurance, this section of the Wall disappoints few travelers. It may be crowded, but so is China, especially at its top sites.

> **Impressions**
>
> *To think that these walls, built in apparently inaccessible places, as though to balance the Milky Way in the sky, a walled walk over the mountain-tops, are the work of men, makes it seem like a dream.*
> —Comte de Beauvoir, *Voyage autour du Monde,* 1867

Construction of this Ming Dynasty section of the Great Wall began in 1368 and continued for almost 200 years. Built of stone, the Wall averages 24 feet in height, 21 feet in width at its base, and 18 feet wide on top. The interior is a mixture of tamped soil and rubble. The sides are covered in stone, the top in layers of brick. In fact, the bricks we associate with the building of the Great Wall weren't introduced until the Ming builders set to work here, northwest of Beijing.

The wall at Badaling has been restored to reflect its Ming Dynasty grandeur. Gateway arches and watchtowers run the length of the Wall, which served as a highway through the mountains. Five horses could ride abreast, drawing carriages. Today, the main parking lot and squares, filled with vendors, are a reflection of China's modern economic boom.

ESSENTIALS
VISITOR INFORMATION The Great Wall at Badaling (✆ **010/ 6912-1308**) is open daily from 6am to 6:30pm (until 10pm on summer weekends). Admission is 30RMB ($3.60). The cable car costs 50RMB ($6) round-trip.

GETTING THERE **China International Travel Service (CITS),** with headquarters at 103 Fuxingmennei Dajie (✆ **010/6601-1122**), arranges guided tours to the Great Wall at Badaling. CITS maintains convenient branches in most hotels. Group tours to the Great Wall at Badaling leave from various hotels at 8:30am daily and cost about 400RMB ($48) per person, including lunch and stops at the Ming Tombs, souvenir stores, and other regional sites. Time on the Wall itself is usually limited to under 2 hours.

To hire a driver, car, and guide for the day costs about 1,200RMB ($144). To hire just a car and driver costs less (about 800RMB, $96). The cost to hire a taxi on your own from the street for the day depends on your powers of negotiation, but it can cost less than 400RMB ($48).

A new expressway connects Beijing to the Great Wall at Badaling. Tour buses make the trip in about 90 minutes unless the expressway is clogged with other buses or there's been an accident (which is not uncommon).

> **Tips   For Travelers with Disabilities**
>
> The Great Wall is tough enough for people in reasonably good walking shape to reach and tour; the treks can be steep and a bit precarious. For those with disabilities, touring the Wall is a challenge—and often a nightmare. If walking is difficult, take a cable car to the top and enjoy the view and atmosphere. The Badaling section is recommended because the cable car provides fairly smooth access to the Wall itself. There are no elevators or wheelchair assists at any of the Great Wall sections.

Government-sponsored tour buses (the green #1 buses) make the run every 20 minutes in the morning, beginning at 6am and leaving from in front of Qianmen Gate (at the south end of Tiananmen Square) for 40RMB ($4.80) round-trip. Other buses depart from the Beijing Railway Station southeast of Tiananmen (bus no. 2); from Dondaqiao, near the Silk Alley Market (bus no. 3); from the Beijing Zoo (bus no. 4); and from Qianmen Xi Dajie, west of Tiananmen Square (bus no. 5). Bus no. 919 (5RMB, 60¢) also serves Badaling from near the Deshengmen subway station in north Beijing.

The train from Beijing to Hohhot stops near the Badaling section of the Wall at Qinglongqiao West train station. The rail journey (train no. 527) takes about 3 hours from Beijing's Yongdingmen train station, departing at 9:40am (one-way fare 20RMB, $2.40). There are many other trains as well. The Qinglongqiao West train station, part of the first railroad to be built entirely with Chinese labor and funds (1909), is near the southern end of Badaling. It tunnels under the Great Wall. In the winter, when the Great Wall at Badaling is dusted with snow, a train trip from Beijing is a delight. There are almost no tourists on the Wall then, the sun is bright, and the mountain peaks and guard towers are gorgeous.

EXPLORING THE WALL

A long stairway runs up to the Wall. You can head northeast or southwest and walk a mile or so in either direction. The incredible steepness of the Great Wall and the high rise of its stairs always astound visitors. Walking up to the highest watchtower is often enough to thoroughly exhaust you, especially on a hot day. There's no reason to hurry. The scenery is splendid. The two-story watchtowers, consisting of a guardroom below and an observation house above, are fine places to recuperate.

If you walk along the southwest section of the Wall about two-thirds of a mile, you'll come to an unrenovated spine of the Wall that has a much more primitive feel. Few tourists venture out this far. The stairs are crumbling and the sides of the Wall are broken, exposing the earthen filling.

If you choose to walk Badaling in the other direction, you'll come to a terminal for the Great Wall cable car that takes you down to another parking lot. Beyond the cable car, the Great Wall also reverts to its former ruins, and you're again free to explore the Wall as it was centuries ago.

The way back down the Wall where you came in requires a steep descent down high stairs. Some travelers walk back down facing backwards. The modern handrails help. At the bottom of the Wall is a "Great Mall" of endless souvenir stands, a movie hall, and cafes. Prices are exceptionally high for trinkets, crafts, and "I Climbed the Great Wall" T-shirts, even when you bargain like mad.

THE GREAT WALL AT MUTIANYU ★★
55 miles NE of Beijing

The Great Wall at Badaling proved so popular that authorities restored a second section of the Wall at Mutianyu in 1986. Mutianyu was supposed to relieve the overcrowding at Badaling, particularly on weekends. The ploy has not been completely successful, but Mutianyu is often less busy than Badaling. Its setting is more rough and rugged than that at Badaling, even if it now has summer traffic jams of its own.

ESSENTIALS
VISITOR INFORMATION The Great Wall at Mutianyu (✆ **010/ 6964-2022**) is open daily from 6:30am to 6pm (until 10pm in the summer). Admission is 30RMB ($3.60). The cable car costs 50RMB ($6) round-trip. For the same price there is a new **rollertrain** that winds up and down the hillsides along the Wall for about two-thirds of a mile, reaching speeds of 20mph.

GETTING THERE **China International Travel Service (CITS),** with branches in most hotels and headquarters at 103 Fuxingmennei Dajie (✆ **010/ 6601-1122**), arranges guided tours to the Great Wall at Mutianyu. Group tours leave at noon on Tuesdays, Thursdays, and Saturdays from various hotels and cost about 250RMB ($30) per person. Like the tour to Badaling, these tours usually make stops at a pearl factory or similar outlet on the way and also include tours of other sites in Beijing, leaving less than 2 hours on the Wall itself.

If you are not on a tour, you can catch a minibus to Mutianyu in front of the Great Hall of the People. A kiosk sells tickets (10RMB, $1.20 each way) the day before. Morning departure times vary, so check ahead. There is no train service.

To hire a driver, car, and guide for the day costs about 1,200RMB ($144). To hire just a car and driver costs less (about 800RMB, $96). The cost to hire a taxi on your own from the street for the day depends on your powers of negotiation, but can cost less than 400RMB ($48).

EXPLORING THE WALL
The mile-long segment of the Great Wall of Mutianyu was among the first built during the Ming Dynasty, beginning over 500 years ago. As at Badaling, a long stairway leads up to the Wall. The hike can take up to 20 minutes, so you may want to use the nearby cable car. If you turn right at the top of the entrance, you can walk the ramparts for over half a mile. At the end, there is a barrier. Visitors are not permitted to venture beyond this point. All you can do is contemplate the Wall in ruins, which gives you an excellent idea of what most of the Great

---

⌒Tips Great Wall Travel
To avoid the thickest crowds, visit the Great Wall at Badaling or Mutianyu on weekdays rather than weekends, and in the morning if possible. Early spring and late fall are the most pleasant times of year to go; June through September is high tourist season. If you're visiting the Great Wall on a tour that includes lunch, you'll dine at one of the restaurants catering to foreign groups with set Chinese lunches. The Great Wall at Badaling even has a branch of Kentucky Fried Chicken. If you're on your own for food, it's best to pack a lunch in Beijing and enjoy it on the Wall.

Wall, even those sections built just a few hundred rather than a few thousand years ago, looks like now.

If you turn left after reaching the Wall, there are several steep and scenic guard towers ahead. The view of the undulating Wall and forested mountains is stunning. There's also a cable car station here, which is the kindest way back down (with respect to your knees and thighs). The vendors who line the path at the base of Mutianyu are friendly but persistent. They will probably remember you. The prices on souvenirs tend to drop dramatically as you descend.

THE GREAT WALL AT SIMATAI ★★★
77 miles NE of Beijing

The Great Wall at Simatai is quiet, remote, and virtually unreconstructed; it is far less crowded than other sections of the Great Wall near Beijing. Locals proclaim it the most dangerous section of the Great Wall. Because it is largely unrestored, it does indeed have difficult and dangerous passages to hike. Fortification aficionados consider Simatai the most beautiful section of the Great Wall. It is beautiful, but its main aesthetic attraction is its state of ruin. This is how the Great Wall really looks 500 years after the Ming constructed it. Simatai is also a paradise for hikers and hill walkers with its dramatic natural scenery, the contours of the sharp peaks heightened by the outline of the Great Wall and its crumbling watchtowers.

The Chengde highway to Simatai is smooth; the countryside, green. At Miyun Reservoir, the terrain steepens. The roadside is clotted with fishing families selling their catch, enormous reservoir trout, many 3 feet long, sheathed in plastic and suspended on posts like lanterns. At Gubeikou, 70 miles northeast of Beijing, a country lane winds 7 more miles through the foothills to Simatai Village and the entrance to the Wall. The town at the base is tiny. The main street leading to the Wall has a few beef noodle cafes, souvenir shops, and vendor shelters stocked with T-shirts and Great Wall tablecloths, but this is a mere minnow pond of sellers compared to the ocean of hawkers flooding the gates to Badaling and Mutianyu. Towering high over the village is the formidable outline of the Great Wall at Simatai, slithering like a dragon's back over a series of sharp, clipped peaks.

ESSENTIALS
VISITOR INFORMATION   The Great Wall at Simatai (© 010/6993-1095) is open daily from 8am to 5pm (until 10pm in the summer). Admission is 20RMB ($2.40). The cable car costs 50RMB ($6) round-trip.

Food stands at the base sell simple dishes for about $2 a plate. You can also pack a lunch in Beijing and enjoy it on the Wall.

GETTING THERE   China International Travel Service (CITS), with headquarters at 103 Fuxingmennei Dajie (© 010/6601-1122), can arrange private guided tours with a driver and an English-speaking guide to the Great Wall at Simatai. The cost for a solo traveler is about 1,200RMB ($144). CITS maintains convenient branches in most hotels.

You can also hire a taxi, without a guide, for about 400RMB ($48), or book a minibus (60RMB, $7.20, round-trip) at the tourist office in the Jinghua Hotel, Nansanhuan Xi Lu (© 010/6722-2211).

EXPLORING THE WALL
Beyond the village, there is a half-mile walk up to the first stairway and watchtower. The sandy path rises and skirts the small Simatai Reservoir, where in the

heat of summer, tourists from Beijing board pleasure boats for a sail along the Great Wall. But from the water, the Wall remains high and remote. The reservoir lies in a deep crease dividing two sections of the Wall, Simatai to the east, Jinshanling to the west.

Ascending the stairs to the first watchtower at Simatai is a matter of pounding a few hundred stone steps, the treads of this staircase often just half as deep as an average foot length. The climb is a struggle, but the view from the first of the ascending towers, taken through open cannon archways, is magnificent: endless mountain chains to the deserted north; watchtowers crowning the ridgelines east and west; and the reservoir, village, and farmlands far below, rolling southward toward Beijing.

This first portion of the Great Wall at Simatai has been restored, as have virtually all the walkways and towers tourists see along Badaling and Mutianyu, but from here on at Simatai, the Wall has been left to crumble. The grand stairways disappear. The pathway becomes a ledge of rock and sand along the outside of the rising Wall, narrowing to sheer drop-offs. Sometimes, there are no footholds at all. Shedding its stair treads over the centuries, the Wall is as treacherous to scale as a water slide of gravel.

The Wall's bricks, each with its own stamped number, date from the Ming Dynasty. Many of the bricks have fallen away, exposing the original earthen core with which the large work gangs capped the mountain peaks. From the towers on the Wall, signals of fire and smoke once alerted those inside the Wall to impending invasions from without.

At Simatai, one can still see the results of the Ming Dynasty building program in high relief. The toll taken by 5 centuries of weather and civilization is substantial but far from complete. Simatai survives as a wild run of ruins, its main outline intact, stretching from peak to chiseled peak on ridges sometimes pitched to 70-degree inclines. Best of all for the traveler, Simatai is as peaceful as it is untouched—and as beautiful as the mountains it dances across. There are 14 watchtowers at Simatai, stationed at quarter-mile intervals and strung across the peaks until the Wall dissolves into scattered bricks, piles of sand, and fragments of bone from the workers who were buried within the Wall.

Coming down Simatai is more daunting than going up. Locals recount stories of visitors who have broken into tears during the descent, unnerved by the steepness, the lack of stairs, the unstable footings. Some come down the stairless top of the Wall backwards, on all fours. The name "Simatai" shares the same sounds in Chinese as the words "Dead Horse Platform," a reference to a horse that fell in a famous battle fought beneath the Wall here. So far, no tourists have added their names to this venerable tradition.

In fact, there is a safer way to scale Simatai. East of the entrance is a gondola. Visitors can hop a ride partway up and climb a new, safer set of steep stairs to the 2,624-foot-high eighth tower on the Wall. From here, on a clear evening, you can even see the lights of Beijing.

WHERE TO STAY

Adventurous travelers may want to stay overnight at the rustic accommodations provided by **Simatai Village** (© **101/6903-1221**), a compound with cabins and dormitories. The cabins, which sleep up to four people, come with clean private bathrooms (toilet and hot water shower) and rent for 606RMB ($73) a day. Four-person dormitory rooms cost RMB96 ($12) per person. The compound boasts its own restaurant and snack bar.

The "Newest" Section of the Great Wall

In 1998, China opened another section of the Great Wall to tourists at **Juyongguan** . Juyongguan lies 36 miles northwest of Beijing, making it the closest point to the capital for a view of the Wall. There, a 2.5-mile section was renovated under a 5-year program costing $14 million. Juyongguan is the site of one of the Great Wall's most famous mountain passes, and the massive guard towers there are quite impressive, as is the Wall itself, which undulates over the peaks and ridges of the Taihang Mountains. Several of the many temples and gardens that were located at the pass have also been restored.

Juyongguan (meaning the "Tower That Bestrides the Road") was erected in A.D. 1345, predating the Ming Dynasty. It is famous for its Buddhist bas-relief carvings and the inscriptions in six languages (Chinese, Uighur, Tangut, Mongolian, Tibetan, and Sanskrit).

At present, there are no regularly scheduled group tours to Juyongguan, but it is only 6 miles southeast of the Great Wall at Badaling, on the same main highway, so check with hotel tour desks and CITS when you arrive. In the meantime, adventurous travelers rely on the slow but cheaper (40RMB, $4.80 round-trip) tourist buses that depart for Badaling from five Beijing locations every morning at 8:30am (Tourist Bus no. 1 from Qianmen, the gate at the southern end of Tiananmen Square; no. 2 from the Beijing Railway Station southeast of Tiananmen; no. 3 from Dondaqiao, near the Silk Alley Market; no. 4 from the Beijing Zoo; and no. 5 from Qianmen Xi Dajie, west of Tiananmen Square).

2 The Western Hills (Fragrant Hills Park)

17 miles NW of Beijing

The **Western Hills (Xi Shan)** have been a refuge from the summer heat for China's rulers since the Liao Dynasty (907–1125), when the first Imperial villas appeared on these shady slopes. Under Qing emperor Qianlong in the 18th century, the mountainside retreat became the site of a formal park, with temples, pavilions, 28 officially designated scenic locations, and an exotic wildlife park stocked with white deer. This portion of the Western Hills, now the destination of ordinary Beijingers desiring to escape the city heat, is known as **Fragrant Hills Park (Xiangshan Gongyuan).** The Fragrant Hills Park, which encompasses 4,000 acres, has been a public park since 1957. The highlights for most park-goers: hiking the trail or riding the chairlifts to the summit of Fragrant Hills, known as Incense Burner Hill, particularly in the late autumn when the leaves of the Huanglu smoke tree are changing color.

ESSENTIALS

Fragrant Hills Park (© **010/6259-1155**) is open daily from 8am until 5pm (until sunset in the summer). It is sometimes included on CITS group tours offered through hotels. The park is just 6 miles from the Summer Palace. From downtown, taxis can reach the Fragrant Hills in about 1 hour at a cost of about

100RMB ($12) one-way. Bus no. 360 from the Beijing Zoo and bus no. 333 from the Summer Palace also serve Fragrant Hills. Admission is 5RMB (60¢). The chairlift to the summit of Incense Burner Peak costs 30RMB ($3.60) each way.

EXPLORING THE AREA

There's plenty to see in the Western Hills. A mile east of the north gate to Fragrant Hills Park is the **Temple of the Sleeping Buddha (Wo Fo Si).** Its most famous attraction is a lacquered, reclining statue of Buddha about to enter Nirvana, located in the last of four halls (Wo Fo Dian). The figure's age is in some dispute (some think it dates back as far as 1321), but its length is easily fixed, stretching the tape to 16 feet (5m). The enormous shoes displayed in the flanking cases are gifts presented to the Buddha by devout worshippers, perhaps even some Qing Dynasty emperors. The temple is open daily from 8am to 4:30pm; admission is a modest 2RMB (24¢).

Located just inside the northern gate to the Fragrant Hills Park (immediately to the right and north across the bridge) is the **Temple of the Azure Clouds (Bi Yun Si)** (© 010/6259-1205). It is a large complex that climbs the hillside, courtyard by courtyard and hall by hall, and is crowned by the Diamond Throne Pagoda, built in the style of India's *stupas* in the late 18th century and decorated with well-restored Buddhist sculptures. The **Diamond Throne Pagoda (Jinggang Baozuo Ta),** built in 1748, consists of a white marble pagoda 115 feet tall and a cluster of four lesser pagodas and two dagobas (bulb-shaped towers). The most interesting display is in the Luohan Hall, where there are 508 lifelike, lively, and sometimes gruesomely surreal gilded statues of Buddha's disciples, glumly displayed in dusty glass cases. One of the middle halls memorializes Sun Yat-sen, founder of the Chinese Republic, who lay in state in this temple complex until his body was moved to Nanjing. His steel and crystal coffin, a gift from Russia, is still on view, and his hat and coat were left behind, sealed up in the Diamond Throne Pagoda. Open daily from 7:30am to 4:30pm, the temple charges an admission of 10RMB ($1.20).

The ticket office for the chairlift to the summit of the Fragrant Hills is also just inside the northern entrance. This is the park's top attraction, affording marvelous panoramic views of the forested hills. The summit is called **Incense Burner Peak (Xiang Lu Feng)** ✹ because of the enormous incense burner–shaped dual rock formation on its crown. Open daily from 8am to 5pm, the two-person chairlifts take about 20 minutes to make the ascent through its 20 numbered stations to the top (elevation: 1,827 ft., or 557m). Fuzzy recorded music accompanies every chairlift passenger from cable tower to cable tower. On the right, as you ascend, you can see the Temple of Azure Clouds and its lovely pagoda; on the left, Spectacles Lake (Yanjing Hu), two lakes joined by a bridge that resemble a pair of eyeglasses; and farther away, a 16th-century garden, the Pavilion of Introspection (Jian Xin Zhai), with a moon-shaped pool. Nearby are the remains of a lama temple (Zhao Miao) and its seven-story pagoda (Liu Li Ta), noted for its glazed tiles and its bronze bells dangling from the eaves. You can take a closer look at these sites on foot after you descend.

The peak is a spacious one, with pavilions, courtyards, vendors, and a plethora of paths leading up and down further peaks in every direction. To the east, it is possible to see the Summer Palace. If you come to the Fragrant Hills in its prime season, when the leaves change to a sizzling red in the autumn (late Oct or early Nov), you'll see thousands of young couples, as well as families, on the peak, lured by the romance conferred by the foliage and advertised by classical poets since the Tang Dynasty. Young women and girls all seem to wear wristbands and headbands of fresh flowers. The fall foliage is a nice change from the drab urban landscapes, but don't expect it to be quite as luxuriant in the Fragrant Hills as it is in New England and northeast Canada.

The chairlift makes for a quick, scenic descent, but the most healthful way down from the peak is a 45- to 60-minute walk on the zigzagging path, which consists of over 2,000 steps. The path is known as Guijianchou ("Even the Devil Is Scared"), but it is far from tortuous or dangerous. If you keep to the right as you descend, you'll end up at a road that leads north (a left turn) to the basic, poorly managed **Fragrant Hills Hotel (Xiangshan Mengyangyuan Binguan)** (© **010/6259-1155**), designed by I. M. Pei, the renowned Asian-American architect. A blend of Western and Chinese, as well as ancient and modern styles, the hotel and the grounds invite strolling. The hotel also serves the best food in the park (Western and Chinese); its restaurants accept credit cards. From the hotel you can walk back to the north entrance, taking in the temples, pagodas, and gardens you spotted from above.

3 Museum of Peking Man

31 miles SW of Beijing

A team of archaeologists excavating a site known as **Dragon Bone Hill (Long Gu Shan),** near the village of Zhoukoudian, made one of the great discoveries in modern paleontology on December 2, 1929, when they turned up the skull of a new human ancestor: *homo erectus pekinensis,* better known as **Peking Man.** This and other remains of Peking Man, who is thought to have lived here as long ago as 690,000 years, means that man's closest ancestor probably evolved in Asia. The cave where Peking Man dwelt measures 460-feet-wide by 130-feet-deep. Up the north-facing hillside, researchers located a second cave, the Upper Cave, where Stone Age Man dwelt a mere 20,000 to 50,000 years ago. The Upper Cave yielded the remains of eight people, their stone tools, bone ornaments, and a sewing needle. The much older Peking Man cave yielded six complete skulls, nine skull fragments, and 152 teeth—the remains of as many as 40 cave dwellers—as well as evidence of the use of fire and stone tools. Following an intensive period of excavation from 1927 to 1937, almost all of these fossils disappeared en route to America for safekeeping during the war, apparently pilfered along the way (some say by the Japanese, some say by the Taiwanese, and some say by American archaeologists or collectors).

ESSENTIALS

Located at Zhoukoudian Village, Fangshan District (© **010/6930-1272**), the **Peking Man Museum (Zhoukoudian Beijing Yuanren Bowuguan)** is open daily from 8:30am to 4:30pm. Admission is 20RMB ($2.40). If you wish to visit in the company of an English-speaking guide (which I recommend) contact your hotel concierge or **China International Travel Service (CITS),** 103 Fuxingmennei Dajie (© **010/6601-1122**).

EXPLORING THE AREA

For those with a keen interest in archaeology or paleontology, the Peking Man Museum at Zhoukoudian is an absolute must, but for most tourists it is best skipped. The museum, rebuilt in 1972, houses the remains of Peking Man's cave on one side and an Exhibition Hall on the other. The educational displays in the

Exhibition Hall are ponderous, there's not much information in English, and the fossils and relics aren't terribly impressive, consisting largely of plaster molds of the missing skulls, prehistoric animal bones, some stone tools, and statues of Peking Man. There are trails to the excavation sites (which are numbered) and to the Upper and Lower caves on Dragon Bone Hill, so named because local peasants had been digging up the bone fragments of prehistoric man for years, thinking they were the bones of ancient dragons.

4 The Ming Tombs

31 miles NW of Beijing

Of the 16 emperors who ruled China during the Ming Dynasty (1368–1644), 13 are buried in elaborate complexes in the valley of the Ming Tombs north of Beijing. Tomb construction began here in 1409 and continued for 2 centuries. The valley was sealed off by a red gate at its only entrance, guards were posted to keep out the people, and no one, not even the emperor, could ride a horse on these grounds. The site of this huge cemetery was chosen by the same emperor, Yongle, who oversaw the construction of the Forbidden City. The tombs reflect a similar conception of Imperial architecture, consisting of walls, gates, court-yards, stairways, and elaborate pavilions with roofs of yellow tiles (yellow being the color of emperors). The actual burial chamber (a *tumulus*) is underground. The emperor, his wife, and his favored concubines were the only people buried there, along with enough royal treasure to stuff a small museum. Yongle's two Ming Dynasty successors are entombed in Nanjing, and the seventh Ming emperor chose to be buried nearer to Beijing (on Jinshan Hill). Otherwise, this is Ming China's ultimate old boy's club (afterlife branch).

The entrance to the Ming Tombs, a long and celebrated Spirit Way, is lined with statues of guardian animals and officials. The tombs are dispersed around the edges of a box canyon. Three of the tombs have been restored (Ding Ling, Chang Ling, and Zhao Ling). The rest can be visited but not entered. The 10 unrestored tombs are among the favorite summer picnic spots of resident foreigners in Beijing. This "Forbidden Valley" of dead kings covers about 15 square miles.

ESSENTIALS

The Ming Tombs (known in Chinese as *Shisan Ling,* the "Thirteen Tombs"), in Changping County (© **010/6976-1424**), are open daily from 8am to 5:30pm. Admission, collected at the Spirit Way entrance to the tombs, is 20RMB ($2.40). Admission to each of the three restored tombs is an additional 20 to 30RMB ($2.40–$3.60). Many group tours to the Great Wall at Badaling stop here. Check with your hotel about group tours or contact **China International Travel Service (CITS),** 103 Fuxingmennei Dajie (© **010/6601-1122**). On your own, you can hire a taxi or take any of the special Tourist Buses (40RMB, $4.80) that stop here on the way to the Great Wall. These buses depart Beijing every morning, starting at about 8:30am (Tourist Bus no. 1 from Qianmen, the gate at the southern end of Tiananmen Square; no. 2 from the Beijing Railway Station southeast of Tiananmen; no. 3 from Dondaqiao, near the Silk Alley Market; no. 4 from the Beijing Zoo; and no. 5 from Qianmen Xi Dajie, west of Tiananmen Square).

The Ming Tombs are at their most charming along the Spirit Way entrance and off-the-beaten-track on the grounds of the unrestored tombs (to which there is no admission fee). The three restored tombs, where tour groups are funneled by their leaders, are largely uninspiring, dank, and usually too crowded to enjoy. In fact, the Ming Tombs are so unpopular with foreign tourists that they are now more often than not excluded from the group itinerary.

A more impressive cemetery of kings is the Eastern Qing Tombs (see below).

EXPLORING THE AREA

The **Spirit Way (Shen Dao)** ⊛, the formal entrance to the Ming Tombs over which the funeral processions from the Forbidden City would have trod, extends almost 4 miles from the entrance gate to the first of three restored tombs. The five-arched marble entrance gate, 95 feet wide, was carved in 1540. A second passageway, the **Great Red Gate (Da Hong Men),** served as the old entrance to the valley, its middle door opened only to admit an emperor about to be entombed. The next relic is a carved stone tablet (*stele*) dating from 1426, with an inscription added by Qing Emperor Qianlong 3 centuries later. This is followed by the most famous site at the Ming Tombs, the **Avenue of the Stone Animals** ⊛. Most royal tombs have such an avenue of sculptures, but none is as impressive as that of the Ming Tombs. There are 12 pairs of animals, including elephants, lions, and mythological beasts, and 6 pairs of court and military officials. It is worth walking this portion of the entrance, as the old sculptures, some dating from 1435, are a delight.

The tombs lie at the end of the Spirit Way, which passes through the **Dragon Phoenix Gate (Long Feng Men)**—said to separate the living from the dead—and across the **Shisanling (13 Tombs) Reservoir.** The largest and best preserved of the tombs is straight ahead: **Chang Ling,** the tomb of Emperor Yongle, the third Ming ruler who presided over China from 1403 to 1424 and created the Forbidden Palace and Temple of Heaven. He is buried here with his wife, Empress Xu. Above ground, the complex is like a miniature Forbidden City, with gates, courtyards, and halls mounted on tiers of marble terraces. Stairways are divided by slabs with engraved dragons and phoenixes. The yellow-tiled roof of the massive **Hall of Eminent Favors (Ling En Dian)** is supported by scores of sandalwood columns, transported from distant Yunnan Province in the 15th century. It now contains a gallery of treasures extracted from another Ming Tomb (the **Ding Ling** tomb), including armor and Imperial gowns. The **Soul Tower,** containing a stone tablet and marble altar, is located behind the Hall of Eminent Favors in the third courtyard. Then comes the underground burial palace, surrounded by the 1,640-foot-long circular **Precious Wall (Bao Cheng).** Unfortunately, archaeologists have not yet figured out how to safely enter the tomb below. There are 16 satellite graves at Emperor Yongle's tomb, one for each of his concubines, who are said to have been buried alive.

To enter a Ming Dynasty underground burial vault, visitors must line up at **Ding Ling,** the tomb of the 13th Ming Emperor, Wanli; his wife, Empress Xiaoduan; and his number-one concubine, Xiaojing. Wanli ruled from 1573 to 1620. He had been overseeing the construction of his Underground Palace from the age of 22. When it was completed, he threw a party in the funeral vault, where he was buried 30 years later. Ding Ling was the first Imperial tomb ever officially excavated in China, opening in 1958. The 13,000-square-foot Underground Palace, a marble vault divided into five chambers, lies 88 feet below ground. The stairway down is cold and claustrophobic. Each carved archway once contained an ingenious system of "self-acting stones" that fell into place as locks the first time the door was closed, sealing in the dead.

Ding Ling still contains the white marble throne of the emperor and the large porcelain jars outfitted with sesame oil and wicks so as to burn eternally underground. In the Burial Chamber are three red coffins—the emperor's is in the middle, flanked by those of his wife and concubine. There are also 23 wooden chests filled with jewelry, costumes, cups, silk, jade belts, and gold chopsticks—about 3,000 precious objects, many now on display at the Chang Ling tomb. It was in this emperor's casket that researchers made a rare discovery, a winged-crown of gold mesh with coiling dragons and a pearl, the only Imperial crown ever excavated in China.

5 The Eastern Qing Tombs (★/★

78 miles NE of Beijing

The eastern tombs of the Qing Dynasty (1644–1911) far surpass in splendor and majesty their more famous predecessors, the Ming Tombs, but they are seldom visited, owing to their relative remoteness from Beijing (often a 4-hr. drive). They form a countryside version of the Forbidden City and are nearly as elaborate. Tastefully restored for the most part, this Imperial city is vast, grand, and uncrowded.

The **Eastern Qing Tombs (Dong Qing Ling)** are the final resting place of the three rulers who did the most to preserve the historic treasures of Beijing that we see today. Emperor **Kangxi** (1654–1722), his grandson Emperor **Qianlong** (1711–99), and Empress Dowager **Cixi** (1835–1908), whose lives spanned that of China's last dynasty, are all buried in splendid underground palaces at this site. Also interred in the same royal cemetery, which extends over a valley 21 miles wide, is Emperor **Shun Zhi** (1638–61), founder of the Qing Dynasty. While on a hunting trip, he came upon this valley and reserved it for the Imperial burial ground. It would become China's largest dynastic cemetery, entombing 5 emperors, 15 empresses, and more than 100 concubines, princes, and princesses—even Emperor Kangxi's teacher. Tomb construction began in 1661 and required 274 years to complete, not ending until the last Imperial concubine was interred in 1935, 24 years after the Qing Dynasty itself ended. Altogether, five tombs were built for emperors, four for empresses, five for concubines, and one for a princess. A total of 161 members of the royal family and court are buried here.

The layout of the Eastern Qing Tombs is orderly and traditional, and follows the outlines of the Forbidden City because this was to be the Imperial Palace of the Afterlife. A long Sacred Way leads to the tomb of the first Qing emperor, and secondary Sacred Ways branch off to the tombs of succeeding emperors. Leading to the tomb is a series of gates, courtyards, bridges, and halls. The tomb, located at the northern end of the complex, is covered with a circular mound of raised earth (a *tumulus*). This "Precious Citadel" is fronted by a raised pedestal and tower called a "Square City." In Chinese cosmology, a square represents the Earth, a circle the Heavens. The burial chamber beneath the mound, the "Underground Palace," is created in the typical style of burial chambers—a full palace, built of stone, divided into vaults, and filled with Imperial treasures for enjoyment in the next world.

At the Eastern Qing Tombs, two of the "Underground Palaces" are open: that of Emperor Qianlong and that of Empress Dowager Cixi, hers being perhaps the most lavish burial chamber ever built in China.

ESSENTIALS

The Eastern Qing Tombs (Dong Qing Ling) are a 4-hour drive northeast of Beijing, 47 miles beyond the Beijing Capital Airport, just across the municipal border at the town of Malanyu in Zunhua County, Heibei Province. The most practical way to get there is by hiring a private car or taxi from your hotel or arranging for a special tour with an English-speaking guide and car through **China International Travel Service (CITS),** 103 Fuxingmennei Dajie (*C* **010/ 6601-1122**). Open daily from 8:30am to 4:30pm; admission (which goes up quickly these days) is 55RMB ($7). CITS has an office here and it provides English-speaking guides if you arrive independently. The **Qingdong Tombs Guest House** (*C* **0315/694-4061**) is within walking distance and provides barely acceptable overnight accommodations starting at about 250RMB ($30) for a double with private bath and no amenities.

EXPLORING THE AREA

Running north for 3 miles, the **Sacred Way** is lined with 18 pairs of stone sculptures, splendid renderings of lions, elephants, horses, camels, and unicorns, as well as army generals and court advisors. The path, which royal funeral processions would have followed after the long journey from Beijing, ends at the oldest tomb, **Xiao Ling,** where Shunzhi, first emperor of the Qing Dynasty, is buried. The grounds are vast, encompassing 28 clusters of buildings, but the tomb itself is not open. To the east, about a third of a mile away, is **Dong Xiao Ling,** a tomb complex built for Emperor Shunzhi's wife (Empress Xiaohui Zhang) and his 28 concubines.

Jing Ling ⚝, the tomb of Emperor Kangxi, has not been excavated either, but it is worth visiting for its magnificent halls. Kangxi's tomb has its own Spirit Way, lined with five pairs of stone sculptures, which curves along a riverbank. This tomb is southeast of the first Qing emperor's tomb, and it is reached by crossing the 350-foot-long **Five-Arch Bridge,** the grandest of the many stone bridges in the Eastern Qing cemetery. Among the treasures contained in the sacrificial halls is Emperor Kangxi's ceremonial Dragon Throne.

Yu Ling ⚝⚝ is the tomb of Emperor Qianlong, the longest ruling monarch in Chinese history. It has been excavated, and the elaborate Underground Palace is open to visitors. Consisting of nine elaborately decorated vaults and located 177 feet below the ground, this palace is divided by a series of marble doors 10 feet thick. The burial chamber contains the sarcophagi of the emperor and five of his consorts. Qianlong also built round earthen mounds at the rear of this complex to entomb his Imperial concubines.

Ding Dong Ling ⚝⚝⚝, the tomb of Empress Dowager Cixi, although not as large as that of Emperor Qianlong, is even more lavish. Her tomb has also been excavated, and it is open to visitors. Inside the sacrificial hall (Long En Dian), above her Underground Palace, there is today a life-size waxwork diorama showing the Empress Dowager as the goddess of mercy (Guanyin) in a Buddhist robe, crown, and beads, attended by a young woman and her favorite court eunuch. In the underground burial chamber, Cixi's sarcophagus is still in place. She was entombed inside it, within a wooden double coffin painted with lacquer and gold powder. In 1928, the warlord Sun Dianying opened this tomb and plundered its treasures, removing and scattering the Empress Dowager's corpse. The body was later retrieved and placed back in the tomb, but most of the Imperial treasures buried with the Empress Dowager—which included 25,000 pearls, 200 pieces of jade, 80 gems, and a pearl burial quilt 7 inches

Location, Location, Location!

Why did the Qing Emperors decide to be buried so far from their home, the Forbidden City in Beijing, when the only way to reach their remote cemetery grounds was by horseback or on foot? In a word, the reason was location. The site of the Eastern Qing Tombs possessed unparalleled, irresistible *feng shui.* By ancient tradition, geomancers were always consulted to determine where best to locate a new building or monument. The chosen ground should have protective natural elements to screen off the threat of evil forces both from the front and the rear. The mountain ranges in this remote valley formed perfect protective screens, blocking the northward flow of evil. A peak to the south would protect the dead from the wind, and hills to the east and west stood guard. Twin rivers embraced the cemetery as well.

Although *feng shui* failed to deter grave robbers, to this day many Chinese regard the Eastern Qing Tombs to be in a cosmically fortified location. Locals point out that floods, droughts, and other natural disasters have never visited these tombs in recorded history. Even the 1976 earthquake that leveled Tangshan, 60 miles away, and killed 250,000 in a single blow caused no damage. Moreover, it is said that at the Eastern Qing Tombs, the rain falls precisely 72 times each year, no more and no less, even in years of severe drought—a phenomenon worthy of the Chinese X-Files.

thick—disappeared with the looters. Nevertheless, many of Cixi's treasures have been rescued and are on display in two galleries at her tomb, including her summer robe, jewels, enamels, and carved ivories. Even the pictures that decorate the walls of the pavilions and Underground Palace are lavish, each colored in gold foil, a process employing some 300 pounds of the precious metal.

Appendix A: Beijing in Depth

1 Beijing Today

Many a traveler's first impression of Beijing is of a flat, sprawling metropolis, steeped in smog and dust and devoid of Chinese architecture, a city that is being systematically ripped apart at the seams by an endless procession of construction teams intent upon turning an ugly Stalinesque city into a characterless Western-style capital. In fact, although Beijing does not yet rank among the world's most beautiful capitals, it can claim to be one of the world's most interesting, dynamic, and culturally enriching cities. And for the most part, the recent explosion of skyscrapers, malls, and plazas has given the city a welcomed shine.

Statistics tell one story of modern Beijing, starting with its population: More than 11 million people occupy the metropolitan area, including 7 million that live within the city limits. This makes Beijing a bit smaller than Shanghai, but the capital still ranks as the 12th largest city in the world. Of Beijing's millions, more than 100,000 are foreign-born; many of them reside in the capital as diplomats, teachers, students, or employees of overseas companies. For foreign residents, Beijing can be brutally expensive. In a recent survey of the 20 most expensive cities in the world in which to live and do business, Beijing ranked third, far ahead of London, Geneva, and New York City.

Although Beijing has overnight millionaires, China's highest-ranking politicians, and many of the nation's top academic minds, ordinary Beijingers must be counted as residents of a developing rather than a developed nation, even though the pace of development has quickened. Living space, a slim 140 square feet per person a few years ago, has increased to 175 square feet, although the shortage of adequate housing persists. Beijing's per capita Gross Domestic Product (GDP) for 2000 was $2,651, a 10% jump over the previous year and a 61% increase in just 5 years. In the early 1990s, Beijing consumers spent 90% of their income on food, clothing, and daily commodities; after 2000, that figure had dropped to 60%. On the other hand, thousands of Beijingers scrimp by on less than the UN-established world minimum wage ($1 per day), holding either menial jobs or no jobs at all. The unemployed, arriving in Beijing from the countryside illegally, without residence permits and hoping for a better life, can be sighted sleeping under bridges, awaiting work. Some find jobs. As many as 100,000 women from the rural areas now work in Beijing as maids (officially called "home helpers").

Overall, Beijing has a definite air of prosperity, deservedly so after a decade of double-digit economic growth, and there are numbers to bear this out, too. While 67% of Beijingers commute to work on bikes and 25% by bus, a surprising 17% are rich enough to go to work by car or taxi. And Beijing, the city of the bicycle, is rapidly becoming the city of the automobile. There are up to 8 million bikes on the streets of the capital, but cars now number well over 1 million. The car population has been growing at a steady and quite dizzying rate of 15% yearly. At the same time, the capacity of the roads has risen no more than 0.4% annually, and there are currently only enough parking places for one in four Beijing cars and trucks.

Numbers tell only one story, however. The real flesh and blood tale of Beijing today concerns the pull of two polar opposites: progress and preservation. The future and the past, the modern and the ancient, could not stand in starker contrast than in present-day Beijing. In a frenzy to rebuild itself as a modern capital worthy of a powerful new China in the 21st century, Beijing is a city that is altering its face as each day passes. In 2001, a massive reconstruction of the central business district (encompassing 100 million sq. ft. of offices, retail outlets, residential units, and cultural projects) was announced, the designers to be a Los Angeles firm (Johnson Fain Partners). For the immediate future, construction sites, smog, traffic jams, and shopping plazas are likely to dominate Beijing, rather than *hutongs* and parks, lakes and temples, or even the grand edifices of the Forbidden City and the Great Wall.

Material progress comes first these days; preserving the past is one of Beijing's most difficult challenges. Many locals view the past with little sentimentality. As narrow lanes and tile-roofed courtyard houses disappear in the wake of new housing projects and expanded road systems, many Beijingers dwell on the necessity of change and the benefits of progress. And the benefits are real enough in this crowded city where only a few are wealthy and everyday amenities do not begin to match those of Western capitals.

How much is left to preserve? In 1958, as the old city walls and most of the monumental city gates were being removed from Beijing, the government completed a survey of all sites with any historic, religious, or artistic value whatsoever, coming up with a grand total of over 8,000 such monuments—from which just 78 were culled for preservation. A quarter of a century later, in 1982, following the wholesale destruction of cultural relics during the Cultural Revolution, surveyors were able to add just 70 more sites to the original 78 that were tabbed for preservation. Many of the city's remaining 148 treasures were themselves in need of renovation.

The pendulum is always swinging in Beijing. Pleas to preserve old Beijing have reached as high as the National People's Congress, where in 1998 delegates submitted a motion to the annual legislature. "As an ancient cultural city, Beijing belongs to the whole Chinese nation and to the world as well," the motion proclaimed. "Greater efforts should be made to protect existing cultural sites and old buildings." The capital, after all, is China's most visited city precisely because it has a past worth seeing. With the arrival of the millennium (and the 50th anniversary of the founding of the People's Republic) in 1999, Beijing launched a concerted program of cleanup and restoration, scouring its parkland lakes, banking its waterways in stone, refurbishing many of its temples and pagodas—even replacing Tiananmen Square's humble cement blocks one by one with stately granite. A more direct highway now connects Beijing to the Great Wall, and more sections of the Great Wall have been opened to receive the overflow of visitors. In the heart of the city, 25 old streets, including 260 *hutongs* and 2,000 courtyard houses, have been placed in "first-phase cultural protection zones."

As Beijing preserves and beautifies its past, it is also rapidly upgrading its tourist services and facilities. Scores of Beijing hotels have achieved international standards of service. Restaurants and bars catering to Westerners are proliferating. There are Internet cafes, plenty of McDonald's and Starbucks, and even a Hard Rock Cafe. Western fast food, brands, stores, and necessities are widely available—strong hints that Beijing is becoming an international as well as a Chinese capital. For the first time in history, in fact, it is possible to spend a comfortable week in China's capital as an ordinary tourist without once eating in a Chinese restaurant, sleeping in a Chinese hotel, shopping in a Chinese store, or speaking anything but English—should you choose to experience Beijing in this rather strange and insulated way.

One of modern Beijing's most publicized plagues is its air pollution. Headlines in the West have declared that the air in Beijing is five times filthier than the air in Los Angeles, and that breathing in Beijing for a day is equal to smoking three packs of unfiltered cigarettes. Indeed, some days the pollution is quite visible, and the city, along with the surrounding mountain ranges, is wrapped in a dark, soupy shroud. On the other hand, many a day, particularly in late autumn, is blessed with brilliant blue skies. Moreover, the government is moving on several fronts to reduce the level of the two chief pollutants, coal (for heating and industry) and petroleum (for vehicles). Beijing was the first major Chinese city to phase out leaded fuel. New cars must be fitted with catalytic converters. Buses that chug up and down Chang'an Avenue, the main east–west thoroughfare through the heart of the city, must now be fueled with natural gas, and police conduct spot checks of tailpipe emissions. Even spitting in public, once a tradition across China, has been outlawed in Beijing, where those expectorating on the streets are fined a fat 50RMB ($6) when caught in this act of polluting.

Meanwhile, Beijing has shut down hundreds of its dirtiest factories. New apartments use natural gas for heating and cooking, instead of coal (which provides 75% of China's entire energy needs). The media has begun to publish and broadcast weekly figures on air quality. Although Beijing still ranks among the top ten most polluted cities in the world (according to the World Bank), it is attempting to reverse the ravages of rapid industrialization and rising affluence. A 5-year, $1.25-billion anti-pollution campaign, starting in 2001, is designed to make Beijing as clean and green as major Western capitals, such as Paris. In a popular measure that both reduces pollution and saves on taxes, the State Council has mandated that all bureaucrats below ministry level trade in their official cars for travel allowances, with the old black sedans going to auction.

As for Beijingers themselves, visitors today will find them generally warmer, more open, and jollier than residents to the south in the frantic cities of Shanghai, Guangzhou, and Hong Kong—and taller, too, as many northerners tend to be larger in stature than their southern compatriots. Beijingers are quite friendly to outsiders. The capital is used to visitors. As China's political capital, Beijing has long been exposed to foreigners in their streets, and residents do not look upon "big-nosed" Westerners as escapees from sideshows, as often happens in more provincial regions of China. The capital has a cosmopolitan atmosphere. Although the pace of life is relaxed, residents do keep up with the latest trends

---

⸢Fun Fact⸥ The Color of Beijing

In November 2000, city planners announced that they had ordered the buildings of the capital to assume a uniform color scheme to make Beijing more visually appealing. The official color? **Gray.** The reason? According to city planner Fu Bonan, gray is "the dominant tone formed naturally during the history of the city."

and fashions from the West, indulging in both when they can afford them. Beijingers are dedicated window-shoppers, making a stroll on the busy streets a delightful exercise in people-watching. Like other Chinese, they remain quite family-oriented, and with the one-child-per-family mandate formally in place here, they can often be seen spoiling their "Little Emperors" or "Little Empresses" excessively. Despite having the problems of an emerging modern city, Beijing remains a comfortable place to experience Chinese life up close and to explore a large number of the supreme cultural remains of Imperial Cathay freely and with few hassles.

2 Beijing History 101

FROM PEKING MAN TO THE MING DYNASTY

The remains of Beijing's oldest residents, the skulls of **Peking Man,** date back as far as 500,000 years, although the caves where China's *homo erectus* once dwelled actually lie over 30 miles southwest of the city, at Zhoukoudian. No evidence of prehistoric settlement within the capital surfaced until 1996 when construction workers unearthed a Stone Age site 20,000 years old just a mile from the Forbidden City.

Historic records first mention a fiefdom existing within modern Beijing's city limits at the beginning of the **Western Zhou Dynasty** (1100–771 B.C.), but Beijing did not become a major Chinese city until almost 2,000 years later, after the **Tang Dynasty** collapsed. The **Liao Dynasty** (916–1125), made up of Khitan invaders from the north, controlled northern China and made Beijing for the first time a regional, if not a national, capital. The Liao were succeeded by the **Jin Dynasty,** which built a new capital on Beijing's outskirts. In turn, **Genghis Khan** and the Mongols overran the Jin rulers, leveling the Imperial city. **Kublai Khan** eventually built his own capital, with his Imperial palace situated on the shores of Beijing's Beihai Lake, in 1279, initiating the **Yuan Dynasty** (1279–1368). For the first time, Beijing was the capital of a unified China, and it was this city, then

Dateline

- **500,000 B.C.** "Peking Man" occupies caves near present-day Beijing.
- **20,000 B.C.** Early man establishes settlements in what is today downtown Beijing, hunting buffalo and elephants.
- **916–1125** The Liao Dynasty establishes its northern capital, Yanjing, at Beijing.
- **1153** The Jin Dynasty establishes its capital, Zhongdu, at Beijing.
- **1275** Marco Polo visits Beijing and later writes the first Western account of the capital.
- **1279–1368** The Yuan Dynasty establishes its capital, Khanbaliq, at Beijing.
- **1402** The Ming Dynasty moves its capital to Beijing and begins building the Forbidden City.
- **1601–10** Jesuit father Matteo Ricci lives in Beijing as court mathematician and astronomer, making few converts but sending detailed description of China to Europe.
- **1644–1911** The Qing (Manchu) Dynasty inherits the capital, builds the Summer Palace, extends the Great Wall, and refurbishes the temples and parks.
- **1860** French and English armies reduce the Summer Palace to ruins during the Second Opium War.
- **1900** Foreigners in Beijing are attacked during the Boxer Rebellion.
- **1903** The Empress Dowager Cixi restores the Summer Palace.
- **1911** The Qing Dynasty ends, and the Republic of China is formed.

continues

known as Khanbaliq or Dadu (Great Capital), that **Marco Polo** visited in the late 13th century.

When the Yuan Dynasty fell to the all-conquering **Ming Dynasty** (1368–1644), the Imperial capital at Beijing was again razed, rebuilt, and renamed. Although almost nothing of the three earlier dynasties that ruled from Beijing remains today, much of the Ming Dynasty capital has survived in glorious condition. Emperor Yongle renamed the capital Beijing (Northern Capital) in 1403, finished the Forbidden City in 1421, and erected the Drum Tower, the Bell Tower, and the magnificent Temple of Heaven—all of which still grace Beijing. The Ming also saw to the restoration and lengthening of the Great Wall near the capital in a futile attempt to keep their dynasty safe from still more invaders.

THE LAST EMPERORS

The Ming emperors ruled China from the Forbidden City for most of three centuries, but they were finally toppled by the Manchus, another northern tribe. The Manchus formed the **Qing Dynasty** (1644–1911), but happily, for a change, they did not tear down the old capital and build a new one. As a result, Beijing has been able to preserve many of the Imperial monuments and treasures of China dating back over 500 years.

The Qing rulers expanded Beijing's *hutong* (alleyway) neighborhoods of gray tile-roofed courtyard houses and undertook building the Summer Palace in 1750. The two great emperors of the time, **Kangxi** and his grandson **Qianlong,** each ruled 58 years and both had an enormous impact on the shape and appearance of Beijing that lasts to this day. Many items from their royal collections of art and artifacts are still on display in the Forbidden City.

By the 19th century, the Qing Dynasty was waning and Western nations were exacting concessions

- **1919** Students and others protest China's weakness in the "May Fourth Movement" on Tiananmen Square.
- **1923** The "last emperor" is evicted from the Forbidden City.
- **1928** Chiang Kai-shek makes Beijing the capital of the Republic of China.
- **1937–45** The Japanese occupy Beijing.
- **1949** Mao Zedong proclaims the creation of the People's Republic of China to those assembled on Tiananmen Square.
- **1958–59** Tiananmen Square is expanded, the Great Hall of the People is built, the city walls are destroyed, and China's first subway begins to operate in Beijing.
- **1966–76** Beijing is effectively closed to foreign visitors during the turmoil of the Cultural Revolution, as many temples and historic sites are damaged by Red Guards.
- **1972** U.S. President Richard Nixon visits Beijing and the Great Wall, signaling a reopening of China to the West.
- **1976** Thousands amass on Tiananmen Square to protest the excesses of the Cultural Revolution.
- **1976–78** After the death of Chairman Mao and the arrest of the Gang of Four, Deng Xiaoping launches a program of economic reform.
- **1979** Democracy Wall Movement ends with arrest of "dissidents" who wrote wall posters in Beijing criticizing Mao and the Cultural Revolution.
- **1987** World's largest KFC (Kentucky Fried Chicken) fast-food outlet opens near Tiananmen Square.
- **1989** Students leading massive pro-democracy demonstrations occupy Tiananmen Square before a forcible eviction, June 3–4.
- **1990** Beijing's first successful independent Western bar and grill, Frank's Place, opens its doors.
- **1992** McDonald's opens its first Beijing outlet on Wangfujing Street.
- **1994** First Internet server in China established at the Chinese Academy of Science in Beijing.

continues

from China, including the right to live in the capital itself. Foreign delegations, businesses, traders, and missionaries carved out their own special domain in Beijing, known as the Foreign Legation Quarter, south of the Forbidden City. In 1900, a native rebel group known as the Brotherhood of Righteous Fists, or the **Boxers,** entered Beijing and, as the Qing court stood by, laid siege to this foreign stronghold for 55 days. Eight Western nations struck back, even setting fire to the Summer Palace. The last of the Qing Dynasty's most powerful rulers, **Cixi,** the Empress Dowager, was blamed for Beijing's humiliation. She rebuilt the Summer Palace as we see it today, but she could not maintain her dynasty's "Mandate of Heaven." The Republic of China, founded by **Sun Yat-sen,** toppled the last official Imperial dynasty in 1911, and in 1923, the last emperor, **Pu Yi,** was evicted from the Forbidden City.

- 1995 Beijing hosts the United Nations' Conference on Women. Beijing's mayor, Chen Xitong, is indicted for official corruption.
- 1997 Beijingers line the streets for the funeral of Deng Xiaoping, who is succeeded as paramount leader by Jiang Zemin.
- 1998 Puccini's *Turandot* is staged in the Forbidden City, while bicycles are banned for the first time on a downtown Beijing street.
- 1999 China celebrates the Golden Anniversary of the founding of the People's Republic (1949–99) on a newly renovated Tiananmen Square.
- 2000 The fifth official Chinese census since 1953 is launched in Beijing.
- 2001 Beijing awarded 2008 Summer Olympics.

THE CULT OF CHAIRMAN MAO

In 1928, the Guomintang Party, led by **Chiang Kai-shek,** seized Beijing, and made it the capital of the Republic of China, but Japan would soon invade. In 1937, after a valiant battle at the Marco Polo Bridge, Beijing fell and Japan occupied the city until 1945. With Japan's defeat in World War II, the ruling Guomintang Party and the revolutionary Chinese Communist Party, led by **Mao Zedong** (who had once worked as a library assistant in Beijing), resumed a civil war that had been ebbing and flowing for several decades. The communist forces soon triumphed, the Guomintang survivors fled to Taiwan (establishing the Republic of China there), and a new era in China's long history unfolded.

Chairman Mao Zedong proclaimed the People's Republic of China in Beijing on October 1, 1949. The classic grid of the capital, laid down in the Ming Dynasty and elaborated by the Qing, had survived repeated wars and regimes, but now the city walls, which had stood for 400 years, were pulled down, Tiananmen Square was enlarged, the Great Hall of the People was erected, and the Great Wall was opened to tourists. An underground subway system was constructed along the path of the old city wall. Much of the new architecture that took shape in Beijing from 1950 to 1980 bore the stamp of Russia's "socialist realism" school—which translated into large, ugly cement boxes and wide, dreary concrete avenues.

Under Chairman Mao, the capital and all of China were rebuilt politically, culturally, and spiritually. The old social ills were removed (prostitution, gambling, and drug addiction disappeared from the streets) and the economy was reorganized along strict egalitarian and socialistic lines, with **communes** in the countryside and structured **work units** in the cities, but China remained poor, if more self-sufficient. Beijing and the nation were racked by a series of disastrous political campaigns, beginning with the **Anti-Rightist Movement** (1957), which brought persecution of capitalists and Western-leaning intellectuals, and the **Great Leap Forward** (1958–60), an attempt to mobilize the populace to create an industrialized society overnight that ended in mass starvation.

These and other political movements culminated in the **Cultural Revolution** (1966–76), in which Chairman Mao's youthful followers, known as the Red Guard, held mass rallies on Tiananmen Square and elsewhere, swore their fervent devotion to Mao and his doctrine of extreme and constant revolution, and went on a prolonged rampage, destroying cultural landmarks, closing China's schools, and holding political trials. The whole country was torn apart in the ensuing chaos, many lost their lives or were sent down to the countryside for "re-education" in the doctrines of Mao, and China was sealed off from the outside world.

With Chairman Mao's death in 1976 and the return from disgrace of **Deng Xiaoping,** China slowly entered the most open and liberal era in its history. There were still bumps in the new road ahead. Beijing was the site of the **Democracy Wall Movement** of 1979, when at the bidding of Deng, the people were encouraged to create wall posters that were critical of political leaders and policies. Deng quickly reversed himself as the Democracy Wall Movement blossomed into calls for greater democracy. Eventually, similar protests erupted in a far more threatening form in Beijing, with the occupation of **Tiananmen Square** in 1989, and again it was Deng who crushed the pro-democracy opposition.

Deng's liberal side was economic, rather than political. Under his leadership, the disastrous economic programs of Chairman Mao were reversed, capitalism was injected into the marketplace, Western investment and ideas were welcomed, and Beijing, as China's political and cultural center, became increasingly international, technological, and prosperous. The modernization of Beijing, achieved in just a few decades, has flooded the city's thoroughfares, while the emperors and revolutionaries who shaped Beijing over the centuries are remembered only in certain side streets where museums, monuments, and temples still stand.

3 Chinese Ways & Manners

East is East and West is West, as the old adage goes—but in Beijing the two often meet, mingle, and occasionally collide. As visitors to China and guests of Beijing, travelers should be aware of differing customs and make adjustments accordingly. Of course, as Beijing modernizes, traditional ways are disappearing. Many Beijingers are worldly enough to have been exposed to Western behaviors. English-speaking tour guides, for example, have set answers to "embarrassing" questions that visitors sometimes ask. Uncomfortable topics include China's handling of political and religious dissidents, the status of Tibet and Taiwan, restrictions on the media, abortion, prison labor, and the Tiananmen Square massacre—although many younger Beijingers seem eager to tackle these topics head-on. The problem is that visitors can put their hosts—who may have government jobs—in the hot seat by posing politically sensitive questions. Feel free to ask the locals about anything, but remember that even in China's political capital, politics is still taboo.

Face Value

In social settings, the Chinese often take great pains to preserve "face," which involves maintaining one's self-respect while deferring important decisions to those of higher rank within a group. To "lose face" means to suffer embarrassment before others. To be criticized roughly by a visitor, for example, or to be asked to do something that is impossible puts a Chinese person in a dangerous position. "Saving face" is achieved by compromising, or sometimes by ignoring a problem altogether. Many Chinese go to extremes to avoid settling a dispute or handling a complaint, since any loss of face could reflect badly upon their family and China, as well as on themselves.

What visitors need to do when making requests or issuing complaints in Beijing, then, is to control their tempers, avoid assigning personal blame, seek compromise when possible, and practice patience. A polite approach has a better chance of success than a more aggressive, brutally frank, or simply angry outburst. In a nation renowned for the size and inertia of its bureaucracy, some things are slow to be done, and some things are never done at all. It often helps to ask a person to relay your complaint or demand to a superior, remembering that a response may not be immediate.

Recently, the government mandated a 5-day workweek. Most Chinese now work Monday through Friday. The workday begins about 9am, sometimes later, enabling thousands of Beijingers to do their morning exercises. The parks fill up with locals performing traditional *tai chi* or *chi gong* and sometimes even Western ballroom dancing. No one seems to mind being watched, and foreigners sometimes join in, but it is the most quiet and private time of the day. Lunch comes at the noon hour, although most shops no longer close down for afternoon siestas. Dinner is fairly early, usually around 6pm, followed by time spent at home with the family. Saturday and especially Sunday are spent in s hop-ping and enjoying the family in the parks and other attractions.

This typical weekly schedule overlooks a fundamental difference in viewpoints between East and West. The Chinese tend to view the individual as part of greater wholes—of the family, foremost; of the workplace; and of the nation. The group has more power than the individual, and it must be consulted before decisions are made. In practical terms, this translates into a respect for hierarchies. Those of higher rank within any organization, be it a family or a business, hold the power over others and decide what those of lower rank may do. The individual often has far less autonomy and power in Chinese society than in Western societies—even when it comes to apparently insignificant matters.

In the days of dynasties and eunuchs, China's tiny upper class practiced a number of elaborate courtesies that have all but disappeared from the modern People's Republic. Beijingers are not formal, nor do they have a set of enigmatic social rules that excludes outsiders. The Chinese do not bow (as the Japanese do), and they do not remove their shoes upon entering a house. Beijingers tend to be frank, and they do not, as a rule, thank others for favors, except by later actions. They shake hands but seldom embrace or kiss in public. They joke, but they do not speak loudly; and they seldom brag about their own accomplish-ments. Until recently, spitting in public and smoking whenever and wherever one pleased were common habits, but in recent years in Beijing, spitting has become unacceptable and smoking, in many public areas, has become unlawful.

Beijingers are quite inquisitive and direct, asking some questions that are per-fectly acceptable in China, if not in the West. Questions from Beijingers you have just met can include details about your salary and the number of children in your family. You can answer such queries as you see fit, vaguely if you wish.

Among ancient customs that do endure in modern Beijing are the respect for age, which is synonymous with wisdom and stature; the respect for higher edu-cation; and the respect for family matters, which are of more importance than those of work, politics, or world affairs. Among new customs, perhaps the most ubiquitous is an exaggerated respect for money: The millionaire now seems more respected than the scholar, a reversal of 2,000 years of Confucian thought.

Although women are equal to men by law and by Communist dogma, in fact women are often considered as they once were in traditional Chinese society: second-best to men. Male children, who alone continue the family line, are still preferred over females by many couples. Even among foreigners, men are often treated with slightly more respect than women, although modern education and the influx of Western ideas have begun to erode such prejudices.

A few other differences in customs are worth noting. The Chinese give their family names first, followed by their personal names, in the reverse order of most Western societies, and it is perfectly proper to refer to Chinese by their last names. Some Beijingers use English first names that they have either chosen or received at school. Despite Beijingers' fascination with the latest Western fash-ions, it is still advisable for Westerners to dress conservatively and to wear less jewelry than usual, if for no other reason than to avoid broadcasting their wealth to shopkeepers, vendors, touts, and pickpockets. Finally, before snapping a close-up photo of a fascinating Chinese face, ask permission, by pantomime if necessary. Many Beijingers do not want their photographs taken, although they usually give in when asked permission to take a picture of their children—whom the Chinese find as adorable as foreigners do.

4 Beijing in Print & on the Silver Screen

RECOMMENDED BOOKS

Two of the best introductions to modern Beijing (and to modern China) are by former bureau chiefs stationed in the capital for the *New York Times.* Fox Butterfield's classic account of Beijing in the aftermath of the Cultural Revolu-tion, *China: Alive in the Bitter Sea,* written in 1982, should be compared with the more optimistic vision of Nicholas Kristof and Sheryl Wudunn's study, *China Wakes: The Struggle for the Soul of a Rising Power,* written a scant 12 years later. These journalists seem to have covered completely different cities.

Old Beijing comes alive in a number of engrossing memoirs, including *Twilight in the Forbidden City* by Reginald F. Johnston (the Englishman who served as tutor to the last emperor, Pu Yi, in the Forbidden City 1919–24), *Old Madam Yin: A Memoir of Peking Life, 1926–1938* by Ida Pruitt (which gives a Chinese woman's view of life in the capital), and *The Years That Were Fat* by George N. Kates (who immersed herself in the romantic life of Old Peking 1933–40). More recent events in Beijing are the focus of a sensational memoir, *The Private Life of Chairman Mao,* by Li Zhisui, the Great Helmsman's personal physician; the *Tiananmen Papers,* based on an insider's leak of government documents; and Bette Bao Lord's *Legacies: A Chinese Mosaic,* which weaves together stories of the Cultural Revolution, accounts of diplomatic life in Beijing from 1985 to 1989, and the author's experiences at Tiananmen Square.

Two engrossing page-turners by Sterling Seagrave provide unforgettable portraits of two of Beijing's most notable personalities. In *The Soong Dynasty,* a biography of the Soong sisters, whose lives were intimately entwined with those of Sun Yat-sen and Chiang Kai-Shek, there is a moving portrait of the Soong sister who stayed behind in Beijing, where her house is now a museum. In *Dragon Lady: The Life and Legend of the Last Empress of China,* the myth of the Empress Dowager Cixi as China's Lady Macbeth is convincingly debunked, along with the popular version of the events known as the Boxer Rebellion. The more common but thoroughly Western version of the "Siege of Peking" during the Boxer Rebellion in 1900 is *55 Days at Peking* (1963), filled with heroes (Charlton Heston), heroines (Ava Gardner), and histrionics.

RECOMMENDED FILMS

Two of the best films both set and actually filmed in Beijing concern the fall from grace of an opera singer on one hand and an emperor on the other. The world of Beijing Opera is rendered with shattering effect in the film *Farewell, My Concubine,* starring China's best-known actress, Gong Li, and directed by Chen Kaige, who has helped place China on the world map of modern cinema. An epic film version of China's last dynasty, filmed on location in the Forbidden City, is Bernardo Bertolucci's *The Last Emperor.* A "director's cut" of this 1987 Oscar-winning film was released in 1998, its running time extended to 219 minutes—well worth an evening's viewing before visiting Beijing. Or if you are in a grim mood, rent *The Gate of Heavenly Peace,* a controversial but gripping documentary of the Tiananmen Square massacre. Donald Sutherland, Ge You, and other actors were rumored to be in Beijing for the filming of Chinese director Feng Xiaogang's *Big Shot's Funeral,* but its release in the West would not be until 2002 at the earliest.

5 Food & Drink

By virtue of its antiquity, continuity, and complexity, Chinese cuisine is frequently heralded as the world's supreme dining fare, although for decades, Beijing and other Chinese cities were dismissed as culinary backwaters. China's great chefs and its cooking traditions were often seen at their best in Hong Kong, Taipei, Singapore, San Francisco, New York, or London—but not in the capital of the country where they were born. Fortunately, this situation began to reverse itself as China instituted its "reform and opening" programs in the 1990s. Chefs were welcomed back and affluence led to a demand for fine dining. Beijing today can once again point to its own cooks and restaurants with pride.

Beijing's own contributions to Chinese eating are legendary. Sampling them at their source is among the chief delights of the traveler. The capital's most famous dish is Beijing duck, also called Peking duck, in which the bird is air-dried and coated in soy sauce and syrup, roasted until the skin is crispy, and sliced at the table. Best enjoyed amongst a large circle of friends, Beijing duck is served with thin pancake wrappings, seasoned by the diner with spring onions and plum sauce, and eaten with the fingers or chopsticks. (Chopsticks, of course, are often the great challenge for the foreign diner in China, but practice beforehand should guarantee adequate dexterity.) Chinese restaurants in leading hotels and a half-dozen Beijing duck specialty restaurants serve thousands of ducks daily.

Another noted Beijing original is Beggar's Chicken. Stuffed with Chinese vegetables and herbs, wrapped in lotus leaves and clay, then baked for many hours, Beggar's Chicken is a tender delight. Usually ordered the day before, this dish is broken apart at the table by use of a little hammer.

Beijing cuisine is actually part of Northern Chinese cuisine, which evolved in a cold environment that favored steaming, stir-frying, and strong seasonings (such as garlic and star anise)—as well as the use of wheat noodles and steamed breads over the great staple of southern and central China: rice. One of the most popular staples for northerners is boiled dumplings (*jiaozi*), stuffed with a variety of fillings. Similar to dim sum, *jiaozi*, noodles, and spring rolls constitute an authentic Beijing dining experience, and when prepared expertly, an excellent repast.

The northern cuisine would be regarded as hearty and simple were it not for two notable influences. The first is Mongolian. The Mongolian hot pot, with its slices of potatoes, cabbage, lamb, and beef that diners cook to taste in pungent hot oil, makes a superb one-dish meal. The other contribution of the capital is its Imperial cuisine—with dishes based on the recipes of the Qing Dynasty emperors and empresses. Imperial dining, with its fresh, natural ingredients and main dishes such as Mandarin fish and General Gong's chicken, has been the rage of Beijing in recent years—China's answer, perhaps, to nouveau California cuisine. Several Beijing restaurants serve Imperial fare in ornate pavilion restaurants, complete with traditional entertainment.

Beijing does not restrict its fine offerings to its own regional favorites. In fact, the capital has the most varied dining fare in China, with cafes representing nearly every province and region, from Hunan to Yunnan. In addition to Confucian and Cultural Revolution (Maoist) restaurants, Beijing is particularly noted for its superb Cantonese, Sichuan, and Shanghainese restaurants (the latter being the trendiest). With a large Uighur population from the far western province of Xinjiang, Beijing also boasts some superb Muslim eateries.

The recent increase in Asian businessmen and travelers to Beijing has spurred a growth in the number and quality of Japanese, Korean, Indian, and Thai restaurants. Above all, there has been a boom in Western cuisine. From Italian to Brazilian and French to Russian, Beijing can now satisfy a full palate of foreign tastes, offering a selection of fine restaurants with foreign chefs (at prices ranging from the economical to the astronomical). For the truly homesick, of course, there are the Western fast-food outlets that are sprouting up in every neighborhood of Beijing. McDonald's, Pizza Hut, Subway, KFC, Domino's, A & W, and even Dunkin' Donuts—they've all successfully invaded every corner of the capital and are a particular favorite of many Beijingers, who treat themselves to a real overseas culinary experience (American-style) whenever they can afford it, which is not so often because menu prices match those in the West, while Beijingers' wages do not.

The most popular drink in Beijing is perhaps still tea, sipped by ordinary citizens from jars all day long, but running a close second is bottled water, available everywhere as it is in the West. This is fortunate because the water from taps in Beijing, as in all of China, is still almost never considered hygienic enough to drink. Colas have long been available in Beijing, too, but they are still more popular with visitors than locals. Coffees are just starting to find a young audience, and coffeehouses may be the next trend, especially since Starbucks opened its first Chinese outlet in Beijing (and is immediately spreading its outlets throughout the city). Among harder drinks, the hotel lounges and Western-leaning bars offer all the imported spirits and beers. In addition to Tsing-Tao, China's national beer, and the locally brewed favorite, Yanjing Beer, one can even find genuine German microbrews. Chinese wines have improved over the years, especially those made by the joint-venture wineries, but they still have not achieved the quality and consistency of French, European, Australian, or Californian and Oregonian wines, particularly among reds. Finally, there's the bane of many a banquet, the local mai tai, the clear, gasoline-like liqueur used for rounds of toasts, in which *"gambei"* ("bottoms-up") signals the emptying of the glass.

6 Religion

Some of Beijing's most stunning monuments are its temples and other religious sites. As capital, Beijing is the location of many of China's leading shrines. Today, many of these holy sites are not only open to tourists, but are also active places of worship for modern followers of the ancient religions, both native and foreign, that shaped traditional Chinese culture and art. Monks, nuns, abbots, priests, and other religious leaders have again taken up residence at Beijing's temples, mosques, and churches after being expelled during the anti-religious fervor of the Cultural Revolution (1966–76), during which many sacred complexes were heavily damaged, closed, or converted to secular enterprises.

Beijing's temples, which number in the hundreds, all adhere to the same basic arrangement, regardless of the religion they serve. The walled grounds are entered from the south, usually through a gate and gatehouse that may contain large statues of four guardian figures. A series of pavilions, each enshrining statues of major deities, runs northward in ascending order of importance through the heart of the courtyards, with halls devoted to minor deities and living quarters lining the east and west edges. Incense is usually burned at large burners in front of each pavilion. Inside, worshippers kneel before the image of a deity, praying and burning more incense. The final shrine is often the largest and most grand in the temple complex. Incense and souvenirs are frequently for sale by monks inside each shrine. Several temples (notably, the newly restored White Dagoba Temple and the Temple of Everlasting Peace in Beihai Park) also contain pagodas or pagoda-like structures called *dagobas,* immense bulb-shaped monuments that contain holy relics and remains of gods or celebrated religious figures. Temples give visitors a fine chance to see the old religions in operation and modern Beijingers praying at shrines for a variety of usually quite practical ends: the birth of a child, the healing a disease, the granting of wealth or employment. Temples also preserve some of China's most beautiful architecture and art works.

China's own major organized religion, Daoism (or Taoism), with its emphasis on nature, mysticism, and the individual, is best represented in Beijing by the White Cloud Temple (Baiyun Guan), where a variety of shrines receive active petitioners, and by the recently renovated Eastern Mountain Temple (Dongyue Miao). Daoist practices date back more than 2,000 years. Buddhism, which had a profound influence on Chinese art, was heavily influenced in Beijing by the presence of northern and far western peoples who followed the Buddhist sect of

Lamaism. Beijing's Lama Temple is the capital's most visited religious site today, and its five main halls make up the most important lamasery in China.

Next door to the Lama Temple is the Confucius Temple (Kong Miao), the largest in China outside of Qufu, the birthplace of Confucius. While Confucius is regarded primarily as a philosopher and his followers were frequently members of the empire's vast bureaucracy and Imperial court, temples to the great sage were built across China. The Confucius Temple in Beijing is more a quiet museum of monuments and relics to Confucius than a sacred shrine for the performance of Confucian rites; it is also the site of the Imperial College, where China's emperors once addressed professors, students, and candidates successful in the national Imperial examinations.

Several of Beijing's finest temple complexes are devoted to artistic and cultural endeavors, rather than religious pursuits. The Great Bell Temple (Dazhong Si) houses China's largest bell. The Five Pagodas Temple (Wuta Si) has a splendid Indian-style hall and an outdoor display of historic carved tablets and statues. The Wanshou Temple serves as the Beijing Art Museum.

Beijing's 200,000 Muslims (the Hui minority, who are ethnically Chinese) maintain over 40 mosques in the capital. The Niujie (Ox Street) Mosque, located southwest of Tiananmen Square in Beijing's largest Muslim neighborhood, is open to visitors and resembles a Chinese temple in much of its architecture. Only followers of Islam are allowed inside its main prayer hall.

Christianity came to Beijing as early as the 14th century. In the 17th century, the Jesuits, led by Matteo Ricci, became favorites of the emperors. Ricci lived in a house on the site of what is today the South Cathedral (Nan Tang), Beijing's largest functioning Catholic cathedral, where visitors can attend masses conducted in Chinese, English, and even Latin. Other cathedrals and Protestant churches dating from the late 19th and early 20th century, when Christian missionaries from abroad last lived and worked in Beijing in large numbers, have also reopened to local and visiting worshippers.

Despite a number of functioning temples, mosques, and churches, Beijing, like most of China, is no longer a religious society. Current figures place the number of practicing Buddhists in China at 6% of the population, Muslims at 1%, Daoists at less than 1%, and Christians at 0.2%. Nevertheless, the surviving temples are crowded, the mosques quite active, and the churches overflowing as many locals take to Western religion as well as culture. Visiting Beijing's wide range of religious sites is rewarding not just for viewing ancient treasures but also for sampling what some see as a religious revival in China.

Appendix B:
The Chinese Language

Speaking no Chinese is hardly an obstacle in Beijing these days, particularly if one sticks to big hotels, guided tours, Friendship Stores, tourist sites, and restaurants catering to foreigners. But once visitors venture out on their own, hailing taxis, shopping local stores, buying admission tickets, getting lost on the streets, or ordering at an out-of-the-way restaurant, speaking English—no matter how loudly or clearly—isn't always enough. Nevertheless, there are measures a smart traveler can take when confronted with the baffling mysteries of the Chinese language, whether spoken or written.

The Chinese language is ancient, complex, and quite alien to those who know only the languages of the West. In Beijing, nearly everyone speaks the official dialect, called *putonghua,* or Mandarin Chinese. This is also the dialect that students throughout China learn to speak in school. (Chinese students are now taught English, as well, although seldom in a thorough manner.) Beijing natives, about two-thirds of the capital's population, actually prefer to speak the language of the streets, *Beijinghua,* which is a harsher version of standard Chinese. In the capital, at least, if you speak Mandarin, you are understood—but there's the rub, because even the rudiments of Mandarin can be difficult for those grounded in English or European languages. The four tones employed in pronouncing each syllable of Mandarin (each generally equivalent to a word or written Chinese character) are crucial to being understood. Chinese is rife with homonyms—words that sound alike except for the tone.

Nevertheless, if travelers have time beforehand, it is fairly easy to learn a handful of basic spoken phrases that can be useful. Correct pronunciation can be learned as you go by listening carefully while in Beijing. Because few travelers have time to take a Chinese language course before visiting China, a Mandarin phrase book becomes essential, especially one that has the words and phrases printed in Chinese characters. The written language is universal in China, regardless of local dialects.

In addition to a phrase book, an essential traveler's companion is a trilingual (in English, Chinese characters, and *pinyin*) map of Beijing. If the map contains Chinese script in addition to English, helpful strangers in the street can consult it and point a wandering traveler in the right direction. Street signs, where they exist, can also be useful if they contain *pinyin* in addition to Chinese characters. *Pinyin* is the official transcription of Chinese into an alphabetical form. For example, a sign reading *Tiantanyuan* means Temple of Heaven Park. Street signs often have the name of the street in *pinyin* followed by the transcription of one of the words for street (such as *dajie*).

The written form of Chinese is even more difficult to learn than the spoken form because it does not employ an alphabetical system. Students must memorize the meaning (and pronunciation) of thousands of written characters, a time-consuming challenge even for native speakers. Travelers must rely again on phrase books, bilingual maps, and hotel staff to unravel these enigmatic signs, although many visitors quickly learn to recognize some of the simpler and more

> **Tips It's All in the Cards**
>
> Another aid for travelers who don't speak Chinese are small cards offered at most hotels that have the name of the hotel and the name of your destination printed in Chinese characters. You can show the card to your taxi driver or to others along the way. These cards make getting to and returning from a site, restaurant, or shop quite easy.

common characters as they travel. It can be particularly useful at times to recognize the difference between the symbols for male and female when approaching an otherwise unlabeled public toilet.

Probably the most common question asked of travelers in Beijing is "*Ni shi cong nar lai de?*" or "Where are you from?" The answer is "*Wo shi Meiguo lai da*" if you're from America. *Meiguo* means America, so if you're from another country, use it instead: *Aodaliya* means Australia, *Jianada* means Canada, *Yingguo* means England, *Faguo* means France, *Deguo* means Germany, *Helan* means Holland, *Aierlan* means Ireland, and *Riben* means Japan. China, by the way, is *Zhongguo* in Chinese.

Even if your pronunciation is poor at first, it's worth making an attempt. Beijingers are not only amused, but also impressed, when foreigners take a stab at using Chinese, the language they regard as supreme.

English	Pinyin	Chinese
BEIJING	**Beijing**	北京
Ancient Observatory	Guguanxiangtai	古观象台
Chairman Mao Mausoleum	Mao Zhuxi Jiniantang	毛主席纪念堂
Forbidden City	Gugong	故宫
Lama Temple	Yonghegong	雍和宫
Old Summer Palace	Yuanmingyuan	圆明园
Summer Palace	Yiheyuan	颐和园
Temple of Heaven	Tiantan Gongyuan	天坛公园
Tiananmen Square	Tiananmen Guangchang	天安门广场
Useful Phrases		
Hello	Ni hao	你好
How are you?	Ni hao ma?	你好吗？
Good	Hen hao	很好
Bad	Bu hao	不好

English	Pinyin	Chinese

Useful Phrases

English	Pinyin	Chinese
I don't want	Wo bu yao	我不要
Goodbye	Zai jian	再见
Thank you	Xie xie	谢谢
Yes	Dui	对
No	Bu dui	不对
How's it going?	Ni chi le ma?	你吃了吗？
When?	Shenme shihou?	什么时候？
Excuse me, I'm sorry	Dui bu qi	对不起
How much does it cost?	Duoshao qian?	多少钱？
Too expensive	Tai guile	太贵了
It's broken	Huaile	坏了
May I take a look?	Wo neng bu neng kan yi kan?	我能不能看一看？
Do you speak English?	Ni shuo Yingwen ma?	你说英文吗？
What's your name?	Ni gui xing?	你贵姓？
My name is ____	Wo xing ____	我姓 ____
I'm lost	Wo milu le	我迷路了
I don't smoke	Wo bu chouyan	我不抽烟
I'm ill	Wo shengbing le	我生病了
Bill please!	Qing jiezhang!	请结帐！
I am vegetarian	Wo shi chisude	我是吃素的
Can I take a photograph?	Wo keyi zhao ge xiang ma?	我可以照个相吗？
I can't speak Chinese	Wo buhui shuo Zhongwen	我不会说中文
I don't understand	Wo ting bu dong	我听不懂
It doesn't matter	Mei guanxi	没关系
No problem	Mei wenti	没问题
Where are you from?	Ni shi cong nar lai de?	你是从哪来的？
I am from	Wo shi cong ___ lai de	我是从 ____ 来的
America	Meiguo	美国
Australia	Aodaliya	澳大利亚
Canada	Jianada	加拿大
England	Yingguo	英国

France	Faguo	法国
Germany	Deguo	德国
Holland	Helan	荷兰
Ireland	Aierlan	爱尔兰
Japan	Riben	日本
Do you have a ____?	Ni you mei you ____?	你有没有 ____？
Do you know ____?	Ni zhi bu zhidao? ____	你知不知道___？
What do you call this?	Zhe jiao shenme?	这叫什么？
I want to go to ____	Wo xiang qu ____	我想去 ____
Where is ____?	____ zai nar?	____ 在哪儿？
I want ____	Wo yao ____	我要 ____
Airport	feji chang	飞机场
Bank	yinhang	银行
Beer	pijiu	啤酒
Bicycle	zixingche	自行车
Boiled water	kai shui	开水
Bus	gonggong qiche	公共汽车
Bus station	qiche zong zhan	汽车总站
Chinese "dollar" or renminbi	yuan or kuai	元，块
CITS	lüxingshe	旅行社
Credit card	xinyong ka	信用卡
Hot water	re shui	热水
Hotel	binguan, dajiudian, fandian	宾馆，大酒店，饭店
Map	ditu	地图
Mineral water	kuangquanshui	矿泉水
Passport	huzhao	护照
Police!	Jingcha!	警察！
Restaurant	fanguan	饭馆
Soft drink	qishui	汽水
Taxi	chuzu qiche	出租汽车
Telephone	dianhua	电话
Toilet	cesuo	厕所
Toilet paper	weisheng zhi	卫生纸
Train	huoche	火车
Train station	huoche zhan	火车站

English	Pinyin	Chinese
Zero	ling	零
One	yi	一
Two	er	二
Three	san	三
Four	si	四
Five	wu	五
Six	liu	六
Seven	qi	七
Eight	ba	八
Nine	jiu	九
Ten	shi	十
Eleven	shi yi	十一
Twelve	shi er	十二
Fifteen	shi wu	十五
Twenty	er shi	二十
Twenty-one	er shi yi (and so on)	二十一
Thirty	san shi	三十
Thirty-one	san shi yi (and so on)	三十一
One hundred	yi bai	一百
Two hundred	er bai	二百
Three hundred	san bai	三百
Four hundred	si bai	四百
One thousand	yi qian	一千
Two thousand	er qian	二千

Days of the Week

Sunday	Xingqitian	星期天
Monday	Xingqiyi	星期一
Tuesday	Xingqier	星期二
Wednesday	Xingqisan	星期三
Thursday	Xingqisi	星期四
Friday	Xingqiwu	星期五
Saturday	Xingqiliu	星期六
Yesterday	zuotian	昨天
Today	jintian	今天
Tomorrow	mingtian	明天

Index

See also Accommodations and Restaurant indexes, below.

RESTAURANTS

FROMMER'S® COMPLETE TRAVEL GUIDES

Alaska
Amsterdam
Argentina & Chile
Arizona
Atlanta
Australia
Austria
Bahamas
Barcelona, Madrid & Seville
Beijing
Belgium, Holland & Luxembourg
Bermuda
Boston
British Columbia & the Canadian
  Rockies
Budapest & the Best of Hungary
California
Canada
Cancún, Cozumel & the Yucatán
Cape Cod, Nantucket &
  Martha's Vineyard
Caribbean
Caribbean Cruises & Ports of Call
Caribbean Ports of Call
Carolinas & Georgia
Chicago
China
Colorado
Costa Rica
Denmark
Denver, Boulder & Colorado Springs
England
Europe
European Cruises & Ports of Call
Florida
France

Germany
Great Britain
Greece
Greek Islands
Hawaii
Hong Kong
Honolulu, Waikiki & Oahu
Ireland
Israel
Italy
Jamaica
Japan
Las Vegas
London
Los Angeles
Maryland & Delaware
Maui
Mexico
Montana & Wyoming
Montréal & Québec City
Munich & the Bavarian Alps
Nashville & Memphis
Nepal
New England
New Mexico
New Orleans
New York City
New Zealand
Nova Scotia, New Brunswick &
  Prince Edward Island
Oregon
Paris
Philadelphia & the Amish Country
Portugal
Prague & the Best of the Czech
  Republic

Provence & the Riviera
Puerto Rico
Rome
San Antonio & Austin
San Diego
San Francisco
Santa Fe, Taos & Albuquerque
Scandinavia
Scotland
Seattle & Portland
Shanghai
Singapore & Malaysia
South Africa
South America
Southeast Asia
South Florida
South Pacific
Spain
Sweden
Switzerland
Texas
Thailand
Tokyo
Toronto
Tuscany & Umbria
USA
Utah
Vancouver & Victoria
Vermont, New Hampshire
  & Maine
Vienna & the Danube Valley
Virgin Islands
Virginia
Walt Disney World & Orlando
Washington, D.C.
Washington State

FROMMER'S® DOLLAR-A-DAY GUIDES

Australia from $50 a Day
California from $70 a Day
Caribbean from $70 a Day
England from $70 a Day
Europe from $70 a Day

Florida from $70 a Day
Hawaii from $80 a Day
Ireland from $60 a Day
Italy from $70 a Day
London from $85 a Day

New York from $90 a Day
Paris from $80 a Day
San Francisco from $70 a Day
Washington, D.C., from $70
  a Day

FROMMER'S® PORTABLE GUIDES

Acapulco, Ixtapa & Zihuatanejo
Alaska Cruises & Ports of Call
Amsterdam
Aruba
Australia's Great Barrier Reef
Bahamas
Baja & Los Cabos
Berlin
Big Island of Hawaii
Boston
California Wine Country
Cancún
Charleston & Savannah
Chicago
Disneyland

Dublin
Florence
Frankfurt
Hong Kong
Houston
Las Vegas
London
Los Angeles
Maine Coast
Maui
Miami
New Orleans
New York City
Paris

Phoenix & Scottsdale
Portland
Puerto Rico
Puerto Vallarta, Manzanillo &
  Guadalajara
San Diego
San Francisco
Seattle
Sydney
Tampa & St. Petersburg
Vancouver
Venice
Virgin Islands
Washington, D.C.

FROMMER'S® NATIONAL PARK GUIDES

Family Vacations in the National
  Parks
Grand Canyon

National Parks of the American
  West
Rocky Mountain
Yellowstone & Grand Teton

Yosemite & Sequoia/
  Kings Canyon
Zion & Bryce Canyon

Frommer's® Memorable Walks

Chicago	New York	San Francisco
London	Paris	

Frommer's® Great Outdoor Guides

Arizona & New Mexico	Northern California	Vermont & New Hampshire
New England	Southern New England	

Suzy Gershman's Born to Shop Guides

Born to Shop: France	Born to Shop: Italy	Born to Shop: New York
Born to Shop: Hong Kong, Shanghai & Beijing	Born to Shop: London	Born to Shop: Paris

Frommer's® Irreverent Guides

Amsterdam	Los Angeles	San Francisco
Boston	Manhattan	Seattle & Portland
Chicago	New Orleans	Vancouver
Las Vegas	Paris	Walt Disney World
London	Rome	Washington, D.C.

Frommer's® Best-Loved Driving Tours

Britain	Germany	New England
California	Ireland	Scotland
Florida	Italy	Spain
France		

Hanging Out™ Guides

Hanging Out in England	Hanging Out in France	Hanging Out in Italy
Hanging Out in Europe	Hanging Out in Ireland	Hanging Out in Spain

The Unofficial Guides®

Bed & Breakfasts and Country Inns in:	Florida with Kids	New Orleans
California	Golf Vacations in the Eastern U.S.	New York City
New England	The Great Smokey & Blue Ridge Mountains	Paris
Northwest		San Francisco
Rockies	Inside Disney	Skiing in the West
Southeast	Hawaii	Southeast with Kids
Beyond Disney	Las Vegas	Walt Disney World
Branson, Missouri	London	Walt Disney World for Grown-ups
California with Kids	Mid-Atlantic with Kids	Walt Disney World for Kids
Chicago	Mini Las Vegas	Washington, D.C.
Cruises	Mini-Mickey	World's Best Diving Vacations
Disneyland	New England & New York with Kids	

Special-Interest Titles

Frommer's Adventure Guide to Australia & New Zealand
Frommer's Adventure Guide to Central America
Frommer's Adventure Guide to India & Pakistan
Frommer's Adventure Guide to South America
Frommer's Adventure Guide to Southeast Asia
Frommer's Adventure Guide to Southern Africa
Frommer's Britain's Best Bed & Breakfasts and Country Inns
Frommer's France's Best Bed & Breakfasts and Country Inns
Frommer's Italy's Best Bed & Breakfasts and Country Inns
Frommer's Caribbean Hideaways

Frommer's Exploring America by RV
Frommer's Gay & Lesbian Europe
Frommer's The Moon
Frommer's New York City with Kids
Frommer's Road Atlas Britain
Frommer's Road Atlas Europe
Frommer's Washington, D.C., with Kids
Frommer's What the Airlines Never Tell You
Israel Past & Present
The New York Times' Guide to Unforgettable Weekends
Places Rated Almanac
Retirement Places Rated

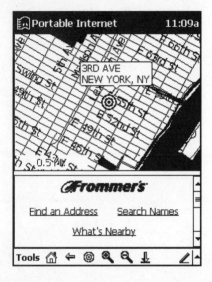